DATE DUE

MAR 1 1 2010	

Family Caps, Abortion, and Women of Color

FAMILY CAPS, ABORTION, AND WOMEN OF COLOR

Research Connection and Political Rejection

Michael J. Camasso

OXFORD
UNIVERSITY PRESS

2007

OXFORD
UNIVERSITY PRESS

Oxford University Press, Inc., publishes works that further
Oxford University's objective of excellence
in research, scholarship, and education.

Oxford   New York
Auckland   Cape Town   Dar es Salaam   Hong Kong   Karachi
Kuala Lumpur   Madrid   Melbourne   Mexico City   Nairobi
New Delhi   Shanghai   Taipei   Toronto

With offices in
Argentina   Austria   Brazil   Chile   Czech Republic   France   Greece
Guatemala   Hungary   Italy   Japan   Poland   Portugal   Singapore
South Korea   Switzerland   Thailand   Turkey   Ukraine   Vietnam

Published by Oxford University Press, Inc.
198 Madison Avenue, New York, New York 10016

www.oup.com

Oxford is a registered trademark of Oxford University Press

Library of Congress Cataloging-in-Publication Data
Camasso, Michael.
Family caps, abortion, and women of color : research connection
and political rejection / Michael J. Camasso.
    p.   cm.
Includes bibliographical references and index.
ISBN 978-0-19-517905-7
1. Welfare recipients—Government policy—United States.   2. Family size—
Government policy—United States.   3. Low-income single mothers—Government
policy—United States.   4. Public welfare—United States.   5. Public welfare—Law
and legislation—United States.   6. Abortion—United States.
I. Title.
HV95.C314 2007
362.5'561—dc22   2006101654

9 8 7 6 5 4 3 2 1

Printed in the United States of America
on acid-free paper

To my father who, through example, demonstrated the difference between moral earnestness and real morality

Preface

The primary purpose of this book is to acquaint readers with a welfare reform initiative known variously as the "Family Cap" or "child exclusion provision." But as the title suggests, the contents are not limited to research findings and data-based analysis. I use the Family Cap research, primarily research I have conducted, to take the interested on a journey—a rather bumpy ride, in fact—into the estate where politicians and their anxious companions, the policy experts, dwell. For many public policy researchers this can be an unfriendly land, especially for those who fail to heed Henry Brooks Adams's warning that "practical politics consists in ignoring facts." As we shall see, however, some policy experts are quite at home in this environment—indeed, some could not survive outside of it.

The attention of the book is focused on New Jersey, the state where the first Family Cap was implemented. From 1993 through 1999 I served as the principal investigator, responsible for the federally mandated, independent evaluation of New Jersey's welfare reform called the Family Development Program. The Family Cap, which was a centerpiece of the program, ignited national controversy and debate from the moment it was implemented in October 1992. The research undertaken by my colleagues and me, as sometimes happens with social science research, rather than being ignored, was seized upon by politicians, journalists, academics, legal analysts, and especially policy experts as they sought to make sense out of the legislation. The results from these efforts, while they were at times enlightening, created a haze of confusion in the general public about Family Cap impacts that persists even now as the dance over welfare reform reauthorization, after passage of the Deficit Reduction Act of 2005, begins to change rhythm. It is hoped this book will help inform a public that could benefit from a few more facts about how and why Family Caps affect the fertility decisions of women on public welfare.

Acknowledgments

The evaluation of New Jersey's Family Development program was supported under contract number A63003 by the New Jersey Department of Human Services, by the Administration for Children and Families (ACF), United States Department of Health and Human Services (USDHHS), and by the Assistant Secretary for Planning and Evaluation (ASPE), USDHHS. Additional funding was provided by the Henry J. Kaiser Family Foundation. Rudy Myers, assistant director for planning and operations, New Jersey Division of Family Development, played a pivotal role in supplying public assistance, labor, and Medicaid administrative data. Without his help it is difficult to imagine how this evaluation project would ever have been completed.

The same can be said for my colleagues on the Rutgers evaluation team: Carol Harvey, Mark Killingsworth, and Radha Jagannathan. Carol Harvey served as the project's co-principal investigator and cost-benefit expert. As the criticism of our research increased in both volume and shrillness, Carol's faith in the conceptual and methodological soundness of our work never wavered. Mark Killingsworth brought his superb skills in econometric modeling and a certain stoicism to the project, a combination of rigor and detachment that kept our interpretation from straying too far from the data. Radha Jagannathan began the project as a Rutgers student, provided virtually all of the critical programming on the project while completing her doctorate at Princeton University, and finished the project as a Rutgers University faculty member. To say that Radha was the glue that held the team together would be to vastly understate her role. Her analytic and conceptual contributions are essential to many of the empirical arguments made in this book.

Several other individuals also played important roles in the development of the book. I thank Usha Sambamoorthi, late of the Rutgers Center on Heath, Health Care Policy, and Aging for her work on making sense out of New Jersey's Medicaid claims files. My colleagues, Al Roberts and Paul Lerman, like me, former members of the Rutgers School of Social Work faculty, provided numerous reasons why this book needed to be written. David Rumbo, project officer from the Rutgers University Division of Research and Sponsored Programs, was supportive when other voices in the administration fell silent. I will never forget his gentle scolding of New Jersey State administrators and lawyers, who sought to limit our publication rights, with the affirmation "Rutgers University does not do secret research." In addition, I am very grateful for the editorial assistance I have been given by Maura Roessner of Oxford University Press. Her patience was the perfect antidote for my procrastination. The book benefited considerably from the comments provided by three anonymous reviewers. Typing and editorial assistance provided by Meera Jagannathan are also greatly appreciated.

Finally, these acknowledgments would not be complete without my recognition of the role played by my wife, Anne, who encouraged me to close some of these chapters in my life.

Contents

Family Caps, Abortion, and Women of Color

1

Reforming Welfare with Family Caps

Introduction

The Family Cap or child exclusion, as it is often called, attempts to reform welfare by targeting a woman's decision to conceive and bring a baby to term while she is receiving cash benefits under the Temporary Assistance for Needy Families (TANF) program. Prior to the passage of the Personal Responsibility and Work Opportunity Reconciliation Act (PRWORA) in July 1996, Family Caps focused on this decision while women were receiving public assistance under Aid to Families with Dependent Children (AFDC). Currently 23 states have some form of Family Cap in place with most following the "gestation period" model first implemented by New Jersey in October 1992.[1] Under this model benefit caps apply to any child who is born 10 or more months subsequent to the mother's application for or receipt of TANF or AFDC.[2] Since a woman must have given birth to a child (or children) in order to qualify for TANF/AFDC in the first place, Family Caps cannot be applied to a child (or children) born outside of welfare or to a child (or children) receiving benefits prior to a Cap's implementation. Hence, Family Caps can only target subsequent births.

Seventeen of the 23 states that adopted a Family Cap did so before the authorization of PRWORA,[3] with New Jersey leading the way. Family Caps in these states were initiated under provisions of Section 1115 of the Social Security Act that allowed states to waive specific provisions of the Act to experiment with initiatives that would improve the AFDC program. The federal government especially encouraged experiments or demonstration projects designed to reduce welfare recipiency, ease the transition of welfare recipients into the labor market, or advance the work objectives of the AFDC program.[4] The New Jersey evaluation, conducted by my colleagues and me at Rutgers University, was one of the very few that focused on the potential impacts of Family Caps on the fertility outcomes of women on AFDC. All of the states that implemented a Family Cap under Section 1115 chose to continue Family Caps after the passage of PRWORA with six additional states making Family Caps a rule under their TANF programs. The remaining states chose not to implement any sort of child exclusion provision, which is their prerogative under PRWORA.

The fact that fewer than half the states have opted for a Family Cap is indicative of the great passion this particular welfare reform policy has engendered across the country. This is because Family Caps seek to promote self-sufficiency in welfare recipients through an alteration in family culture, that is, the norms and preferences that are viewed as supporting welfare dependency. Richard Fording recognizes this thrust when he identifies Family Caps as "value-instilling" waivers; so does Gwendolyn Mink when she refers to Caps as the replacement of a simple "means test for welfare with a means and morals test" that assesses the legitimacy of poor mothers' economic need in terms of the marital conditions under which they bore their children.[5]

Family Caps presented several problems for the U.S. Congress and President Bill Clinton that eroded support for their federal implementation. There was the historical conflict between the rehabilitation and values creation goals of welfare reform, embodied in a basic Democratic-Republican party split. Clinton was apparently never a big supporter of a policy he saw as having nothing to do with work and everything to do with harming children,[6] and there were two additional issues surrounding Family Caps that created fractures both across and within party lines: namely, alleged racism and abortion.

Welfare reform discussions targeting illegitimacy, out-of-wedlock births, and single-parent households made many Democratic representatives and senators uneasy, conjuring up again the race-laden images of the 1965 Moynihan Report, Charles Murray and the black underclass, and "eugenics for the Negroes."[7] Theodore Cross uttered the thoughts of many blacks when he asserted that "out-of-wedlock births among blacks appear, in large measure, to account for PRWORA."[8] Ron Haskins, a former congressional staffer, who had worked with Newt Gingrich, Dick Armey, and House Republicans to pass "The Contract with America" in 1994, made this linkage between welfare reform and black birth control explicit in his discussion of the illegitimacy bonuses available through PRWORA. "The District of Columbia has won the bonus twice, but the most significant factor contributing to this success appears to be that the nonmarital birth rate has been declining faster than in any other group and Washington, D.C. has the highest percentage of blacks nationwide."[9] Haskins notes elsewhere that bonuses were the consolation prize to House Republicans who could not get a Family Cap through the Senate.[10]

There was also the fear that utilizing Family Caps to reduce illegitimacy would increase the number of abortions to women on welfare. This specter not only divided Republicans and Democrats, but was divisive among a great many Republicans as well. Organizations like the Heritage Foundation, Family Research Council, and the Christian Coalition favored Caps even at the risk of increasing abortions. Gary Bauer and Senator Phil Gramm, strong supporters of Family Caps, held that Caps could reduce both illegitimacy and abortions by helping to instill personal responsibility.[11] Charles Murray declared that Caps should have any number of healthy effects. "It will lead many young women who shouldn't be mothers to place their babies for adoption. This is good. It will lead others, watching what happens to their sisters, to take steps not to get pregnant. This is also good. Many others will get abortions. Whether this is good depends on what one thinks of abortion."[12] The National Right-to-Life Committee, the U.S. Catholic Bishops Council, and other pro-life groups, in fact, did not think much of abortion and expressed unwavering opposition to Family Caps.[13] To bolster their position, foes began to cite research on the Cap that was being conducted in New Jersey, indicating a possible relationship between Family Cap implementation and abortion.[14] This research, my research, was beginning to receive close scrutiny by politicians and the interest groups and policy experts who sought to influence the future course of welfare reform as a values-instilling initiative. What I was about to learn was that the Family Cap research conducted by my colleagues and me was released into an environment where, Hugh Hecho describes, "the past lack of trustworthy, understandable information has poisoned both public understanding and the politics of welfare reform,"[15] where emotion and reason blend too easily in a red state-blue state kaleidoscope, and where, in Larry Mead's words, political groups appear neither accountable to each other nor to the facts.[16] As we shall see, it is an environment where great efforts are expended to control the meaning and influence of research findings.

Public Welfare and Rehabilitaton

Since its inception under Title IV-A of the 1935 Social Security Act, Congress has typically avoided attempts to reform the Aid to Dependent Children (ADC), renamed AFDC in 1962, through values-instilling initiatives such as Family Caps. Instead, most of the attempts at reform have centered on work requirements for recipients and on punishments for the violation of those work rules. Such an emphasis on the (re)development of the welfare recipient's human capital, that is, her work skills and knowledge, might be expected from a program whose origins lay in misfortune and not in misconduct.[17]

When the program began in 1935, ADC/AFDC was written as an extension of the mother's pension programs that a number of states had created for widows and, as Hecho notes, in some cases for desertion.[18] For the first several years of the program a lump sum payment was made to the estate of the children under 16 years of age, who were deprived of parental support due to parental death, incapacitation, or unemployment. The 1939 Amendments to the Act ended lump sum payments and made monthly payments to these children. Older children were covered in 1940 and spouses began to receive benefits themselves in 1950.[19] Until about 1950, death, incapacitation and, to a much lesser extent, unemployment of the father were the principle reasons for granting ADC/AFDC payments to children. This all changed in 1951 when, for the first time, desertion of the father accounted for more than 50 percent of the child cases. By the time the first welfare-to-work reforms to AFDC were passed under President John Kennedy in 1962, father desertions were implicated in about 65 percent of the children receiving AFDC.[20]

The 1962 Amendments to the Social Security Act marked the first major attempt by the federal government to address the growing problem of dependency on AFDC that had emerged following World War II. From 1946 to 1962, the number of children on AFDC had increased from 800,000 to nearly 3 million, about 256 percent, and pressure mounted in Congress and in state legislatures to pressure deserted women into the workforce. But as Nancy Rose and others have observed, when Kennedy signed these amendments into law he explained that they were intended to help the system provide rehabilitation instead of relief and training for useful work instead of prolonged dependency.[21] The centerpiece rehabilitation program of the 1962 Amendments was the Community Work and Training (CWT) initiative, which sought to increase the human capital of mothers through training support services like child care and transportation reimbursement and orientation into productive work habits.

In the midst of his "War on Poverty," Lyndon Johnson attempted to further the welfare goal of rehabilitation through a new set of Amendments to the Act in 1967. Community Work and Training and several other small work experience and training programs were replaced with the Work Incentive (WIN) program, which expanded the job training, work readiness, monetary work incentives, and funding for child care that were initiated in 1962. But perhaps the most significant incentive in the 1967 amendments was the "thirty and a third rule." Prior to this rule all earnings by a mother were deducted from the AFDC grant amount. The thirty and a third provision allowed recipients to keep the first $30 per month of any earnings plus one-third of their remaining pay.[22] This amendment led to more working mothers and also led to dramatic increases in the size of the AFDC caseload. In 1970 the number of children on AFDC had reached 5.5 million and by 1981 the number was more than 7.6 million.[23] Equally troubling to federal and state officials was the fact that the proportion of working or unemployed parents did not increase substantially despite 20 years of rehabilitative efforts, with consistency hovering around 4 percent.

Fueled by the rising welfare caseload, Ronald Reagan worked with a Democratic Congress to pass the 1981 Omnibus Budget Reconciliation Act (OBRA) and the Work Incentive (WIN) Demonstration Programs. While viewed by many as the beginning of the truly punitive era of welfare reform,[24] OBRA did a great deal to provide operational definitions for the term "welfare recipient rehabilitation." To be sure, the Act did place substantial limits on deductions for work-related expenses, income disregards under the thirty and one-third rule, child care subsidies, and WIN income disregards. And OBRA resulted in 300,000 families losing AFDC benefits and an estimated 400,000 families losing eligibility.[25]

Under OBRA and the WIN Demonstrations a broad range of rehabilitation approaches was entertained and encouraged. Welfare recipients were assisted through a variety of human capital development programs including General High School Equivalency Degrees (GEDs), remedial adult education, two- or four-year college, English as a Second Language (ESL), basic education and academic classroom activities, and vocational training. These programs, while preparing welfare recipients for the world of work, often did not yield immediate employment. This goal was met more quickly through labor force attachment programs like job search, life skills training, work supplementation, on-the-job training (OJT), and work experience programs.[26] Job search was facilitated through the formation of "job clubs"; work experience was aided through government-sponsored Community Work Experience Programs (CWEPs).

The Family Support Act (FSA), passed by Congress in 1988, made many of the work initiatives of OBRA and the WIN Demonstrations a statutory part of the AFDC program. WIN and the WIN Demonstrations were replaced with the Job Opportunities and Basic Skills Training (JOBS) Program. Reflecting the experience with the WIN Demonstrations, Congress offered a broad range of education and training services but required that states "must include at least two of the following four activities: job search, CWEP or other work experience, grant diversion (work supplementation) or on-the-job training."[27] As Mary Jo Bane and David T. Ellwood note, however, JOBS went a good deal further than WIN in promoting work for wages. Whereas WIN required women to register for work or work-related activities, JOBS required actual participation in these activities. Exemptions from work activities were tightened: women with children as young as three years of age were now required to engage in activities; under WIN women with children six or younger could decline work or work training.[28]

In the years between the passage of OBRA and FSA, welfare remained relatively stable with, on average, about 7.3 million children receiving benefits each year. But many state governors and legislators complained that few women on AFDC were actually getting jobs, leading to a "revolving door" of eligibility. Indeed, it was a number of governors, including the soon to be

President Clinton, who pushed for an FSA that would be more supportive of families working to leave AFDC.[29]

FSA required that states guarantee child care and transportation services for women engaged in employment and training. It also required states to provide one year of transitional child care and Medicaid coverage to women who leave AFDC because of work.[30] The earned income disregard was raised from $75 a month under OBRA to $90 a month, and participation standards for the JOBS program were established for fiscal years 1990 through 1995. States were expected to have 20 percent of AFDC mothers involved in work or work training by 1995.

The Family Support Act did not yield the outcomes expected by its advocates. Beginning in 1990, the AFDC caseloads began a rapid ascent. In 1994 the number of children on public assistance reached an all-time high of over 9.5 million[31] and, like WIN, the legacy of JOBS was inefficient bureaucracy and too few jobs.[32] Welfare reform as an almost exclusively rehabilitation-through-work effort ended with the passage of PRWORA.

Public Welfare Values Subtext

While it may have taken 60 years for personal values to assume prominence in public welfare legislation, the morality of cash assistance was never left unaddressed. Martin Gilens reminds us that even as Franklin Roosevelt established the first federal welfare programs in 1935 he referred to welfare as a "narcotic" and a "subtle destroyer of the human spirit." In his annual message to Congress in 1935, Roosevelt proclaimed that "continued dependence on relief induces a spiritual and moral disintegration fundamentally destructive to the national fiber."[33] The 1939 Amendments to the Social Security Act also made a rather explicit values statement when it pulled widows and children of workers out of ADC and allowed them to receive benefits under the Old Age Insurance Program. Robert Lieberman remarks that pulling the worthy widows out of ADC left the program with "abandoned and unmarried mothers, mothers with husbands in jail or widows whose husbands had worked in noncovered occupations or who had never worked."[34]

The changing caseload of AFDC precipitated some initial, if halting, attempts at instilling values or "legislating morality," as some began to call it, in women receiving public assistance.[35] In 1950 Congress amended ADC to require states to notify law enforcement agencies if welfare was being given to a child who had been deserted. It was hoped that local government would track down fathers and force them to pay child support. In 1975 a new statute was added to the Social Security Act Title IV-D, which provided federal funds for enforcing child support. These monies were to be used to locate nonresident parents, establish paternity, establish child support awards, and collect money.[36] AFDC was amended in 1974 to make maternal cooperation in the establishment of paternity a condition of receiving welfare.[37] The Deficit Reduction Act of 1984 required states to adopt numerical guidelines for determining federal child support awards and to garnish the wages of fathers who were more than one month behind in their child support payments.[38]

The Family Support Act (FSA) went even further in efforts to make fathers responsible for their children. The first section of the Act promulgates guidelines for computing child support amounts, establishing paternity through genetic testing, tracking nonresident fathers, withholding wages, and placing unemployed fathers in the JOBS program. The Act also dropped the pretense, hazily visible in the 1950 Notification of Law Enforcement Officers (NOLEO) provision of ADC, that child support enforcement was simply all about fathers. Winifred Bell argues convincingly that child enforcement measures have been subtle ways of calling attention to illegitimate births; that is, AFDC homes where women had children outside of marriage.[39] The FSA leaves less ambiguity when setting federal standards for state efforts to establish paternity. "The standard relates to the percentage obtained by dividing the number of children in the state who are born out of wedlock, are receiving cash benefits or IV-D child support services, and for whom paternity has been established by the number of children who are born out of wedlock and are receiving cash benefits or IV-D child support services."[40]

The FSA attempted to reform welfare primarily by developing self-sufficiency in recipients through participation in JOBS. Bane and Ellwood, among others, also contend that FSA held out the promise "for changing the culture of the welfare system" by required work and sanctions for nonparticipation.[41] In its own fashion, then, FSA relied on rehabilitation; values-instilling measures were limited to the child support provisions of the Act. The role of family values modification in a changing welfare culture was to become much more substantial with the passage of PRWORA in 1996.

The PRWORA legislation ended the AFDC entitlement program and, in so doing, provided state governors and legislatures much more flexibility in crafting approaches to welfare and work programs. Two block grants to states formed the financial core of PRWORA: TANF, which funded cash grants to needy families, and a child care block grant that subsidizes child care for families on welfare, families leaving welfare, and other low-income families who could be vulnerable to welfare spells.[42] Some other noteworthy changes that PRWORA accomplished in welfare policy include the following:

- Placed a two-year time limit on cash assistance if a recipient has not worked, and a five-year lifetime limit on cash assistance with exemptions for up to 20 percent of the caseload.
- Made states responsible for the labor force participation of 25 percent of single-parent recipients by 1997 and 50 percent of recipients by 2002.

- Imposed penalties on states if they failed to meet these above-mentioned employment goals.
- Instituted a maintenance-of-effort provision that required states to continue spending 75–80 percent of their pre-PRWORA welfare funding.
- Defined work activities as comprising unsubsidized employment, subsidized private employment, subsidized public employment, work experience, on-the-job training, job search and job readiness assistance, community service, vocational education training, provision of child care to TANF recipients, job skills training directly related to employment, education directly related to employment, satisfactory attendance in secondary education or a GED program if the recipient is a dropout.
- Provided Medicaid coverage to families ineligible for cash assistance for work (18 months), families ineligible because of earnings from child support (14 months), and families that would have been eligible for AFDC.[43]

The impact of this new rehabilitation package continues to be the topic of ongoing debate. After peaking in 1994, caseloads began a sharp descent. In 1996 the average monthly count of children on AFDC/TANF was 8.7 million; by 2000 the number was just under 4 million.[44] Studies of recipient transition from welfare to work have revealed that more than 60 percent of the women who left TANF cash assistance in 1997 and 1999 were employed.[45] Pamela Winston, however, cites a major "leaver study" that indicates that most of the recipients who left welfare did not escape poverty. Low-paying jobs with few or no benefits resulted in about 30 percent returning to public assistance.[46] I will have a bit more to say about the success of welfare reform's rehabilitative strategy later.

Rehabilitation through work was just one of the principal goals of PRWORA. Under Section 401 of the Act, Congress clearly views the barriers to self-sufficiency not merely as an employment skills problem but as a family structure and values problem as well. States are expressly called upon to operate TANF to "prevent and reduce the incidence of out-of-wedlock pregnancies and establish annual numerical goals for preventing and reducing the incidence of these pregnancies" and, additionally, "encourage the formation and maintenance of two-parent families."[47]

To help achieve these goals of family formation and responsible child-bearing, PRWORA made nearly 50 changes to the existing child support law. Payments to families leaving welfare were increased and states were given increased financial support to develop a computerized registry of IV-D cases. Employers were required to send information on new employees to a centralized State Directory of New Hires. Child enforcement agencies were given computer access to the motor vehicle and law enforcement locator systems of all states to facilitate tracking. The establishment of paternity through DNA testing for children 18 years of age and under, even in cases that had previously been dismissed because of the expiration of previously established statutes of limitations, was required.[48] Finally, TANF cash assistance was made contingent on a woman's supplying specific identifying information on the father (or fathers) of her child (children).

The PRWORA legislation, even without a mandatory Family Cap, still included a number of provisions designed to reduce out-of-wedlock child-bearing, defined in the Act as births to never married women. Monies were allocated through the TANF block grant and additional funds to fund abstinence education, and programs to combat teenage pregnancy and encourage male responsibility. But the principal initiative outlined in PRWORA to address out-of-wedlock births was a set of numerical standards aimed at a state's "illegitimacy ratio" (Section 403 (a)(2)(b)). This ratio is really a combination of two ratios: the first is the comparison of a state's out-of-wedlock births during the most recent two-year period with the number of such births in the previous two-year period, and the second is the number of induced pregnancy terminations (abortions) in the state for the fiscal year compared to the number of abortions in 1995. Each year the five states with the largest decrease in births that do not experience an increase in abortions were each to be awarded a $20 million bonus, an amount that could $25 million if fewer than five states proved eligible. Moreover, states successful in reducing their illegitimacy ratios were eligible for a share of a $9 billion "performance bonus" fund.[49]

Welfare Provision and States' Rights

Quite correctly, critics of the 1935 Social Security Act describe a mindfully constructed, two-track system—one for the "deserving" or "worthy" poor and the other for the undeserving—in which individual states have played a major role in constructing the second track.[50] On the first track is the Old-Age Insurance Program, which today is technically known as the Old Age, Survivors and Disability Insurance (OASDI) program, but is simply called Social Security by most Americans. Social Security provides monthly benefits to retired and disabled workers, their dependents and/or survivors, and is funded through payroll deductions contributed by these workers. Others on the track are workers who are laid off and who receive wage replacement under the Unemployment Insurance (UI) or Compensation (UC) program. Unemployment Compensation is also funded by payroll deductions, paid for by the employer on the worker's behalf, in exchange for credits on state unemployment taxes. Unlike Social Security, which is a federal program, UI was established as a joint federal-state program with states responsible for setting tax levels, eligibility requirements, and benefit levels.[51]

ADC, along with Old Age Assistance (OAA) and blind assistance, formed the second track under Social Security.[52] These programs were designed as income-tested or need-based benefits and are funded from general tax revenues. Like UI, ADC represents a federal-state partnership, except in this case there is no contributory component on the part of the individual or a third-party employer. Arguably, moreover, the policy role played by states in setting administrative procedures, eligibility requirements, and benefit levels has been far more pronounced than what has occurred in the UC program.

The evolution of ADC/AFDC/TANF is perhaps best viewed as an ongoing conflict between state and federal perspectives on the relevance of non-contributory welfare payments for the healthy functioning of society. Lieberman points out that this battle has been fought continually in administrative, legislative, and legal venues.[53] It is of interest to note that when the course of the conflict is charted by many policy experts in Washington, it is characterized as "devolution," for example, a kind of retrograde evolution where the central government has surrendered its powers to state and local agencies.[54]

At its inception in 1935, ADC was funded as a federal-state, 50-50 matching program with states allowed to set their cash assistance grants at any level deemed necessary to meet need. In 1958, variable matching formulas were introduced with the federal share ranging in states from 50 percent to as high as 78 percent.[55] Wide variations in benefit levels have always been a hallmark of AFDC and these differences continue through the implementation of TANF. In 2000, for example, the Administration for Children and Families (ACF) and the USDHHS reported that monthly benefit levels for a family of three were $164 in Alabama, $204 in Arkansas, $424 in New Jersey, and $577 in New York. These amounts remained unchanged from the years immediately prior to the passage of PRWORA.[56]

The issue of cash grant amounts is, of course, inextricably bound up with the criteria used to define need and states vary considerably in eligibility thresholds they applied and continue to apply to this day. Francis Piven and Richard Cloward note that a number of states applied the principle of "less eligibility" to ensure that welfare grant levels were always kept lower than wages from the lowest paying jobs in the state.[57] Many states adopted or attempted to institute one- or two-year residency requirements to guard against the "welfare magnet" phenomenon. Compulsory work rules attempted to tie welfare payments to seeking work in appropriate seasons when farm or tourism help was needed.[58] Some states made a welfare claimant's morality a criterion of need. Among the more notorious values-centered measures were "man-in-the-house" rules and "suitable home policies."[59] The former were surveillance procedures used to determine if able-bodied men were obtaining income through their wives, paramours, or children instead of through employment. By 1960, 23 states also had put in place policies that defined the homes of unwed mothers as unfit to raise children and referred the children in such homes as "illegitimate." Unsuitable homes and the unfit mothers and illegitimate children who inhabited them were ineligible for ADC/AFDC. Court intervention, precipitated by the welfare rights movement of the 1960s, was successful in striking down a great many of these eligibility criteria.

It is also true that states were often loath to put in place welfare initiatives highly recommended, if not required, by the federal government. The 1962 amendments to ADC permitted federal reimbursement to states for the creation of Aid to Dependent Children with Unemployed Fathers (ADC-UP later AFDC-UP). A great many states, particularly in the South, were slow to adopt this option, often citing its potential to extend, not reduce, welfare dependency.[60] In 1988 the Family Support Act required all states to establish an AFDC-UP program.[61] Another example of states' resistance was in the provision of social services, that is, counseling and other noncash benefits, to welfare recipients. In this case, the federal government offered a 75 percent (federal)-25 percent (state) matching grant formula to states for training social workers and the provision of support services.[62]

The first 40 to 45 years of the state role in the delivery of AFDC casts state and local governments in a perhaps well-deserved Dickensian light. Lieberman describes the state posture as parochial, discretionary, and unstable.[63] Pamela Winston, citing John Madison in Federalist Paper #10, warns that smaller jurisdictions contain a narrower diversity of interests that increase the danger that a powerful majority faction will oppress a minority. She remarks that "from this perspective, localism may be less democratic and could be dominated by local elites."[64] Unfortunately, such portrayals, which are commonplace in the devolution literature, neglect to acknowledge how states have advanced our empirical knowledge base on the effects of public assistance and welfare reform.

A number of states used the guidance promulgated in OBRA, and the WIN Demonstrations, to develop innovative demonstration programs and to evaluate their effectiveness in reducing welfare dependency. States like Arkansas, Kentucky, Illinois, West Virginia, Virginia, California, Maryland, Maine, and New Jersey formed partnerships with the federal government, foundations and evaluators such as Abt, and the Manpower Demonstration Research Corporation (MDRC) to examine the outcomes and costs of a variety of rehabilitation approaches. These research/demonstrations, particularly those involving MDRC, had much to do with the structure and passage of the Family Support Act.[65]

Use of Section 1115 of the Social Security Act by states to examine new welfare delivery strategies increased dramatically under the first George Bush and Clinton administrations. President Clinton approved a total of 83 waiver applications from 43 states and the District of Columbia; many of these applications proposed experimental or strong quasi-experimental designs to assess expected program impacts. States experimented with changes in the treatment of earned income disregards, the treatment of countable assets, eligibility rules such as time limits on recipiency and Family Caps, increased work responsibilities, modifications of the JOBS program, transitional employment, and new approaches to child support enforcement.[66] The Greater Avenues for Independence (GAIN) demonstration, evaluated by MDRC, provided convincing evidence to Congress for the efficacy of a labor

force attachment approach to work rehabilitation.[67] The PRWORA work activities draw heavily on this research and a set of related welfare-to-work
program evaluations.[68] If anything, the willingness of states to engage in demonstrations and their evaluations, in David Ellwood's words, helped bring
"reason and research in an area swamped by anecdote and emotion."[69]

The PRWORA legislation contained two provisions that continue the
federal-state partnership to build a research-grounded, welfare reform strategy.
One allows states to maintain waivers if the waiver will not result in increasing federal welfare spending above TANF block grant levels.[70] The second,
contained in Section 413, directs the development of "studies on the effects of
different [state] programs and the operation of such programs on welfare dependency, illegitimacy, teen pregnancy, employment rates, child well-being,
and any other area."[71] Scores of studies conducted under the auspices of the
U.S. Department of Health and Human Services–Administration for Children and Families (USDHHS–ACF) and the Office of the Assistant Secretary
for Planning and Evaluation in the U.S. Department of Health and Human
Services (ASPE–USDHHS) added to our understanding of the impact(s) of
welfare reform.[72]

A number of policy analysts have tried to make sense out of state variability under PRWORA through the classification of state program implementation strategies. Most of these taxonomies focus on the level of punishment believed to be inherent in a state's package of welfare reforms.
LaDonna Pavetti and Dan Bloom organized states in a two-dimensional
matrix with states adopting time limits of less than five years and work
requirements/sanctions stricter than in basic PRWORA called "stringent"
and their antipodes "lenient."[73] Alan Weil combines Pavetti and Bloom's
dimensions into one-dimension "state limitation on welfare receipt without
work" and cross-classifies states on this factor and the state level of support
offered welfare recipients under the Earned Income Tax Credit (EITC). Low
levels of income support and strict welfare policies define "barrier" states.[74]
When states combine Family Caps with tougher work rules and sanctions,
as does New Jersey, they are consistently classified by policy analysts in
Washington as the harshest or toughest on welfare recipients.[75] Hence,
while the Dickensian light has dimmed, it still remains bright enough to
guide many a discussion on welfare reform and the role played by states.

2

New Jersey—Birthplace of the Family Cap

Introduction

New Jersey would seem a very unlikely place for the implementation of the first Section 1115–waivered Family Cap. The state's politics are dominated by liberal Democrats and moderate Republicans who might be expected to steer away from values-instilling approaches to welfare reform. The 2000 U.S. Census describes New Jersey as the most urbanized state in the nation with a population of about 8.4 million, most of whom live in small municipalities, segregated to a large extent by income and by race. The state's annual per capita income of nearly $30,000 is second only to Connecticut; approximately 12 percent of residents are black and 15 percent are Hispanic. New Jersey has only three municipalities with more than 100,000 residents: namely, Jersey City, Camden, and Newark, and the latter two rank among the poorest cities in the country. In recent years New Jersey has been confronted with a number of social issues—affordable housing, public school education, law enforcement—where racial bias has figured prominently in discussions of cause and consequence. The Supreme Court of New Jersey has never been reluctant to enter this public policy arena with remedies the Court believes promote social justice.[1] It is difficult to conceive of a more racially linked policy than welfare reform or a state where the legislative and court environments for a Family Cap would be more inhospitable.

The Racial Undertow in AFDC and TANF

The early annals of ADC/AFDC and the entire Social Security Act have been laced with statutory and administrative features that many welfare historians have pointed to as race-based or racially motivated. Michael Brown, for example, chronicles the political processes in Congress and in the Roosevelt administration that led to the exclusion of three-fifths of black workers from coverage under Old Age Insurance and Unemployment Insurance. He remarks that "after Congress excluded domestic and agricultural workers, public employees and workers in nonprofit, voluntary organizations (the occupations in which most blacks worked) just 53 percent of all gainful workers were covered."[2] The means-tested ADC and general relief programs, on the other hand, paid benefits to a disproportionate number of blacks, that is, disproportionate to their numbers in the general population, a service pattern that has remained unchanged from the Depression to today.[3] But this is to be expected, says Brown, because "white and black women have had different relationships to the welfare state, even though both have been burdened by the implicit patriarchal assumptions of social policy and by labor market discrimination. The cash transfer system protects white women against husband failure in addition to helping never-married mothers. White women rely less on AFDC than black women and they have greater access to social insurance and veterans programs, whether through marriage or through independent, work-related entitlements. For most black women the only alternative to AFDC is work, but not the kind of work that would typically support a family."[4] Race, moreover, is seen by many welfare policy analysts as the principal factor behind state differences in eligibility rules and benefit levels. Robert Lieberman finds that, as early as the late 1930s, higher concentrations of blacks in counties in the South and in northern cities were indicative of less ADC coverage.[5] Francis Piven and Richard Cloward trace the institution of eligibility rules like "man-in-the-house," "suitable home," and "less eligibility" to state and city concentrations of potential black recipients.[6] And in their independent tests of the racial hostility hypothesis posited by Jill Quadagno and the group threat thesis advanced by V. O. Key, some political scientists have found a strong correlation between state adoption of stringent welfare reform measures and the proportions of blacks in that state's general population.[7] Fording reports that Family Caps are a consistent 1115 waiver response of states with higher percentages of black women on AFDC[8]; Soss and his colleagues find an equally strong relationship between the number of marriage-aged black women (aged 15–44 years) and states opting for Family Caps, stricter work requirements, and time limits under PRWORA.[9]

The issue that continues to bind AFDC, welfare reform, and Family Caps most tightly with race is the dramatic increase in the number of "out-of-wedlock" (nonmarital) births that have occurred in our country from 1940 to the present. "Illegitimacy" has always been viewed as a black problem by many white Americans and is the primary motivation behind values-instilling forms of welfare reform.[10] In the historical background documentation that accompanies the PRWORA legislation, Congress presents black-white differences in illegitimacy rates which, since 1960, are, on average, nine times higher for black women.[11]

The link between black illegitimacy and AFDC utilization dates back to congressional and state concerns about the growing number of children on ADC with absent and/or deserting fathers. The event, however, that was instrumental in etching this relationship into the minds and discourse of politicians and the general public was the report coauthored in 1965 by Daniel Patrick Moynihan entitled "The Negro Family: The Case for National Action." Subsequently termed "The Moynihan Report," the authors present blacks caught in a "tangle of pathology" where male desertion and female illegitimacy have led to "a startling increase in welfare dependency."[12] The research of Charles Murray in the early 1980s reinforced the notion that black illegitimacy and AFDC were strongly related; in fact, he asserted that welfare payments promoted this illegitimacy.[13] Murray's later research, which appeared in the prestigious *Journal of Labor Economics*, went further: welfare benefits increased illegitimacy among black women in states where black populations were most highly concentrated.[14] Whether or not welfare causes illegitimacy, a subject of ongoing debate,[15] their simple correlation has certainly helped put a black face on both out-of-wedlock births and on AFDC/TANF in the mind of the general public.[16]

Using Family Caps to mitigate illegitimacy, especially black illegitimacy, also revives unpleasant memories among many who see the Cap as a reincarnation of the eugenics thinking of the 1960s and 1970s. Dorothy Roberts views Family Caps in the same light as birth control programs like Norplant and Depo-Provera and reproductive punishments like sterilization and family planning, programs eugenicists argued would "not only improve the race but also would reduce the cost of subsidizing the unfit."[17] Others have argued that Family Caps must increase abortions among black women because marriage or going it alone off welfare are even less attractive options.[18] Kenneth Neubeck and Noel Cazenave have termed current welfare reform efforts like Caps and time limits as "procreation-focused race control," policies that take choice away, even from the pro-choicers.[19]

There are some recent indications that welfare reform is not engendering self-sufficiency to the same extent in black families that it is among whites. Using data from the University of Michigan, Panel Study of Income Dynamics (PSID) and from USDHHS–ACF, Schram finds that since 1995 blacks consistently compose a larger percentage of the AFDC/TANF caseload than do whites.[20] The welfare spells of black women are likely to be longer than those of whites and the probability of blacks experiencing repeat spells is considerably greater.[21] Black women, moreover, tend to be disproportionately represented among the welfare recipients who are terminated from TANF not because of employment but for administrative sanctions and time limits.[22]

The racial baggage accompanying welfare reform with a Family Cap component would appear a bit too heavy and cumbersome for the politicians in New Jersey. Institutional racism, race-based population control, and increased dependency on TANF by black and Hispanic families are issues not likely to be confronted by the fainthearted. Unfortunately, or fortunately, depending on your feelings about Family Cap, New Jersey had a politician willing to do the heavy lifting—his name, Wayne Bryant.

Wayne Bryant's Family Cap

Family Caps or child exclusions had been proposed long before state Assemblyman Wayne Bryant brought his proposal for a Family Cap to the New Jersey governor and legislature in 1991. Such proposals were typically met with indifference or open rebuke. In 1960, Louisiana implemented a child exclusion policy cutting aid off to more than 23,000 children because their mothers had given birth to an out-of-wedlock child. The federal government quickly reinstated these children.[23] Joseph McD. Mitchell, city manager for Newburgh, New York, proposed a plan to control ADC spending in 1961 that also included benefit caps on women who had an additional birth while on welfare. The emotion with which the plan was greeted in much of the media and in the academy is captured in this thumbnail sketch offered by Robert Lieberman. "Mitchell himself was a right wing fanatic—a grotesque—comic character and an exemplar of the paranoid style—and he pandered to the ugliest strains of racism in a community that was just entering the decline that overtook so many Northern cities in the 1960s."[24]

When Wayne Bryant proposed his Family Cap he had two advantages his predecessors lacked. The mood of the country was undergoing a significant change and what were once termed punitive or draconian welfare reforms were now receiving much wider acceptance.[25] Bryant's second advantage was that he was a black legislator representing a minority constituency in Camden, the poorest municipality in New Jersey. Nina Perales, in her unflattering portrait of the evolution of New Jersey's Family Cap, acknowledges the importance of Bryant's race for other potential Family Cap supporters: "One white New Jersey senator stated that it would be very difficult for a white to raise the subject of welfare dependency. A white raising the same concerns would be called a racist. Wayne Bryant is doing us all a favor by focusing the debate."[26] The Bryant strategy for moving a Family Cap through a Democratically controlled legislature for signature by a Democrat governor demonstrated three qualities that helped ensure success: for example, (1) embedding the Cap within a rehabilitation context, (2) discussing Family Cap objectives with shibboleth and generality while avoiding any

reference to illegitimacy or out-of-wedlock births, and (3) expressing solidarity with the black welfare recipients most likely to be affected by a
Family Cap.

In testimony at public hearings held in the summer and fall of 1991, Bryant
made clear the importance of his pedigree for creating meaningful welfare
reform legislation. Citing the fact that black families composed 50 percent of
the AFDC caseload in the state, Bryant said that "as an African-American, I
will not tolerate anyone having my people disproportionately in a system that
is going to keep them permanently in poverty, without them having some
responsibility."[27] As to why a Cap was needed, Bryant offered this reasoning:
"So, therefore, when folks say it's a denial of benefits—no, I just came up with
another way that folks could be responsible like the rest of us. I often wonder
why no one focuses on that point, that we have given folks an opportunity to do
like other folks do—work for their kids."[28] Bryant's expressions of solidarity
with the very individuals targeted by the Family Cap proved to be very effective in blunting criticisms expressed by many statewide, liberal advocacy
groups. Goertzel and Hart remark that Bryant's race denied the opposition the
argument that the reform was motivated by racism or mean-spiritedness.[29] In
responding to charges by the National Organization for Women (NOW), the
American Civil Liberties Union (ACLU), the National Association of Social
Workers (NASW), and the Association for Children of New Jersey (ACNJ) that
Family Caps punish children, the Bryant reply was to recriminate; to ask why
organizations professing to help minorities were supporting a welfare system
that ensured a life of poverty.

As Wayne Bryant began to craft his welfare reform, called the Family
Development Program (FDP), he was very careful to avoid references to
program objectives that connoted population control. You will not find any
substantive discussion of nonmarital birthrates in the state assembly bills
that Bryant used to structure and pass his program.[30] Program guidelines
provided to county planning departments, welfare agencies, advocacy
groups, and the general public identified three Family Development Program goals: "breaking the cycle of poverty," "strengthening and reuniting
families," and "enhancing the role of individual responsibility."[31] A mechanism for achieving this last goal was a Family Cap, described in this language: "FDP encourages individuals to be responsible by empowering them
to make decisions for themselves. One important way the FDP encourages
decision making is to offer parents a choice regarding their decision to have
another child while receiving public assistance. As of October 1, 1992, an
AFDC recipient will not receive a benefit increase for an additional child
born on or after August 1, 1993."[32] As we shall see, the vagueness of these
program objectives created a political environment that made it rather easy
for state officials to gainsay any measures of program impact I and my colleagues used in our independent evaluation of FDP.

The Family Cap legislation in New Jersey was certainly made more palatable by placing it in a bundle of reforms that were directed at improving

the effectiveness of the JOBS component in the Family Support Act. Indeed, Bryant justified the need for FDP by citing the failure of REACH, New Jersey's name for its welfare program under the Family Support Act, "to provide the variety or intensity of services to address the many and deep-rooted needs of the populations of these counties and municipalities."[33]

Table 2.1 provides a side-by-side comparison of the differences between FDP and AFDC under FSA. The first nine components of FDP were promoted as improvements to JOBS and were termed elements of "Enhanced JOBS."

Family Cap under FDP also was a bit more complex than early media accounts and some social science analyses seemed to portray. A segment on the CBS news program *60 Minutes*, called "The $64 Question," focused on the amount of cash assistance that would be lost to an AFDC family of three, a mother and two children, if the mother were to have a third child.[34] If, however, the mother had only one child and was about to bear a second while on welfare for ten or more months, the cash loss would be $102, not $64. The Cap was, in effect, family-size sensitive. Capped families also received additional food stamps to help offset their cash loss.[35]

FDP was signed into law by the governor of New Jersey in January 1992. The state requested federal consideration of the program under Section 1115 Waiver provisions in July. One month later FDP was approved and on October 1, 1992, FDP and its Family Cap began operating.

Family Cap in the Courts

Two months after the FDP program was implemented, the National Organization for Women Legal Defense Fund along with the New Jersey Chapter of the ACLU and Legal Services of New Jersey filed a class action suit against Donna E. Shalala, U.S. Secretary of Health and Human Services, and William Waldman, New Jersey Commissioner of Human Services, in U.S. District Court. The suit, *C.K. v. Shalala*, alleged that Family Cap was a government-sponsored program of discrimination against poor women that improperly intruded into their personal decisions to bear children.[36] The National Organization for Women's argument proceeded along two pathways: the first disputed the administrative process used to implement FDP while the second questioned the constitutionality of the Family Cap.

The focus of the administrative challenges centered on the application of the 1115 waiver process by the state and federal government. The attorneys representing NOW charged that neither the state nor federal defendant had explained how the Family Cap waiver satisfied the improvement requirements of Section 1115 and that the secretary had exceeded her authority in approving such a program. The plaintiffs also stated that the evaluation component of the 1115 waiver process violated federal guidelines for the protection of human subjects.[37]

Table 2.1. Comparison of Program Components under New Jersey's Family
Development Program and the Family Support Act of 1988

Family Development Program	Family Support Act
1. Recipient with child under 2 must participate in counseling and vocational assessment.	Exempt if child is under 2, but may volunteer.
2. Recipient with child 2 years or older must participate in FDP activities.	Recipients who have a child 3 years or older and are in a federal target group must participate.
3. Participants must complete a Family Plan, including a written contract, outlining the participant and each family member's educational and job goals.	Participants complete an Employability Plan and a signed agreement.
4. The Family Plan includes support services (child care, transportation, Medicaid for up to two years if eligibility lost due to earned income). Post-AFDC families must have been on AFDC for three out of six months prior to loss of benefits to receive extension.	Provides same support services, however, Medicaid benefits extended only for one year and families are required to have been on AFDC for one month prior to loss of benefits.
5. Job development and placement, counseling, vocational assessment, intensive remedial education, job search assistance, community work experience, job-specific employment skills training, on-the-job training. Services are provided to all family members.	Services are the same except they are not extended to family members.
6. High school diploma or equivalency for each participant and family member before assignment to vocational activity. Exemptions granted if there is a legitimate inability to complete. If exempt, referred to alternative educational programs, employment, job training, job search.	High school diploma or equivalency mandated only for custodial parents under age 18. Needs assessment and individual employment goal determine education requirements. Only participants under 25 must acquire a high school diploma regardless of whether or not employment goals require it.
7. Case management must conduct an assessment of health-related, educational, social, and vocational needs for the participant and family members.	Participants are eligible for determined services and activities.

Table 2.1.   (*continued*)

Family Development Program	Family Support Act
Services to the participant and the family must include remedial education and/or training and parent skills training.	Services extended to family members are less comprehensive.
8. A Family Resource Center must be established in each county. Services will be collocated to the maximum extent possible.	Is not required.
9. Failure to participate without good cause will result in a reduction in benefits of at least 20 percent or ineligibility for at least ninety days.	Failure to participate without good cause will result in a reduction in grant by per capita share for that person for 1) a minimum of thirty days, 2) for six months or longer, or 3) based on the number of noncompliances.
Elimination of the "marriage penalty" i.e., a woman can continue to receive cash benefits for her biological children when she marries a man who is not the children's father so long as the annual income of the household does not exceed 150 percent of the poverty level.	If a woman marries the income of a spouse is countable in the computation of cash benefits for children in the household.
Family Cap: A woman who gives birth to a child 10 or months from their AFDC application date will not receive full cash benefits for the child.	Benefits increase with each child added to the eligible household.

New Jersey Department of Human Services, Division of Family Development, Program Comparison Summary, October 1992.

The constitutional argument offered by NOW held that the Family Cap violated the guarantees of due process and of equal protection under the Fourteenth Amendment by penalizing vulnerable children for the behaviors of their parents. In effect, it was alleged that the Family Cap created two classes of children, some of whom receive welfare benefits and some who do not based only on the timing of their births. The *C.K. v. Shalala* brief also stated that New Jersey's Family Cap violated the procreative privacy of a woman by interfering with her decision of when and under what circumstance she could bear a child.[38] The structure of this lawsuit was to be duplicated in a number of other states that were attempting to implement their own Family Cap.[39]

None of these arguments proved persuasive to the federal judge hearing the case. In May 1995, Judge Nicholas Politan concluded that New Jersey's FDP law had rational, legitimate goals and that it did not violate the reproductive rights of women receiving welfare. Susan Appleton points out the basis for the judicial reasoning in the case emanated from a series of abortion funding decisions that ruled that the right of procreative choice did not mean state or federal government was obligated to pay for the choice.[40] In *Mahrer v. Roe* (1977) the U.S. Supreme Court upheld a Connecticut law that paid for childbirth but not for nontherapeutic abortion. Here state "value judgments favoring childbirth over abortion" were seen as providing a sufficiently reasonable basis to justify the state's funding choices.[41] In *Harris v. Mc Rae* (1980) the Supreme Court was even more direct in its opinion that states are not obligated to subsidize any reproductive choice. The distinction between a state's direct interference with a protected right (to have a child or abortion) and a state's refusal to subsidize a protected right is clear in this summation: "Although government may not place obstacles in the path of a woman's choice, it need not remove those not of is own creation. It simply does not follow that a woman's freedom of choice carries with it a constitutional entitlement to the financial resources to avail herself of the full range of protected choices."[42] Finally, in *Planned Parenthood of S.E. Pennsylvania v. Casey* (1992) the U. S. Supreme Court ruled that state restrictions on choice would generally be upheld unless the restrictions placed "an undue burden" on a woman seeking abortion.[43] The Family Cap ruling extended the federal court interpretation to a woman seeking to have a birth.

With respect to violations of the equal protection clause, Judge Nicholas Politan cited the U.S. Supreme Court's reasoning in *Dandridge v. Williams* (1970).[44] Here the Court held that a Maryland regulation that placed a ceiling of $250 per month in welfare benefits for a family, regardless of family size or need, was a rational way for a state to further its interest in employment and poverty reduction. Furthermore, because Maryland had no duty to provide public assistance, let alone provide any particular levels of welfare payments, the Court indicated it could not compel the state to enforce any pro rata policy. New Jersey's Family Cap, according to Politan's ruling, was a "reasoned legislative determination that a ceiling on benefits provides an incentive for parents to leave the welfare rolls for the workforce."[45]

The National Association for Women appealed the federal district court ruling almost immediately with the same results. In August 1996 the U.S. 3rd Circuit Court of Appeals upheld the Politan ruling that FDP places welfare households on a par with working families and that this purpose is a reasonable and appropriate goal of welfare reform. The Court specifically viewed the state's Family Cap, through its maintenance of the level of AFDC benefits despite the arrival of an additional child, as placing the welfare household in the same situation as that of a working family, which does not automatically receive a wage increase every time it produces another child.[46]

Rebuffed by the federal courts, NOW and the ACLU sought relief from the Family Cap in state court. On September 4, 1997, the lawsuit *Sojourner, A. v. The New Jersey Department of Human Services (NJDHS)* was filed in Superior Court alleging that the child exclusion provision of New Jersey's welfare reform violated the rights of poor women guaranteed under the privacy and equal protection provisions of the state constitution.[47] Dropped from the plaintiff's complaint were objections to the 1115 waiver process with its requirement for evaluation through experimental design. The plaintiffs, in fact, were now using some of the preliminary data my colleagues and I had collected for the state evaluation as evidence of the Family Cap's ineffectiveness in achieving its intended purposes.[48] This issue, moreover, was largely moot since PRWORA had been implemented, and the evaluation of FDP was winding down as was FDP itself, replaced by Work First New Jersey (WFNJ).[49] The list of expert witnesses used by NOW and the ACLU to buttress their case had also changed. Experts like Jay Katz, a psychiatrist who had railed against social experiments in an affidavit included in the federal lawsuit, were replaced with social scientists who focused more attention on the public policy and child well-being implications of the Family Cap.[50]

I believe it is informative to provide readers with a glimpse into the expert opinion employed by the plaintiffs in the *Sojourner, A. v. NJDHS* case since it is the arguments of these experts that underpinned NOW/ACLU's contention of human suffering. Kathryn Edin, a sociologist, focused her testimony on the economic hardship that would accompany the deprivation of a cash increment to meet the needs of an additional child in the family. Edin cited her study of "a large [nonrandom] sample [N = 214] of low income single mothers" showing that low-income single mothers who worked in low-income jobs were likely to experience great or greater material hardship than women receiving AFDC.[51] She concluded that a Family Cap would only increase a family's likelihood of homelessness, hunger, and lack of basic necessities. Mark Rank, another sociologist, called into question the state's "assumption that denying benefits to children conceived and born on welfare will have the effect of deterring births to welfare recipients."[52] He went on to discuss his own research, which shows that women on welfare [in Wisconsin in 1981] actually had a fertility rate at or below that of the general population [in Wisconsin in 1981]. From this study of one-year fertility rates Rank questioned the effectiveness of a Family Cap in influencing the childbearing decisions of women on welfare. I should note that the bracketed information has been added by me to help the reader gain some appreciation for the data used by the experts drawing these conclusions.

A number of the expert witnesses employed by NOW/ACLU discussed the negative impacts the Family Cap was likely to have on children of welfare recipients. Thomas Cook, a nutritional scientist, swore "without reservation that a policy such as New Jersey's ... will result in increased prevalence of hunger among those children and may lead to serious and possibly permanent damage to their health, cognitive impairments, physical weakness, anemia, stunting and growth failure."[53] Cook did not discuss what, if anything, the increase in food stamp allotments under FDP/WFNJ would do to address any nutritional deficits of Capped children. The testimony of Deborah Frank, a physician, also expressed concern about the "effects of undernutrition on children's behavior,"[54] especially iron deficiency and lead toxicity caused by a Family Cap. Here again the effective increase in food stamp benefits under FDP/WFNJ was not acknowledged or discussed by the expert.

Several of the experts testified on the reproductive decisions they believed Family Caps were constraining pregnant women to make. Wendy Chavkin, for example, saw a direct tie between the denial of benefits and effective contraception use or abortion and characterized New Jersey's FDP/WFNJ as a policy for the population control of poor and vulnerable women.[55] From this perspective Family Cap was less a values-instilling mechanism than it was a systematic effort at coercing behavior modification.

The National Organization for Women and the ACLU had high hopes—not unjustified, it should be added—that the New Jersey court system would be receptive to their arguments of abridged reproductive rights inherent in a Family Cap. They reminded the Superior Court judge in their brief that "as with equal protection claims, the New Jersey Supreme Court has often accorded far greater protection of privacy under Article 1, paragraph 1 of the state constitution than the United States Supreme Court has afforded under the federal constitution."[56] The plaintiffs were acknowledging the Supreme Court's decisions to invalidate the state ban on Medicaid funding for abortions, strike down state illegitimacy statutes, and declare unconstitutional the restriction of a minor's right to an abortion subject to parental notification.

In August 2000 state Superior Court Judge Anthony Iuliani, in a summary decision, rejected the arguments of NOW/ACLU declaring that "while the Family Cap law poses a slight impediment to welfare moms and their newborns, it isn't substantial enough to outweigh the goals of New Jersey's efforts to move residents off welfare."[57] Iuliani remarked that unlike the abortion cases cited by the plaintiffs, which placed real burdens on women's reproductive decisions, the Family Cap did not impose any undue burden on women.

The plaintiffs appealed the Superior Court decision to the State Appellate Division and in April 2002 once again saw their arguments dismissed. The three-judge panel found the judicial reasoning used in the *C.K. v. Shalala* case to be both sound and informative. With respect to the argument that Family Caps forced women "not to have a birth" in the same fashion that ban on Medicaid funding and requirement of parental notification forced women "not to have an abortion" the Court ruled

In *Planned Parenthood of Central New Jersey v. Farmer* (2000), conditioning a minor's right to obtain an abortion on parental notification was found to be a significant burden on minors seeking abortions. The restriction was direct. Here, the state argues the restrictions on a woman's right to procreate by the Family Cap are, at best, indirect and insignificant, and therefore, the rational basis test should be applied. The state is correct. The Family Cap does not substantially interfere with a woman's right to have children; she may still bear children, albeit without a cash subsidy. The failure to provide a cash benefit on the birth of an additional child does not impair a woman's reproductive rights to any significant degree.[58]

Undaunted by a string of four consecutive losses, NOW/ACLU appealed the decision of the Appellate division to the New Jersey Supreme Court in July 2002. The basic equal protection and privacy arguments remained the same but the plaintiffs were relying more than ever before on results from the Rutgers evaluation study. Final reports were available in early 1999 and publications began appearing in scientific journals in 2000. To strengthen their case, NOW/ACLU used this information to develop an empirical component to an argument that had been largely conjectural and hypothetical. Birth and abortion rate data linked to Family Cap exposure now made its way in the Court but apparently too much law had been made for the data to make much difference. In August 2003, by a 7–0 vote, the State Supreme Court upheld the New Jersey Family Cap. The decision written by Chief Justice Deborah Poritz stated the case was not about a woman's right to choose whether and when to bear children but rather about whether that state must subsidize the choice.[59] The same abortion funding reasoning upheld by the U.S. Supreme Court in *Mahrer v. Roe*, *Harris v. McRae*, and *Planned Parenthood v. Casey* to limit a state's obligation to fund abortions was used by the New Jersey Supreme Court to do the same for births.

Judge Poritz explained why the Family Cap case differed from the decision of the New Jersey Supreme Court to provide Medicaid funding for abortion deemed medically necessary for the health and well-being of the mother. In the latter instance, she observed, equal protection was violated because abortion funding was limited to women only if their lives were at stake while funding for childbirth was available for any medical necessity.[60] The old Medicaid law had failed to meet the "balancing test" that the Court uses to decide equal protection and due process challenges. Poritz described this balancing as follows: "a court must weigh the nature of the restraint or the denial against the apparent public justification and decide whether the state action is arbitrary. In that process if the circumstances sensibly so require, the court may call upon the state to demonstrate the existence of a sufficient public need for the restraint or the denial."[61] Any burden or limitation placed on privacy by the Family Cap was viewed by the courts as overbalanced by the pubic good it was doing by creating parity in the birth decisions of welfare recipients and "working people." The New Jersey Supreme Court did not comment on whether or not the Family Cap would influence a poor woman's decision to seek the protected right of abortion.

Nor would one expect the Court to do so inasmuch as such abortion decisions were ostensibly in the interest of the general public in New Jersey also.

Family Cap Success!

In November 1993, as the Rutgers evaluation team began finalizing the research design that would be used to assess New Jersey's FDP and Family Cap impacts, I was startled to read in a local newspaper that the program was well on its way to success. Departing governor Jim Florio called the 16 percent drop in "pregnancies" during the first two months of FDP "encouraging." Human Services Commissioner William Waldman remarked: "Two months is not a lot of time to do statistical analysis. But the drop has been significant." And Wayne Bryant, creator of the Family Cap in New Jersey, stated, "It's gratifying to hear reports indicating that fewer women on welfare are having babies and that our reforms have enabled thousands of Family Development Program clients to get jobs and earn a living."[62] The use of the term *pregnancies* rather than *births* surprised me but then Governor Florio let the other shoe drop: "We didn't see an increase in abortions; what we saw was welfare people doing the same thing that everyone else does, understanding that they have to take responsibility for the consequences of their actions, that there would not be automatic payments for extra children."[63] Inasmuch as pregnancies are equal to births plus abortions, adjusting for small numbers of miscarriages, no abortion increase meant that the governor could indeed talk about pregnancies.

The state claim of declining pregnancy rates was significantly buttressed by the work of June O'Neill, a highly respected economist from City University of New York. In an August 1994 report completed for the New Jersey Department of Human Services and entered by the state into evidence in the *C.K. v. Shalala* case, O'Neill found a decline in birthrates that ranged between 19 and 29 percent, depending on the statistical methodology employed.[64] However, the two-year study (August 1992–June 1994) did not examine abortion rates, so it was unclear if the birth decline depended solely on abstinence and more responsible contraception use, that is, if it was tantamount to a pregnancy decline.

Any further conjecture about abortion rates after implementation of the Family Cap was obviated on May 15, 1995, when NJDHS released information on abortions paid under its Medicaid program. These data showed that the rate of abortions per 1,000 women on welfare had increased from 9.43 to 9.78 (3.7 percent) in the eight months before and after the implementation of the Family Cap.[65] Despite warnings by Commissioner Waldman that it was too early to draw any conclusions about a Family Cap impact, these data had an electric attraction in the Family Cap—abortion debate that was already underway in Congress.[66] Chris Smith, U.S. Representative from New Jersey and a staunch opponent of a Family Cap, told a *New York Times* reporter, "If you take away funding for the poorest of our children and pay for abortions on demand through Medicaid, like New Jersey and New York and many other states do, it doesn't take a rocket scientist to conclude that you are either going to have poorer children or dead children."[67]

The abortion announcement was contemporaneous with new reports from NJDHS on the birthrates for women on welfare. With each state report the amount of decrease since FDP implementation was shrinking, from 16 percent two months after implementation to 13 percent after eight months to 11 percent after a year.[68] In addition to presenting state officials with an apparent credibility problem, this juxtapositioning of births and abortions made it more difficult to cast Family Cap as a pregnancy- or conception-prevention program. A principal mechanism behind Family Cap's effect appeared to be abortion, an observation made by Michael Dorning when he wrote in the *Chicago Tribune* that the "abortion rate ... accounts for about a third of the 11 percent decline in births to welfare mothers ... from New Jersey."[69]

Notwithstanding any potential abortion issue, the Family Cap continued to be termed a success by many New Jersey politicians and some state-based policy analysts as well. Goertzel and Young employed two years of data (1992–1994) from New Jersey's administrative welfare files and hospital records and found a 13.6 percent decline in birthrates. The authors of this study declared that "the New Jersey welfare reform has successfully reduced welfare dependency as well as births to unmarried mothers in poor communities" and, moreover, that "the New Jersey reform worked because it was designed by a politician [Wayne Bryant] with a good sense of timing who was close to the community."[70]

While the expectations of welfare recipients in New Jersey may have been changing, there was another change under way that was difficult to ignore. The Alan Guttmacher Institute, an organization with arguably the best information on abortion incidence, found abortions to be in steady decline nationally since 1985. As can be seen in figure 2.1, this was also the case in New Jersey until 1992 when the trend reversed dramatically. For the same period that O'Neill and Geortzel report dramatic declines in birthrates (1992–1994), the Guttmacher data indicates an 11.5 percent increase in abortion. These data, of course, do not look exclusively at abortions among poor women, the group most affected by Family Cap; however, the data in figure 2.2 do. Here, in an internal New Jersey Division of Medical Assistance and Health Services (NJDMAHS) document not released to the public, the quarterly abortions paid for by NJDMAHS indicate a similar spiking at the end of 1992. From 1992 to 1993 abortions rose by over 10 percent and from that point began a steady trajectory upward.[1] Using descriptive data such as these to impute cause-effect can be a risky practice, however, because other factors may account for this statewide change in abortion incidence. Nonetheless, the information in figures 2.1 and 2.2 is thought provoking, and reasonable individuals could posit a relationship between the implementation of a Family Cap and the rise in abortion.

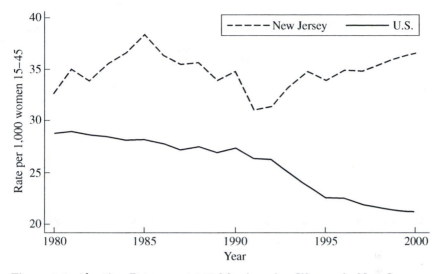

Figure 2.1. Abortion Rates per 1,000 Marriage Age Women in New Jersey and Nationwide (Alan Guttmacher Institute)

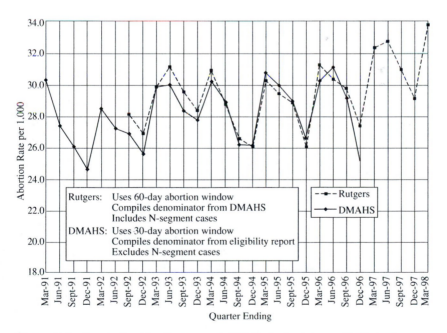

Figure 2.2. Quarterly Abortions per 1,000 Cash Assistance Recipients

Welfare reform would appear to have created a dilemma for many re-formers. As Jacob Klerman notes, the explicit goals of PRWORA were to lower nonmarital fertility without increasing abortions.[71] Could the achievement of the first goal come only at the expense of the second? For the author of New Jersey's Family Cap, Wayne Bryant, this was a Gordian knot that could be easily cut. In his own words, "[Abortion] is a tough decision... but it's a responsible decision for a family that believes it's in their best interest."[72]

3

Family Caps and Nonmarital Births

Introduction

In New Jersey, implementers of the Family Cap took great pains to avoid any program descriptions that linked the Cap to illegitimacy, out-of-wedlock births, nonmarital fertility, or similar terms. State Commissioner of Human Services William Waldman, when interviewed by the media, disputed any notion that the intent of Family Caps was to stop women on welfare from having babies.[1] The "Bryant Bills," which established New Jersey's Family Development Program (FDP) and Family Cap, as I have noted, never use these words, in contrast to the Family Support Act and PRWORA, where they are repeated frequently.[2] When Wayne Bryant has been asked by the press why his Family Cap was any different from Caps proposed by a Republican U.S. Congress, he has offered a variety of reasons. For example, he noted that his Family Cap offered a (small) additional earnings disregard for any excluded child if the mother is employed. "Federal proposals have no such provisions," observed Bryant.[3] On another occasion he distinguishes the New Jersey Cap by its coupling with "a level of training not offered by the Republican Welfare reforms."[4] The Family Cap in New Jersey was always, in the eyes and voices of its authors, about economic self-sufficiency and rehabilitation through work and training.

At the federal level, especially in the House of Representatives, Family Caps were envisioned by many as their principal tool, along with time limits, for combating illegitimate births.[5] The reduction of illegitimacy was a primary theme of Newt Gingrich and the Contract with America;[6] its accomplishment required more than the economic rehabilitation of individuals—it required values transformation. Family Caps, according to politicians like Gingrich, Senator Phil Gramm, and conservative activists like Gary Bauer of the Christian Coalition and Robert Rector of the Heritage Foundation, facilitated the transformation process.[7]

President Bill Clinton, always ambivalent about Family Caps, recognized them as a way of promoting personal responsibility, but was sensitive to their perception by liberals as harsh social engineering.[8] In 1995 and again in 1996 he vetoed reform bills that he believed were "tough on children" or "punished the unmarried."[9] Clearly aware of the goals of Family Cap to reduce out-of-wedlock births, Clinton eventually signed the welfare bill, which punted the Family Cap along with these conscience-wrenching problems to the states, where apparently Clinton and PRWORA believed they belonged.

The Nonmarital Birth Problem

How serious of a problem is illegitimacy or out-of-wedlock childbearing in this country? The question is best answered by examining changes in magnitudes over a number of years and the consequences any changes have had on social health and well-being. Magnitude can be assessed in two ways: the nonmarital birthrate and the nonmarital birth ratio (also termed the illegitimacy ratio). The former measure is computed as the number of nonmarital births per 1,000 unmarried women aged 15–44 years, while the latter is calculated as the number of nonmarital births per 100 live births. A disagreement remains as to which measure is a more valid indicator. Advocates of the nonmarital birthrate claim the ratio confounds marriage and fertility, that is, illegitimate births may actually be going down but the ratio appears to increase because marital births have declined.[10] Proponents of the nonmarital ratio counter that it is the nonmarital rate that confounds how fertile women are and how successful they are in acquiring husbands. The ratio, on the other hand, isolates the incidence of husband-acquiring before a woman gives birth.[11] Until this seemingly intractable dispute is settled it is probably best to look at both of these measures of nonmarital births.

In figures 3.1 and 3.2, I provide data collected by the National Center for Health Statistics on the nonmarital birthrate and ratio from 1980 through 2000. Whichever measure you choose, the rate or ratio, nonmarital births have increased dramatically since 1980. In fact, Stephanie Ventura and her colleagues show that nonmarital births began their rise in the 1940s and trended upward rapidly in the 1970s and 1980s, around the same period that AFDC caseloads also began to expand significantly.[12] In the 1990s, however, nonmarital births began to stabilize—the rate at about 44 per 1,000 and the ratio at 33 per 100.

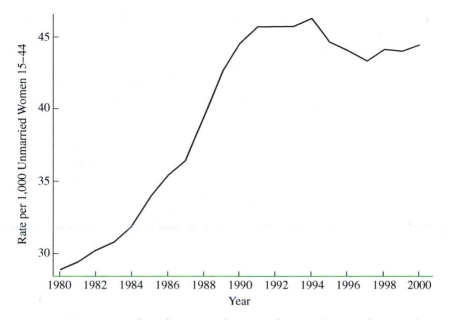

Figure 3.1. Nonmarital Birth Rate in the United States (National Center for Health Statistics, National Vital Statistics System)

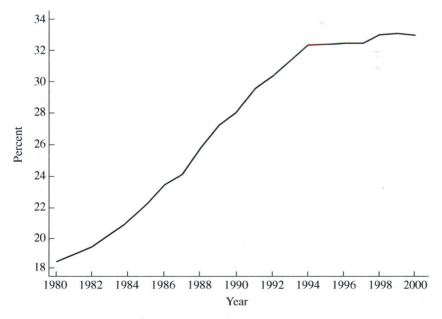

Figure 3.2. Nonmarital Birth Ratio in the United States (National Center for Health Statistics, National Vital Statistics System)

Notwithstanding the apparent stabilization in the 1990s, nonmarital births are still viewed by many politicians and policy experts on both the right and left as one of the most significant social problems facing the country. Their concern stems from three components of the problem that make its solution doubtful: namely, the sheer number of nonmarital births, the proportion of births to never-married women, and great differences across races.

It is clear from table 3.1 that while nonmarital rates and ratios have indeed declined, the number of nonmarital births has actually increased. In fact, from 1980 to 2000 these births doubled from 665,000 to over 1.3 million. The increase in the number of nonmarital births to white women has prompted Charles Murray to predict the procreation of a "white underclass," cut off from mainstream American values and institutions the way many blacks are now isolated.[13] What the table does not show is that approximately 83 percent of all nonmarital births from 1980 and 2000 were to women who had never married. As Haskins and his colleagues at the Brookings Institution tell us, never-married mothers tend to have less education and work experience

Table 3.1.   Indicators of Nonmarital and Marital Births in the United States

	Year		
	1980	1990	2000
Counts			
Number of births	3,731,850	4,158,212	4,058,814
Black	568,080	684,300	622,598
White	2,936,351	3,290,300	3,194,005
Number of nonmarital			
Births	665,747	1,165,384	1,347,043
Black	318,799	445,304	417,270
White	328,984	669,698	835,721
Rates and Ratios			
General fertility rate	68.4	70.9	65.9
Black	84.7	86.8	70.0
White	65.6	68.3	65.3
Nonmarital birth rate	29.4	43.8	43.9
Black	81.1	90.5	70.5
White	18.1	32.9	33.1
Marital birth rate	97.0	93.2	88.3
Black	89.2	79.7	66.3
White	97.5	94.1	87.1
Nonmarital / marital			
Birth ratio	17.8	28.0	33.0
Black	57.2	66.5	67.0
White	10.2	20.0	26.0

Birth data: National Center for Health Statistics, National Vital Statistics System Population data comes from the U.S. Census.

than other single mothers (divorcées, widows), are the most likely to go on welfare, and are the most likely to have long spells on welfare.[14]

Table 3.1 does point up the differences between black and white women in their propensities to experience nonmarital births. In 1980 the rate was 4.5 times higher among black women and the ratio was almost 6 times greater. These disparities have decreased significantly over 21 years' time in the series shown, but still remain over twice as high for black women. And while only about 30 percent of all never-married women are black and about 60 percent are white, 44 percent of the never-married women on AFDC/TANF are black and about 40 percent are white.[15]

Nonmarital childbearing, especially childbearing in the population of never-married women, has been found to have many serious consequences for women, their children, and the larger community. The preamble to the PRWORA legislation lists nearly four pages of negative impacts including lower household income, greater risks of bearing low birth weight babies, lower levels of education aspirations and achievement for both mothers and children, more contacts with the juvenile and criminal justice systems by household members, and a greater likelihood of living in poor and high-crime areas.[16] Sara McLanahan reports that single motherhood is associated with higher rates of depression, unhappiness, low self-esteem, and poor health.[17] Some research has also traced single-parent childbearing to unstable household living arrangements, which can increase the probability that a child will be "fostered" to relatives, friends, or the public child protective service system.[18]

In New Jersey, the nonmarital birthrate and ratio from 1980 through 2000 were consistently lower than national averages. Figure 3.3 shows a rate that ranged between 36 and 38 per 1,000 women over the last 10 years. As we can see in figure 3.4, the ratio had risen steadily until 1999 where it peaked at 29.5 per 100, falling back to 1994 levels in 2000. As was the case nationally, however, the number of nonmarital births rose dramatically in New Jersey over this 21-year period—from about 20,000 in 1980 to over 33,000 in 2000. Racial disparities in the state's nonmarital births mirrored national trends as undoubtedly did the consequences of these births for mothers, their children, local schools, and communities.

Theories of Illegitimacy

While it would be difficult to find individuals who would disagree that nonmarital births pose a significant challenge to the health and well-being of our country, there is much less consensus regarding the causes of this problem. At least four explanations continue to have some currency as this issue is debated in the context of welfare reformation: namely, institutional racism, rational choice, contravening culture, and economic opportunity restriction. The racism and economic opportunity approaches look at nonmarital

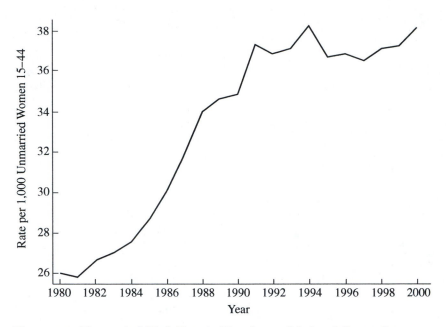

Figure 3.3. Nonmarital Birth Rate in New Jersey (National Center for Health Statistics, National Vital Statistics System)

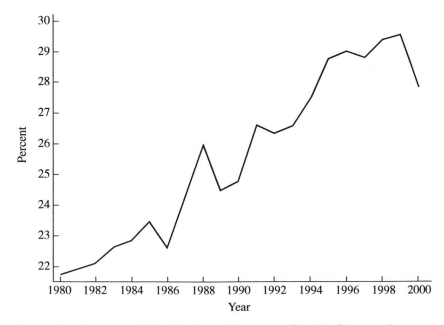

Figure 3.4. Nonmarital Birth Ratio in New Jersey (National Center for Health Statistics, National Vital Statistics System)

births as a consequence of macro institutional processes that victimize individuals without political or economic power. Conceptualizations of nonmarital births within rational choice and contravening culture frameworks focus less on an individual driven by societal forces and much more on the personal capacity to create and control one's own tastes, preferences, intentions, and behaviors.

In chapter 2 I introduced the importance of race in discussions of illegitimacy, AFDC, and welfare reform. The linkage of black women with out-of-wedlock births is evidence enough for some policy analysts to declare that the illegitimacy problem is an overblown, even fabricated, argument designed to reinforce a system of societywide white racial hegemony.[19] Proponents of this perspective call into question the validity of nonmarital birthrate and ratio data or point to alternative interpretations of trend data that they believe reveal the social control interests of state-based racism.

The racism explanation of illegitimacy was first articulated in some detail by William Ryan in his blistering response to "The Moynihan Report." Ryan called the report a new form of subtle racism that might be termed "Savage Discovery" where the "all-time favorite savage" is the promiscuous (black) mother who "produces a litter of illegitimate brats in order to profit from AFDC."[20] Ryan attributes black-white differences in legitimacy to the underreporting of illegitimate births for whites, more shotgun marriages[21] among whites, more access to contraception, abortion, and adoption for whites, and more concealed births and abortions in the white population. Many years later Frances Fox Piven makes much the same point when she argues that out-of-wedlock births have been increasing across the globe and among all income strata in the United States.[22] The focus on low-income illegitimacy, says Piven, obscures the fact that the rate of out-of-wedlock births has been less a function of actual births than it is of fewer marriages. She opines, "A wise observer might suspect that changed attitudes had reduced the stigma of births to the unwed, so there were fewer shotgun marriages which might not be a bad thing at all."[23] For Stephanie Coontz, much of today's talk about the pathology of unwed motherhood can be traced to a victim blaming that is consistent with racism.[24]

From the racism perspective, illegitimacy is less a function of a real social problem than it is, to borrow a phrase from Peter Berger and Thomas Luckmann, a social construction of reality designed to preserve important societal interests.[25] It would be foolish to deny that racism does not play some role in black-white differences in nonmarital births; however, the extent of that role is a subject that reasonable individuals can disagree upon. Racism as an explanation for black-white inequality is itself divided along racial lines with blacks nearly twice as likely as whites (64 percent to 35 percent) to blame past discrimination as the reason for black social problems.[26]

As a coherent exegesis of nonmarital births, racism falls short in several respects. It fails to account for important differences in nonmarital births among minority groups, especially between black and Hispanic women in similar low-income circumstances. Why, for example, does the Hispanic nonmarital birth ratio range between 37 (1990) and 43 (2000) while the ratio for black women has remained in the high 60s over the same period?[27] Can we assume that more discrimination is directed toward blacks than Hispanics? There is also the difficulty of establishing empirical covariations between a longtime, pervasive phenomenon (racism) and changes that have occurred in specific fertility behaviors. This is not to say, of course, that racism may not underpin at least part of the explanation to proposed solutions to the nonmarital birth reality. There is sufficient evidence, for example, to suggest that race is a significant factor in the variation we see across states in the adoption of welfare reform strategies[28] and population control efforts.[29] It would be expected within the framework of the racism explanation for nonmarital births that Family Caps would enforce fertility control on (black) women through the increased impoverishment of women on welfare. This impact, moreover, would be expected to be greatest for black women and (by extension) Hispanic women who are most dependent on welfare benefits for their family's survival.

If racism views nonmarital births through a lens of societal victimization, rational choice interprets the problem more as a family's demand for a durable good, even if the pursuit of this "good" may become a self-inflicted wound. The view of children as desired consumer goods was first proposed and systematically developed by Gary Becker.[30] His economic analysis of fertility assumed that a family's preference of a child or children could be captured by maximizing a utility function that is based on family income, parental "tastes" for children, expected net cost of raising a child (or children), and the amount parents are willing to spend on each child. This last component refers to the family trade-off between the quantity and quality of children. Some parents, says Becker, obtain additional utility from having fewer children on whom they can expend more resource, so called "higher quality" or "more expensive children."[31]

The decision of whether to have a child (or children) outside of marriage is also a matter of preference within rational choice theory. The decision, says Becker, is based on two principles: first, whether marriage can be assumed to increase the person's utility level above what it would be were he or she to remain single; and second, what restrictions on mates are imposed by the "marriage market" conditions facing the person.[32]

Marriage markets, like any consumer market, can be tight or slack. As men compete with other men and women compete with other women for marriage partners, the success of individuals is governed by the supply of men and women (sex ratio) and the incomes of women relative to men's incomes.[33] If men outnumber women or if women's incomes are low compared to men, then a classical marriage market equilibrium obtains, with all women who wish to marry finding mates and by extension all women who wish to have a child doing so within marriage. Under the Becker model the woman's decision to bear a child while married is the only obvious (rational) choice since it is in this arrangement that the joint incomes of partners are most likely to provide sufficient resources for raising children.

Issues with Becker's model arise when individuals are believed to have incomplete information on the costs and benefits of marriage/fertility decisions. This is often the case with teenagers and poorly educated young men and women who do not plan pregnancies very carefully and have less than perfect control over their fertility decisions, and even contraception use.[34] For most individuals, George Homans once quipped, rational choice theory is good advice for human behavior but a poor description of it.[35]

The classical marriage market described by Becker, moreover, may be a poor portrayal of behavior when the male to female sex ratio drops or when women's incomes are relatively high compared to those of men. Under such circumstances individuals may not maximize their utility through marriage and/or conceiving children while married. Both of these conditions prevail in many of today's black communities.

It is clear from even a cursory examination of Becker's approach to marriage and fertility behavior that wages (income) of men and especially women are critical components in these decisions. Wages are used to approximate the opportunity costs faced by women; high opportunity costs would be expected to yield delayed childbearing, better pregnancy planning, and fewer children.[36] In Becker's view, participation in public welfare programs can both reduce these opportunity costs and, in so doing, significantly change marriage and fertility preferences.[37] A Family Cap would be expected to reduce fertility insofar as it makes the preference for childbearing more costly. Any differences in its impact across races would be expected to be greatest where male to female sex ratios or income ratios are lowest, and small to nonexistent where these ratios are larger than 1.

Like rational choice, the contravening culture perspective, as I have termed it, views welfare benefits as a source for nonmarital childbearing; however, variation in welfare benefits alone is not seen as providing a sufficient explanation for the substantial differences that occur between black and white women. Important also are the norms, preferences, and values that develop from neighborhood and community concentrations of poverty and social disorganization, norms that support welfare dependency and nonmarital births.[38] The contravening culture framework for explaining the causes of nonmarital births appears under a variety of labels in the welfare reform literature, including urban underclass theory,[39] conservative culturalism,[40] welfare incentive theory,[41] and the culture of poverty.[42] No matter what it is called it will always be associated with two names: Daniel Patrick Moynihan and Charles Murray.

Earlier, I made brief reference to "The Moynihan Report" in which the author linked growing black nonmarital births and public welfare utilization. Amid the cries of racism, by Ryan and many others, Moynihan had begun to sketch one of the earliest, coherent culture of poverty explanation for nonmarital births. While his efforts may have been somewhat crude, he managed to include in his "tangle of pathology" explanation most of the elements that were to appear in later descriptions of the black underclass: namely, criminality, unemployment, the retreat from marriage, low participation in the labor force, alienation from mainstream societal values, as well as illegitimacy.[43] But Moynihan went much further than supplying a morphology of this culture; he pinpointed its cause in a matriarchal family consisting of a mother, children, and a series of transient males, and the failure of this type of family to function well in a competitive, wage-driven society.[44] His solution was to recast government welfare and economic policies that would discourage desertion, reduce welfare dependency, and increase employment opportunities for unskilled black men. In 1965, in the midst of the civil rights struggle, Moynihan's cultural explanation for black illegitimacy and other social problems became hopelessly conflated with racism. Hugh Hecho observes that "intimidated by charges of racism and blaming the victim, supporters of the pathology interpretation tended to fall silent."[45]

It was not until Charles Murray began his frontal assault on the social welfare system in 1984 with the book *Losing Ground: American Social Policy 1950–1980*[46] that the contravening culture perspective was once again given broad voice in academic and policy circles. Murray's thesis, reiterated in a number of papers on the urban underclass, welfare reform, and the consequences of out-of-wedlock births,[47] can be summarized as follows:

- government welfare programs are responsible for creating a set of incentives that discourage poor men and women from marriage, encourage unskilled men to drop out of the labor force, and cause women to bear children outside of marriage;
- government programs help reinforce an underclass of millions of people cut off from productive work, traditional family and community values, and public safety;
- high density nonmarital parenthood is the driving force behind the creation and persistence of this underclass; and
- rehabilitation in the underclass requires not simply addressing issues of poverty but transforming the "Hobbesian kind of individualism in which trust and cooperation are hard to come by and isolation is common."[48]

Murray's thesis, like Moynihan's before him, has brought out a storm of critics who dispute each and every one of these premises.[49] So has the writing of Lawrence Mead, which discusses a black culture or worldview that is "uniquely prone to the attitudes contrary to work and thus is vulnerable to poverty and dependency."[50] When I was in the initial stages of research on New Jersey's Family Cap I received a manifesto (11/94) from the Center on Budget and Policy Priorities stating that "focusing on welfare as the primary cause of rising rates of out-of-wedlock childbearing vastly oversimplifies this complex phenomenon."[51] The declaration, signed by 77 social scientists including Christopher Jencks, Lee Rainwater, and William

Julius Wilson, went on to question policies suggesting that children born to unmarried parents should not be eligible for AFDC/TANF. Such policies, it was contended, would only hurt children without impacting illegitimacy. I got the message—any test of Murray's or Mead's notion that welfare benefits matter was in the mind of a large segment of the social science community a trivial pursuit, a waste of time.

The Center on Budget and Policy Priorities does, however, contain one small demurrer statement noting that some of the signers believe that welfare does have some modest effect on nonmarital childbearing. In fact, a sizeable number of econometric studies have began to accumulate that show that either the size of the welfare benefit or the marginal benefit received by a woman for an additional child does influence both the decision to marry and to have children outside of marriage and this influence often varies across race.[52] Mark Rosenzweig, for example, found that a 10 percent increase in AFDC benefits increased a woman's chance of a nonmarital birth by about 12 percent[53] while Saul Hoffman and Michael Foster report that a 25 percent rise in benefits leads to nonmarital birth increases of 5 to 6 percent.[54] Traci Mach, obversely, presents data that suggest that a $50 penalty in benefits corresponds to a 19 percent decrease in births among black welfare recipients.[55] Modesty may really be in the eye of the beholder here but if this research is to be believed there appear to be some instances when benefits impacts are substantial. Robert Moffitt has captured this slowly changing assessment of the relationship between welfare, on the one hand, and marriage and fertility, on the other, in his extensive review of the literature. "Based on the early studies (in the 1970's and early 1980) a consensus among researchers developed a decade or so ago that the welfare system had no effect on [marriage or fertility] outcomes. However, a majority of the newer studies show that welfare [benefit increases] has a significantly negative effect on marriage or a positive effect on fertility, rather than none at all. Because of this shift in findings the current consensus is that the welfare system probably had some effect on these demographic outcomes."[56] If the contravening culture perspective provides a realistic picture of the effect of welfare payments on nonmarital births, a Family Cap would be predicted to impact low-income black, Hispanic, and white women differently. Black women on welfare living in high concentrations of poverty and in areas with high density nonmarital parenthood would not be expected to be influenced by a Family Cap while black women who do not live in such concentrations would be expected to respond by limiting births. Racial concentration should not play a role in any Family Cap effect on white or Hispanic women, however, because white women and (by extension) Hispanic women are more closely linked to the value structure of the larger society, although this link is weakening according to Murray.[57] Hence, white and Hispanic women on welfare, irrespective of neighborhood composition, should exhibit lower birthrates when exposed to a Family Cap.

The most popular explanation for the rise in nonmarital births among university-based social scientists is the conceptual framework identified with William Julius Wilson called variously the liberal culture interpretation,[58] the job-shortage theory,[59] or to what I have referred to as the community opportunity structure framework.[60] Wilson places the blame for the rise in single-parent families and increases in nonmarital births on the difficulty that poor women, particularly poor, black women, have in finding a partner with stable employment. Wilson and Neckerman state that "the increasing rate of joblessness among black men merits serious consideration as a major underlying factor in the rise of black single mothers. . . . Moreover, when the factor of joblessness is combined with high black male mortality and incarceration rates, the proportion of black men in stable economic situations is even lower than that conveyed in the current unemployment and labor force figures."[61] Wilson, like Murray, sees a connection between concentrations of poor blacks and that the development of an underclass culture defined by social isolation, absence of conventional role models, circumscribed cultural learning, lack of labor force attachment, casual work habits, and limited aspirations. Unlike Murray, however, he views this culture as contingent on relocated industries and on federal legislation that singled out race as the decisive barrier to economic development. For Wilson the values of the underclass culture are more pliant; remove restraints on mobility and open up opportunities for employment and aberrant norms and preferences will change to conform to those of the larger society.[62] The economic opportunity structure explanation for nonmarital births is certainly less pessimistic than conservative culture as a description and a plan for the ameliorization and this may account for its popularity in academia.

The government policies favored by Wilson and most of the social scientists who signed on to the Center on Budget and Policy Priorities statement focus on programs capable of changing the features of communities that lead to high unemployment and family dysfunction. Therefore, a policy like the Family Cap, which manipulates welfare benefit levels, would be hypothesized to have a negligible influence on childbearing decisions of black, Hispanic, or white women. Lower birthrates would be expected among women who live in communities with adequate employment opportunities, where opportunity costs are high.

There is a growing literature that has attempted to test the efficacy of the community opportunity structure and contravening culture explanations for the rise in nonmarital births. One avenue of research has examined if Wilson's contention that the desiccation of the black male marriage pool coupled with low male wages account for most of the variation we see between white and black illegitimacy. Robert Willis argues that an equilibrium in a "market for out-of-wedlock childbearing" can exist if the ratio of marriageable men to marriageable women is low and if incomes of men are low relative to women's income at the bottom of the income distribution.[63] Both conditions exist in many impoverished, predominantly black communities in the northeastern and north-central United States. These conditions are not nearly as prevalent in predominantly Hispanic or poor white communities. Willis shows how be believes this market functions in figure 3.5. The figure assumes a marriage pool of 100 males and 110 females. A ratio of two un-married female partners per one unmarried male occurs when 90 percent of the males marry and an equilibrium (S_mS_m) is created where 10 percent of the males father children out of wedlock by (20/110) or 18 percent of the women who remain unmarried. If women's incomes rise relative to men's, a new equilibrium $(S_m'S_m')$ obtains indicating that only 1.2 unmarried female partners are now available per unmarried male. In this market 50 percent of the males father illegitimate children by (60/110) or the 54.4 percent of the women who remain unmarried.[64] Conceptually it would appear that an equi-librium could occur, say $(S_m''S_m'')$, where a man would need many female partners in order to choose out-of-wedlock fatherhood over marriage; in this market of relatively high-income males, however, men choosing to father ille-gitimate children would be in short supply.

When the Wilson hypothesis of sex ratio imbalance and marriageable black male shortage is put under empirical scrutiny, much of the difference between black and white marriage and nonmarital both rates (ratios) remain unexplained. Using data from the National Longitudinal Survey of Youth (NLSY) to study the decision to marry, Daniel Lichter reports that when controlling for marriage market difference—"for every three black unmar-ried women in their 20s, there is roughly only one unmarried man with earnings above the poverty threshold"—black transition to marriage is still only 50 to 60 percent of that of white women indicating that poor prospects are not the only reason for low black marriage rates.[65] In subsequent work,

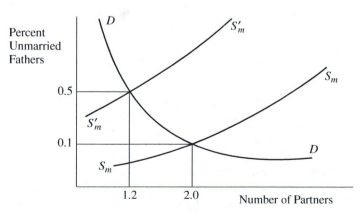

Percent
Unmarried
Fathers

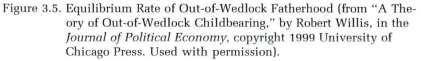

Figure 3.5. Equilibrium Rate of Out-of-Wedlock Fatherhood (from "A The-ory of Out-of-Wedlock Childbearing," by Robert Willis, in the *Journal of Political Economy,* copyright 1999 University of Chicago Press. Used with permission).

using county-level data from the 1980 and 1990 Census Summary Files, Lichter and his colleagues note that while racial differences in marriage market conditions may accentuate differences in U.S. marriage rates, cultural factors including Moynihan's culture of poverty explanation cannot be ruled out, nor can the effects of public assistance.[66] Finally, from an analysis of 443,297 observations from the 1986–1997 Current Population Survey, Lichter concludes, "We cannot dispute claims that the continuing retreat from marriage among African American women has less to do with current economic conditions than perhaps with a race-specific cultural repertoire born of longstanding economic inequality and geographic isolation from mainstream society."[67]

Marriage market imbalance is also far from the whole story in empirical examinations of nonmarital childbearing. Research by Scott South and Kim Lloyd, for example, shows that mate availability has only a modest impact on nonmarital births and this impact is much more pronounced for white women than it is for black women.[68] Similar black-white differences are reported by Mark Fossett and K. Jill Kiecolt in their examinations of marriage markets in metropolitan areas.[69] Such research has prompted Derek Neil to advance a modified formulation of Wilson's shortage of marriageable men thesis.[70] Neil contends that for disadvantaged black women in a market dominated by high male incarceration and unemployment rates, many women face no real prospects for marriage. In such markets, modest changes in the supply of marriageable men primarily affect the choices of women with significant education and earnings capacity. Neil's key point is that many women at the margin in such marriage markets view single motherhood as an inframarginal choice, that is, as a decision in which mate availability has little influence.[71] Neil, like South and Lloyd and Fossett and Kiecolt, however, does not see any influence of public welfare generosity in shaping the birth decisions of poor, less educated women in tight marriage markets.

Abortions and Nonmarital Births

None of the theories of nonmarital births I have discussed addresses the role that abortion may play in the fertility decisions of low-income men and women. There appears to be an assumption in each of these models that abortion is simply a response to contraception availability or failure and, therefore, does not influence decisions to become sexually active or to become pregnant. This is not the view of George Akerlof and his colleagues, who offer the "Technological Shock [of abortion] Explanation" for rising out-of-wedlock childbirth.[72] The Akerlof model posits that the legalization of abortion in the early 1970s exerted a profound impact on both men and women in their decisions to engage in sexual activity, support a pregnancy to term, and to marry once the child was born. For women the increased availability of lower-cost contraception and abortion increased women's willingness to engage in sex without obtaining a promise of marriage if the premarital sexual activity resulted in a pregnancy. Women are placed in an especially disadvantaged position (to men) if the sex ratios are low since they must compete with other females, a proportion of whom do not place high physical and psychic costs on abortion.

Akerlof also offers a set of hypotheses that explains how abortion availability affects the decisions of male partners. He observes that abortion, by making a birth the physical choice of a mother, makes marriage and child support a social option for the would-be father.[73] Low-cost abortion limits potential costs of a pregnancy to the woman and thereby reduces the likelihood that the father feels compelled to marry. The consequences of this decline in the practice of "shotgun marriage"[74] in the presence of low-cost abortion are higher out-of-wedlock birth ratios, higher abortion rates, higher pregnancy rates, and lower marriage rates. Akerlof estimates that about three-fourths of the increase in the white out-of-wedlock first-birth ratio and about three-fifths of the black increase, between 1965–1969 and 1985–1989 are explained by the decrease in the fraction of premaritally conceived first births that are resolved by marriage.

The technological shock theory of nonmarital births, though wrapped in the language of market equilibriums and technology costs, is at its core a normative explanation for nonmarital births. As Akerlof explains, an endogenous consequence of technological shock has been the decline in stigma of out-of-wedlock childbirth.[75] Witness, for example, the general reluctance among policy experts, social scientists, and a large segment of the general public to use the terms "illegitimate" or even "out-of-wedlock" when describing children born to never-married women. Welfare benefits, according to Akerlof, have the same effect on nonmarital births as the decline of social stigma; benefits signal that such childbearing will be accepted and financially supported by state and federal government.

Akerlof's theory that abortion availability can increase *both* abortions and nonmarital births remains controversial and largely untested. The theory fails to explain why nonmarital births remain concentrated among the poorest women. Another limitation pointed out by James Q. Wilson is why poor Hispanic women and men have not responded to technology shock in the same ways that poor black men and women have.[76] Technology shock, moreover, does not provide many cues as to why adoption is so low in poor communities.

One avenue of research that could be used to explore the validity of the theory is the influence that the Medicaid funding of abortion has had on nonmarital births and abortion incidence. Like legalization, Medicaid funding provides another significant diffusion of abortion technology, especially into poor communities. Following the *Roe v. Wade* decision in 1973 to legalize abortion, the Medicaid Program made the procedure available to women who met eligibility criteria as either "categorically needy" or "medically needy."[77] This coverage, however, was short lived when in August 1977 Congress implemented the first version of the Hyde Amendment, which prohibited the use of federal Medicaid funds for virtually all abortions. The constitutionality of the amendment was upheld by the Supreme Court in 1980 in the *Harris v. McRae* decision.[78] The Hyde Amendment was softened by Congress over the intervening years and it allows federal funds to be employed to abort a pregnancy in cases of rape, incest, and life endangerment. States can, of course, fund abortions deemed "medically necessary" with state Medicaid matching funds, and from 1980–2000, as many as 19 states have opted to or have been forced to fund these abortions by court order.[79]

Some indication of Medicaid funding impact on abortion and nonmarital birthrates can be gleaned from table 3.2. The table complements the information presented in table 3.1 for the past three decennial censuses with additional information presented for 1987 and 1994. In 1987, 1994, and 2000, the Alan Guttmacher Institute conducted special surveys of abortion providers to collect information on the socioeconomic and insurance coverage of women obtaining abortions.[80] These data are not typically collected as part of Guttmacher's U.S. Abortion Incidence and Services enumeration.[81]

It is evident that abortion counts, rates, and ratios have declined over the 21 years presented in table 3.2. These drops have occurred at the same time that impressive declines have also occurred in welfare caseloads and women covered by Medicaid. Notwithstanding the shrinking number of AFDC/TANF recipients, abortion rates among the categorically and medically needy rose by 14 percent from 1994 to 2000 according to researchers at the Alan Guttmacher Institute (AGI). The increase from 1994 to 2000 was especially high for women with incomes below 200 percent of the poverty level; here it rose by 24 percent.[82]

It is not, of course, surprising that the availability of lower-cost abortion would increase demand for the procedure. Stanley Henshaw and Kathryn Kost found that in states where Medicaid pays for medically necessary abortion, women covered by Medicaid had an abortion rate almost four times that of women who were not covered.[83] Blank and her colleagues in their analysis of Guttmacher data from 1974–1988 report that the removal of such Medicaid payments reduces abortion by 19 to 25 percent.[84] Similarly, Philip Cook and his associates estimate that about a third of pregnancies that would have resulted in abortion were carried to term because of insufficient Medicaid funds.[85] It is the research conducted by S. Philip Morgan and Allan Parnell on the North Carolina State Abortion Fund (SAF), however, that provides some important insight into how Medicaid may be influencing fertility behavior.[86] From 1988 through 1995, the study period, North Carolina experienced a legislative and legal tug-of-war that resulted in an unstable SAF, with periods of funding for medically necessary abortion followed by funding cutoffs and restoration. Morgan and Parnell found, as expected, a significantly greater probability that pregnancies ended in

Table 3.2. Indicators of Abortion and Welfare Utilization in the United States

	Year				
	1980	1987	1990	1994	2000
Counts					
Number of abortions	1,553,900	1,559,100	1,609,000	1,423,000	1,313,000
White	1,088,176	1,049,274	1,095,729	980,447	896,776
Black	467,724	509,826	513,271	442,553	416,221
Number of abortions paid for by Medicaid	—	371,066	—	377,095	317,746
Number of female-headed families on AFDC/TANF	3,426,094	3,762,109	4,068,434	5,046,263	2,117,658
Rates and Ratios					
Abortion rate	29.3	26.9	27.4	23.7	21.4
White	21.2	21.2	21.0	16.0	13.0
Black	58.0	57.8	56.0	54.0	50.0
Abortion-to-birth ratio	0.416	0.404	0.386	0.362	0.323
Nonmarital abortion-to-nonmarital birth ratio	1.79	1.36	1.08	0.90	0.82
Medicaid abortion rate	—	71.0	—	50.0	57.0

Birth data: National Center for Health Statistics, National Vital Statistics System. Abortion data: The Alan Guttmacher Institute, Abortion Incidence and Services Survey, and from special socioeconomic surveys conducted in 1987, 1994, and 2000. Public welfare data: USDHS, Administration for Children and Families Publication Characteristics and Financial Circumstances of AFDC Recipients.

abortion during periods when Medicaid funding was available. When abortion to birth ratios were examined, important differences between races emerged: black women were affected by the amount of program coverage and not by the substitution of abortions for births; for whites just the opposite was true. These researchers conclude that the "results may reflect a different role of abortions for whites and African Americans in the context of dissimilar life courses.[87]

Could the failure by many poor women to substitute abortion for birth, even when Medicaid funding for abortion is available, account for both high abortion and nonmarital birthrates in welfare populations? In table 3.2 we see that the nonmarital abortion to nonmarital birthrate has declined and by 1994 fell below 1 for the first time since abortion was legalized. Hence, at a time when abortions are rising among the poorest women, births would appear to be increasing even more, if one concedes that the vast majority of poor women are also unmarried. Turning over the Medicaid coin, Philip Levine finds that Medicaid restrictions lower the abortion rate and the birthrate, implying a reduction in pregnancies.[88]

If the Akerlof model is indeed correct, it would be expected that states that fund abortions and provide more generous welfare benefits would experience increases in abortions and nonmarital births. A Family Cap on benefits, in states like New Jersey, which funds abortion through Medicaid, would be hypothesized to reduce nonmarital births only to the extent that the policy increases the costs, financial and social, of childbearing outside of marriage. If, however, the Family Cap does not increase the stigma as well as financial cost of childbearing, the birth impacts should be substantially less than any abortion impacts.

New Jersey, with its unique combination of welfare policies and racial and cultural diversity, provided a research opportunity to test the competing models of nonmarital fertility that I have discussed in this chapter. Testing theory, at least initially in the evaluation, was not among my highest priorities. My immediate focus centered on keeping the evaluation on track and this meant convincing state policymakers, the media, my university, and members of the social science community that the research designs we were utilizing could provide valid answers to the many questions being raised about the Family Cap's impact.

4

Experimenting with a Family Cap

Introduction

New Jersey's Family Cap was initiated under a Section 1115 provision of the Social Security Act that required an independent evaluation of any welfare reform program or policy implemented by states to improve the functioning of AFDC. In 1992, the evaluation methodology preferred by the Administration for Children and Families (ACF), the federal agency responsible for monitoring any welfare waivers and their evaluation, was an experimental design by which welfare clients would be randomly assigned into at least two groups. One group, termed an experimental or treatment group, would be subject to the new welfare program rules and policies. The other group, a control group of recipients, would be subject to the old AFDC and prewaiver rules. Differences in outcomes or costs between the groups in such a research design could in principle be attributed to the new welfare reforms. The simplicity of experimentation appealed to many politicians and policymakers who were often baffled by and mistrustful of econometric and statistical assessments of policy impact.[1] The specific experimental design used in New Jersey and in other states was developed by ACF, typically without input from those contracted to do the evaluation. This practice had the advantage of facilitating cross-state comparison but could place considerable administrative burdens on states with poor client tracking and reporting systems. Fortunately, New Jersey was one of the states that possessed a recipient data management system capable of carrying out a random assignment protocol and providing quarter-by-quarter feedback on how well assignment integrity was being preserved over the life of the experiment.

The Federal Case for Experiments

The federal preference for experimental design in assessing welfare reform impacts under Section 1115 emanated from two interlaced sources. The first of these was the research conducted by the Manpower Demonstration Research Corporation (MDRC) on public assistance and job training in the 1970s and 1980s. Senator Daniel Patrick Moynihan noted that "above all others," MDRC did the research that led Congress to pass the Family Support Act.[2] Pamela Winston asserts correctly that MDRC was seen by much of Congress as a "completely honest" organization with reliable data that helped to shape Personal Responsibility and Work Opportunity Reconciliation Act (PRWORA) legislation.[3]

In that research, MDRC focused its efforts on implementing random assignment experiments into the day-to-day operations of large public bureaucracies including welfare offices, job training centers, community colleges, and community-based organizations. Judith Gueron, the president of MDRC, touts the superiority of social experimentation over other research designs for the manner in which the design answers the question "Is this service effective, compared to what people are already being exposed to?"[4] This attention to the condition of people not exposed to the service, the "counterfactual condition,"[5] embodied in a control group helps avoid the "problem of self-canceling research," according to Gueron.[6] Nonexperiments often fall prey to this problem because they cannot determine precisely what condition serves as a comparison to the treatment.

One MDRC experiment in particular, the Greater Avenues for Independence (GAIN) study, conducted in California from 1988 to 1990, helped shape the form of rehabilitation that welfare reform was to offer AFDC/TANF recipients under PRWORA.[7] As I have noted, rehabilitation had been a contentious issue for many state and federal politicians as they sought to reduce welfare caseloads. The WIN demonstrations and the Family Support Act offered states a long list of education, training, and work-related activities that could be used to move recipients from welfare to work. The carefully implemented, site-based GAIN randomized trial, however, showed that some welfare-to-work strategies were more cost effective than others. Riccio and Orenstein summed up the strategy that appears to work best as "a program that emphasized quick placement into the labor market, direct job development assistance, more equal use of job search and basic education for those found lacking basic skills and comparatively lower levels of personalized attention, backed by a willingness to use formal penalty processes to enforce GAIN's participation mandate."[8]

The GAIN observation that rapid labor force attachment (LFA) led to higher earnings for welfare recipients than more expensive, human capital investment (HCI) approaches has been replicated in a host of subsequent MDRC experiments and by many other researchers as well.[9]

The federal government's second impetus for experimentation, undoubtedly buoyed by the first, was an expanding belief among its service and regulatory agencies that randomized experiments were critical in establishing "strong evidence" or proof of a social intervention's effectiveness. Experiments had been sporadic accompaniments to countless educational, crime prevention, substance abuse, job training, health intervention, and child protective services programs in the 1960s through much of the 1980s. Coincident with the Section 1115 welfare reform and evaluation activity conducted during the first Bush and Clinton administrations, however, there were clear signs that a philosophy about evidence-driven policy was beginning to take form. In 1993, Congress implemented the Government Performance and Review Act, which held federal agencies responsible for identifying measurable program objectives and the interventions capable of reaching them.[10] In that same year the highly influential Cochrane Collaboration in health care became operational internationally and with it the definition of scientific evidence as the product of random clinical trials.[11]

Throughout the decade of the 1990s the connection between evidence and experimentation percolated through the U.S. Departments of Labor, Health and Human Services, and Justice.[12] The Agency for Health Care Research and Quality in USDHHS, for example, began work on a series of evidence-based practice centers (EPCs), which sponsored random trial reports on medical therapies and technology.[13] Discussions also began among social scientists and policymakers in the United States and Europe to expand the Cochrane Collaboration to the areas of criminal justice, education, and social welfare. In 2000 the Campbell Collaboration was inaugurated and a Social, Psychological, Educational, and Criminological Trials Register was created.[14] These developments, in turn, influenced the content of federal legislation like the Scientifically Based Education Research, Evaluation and Statistics and Information Act of 2000 and the No Child Left Behind Act of 2001 where "scientifically-based research," in the form of randomized controlled experiments, was to guide the decisions of policymakers about which programs to implement.[15]

Indeed, there is much to recommend random controlled experiments for teasing out the specific (or marginal) impact of a welfare reform like the Family Cap. Thomas Cook asserts that random assignment experiments provide a counterfactual that is logically more valid, efficient, and credible than any alternative design available.[16]

Larry Orr believes experiments are superior to other multiple group designs because they minimize selection bias and outperform pre-post designs because they minimize errors due to external factors such as maturation processes and regression to the mean.[17] Gary Burtless is among a host of social scientists who posits that random assignment experiments lead to more correct interferences about the direction of causality between treatments and outcomes; that is, that experiments have more internal validity than other research designs.[18] There is also wide agreement that randomization provides the best source of exogenous variation available because it creates variation in the receipt of treatment that cannot possibly be correlated with the behavioral outcome under study. In other words it is the ideal instrument variable.[19]

Experiments are especially well suited to answer what has been called the "efficacy question": Does the policy or social program work when it is implemented properly?[20] By properly here I mean delivered according to program design specifications by qualified personnel to correctly targeted recipients. The researcher can manipulate the treatment in ways that might not occur naturally in ongoing programs. Experiments also allow policy analysts to introduce new and innovative treatments on a limited, demonstration basis, before decisions are made about their incorporation into ongoing programs of service.[21] These efficacy estimates of manipulated, new, or innovative treatment effects often serve as the benchmark measurement for gauging the reliability and validity of treatment results estimated from nonexperimental methods. Daniel Friedlander and Philip Robins, for example, compared the employment and welfare receipt outcomes from four welfare-to-work experiments with the outcomes found when a variety of matched comparison group designs were used. These economists report that the nonexperimental estimates of impact were usually quite different from experimental estimates derived from the same data, a finding they trace to unobserved factors residing in these comparison groups that bias treatment effect sizes.[22] Similar experimental versus nonexperimental differences are reported by Robert Lalonde, Thomas Fraker and Rebecca Maynard, and Gary Burtless and Larry Orr.[23] The benchmark value of experimental studies, moreover, has been carried beyond the assessment of (nonrandom) comparison group performance. Daniel Grissmer and colleagues at RAND advocate the utilization of experimental data for testing assumptions and specifications of econometric and nonexperimental research. These researchers feel that experimental estimates of treatment impact should, in fact, "guide such model specifications."[24]

A final advantage of experiments is their straightforwardness. The simplicity involved in comparing two or more means or percentage point differences has an appeal that transcends the applied research and statistics communities where Occam's razor is too often left in its professional carrying case.

The Case against Social Experimentation

There are a good many social scientists who do not view random assignment experimentation as the benchmark measurement of evidence-based research. Their criticisms range from a variety of practical and methodological concerns to the philosophical propriety of trumpeting experimentation as the "gold standard" of evaluation research.[25] Rigorous experimentation designs are viewed as unworkable in many social settings such as schools, training programs, counseling and service provision agencies because of costs, workflow disruption, and a host of ethical issues. The ethics of randomization in a scarce resource environment, the withholding of potentially effective intervention, the imposition of undesirable interventions, and the possibility of legal action resulting from ethics issues give pause to some researchers who feel the practical and political problems of experimentation do not warrant the effort.[26]

An apparently growing number of program evaluation specialists have resisted experimentation in social settings, not necessarily because they deem experiments to be impractical, but because they view the methodology as epistemologically misguided and theoretically simplistic. It is worthy of note that some of the most stinging criticism of experiments has come from the American Evaluation Association (AEA) and some of that organization's most prominent members. Michael Quinn Patton, as an example, calls for the repudiation of the "dominance of the hypothetical-deductive paradigm with its quantitative, experimental emphasis."[27] Robert Stake sees experiments as one of ten, often competing, dispositions of evaluators that shape policy and program assessments. An "experimental disposition," according to Stake, like the case study, "naturalistic," or any other competing disposition reflects an evaluator's ideology and not any superior pathway to a higher understanding.[28] Yvonna Lincoln and Egon Guba frame the problem of equating evidence with experimentation as the clash of good and evil societal forces:

> It would appear to us that there are two communities engaged in evaluation at the current moment. One community, which early on declared itself the true scientists, continues to deploy experimental and quasi-experimental designs and to treat whole groups of citizens as control groups in vast social experiments. Another group, however, practices alongside this group. In the second community of evaluation specialists, practitioners attempt to remain conscious of value pluralism that marks American life and they tend to engage larger questions of political and social theory in their practice, particularly with respect to issues of social justice, democratic values and the equitable distribution of goods and services.[29]

Proponents of what may be termed "the many ways of knowing" epistemology often link their criticism of experimental one-sidedness to what they believe is an unsophisticated and imprecise rendering of the natural world by experiments. Yvonna Lincoln and Ann Hartman, among others, view behavioral outcomes as the consequences of complex and interacting determinants that are impossible to capture with random assignment experiments.[30] As expected, members of the first community have countered with stout rebuttals to these philosophical arguments.[31]

It is the methodological critiques of experimentation, particularly experimentation in social settings, however, that have shaped the scientific and political debate around the impact of New Jersey's Family Cap. Methodological critiques of experiments follow two general lines of argumentation. The first focuses on how well the research design has maintained its internal validity; while the second attempts to determine if the research results are generalizable; that is, if there is external validity. Inasmuch as the first type of validity is a necessary condition for the second, problems with implementing an experiment can lead to a diminution in the credibility of findings or even to their outright rejection. This is especially true if findings are inconsistent with previous research, expert preconceptions, political interests, or established policy positions.[32]

Threats to the internal validity can occur when individuals are first assigned to treatment and control groups, when actual treatment is given or withheld, or at anytime throughout the life of the experiment. Procedures for random assignment of welfare cases in the 1115 waiver experiments into groups generally involved allocation based on predetermined combinations of case number digits or Social Security numbers. There is no systematic evidence that assignment procedures were not followed in these studies or that they were manipulated by welfare office workers, even though it was often very difficult for many social work and social service providers to accept the notion that they should deny services to a group of welfare clients on the basis of a random draw.[33]

In New Jersey the procedures for random assignment were laid out in a Department of Family Development (DFD) instruction number: 92–9–9. The last four digits of the case head's Social Security number were used to identify group membership: for controls the eighth and ninth digits had to be either "00," "98," or "99"; and the sixth and seventh digits between "00" and "83"; all other combinations marked treatment cases.[34] In independent monitoring of the assignment rules by DFD and by Rutgers, thirteen of the 8,401 cases eventually allocated to treatment and experiment groups were misassigned. In each instance a family that should have been a treatment case was identified as a control. These misassigned cases represented about one-tenth of one percent of all cases and never proved to be a significant factor in either the analysis or interpretation of treatment versus control group differences.

Ensuring the purity of actual treatment delivery in social experiments offers real challenges. Crossover between treatment and control groups can occur when, for example, a family who is originally designed as a treatment (control) case leaves welfare, reapplies elsewhere in the state, and is then selected into the control (treatment) group. Welfare-to-work experiments have also had a difficult time assuring separate orientation processes for treatment and control groups, not just within the welfare program but within other agencies (such as JOBS service providers or Medicaid authorities) who have contact with welfare recipients.[35] As a result, control group subjects may receive information about the contents of the new welfare reform program. Beyond the specific problems that can arise if control group subjects inadvertently receive the wrong information about their specific status or benefits from welfare workers, mixed messages may result if the waivered reforms change the overall orientation of the program. For example, suppose that the existing welfare program stressed the importance of human capital investment such as secondary education while the new program emphasized labor force attachment and immediate employment. In this situation welfare case workers who deal with both treatment and control group cases must take care to communicate the correct, albeit distinctive, messages to clients in the course of their counseling sessions.

A more insidious form of contamination occurs in social experiments when control group families cannot be isolated from the widespread publicity and comment that surrounds welfare reform efforts. Even if welfare recipients completely understand whether or not the treatment applies to them, they may still hear the intended message regarding governmental or societal goals and aspirations for welfare recipients; this message, in turn, may influence recipient behavior.[36]

In some of the 1115 and subsequent welfare reform evaluations, experiments were replaced by nonexperimental approaches. This happened in Wisconsin, after the waiver for the Work Not Welfare (WNW) program was granted in November 1993. State officials successfully argued for a nonexperimental design utilizing historical data to develop a baseline against which WNW outcomes could be assessed.[37] Their reasoning was that WNW, with its time limit on welfare receipt of 24 months on cash benefits and its work requirements for assistance, presented a drastic change in the state's welfare culture that would be effectively communicated to all welfare recipients, including control group members. When WNW was preempted by a new reform program called Wisconsin Works, some state officials were joined by academics at the Institute for Research on Poverty (IRP) who concluded that experimentation was also inappropriate for two reasons: first, it was difficult to isolate a within-state control group from the incentives of a new policy that seeks to change the culture of public support expectations in a state, and, second, the state was required to permit some recipients (e.g., control group members) to continue to rely on the pre-reform system, mandating program administrators to work with these families under the old rules.[38] These problems, critics of experimentation contended, would introduce contamination into both the treatment delivery process and into the management of the environment context.

Other threats to the internal validity of social experiments can arise from the differential attrition of treatment and control cases, noncompliance with experimental conditions, and interfering or multiple treatments. These problems can reduce estimates of average treatment effects, the goal of efficacy studies, to intention-to-treat effects where only impacts on compliers and the treated are measured.[39] The issue of multiple treatments stems from the practice of most welfare reforms to package or "bundle" several financial incentives, rule changes, and services together so as to exert, what is believed to be, a maximum impact on a pervasive welfare culture. In New Jersey, Family Cap was bundled with an enhanced JOBS program and a number of other policy changes. The practice of bundling has caused difficulty when researchers have attempted to isolate which reform component may be responsible for specific recipient outcomes.[40]

Even if random assignment and treatment delivery proceed without serious incident, social experiments may possess, for a variety of reasons, low generalizability or external validity. Experimental estimates of a program's efficacy may or may not tell us much about program effectiveness, that is, whether or not the policy or program works when put into daily practice. Treatment efficacy, as Brian Flay and Linda Collins point out, is a precondition of treatment effectiveness with effectiveness evaluation concerned with "whether more good than harm is done by the efficacious treatment when delivered in the real-world setting."[41] The principal reasons why the experimental effects of New Jersey's Family Cap might not be generalizable across different welfare populations, in distinctive settings, within different bundles of services, and over different time frames include the following.

Randomization Bias

As James Heckman asserts, random assignment may mean that the type of persons who participate in a small-scale experiment will differ from the type of persons who would participate if the social program were global. This could occur in the New Jersey experiment if the recipients in the experimental sample are different from the recipients on the AFDC/TANF caseload in ways that could mitigate the effects of the treatment in the welfare population.[42]

Bias Due to Omission of Entry Effects

A number of researchers have noted that, by virtue of their design, social experiments may ignore "entry effects," even though these effects may be very important responses to policy changes.[43] Most social experiments involving welfare policy include, as experimental and control subjects, only welfare recipients. In theory, such experiments could sample randomly from the entire population of the poor, but in practice that might entail prohibitively high costs for collection of data on persons, many of whom would not be affected in any way by changes in welfare policy. However, as a response to changes in welfare policy, members of the nonwelfare population may change their behavior either (a) in order to join the welfare rolls or (b) to change their expected circumstances in the event that they join the welfare rolls in the future. Focusing exclusively on persons who are already on the welfare rolls will, of course, ignore such responses to the policy change.[44]

Entry effects are often associated in the literature with the experiment's alleged inadequacy in considering macro-level effects such as norm-formation, that is, group-influenced behavioral expectations and low-wage, labor market equilibrium.[45] Robert Moffitt views the entry and macro effect issues as being closely related: "Because the spread of knowledge within community wide information networks is likely to be an important intervening variable in the program entry mechanism, individualized offers of treatment are unlikely to replicate adequately the program environment that would obtain in a permanent communitywide program."[46] If welfare client application, enrollment, participation, and continuation decisions are neglected, as these critics of social experimentation maintain they typically are, then reported impact estimates are bound to differ from the estimates generated by research designs more sensitive to the entry effect problem. Just how or how much the experimental and entry-sensitive impact estimates might differ is not often made clear. Irwin Garfinkel, for example, surmises that norm-formation would lead to an experimental effect that "might be close to or smaller than the change induced by a real shift in policy." On the other hand, information diffusion would suggest "that the real world stimulus would grow stronger while the experimental effect would diminish."[47] These are, of course, guesses because to our knowledge no welfare reform research has actually compared estimates of impact from an experimental sample and the caseload from which the sample was drawn. Biases from randomization and entry effects alert us to the difficulties of generalizing in the face of population heterogeneity, especially when that heterogeneity is stimulated by the experiment itself.

Bias Due to Omission of Community or Scale Effects

As a number of researchers have noted, "community" or "scale" effects might be absent in a small-scale social experiment but might be very powerful in a global program.[48] As a simple model with scale effects, consider

$$Y_i i + bT_i + cP + dT_i P + e_i$$

where i indexes an individual, Y = outcome of interest (e.g., earnings), X = characteristics, T = indicator denoting whether an individual was treated, P = proportion of population subject to the treatment, and e = error term. A "welfare reform," which on a global basis $(p > 0)$ instills a greater "work ethic," may increase work effort $(c > 0$, where Y refers to hours of work) even for individuals who receive no treatment $(T = 0)$; but a small-scale experiment $(p \approx 0)$ may have no such effect. The effect of treatment $(T = 1)$ in a small-scale experiment, with $p \approx 0$, is simply b when it could really be $b + cP + dP$.

The Mixing Problem

The mixing problem addresses the issue of what observations of homogenous treatment outcomes in the sample of study reveal about the outcomes that would occur if a treatment's provisions and parameters were varied across the population of interest.[49] To address this problem, the researcher must be willing to either gather data on the population or impose assumptions on the joint outcome distribution or the nature of the treatment policy Mixing, like the issue of scale effects, calls our attention to the limits placed on experimental generalizability due to treatment heterogeneity.

Setting Heterogeneity

V. Joseph Hotz, Guido Imbens, and Julie Mortimer carefully discuss the problems that arise when attempting to generalize the results of an experiment in one physical location to a new jurisdiction. These researchers note that attempts to adjust for setting heterogeneity require that sites overlap to some degree on population units of study and the treatments. Even then, Hotz and his colleagues find that they are limited to predicting the outcomes of control group members.[50] Research by Friedlander and Robins, moreover, indicates that the greater the geographic distance between the jurisdictions, the weaker the inferences about the program effectiveness become.[51] Setting heterogeneity is also a concern in historical generalizations.

Time-Induced Heterogeneity

In principle, it is possible to address population unit, treatment, and/or setting heterogeneity by ensuring that some degree of overlap exists between the experimental units, treatments, and settings, on the one hand, and the more global subjects, treatments and settings of interest. This same strategy could also be employed to address time-induced heterogeneity, which, to be sure, is a neglected topic in discussions of external validity.

Time-induced heterogeneity is a form of conditioning bias that can arise as a result of the manner in which experimental and/or control subjects are sampled.[52] Although there is no inherent reason why an experiment could not sample randomly from the entire population, for some time period, say t to t + 1, cost and efficiency considerations will usually dictate that sampling for an experiment should proceed conditional on membership in some temporally defined population subgroup. Such conditional sampling may produce a form of selection bias where experimental results based on such sampling may yield erroneous answers to the questions the experiment was intended to address.

An obvious example is the "random" selection of subjects for an experimental welfare program from persons currently enrolled in an existing welfare program. Of course, such sampling necessarily proceeds conditional on—that is, takes as given—actual enrollment in welfare. Even when such sampling selects randomly from all persons currently enrolled in welfare, experiments based on a sample of this kind may yield biased answers. This is because the behavior of persons enrolled in welfare as of time t is not necessarily representative of the experience of persons who will enroll in welfare between time t and time $t + \Delta t$, even in the absence of any macroeconomic, environmental, or other "time effects." For example, persons enrolled at time t may on average be "chronics"—persons who are severely and/or permanently disadvantaged and, as such, are unlikely to respond to any kind of treatment. In contrast, persons who enroll between time t and time $t + \Delta t$ may on average be "acutes"—persons who suffer temporary or intermittent disadvantage and, as such, are likely to respond appreciably to some kinds of treatment. An experiment that randomly samples "chronics" (persons enrolled at time t) may give very misleading estimates of treatment effects for "acutes" (persons who enroll between time t and time $t + \Delta t$)— and vice versa. One or both samples, moreover, might give misleading estimates of a policy's population effectiveness, that is, become out of phase or out of date, if the population's duration mix changes after the experimental sample was drawn.

There is some limited evidence from studies of welfare caseload dynamics to suggest that time-induced heterogeneity may be one of the most pervasive obstacles to the generalizability of experiments. Mark Rank, and David Ellwood and Mary Jo Bane observe that point-in-time random samples will select a very different composition of acute/chronic recipients than will random "opening-cohort" samples.[53] Rank reports that the former sampling strategy nets only about 35 percent acutes ($\leq$ 12 months spent on welfare over a 3-year period) while the latter yields over 60 percent. Of course the welfare population itself might have a variety of acute/chronic compositions.

A sampling strategy that dips into a population pool at t cannot be expected to capture the dynamic flow of cases that comprise a welfare population. Here it is useful to invoke an observation first attributed to Heraclitus: "It is not possible to step twice into the same river, nor is it possible to touch a mortal substance twice in so far as its state is concerned."[54]

The "Heraclitus effect," as I have termed it, alerts us to the possibility that we might find little or no response to a Family Cap in a random sample of chronics (or acutes) but that this estimate of efficacy might seriously understate the possible response in a random sample of acutes (chronics). Moreover, if the welfare population is composed largely of acutes or short-stay recipients, our estimate possesses little external validity.

As with other forms of heterogeneity, the Heraclitus effect might be addressed in a number of ways. One approach would be to suggest a range of joint outcome and treatment distributions that are consistent with the marginal distributions produced by the experimental data. Since the experiment can tell us only about the outcome proportions for those under randomly assigned treatment conditions, there is a need for identifying assumptions about the untreated and/or their outcomes. In the Family Cap experiment, assumptions about the fraction of acute and chronic cases would appear to be appropriate if population data is lacking. These fractions, however, have proven to be somewhat variable in studies of caseload dynamics. Robert Moffitt and Michele Ver Ploeg, for example, report that about a third of the public assistance observations from the National Longitudinal Study of Youth (NLSY) could be considered chronic, long-term welfare users. Ver Ploeg, in her investigation of the Wisconsin caseload, found the proportion of chronic users to be about 50 percent. And in a study of Maryland's caseload, D. Stevens found only about 17 percent of the cases to be chronics.[55]

A Blended Design Strategy

Because of the shadow cast by these many internal and external validity issues, a number of researchers, mainly economists, have proposed a variety of "observational" or quasi-experimental approaches as an alternative to experiments as a way of evaluating policy effectiveness. Chief among these designs are cross-area comparisons, before and after or pre-post analysis, the use of multiple cohorts, and difference-in-difference methods that amount to a combining of cross-area and time-series approaches. While these methods do not necessarily suffer from the entry effect, scale effect, mixing and heterogeneity problems inherent in random assignment experiments, they do suffer from a number of threats that can compromise internal validity. Exhaustive lists of these problems have been published by Thomas Cook, Donald Campbell, and their associates and will not be repeated here.[56] There are several of these threats, however, that do merit attention when attempting to draw inferences about the impact of welfare-to-work reforms. All the designs I have mentioned, with the exception of the pre-post and time-series, are subject to what Moffitt and Ver Ploeg have called "policy endogeneity."[57] This means that, unlike experiments where the policy is allocated through random assignment, observational or "natural" experiments may be examining differences in policy that have come about because of the very outcomes that the policy is being used to explain. What if, for example, the size of the welfare caseloads in states is the principal reason that some states adopt welfare reforms and others do not? An explanation of changes in caseload size, then, as a function of welfare rule or benefits changes would suffer from the confusion of cause and effect.

Any designs that employ an external comparison group, that is, a group from a different jurisdiction than the treated group, may be subject to the problem of selection bias. Selection can occur if the treatment and comparison-group members differ on personal, social, economic, or other characteristics, in addition to the policy treatment(s), and these characteristic differences are themselves correlated with the outcomes under examination. As Bruce Meyer cautions, selection can take many forms: "Observations may be assigned to a treatment based on previous extreme values of the dependent variable or variables associated with the dependent variable. In the training literature, it has been emphasized that a decline in earnings frequently precedes program entry because program operations tend to enroll those individuals with recent labor market problems. This rule for selecting participants makes comparisons of changes in earnings for participants and nonparticipants difficult."[58]

A rather common difficulty with nonexperimental designs is omitted variable bias.[59] If a variable is correlated with treatment status and is also a determinant of the outcome measure but is left out of the analysis, the net effect of the treatment is confounded with this omitted variable. Unlike selection bias, which occurs at the time of assignment to groups, omitted variable bias can occur as a result of the selection process or any event that influences individuals during the entire observation period.

Another neglected topic in the literature on threats to the internal validity of observational studies is the specification error of omitted interactions.[60] As Orr points out, even in experiments we can expect the impact of a policy or program to vary systematically over time.[61] Under a treatment regimen of labor force attachment we might predict that employment effects would manifest themselves while the welfare recipient is still on welfare or shortly after she leaves the rolls. Conversely, any employment and earnings effect in a human capital investment program might not be witnessed for months or even years after the recipients have left the treatment. It is not only time interactions that pose an internal validity problem in observational studies, treatments may interact with individual characteristics or jurisdictions as well. When such conditional relationships between the treatment and time, place or individuals exist and are not included in the analysis of treatment effects in nonexperimental studies, internal validity can suffer in very much the same way it does in random assignment experiments.

Nonexperimental studies that do not use a control group like pre-post panel or time series designs also must contend with the problems of omitted variable bias, policy endogeneity, and omitted interactions. To these threats should be added the natural processes of maturation or life cycle changes that may underlie the observed changes in recipient outcomes.[62] An evaluation following a panel or cohort of women on welfare for three or more years to determine if welfare reform decreases births, for example, should anticipate that aging women would be less likely to bear children, regardless of the policy initiative. These same women might also find employment more feasible as their children age and child-care issues diminish, once again irrespective of the welfare policy.

Given the external validity problems with social experiments and the internal validity threats of the nonexperimental alternatives, it would appear that one obvious way to answer both the efficacy and effectiveness questions would be to augment an experiment with a quasi-experimental or observational design. In fact, this is one of the conclusions drawn by the Panel on

Data and Methods for Measuring the Effects of Changes in Social Welfare Programs. The panel, chaired by Robert Moffitt, a noted labor economist, issued this call of what may be termed a blended strategy: "Experimental methods are a powerful tool for evaluating the effects of broad components and detailed strategies within a fixed overall reform environment and for evaluating incremental changes in welfare programs. However, experimental methods have limitations and should be complemented with non-experimental analysis to obtain a complete picture of the effects of reform. Nonexperimental methods, primarily time-series and comparison group methods, are best suited for gauging the overall effect of welfare reform and least suited for gauging the effects of detailed reform strategies and [are] as important as experiments for the evaluation of broad individual components."[63]

Similar views have been expressed by Brian Flay and Linda Collins when they advocate a sequential analysis of effects under controlled conditions and impacts in the real-world setting.[64] It is also anticipated in the work of Paul Rosenbaum when he contrasts intended and actual treatment application.[65]

It would appear that the obvious way to answer both the efficacy and effectiveness questions would be to augment a welfare reform experiment with a nonexperimental design that avoids the entry effect, scale effect, mixing and heterogeneity problems that can limit the experiment's generalizability. Yet for a variety of practical, political, financial, ethical, and strategic reasons, this blended strategy has not been used in the dozens of 1115 waiver and PRWORA evaluations that have been conducted.[66] That is, with one exception—the evaluation of the New Jersey Family Development Program (FDP) and its Family Cap. As much by accident as conscious planning, my colleagues and I were placed in a position that required us to simultaneously conduct a classic experiment and a pre-post examination of the Family Cap effect on the entire New Jersey welfare caseload from December 1990 through December 1996. Before describing the overall architecture of this blended design I believe it is useful to provide a brief discussion about its origin.

In September 1993 I received notification that our research team at Rutgers had received the contract to evaluate New Jersey's FDP. The contract award was based on a proposal we had submitted to the New Jersey Department of Treasury as part of the competitive bidding process. The scope of work outlined in the contract called for the evaluation team to monitor a sample of 9,000 welfare families, who had been randomly assigned to either FDP or to a control condition of AFDC rules and benefits. This monitoring was to continue through March of 1998 when a final evaluation report on fertility, family formation, employment, and earnings was due. The contract also called for an interim report to be delivered in April 1996.[67] Shortly after receipt of the award, however, the New Jersey Commissioner for Human Services, William Waldman, was contacted by ACF/Office of Policy and Evaluation and by Mary Jo Bane, assistant secretary for planning and evaluation in the U.S. Department of Health and Human Services, to determine if the evaluation team could produce definitive estimates of program impact by April 1996. Given the backdrop of intense political and public interest in the Family Cap the request was understandable—New Jersey was the first opportunity to learn what, if anything, a Family Cap would do to the birth decisions of women on welfare.

In November 1994 we responded to the requests from ACF and ASPE with a research plan that called for the augmentation of the experiment with a before-after analysis of FDP impact on the entire New Jersey welfare population.[68] Using January 1991 as the baseline, I intended to use administrative data to follow all recipients not selected for the experiment until the experiment was completed in 1998. Inasmuch as most recipients of welfare would not be expected to stay on welfare continuously from 1991 through 1998 and new families could join the rolls and leave at any time during this period, the design is best termed an unbalanced panel.[69] Our proposal was approved by state and federal officials in July 1995.

Quicker results, however, may not have been the only motivation behind the ACF and ASPE inquiries; after all, only nine months separated the approved augmentation contract start date and the interim report of experimental impacts. You will recall that in November 1993, Wisconsin welfare reformers had successfully argued for using nonexperimental methods to evaluate their WNW program because of the widespread perception among policymakers and academics in the state that a control group could not be insulated from the drastic welfare culture changes implicit in WNW.[70] There was also news that was beginning to trickle in from Arkansas, from an 1115 waiver evaluation of the nation's second implementation of a Family Cap: Carolyn Turturro and fellow evaluators at the University of Arkansas, Little Rock, School of Social Work reported a "bleeding" of the intervention to the control group via the social experiment.[71] The potential for the contamination of the New Jersey experiment certainly had to weigh on the minds of these welfare policy experts in Washington when they accepted our augmentation proposal. In New Jersey and in Washington this specter of a "bleeding intervention" was soon to be turned into a bloody shirt argument employed by politicians and policy experts who disagreed with our evaluation findings.

The Structure of New Jersey's Evaluation

Random sample assignment for the experiment began in October 1992 with cases drawn from the ten counties in New Jersey that accounted for nearly 85 percent of the state's welfare caseload. Cases were assigned proportionately to the welfare population in that county with Newark (Essex County), Jersey City (Hudson County), and Camden (Camden County) leading the way.[72] The random assignment of the 9,000 families conducted by the state required that 6,000 serve as the treatment group and 3,000 as controls. The rationale for this 2:1 ratio was given as the federal sensitivity to ethical issues of treatment denial, although it is difficult to understand how this particular ratio surmounted this concern.[73] The assignment process was controlled by the state's Division of Family Development through a set of computerized edits linked to eligibility determination. Each welfare recipient assigned to the experiment was required to meet with a case manager or income maintenance worker who informed the recipient of the eligibility rules that applied to her treatment or control group status. The recipient was then asked to indicate her understanding of her experimental status by signing a consent form.

The sampling plan mandated by ACF for the New Jersey evaluation differed from those required in other 1115 waiver assessments in one crucial respect. One-half of the 9,000 cases (4,500) were to be current (ongoing) recipients who had been receiving welfare payments as of October 1, 1992, and the other half were to be new applicants who had a case opened or reopened after that date. The 2:1 treatment to control group assignment was to apply for both types of cases.[74] This stratified sampling design was a crude attempt to deal with the time-induced heterogeneity problem, what I have referred to as the Heraclitus effect. Some important work by Mary Jo Bane and David Ellwood in the 1980s showed that the typical state welfare population was composed of three groups of recipients: namely, short timers in need of transitional cash assistance stemming from an immediate economic emergency, and two types of welfare-dependent recipients—long timers with uninterrupted spells and long timers who cycle on and off welfare.[75] Bane and Ellwood estimated that the welfare caseload was divided equally between the short and long timers. As I have noted, subsequent work by Moffitt and Ver Ploeg and by Moffitt have reported somewhat different proportions of "acutes" and "chronics" in welfare caseloads.[76]

The difficulty with this deliberate sampling for heterogeneity approach required by ACF was that the "point-in-time" sample used to capture ongoing cases as of October 1 may not be yielding an exclusive subsample of chronics. Some short-timers may just happen to have been on the rolls on that date. The same imprecision applies to the "opening cohort sample" entering the welfare system on or after October 1 used to identify acutes. Some of these new cases might actually be long-term cyclers who are once again filing an application for public assistance. How well these subsamples of new and ongoing cases reflect the welfare population composition in New Jersey can only be answered in a blended design where impacts are estimated for the entire caseload as well as for the subsamples.

The experimental sample used in the evaluation fell short of the targeted 9,000 and contained a slightly higher proportion of "ongoing cases" and fewer "new cases." The new case shortfall was a direct consequence of the decline in AFDC caseloads that was beginning to appear in states across the

Table 4.1.   Sample Design Employed in the Experiment

	Treatment	Control	Total
New cases	2,233	1,285	3,518
Ongoing cases	3,268	1,607	4,875
Total	5,501	2,892	8,393

country: fewer women were applying in New Jersey for public assistance and, at the request of the state, sampling was concluded in December 1994. Table 4.1 shows the final sample used in the analysis, cross-classified by treatment versus control group assignment and by new versus ongoing case status. The extended sampling of (new) case status was viewed at the time as a serious problem that could affect statistical power when estimating mean program impacts and the time path of any impacts. While it is true that some cases were not observed for as long a period as was planned, the prolonged sampling interjected, albeit inadvertently, a realism into the case selection process that mirrored the changing characteristics of the caseload.[77]

Each case in the experiment was observed on a quarterly basis using public assistance, Medicaid, and Labor Department administrative data. An observation was kept in the analysis only for those quarters that the case was actually receiving AFDC or FDP payments. This applied to all closed and subsequently reopened cases as well as continuous stayers. The approach is equivalent to what Charles Manski has referred to as the average effect of the treatment on the treated[78] and is consistent with the federal policy guidance that sought to determine if the Family Cap had an impact on births while a woman was receiving welfare benefits. Observations in the experiment were pooled over 17 quarters, that is, from the fourth quarter of 1992 through the fourth quarter of 1996, yielding 66,992 person-quarter observations. Alan Krueger is one of a number of economists who views pooled analysis as the best approach for determining the cumulative effect of an experiment.[79] Data collection in the experiment was terminated in the first quarter of 1997 by the state due to the implementation of PRWORA.

How successfully was the random assignment executed in New Jersey? The answer, at least on the measured characteristics of treatment and control cases and new and ongoing case subsamples, would appear to be quite well. Table 4.2 describes the study sample by experimental status. Here we see that Essex, Camden, and Hudson counties (New Jersey's largest welfare counties) contribute more than 50 percent of the sample cases. Roughly half the sample was black, about 17 percent was white, and nearly a third was Hispanic. While the sample mean age was nearly 32 years, the bulk of the sample was between 20 and 39 years of age. Nearly 37 percent of the sample did not finish high school, about 40 percent of the case participants had

Table 4.2.   Sample Characteristics at Baseline by Experimental Status—All Cases

Characteristic	Treatment Cases	Control Cases
Percentage		
County of Residence		
Atlantic	5.34	5.09
Camden	12.95	13.41
Cumberland	4.70	4.35
Essex	26.73	25.81
Hudson	17.37	16.71
Mercer	5.36	6.39
Passaic	7.72	8.39
Union	6.78	6.43
Race/Ethnicity		
White	16.62	18.01
Black	48.31	49.49
Hispanic	32.90	29.77
Other	1.82	2.00
Age		
Under 20	4.35	4.60
20–24	15.92	14.54
25–29	21.68	23.03
39–34	20.56	20.47
35–39	17.23	15.27
40–44	9.32	9.45
45 and over	8.27	9.13
Education		
Less than high school	36.73	36.66
High school	41.26	40.35
College	10.52	12.13
Other	0.56	0.64
Marital Status		
Never married	62.31	63.36
Married	9.82	9.50
Widowed	0.81	0.66
Separated/divorced	27.06	26.48
Employed	14.13	14.33
Mean		
Age	31.62	31.75
Number of eligible children	1.79	1.82
Earned income averaged over		
entire sample	125.63	134.24
Those working	868.79	910.44
Number of Cases	5,487	2,885

Table 4.3. Sample Characteristics at Baseline by Experimental Status and Case Type

Characteristic	Ongoing Cases		New Cases	
	Treatment	Control	Treatment	Control
Percentage				
County of Residence				
Atlantic	4.13	4.40	7.14	5.97
Camden	13.54	14.39	12.08	12.17
Cumberland	3.95	4.15	5.81	4.61
Essex	30.40	30.55	21.28	19.81
Hudson	18.93	17.54	15.06	15.67
Mercer	4.59	5.53	6.50	7.48
Passaic	6.35	6.98	9.75	10.18
Union	6.57	6.22	7.09	6.68
Race/Ethnicity				
White	14.59	15.96	19.63	20.60
Black	50.67	53.10	44.27	44.72
Hispanic	33.46**	29.33	32.06	30.35
Other	1.11	1.32	2.88	2.86
Age				
Under 20	1.02	0.69	9.29	9.55
20–24	15.36	13.95	16.75	15.27
25–29	22.42	23.95	20.59	21.88
39–34	21.09	20.93	19.77	19.89
35–39	19.18	17.66	14.32	12.25
40–44	10.55	10.25	7.51	8.43
45 and over	9.28	10.94	6.77	6.84
Education				
Less than high school	40.10	40.70	31.60	31.36
High school	38.81	38.05	45.01	43.35
College	8.97	9.60	12.87	15.46
Other	0.77	0.66	0.25	0.61
Marital Status				
Never married	64.52	67.73	58.91	57.57
Married	7.27	6.77	13.78	13.10
Widowed	0.97	0.83	0.58	0.42
Separated/divorced	27.24	24.67	26.73	28.91
Employed	14.46	14.39	13.64	14.24
Mean				
Age	32.47	31.75	30.30	30.36
Number of eligible children	1.88	1.82	1.66	1.68
Earned income averaged over				
entire sample	124.47	134.24	127.42	135.64
Those working	852.98	910.44	893.67	904.78
Number of Cases	3,243	1,591	2,185	1,257

Note: **Indicates p-values < .05.

Table 4.4.   Descriptions of Point-in-Time Caseload, 1992–1996

Variables	Dec. 92	Dec. 93	Dec. 94	Dec. 95	Dec. 96
Mean					
Female head age	28.8	29.1	29.2	29.3	29.4
Eligible children	1.95	1.93	1.84	1.77	1.71
Household size	4.01	4.01	4.01	4	4.02
Percentage					
Race					
White	15.3	15.1	14.9	14.3	13.6
Black	52.7	52.7	52.8	53.1	54.2
Hispanic	31.9	32.2	32.4	32.6	32.3
Education					
High school dropout	40.7	40	39.2	39.6	40.2
High school graduate	39.4	39.9	40.1	40.2	39.6
College	9.2	9.8	10.5	10.6	10.7
Marital Status					
Never married	69.6	70.1	71	72.3	74.4
Number of Cases	79,301	78,689	77,241	72,640	64,567

a high school diploma, and another 10 percent were college educated. A majority of the sample women had never married (nearly 63 percent). About 14 percent of the sample reported earnings from work that averaged a little over $850 a month. There were about two children on average in each AFDC-eligible unit. Table 4.2 also shows equivalence between the experimental and control group members in many of the sample characteristics and provides evidence of proper randomization. In the few instances where there appears to be a difference, for example, the proportion Hispanic or the proportion with a college degree, the difference is not statistically significant.

The stratification of the study sample by ongoing ("chronic") and new ("acute") case types is based on the premise that ongoing or longer-term welfare cases are qualitatively different from new or short-term entrants to the welfare system. The differences between the two types of cases become evident when we examine table 4.3. New cases tend to be younger than ongoing cases, to have fewer children on AFDC, and are more likely to have completed high school and to have attended college. New cases are also less likely to have never married. The racial composition of ongoing and new cases is also different. Among persons in the new case sample, about 44 percent are black and 20 percent are white; in the ongoing case sample the figures are 51 percent and 15 percent, respectively. Within case type, there is only one significant difference, that is, the difference between experimental and control ongoing Hispanic cases.

The unbalanced panel analysis used to augment the experiment examined fertility behavior that was exhibited by welfare recipients on the New

Table 4.5. Distributions of Time on Welfare for AFDC Female Heads in the Experimental Samples and New Jersey Caseload during Study Period

| | Experimental Design Analysis | | | | | | | | Unbalanced Panel Analysis | | | |
| | New Case Sample | | | | Ongoing Case Sample | | | | Caseload | | | |
Number of Quarters on Welfare	% All Heads	% Blacks	% Whites	% Hispanics	% All Heads	% Blacks	% Whites	% Hispanics	% All Heads	% Blacks	% Whites	% Hispanics
1	11.45	8.77	14.08	13.69	4.39	3.24	7.08	5.08	12.24	9.52	16.20	14.35
2	10.72	8.49	13.09	11.75	4.80	4.35	7.70	4.47	10.49	8.18	13.18	12.52
3	9.35	9.56	10.64	8.41	5.34	4.62	7.55	5.76	8.50	7.51	9.78	9.33
4	7.09	6.06	8.18	8.19	3.90	3.86	3.30	4.09	7.20	6.75	8.17	7.36
5	5.62	5.56	7.86	4.42	4.32	3.86	6.60	4.02	5.87	5.74	6.67	5.67
6	5.79	6.78	5.07	4.96	4.25	4.17	4.09	4.55	5.42	5.45	5.79	5.20
7	5.32	5.85	6.38	4.09	4.77	4.31	4.87	5.46	5.06	5.24	5.17	4.71
8	6.79	7.70	5.40	6.57	4.35	4.17	4.87	4.17	4.64	4.95	4.26	4.38
9	6.79	7.28	4.75	7.00	4.32	4.48	4.25	4.02	4.16	4.47	3.79	3.90
10	6.39	6.85	5.73	5.93	3.97	4.17	4.40	3.56	3.83	4.13	3.46	3.57
11	5.99	6.63	4.42	6.03	3.99	4.35	4.40	3.18	3.67	4.10	3.22	3.25
12	4.33	4.49	4.58	4.09	4.44	4.70	3.30	4.32	3.37	3.83	2.92	2.96
13	4.86	5.21	3.44	5.50	4.46	4.88	4.09	3.87	3.19	3.75	2.48	2.72
14	2.96	3.50	1.64	3.02	4.25	4.53	4.25	3.71	3.05	3.55	2.43	2.62
15	2.93	3.28	2.29	3.02	5.41	5.77	4.25	5.31	3.34	3.97	2.32	2.92
16	2.30	2.43	1.47	2.16	7.25	8.39	5.50	6.14	4.04	5.06	2.66	3.23
17	1.33	1.57	0.98	1.19	25.77	26.14	18.55	28.28	11.92	13.81	7.51	11.32
Total cases	3005	1402	611	928	4233	2253	636	1319	163835	78767	28847	56827
Mean quarters	6.9	7.4	6	6.8	10.9	11.3	9.4	10.9	7.8	8.6	6.5	7.3
Median quarters	6	7	5	6	12	12	9	12	6	7	4.5	5
Total person quarters	20,868	10,401	3,717	6,307	46,124	25,403	5,996	14,327	1,278,085	676,837	188,455	412,748

*The total cases and therefore the total person quarters utilized in fertility behavior analyses are less than the actual number in the sample and caseload because female payees over 45 years of age were excluded as not being at risk. In addition cases termed "child only" where no adult payee was on the grant were also excluded.

Jersey caseload two years before and four years after the implementation of the Family Cap. Observations over 24 quarters, from January 1991 through December 1996, for continuous stayers and new or reopened cases were pooled, yielding 1,278,058 person-quarters from approximately 250,000 distinct cases. All cases used in the experiment were excluded from the caseload analysis.

Table 4.4 describes the caseload at each year's end. The average age of recipients was around 29 years. The average household size hovered around four people, while the number of AFDC-eligible children slightly declined over the study period. Black recipients composed over half the caseload, while roughly a third was Hispanic. The caseload contained about equal proportions of high school dropouts and graduates (40 percent), and over 70 percent of the caseload was never married. Table 4.4 also shows clearly that the caseload declined steadily during the study period. Of course, these cross-sectional views of the caseload can be expected to be biased toward chronic cases.[80]

In table 4.5 I compare time on welfare for sample cases with the AFDC caseload for the experimental period (October 1992–December 1996). I also provide this information by race. What is clear from the table is that new and ongoing cases differ dramatically in distributions of welfare duration. Whereas the mean and median numbers of welfare quarters are 6.9 and 6 for new cases, it is 10.9 and 12 for ongoing cases. Moreover, while only about 19 percent of new cases spent 12 or more quarters on welfare, 52 percent of ongoing cases did so.

It is also evident from the table that the new case sample is a closer reflection of caseload over the experimental period. Whereas the typical new case recipient in the sample spends about 7 quarters on welfare, the typical recipient on the caseload spent about 7.8 quarters on welfare. It would be expected then that new case estimate of impact would be closer to caseload estimates than those found for ongoing cases.[81]

Armed with this somewhat inadvertent blended research design, we began the evaluation of New Jersey's Family Development Program in February 1994. In a little over two years we were required to produce our Interim Report on impacts from the caseload analysis. The political pressure for some hard evidence of Family Cap performance, however, was mounting, even before the evaluation team began preliminary data collection. I wondered if our results would be ready soon enough to help politicians and policy experts in their efforts to feed [or extinguish] the congressional fever for reform welfare. I didn't have to wonder very long.

5

Rushing to Judgment about the Family Cap

Introduction

There are two features of social policy experiment evaluations that make them unpopular with politicians: namely, they take too long and they very often bring unwelcome news. It takes several years to assemble the data and assess even the short-run welfare policy impacts of employment, earnings, welfare dependency, and spell length. It takes even longer to determine whether or not welfare reform is changing child and family well-being, marriage, or fertility behavior. Yet elected officials, government bureaucrats, policy experts, advocacy groups, and the media want results quickly.

In New Jersey, within a year of the Family Development Program's implementation, and before my colleagues and I began the official Section 1115 Waiver evaluation, pressure was mounting on the state's Department of Human Services to produce an initial assessment of the impact of the Family Cap. In chapter 2 we saw that these early monitoring and evaluation efforts led to pronouncements of the reform's success by Governor Jim Florio, the commissioner of human services, William Waldman, and the Family Cap's chief architect, Wayne Bryant.[1] New Jersey was not unique in this regard, with what some would say were precocious claims for welfare reform success emanating from a number of states, especially Wisconsin and Michigan.[2]

Then there is the issue of bad news with policies not working as advertised. Evaluations can present problems for elected officials who cannot always control the development and dissemination of evaluation findings.

Evaluation results that do not support a governor's policy stance, that provide ammunition to political opponents, or that are politically damaging in any way are unwelcome. Even seemingly innocuous findings can provide grist for politically motivated attacks against an incumbent legislator or governor. The evaluation of Learnfare in Wisconsin by Lois Quinn and Robert Magill is illustrative of the political consequences of negative research findings.[3] Introduced in 1987 by Governor Tommy Thompson, Learnfare penalized AFDC recipients if teenagers in their families did not regularly attend high school. Quinn and her colleagues at the University of Wisconsin-Milwaukee issued a report in 1991 that found that the program had no effect on increasing school attendance. The report was greeted by Governor Thompson's staff with little enthusiasm, in fact,

> state officials presented the evaluators with written instructions to suppress portions of the evaluation report and to redo the evaluation study according to new specifications developed by the Department of Health and Human Services staff. In addition to the deletion of the evaluation findings that the Learnfare requirement yielded no improvement in the school attendance of AFDC teens in any of the six school districts studied, evaluators were ordered to suppress a section of the evaluation reporting on the number of Learnfare teens who missed more than 20 days of school a semester and to suppress another part of the report providing data on the percentages of Learnfare teens with improved or worsened attendance after a year of the experiment.... After the evaluators refused to suppress the evaluation study, the state canceled the contract with the University for completion of the Learnfare study and attacked the professionalism of the evaluators.[4]

As we shall see, governmental antipathy to displeasing welfare reform evaluation findings was not limited to Wisconsin.[5]

Rough handling of academic researchers by politicians is, of course, old news with scores of evaluation texts and journal articles recounting what can be termed the "Rodney Dangerfield treatment" of researchers and their research by congressional committees, judges, state panels of inquiry, and individuals seeking election or reelection.[6] The Moynihan Report discussed in chapter 3 is only one example of research running afoul of party politics and advocacy group agendas. The work by James Coleman on student achievement and school resources[7] and on the impact of busing, school desegregation, and white flight from cities[8] offers other examples of research resulting in the considerable discomfort of the researcher. More often than not, however, this lack of respect is communicated through an indifference to research findings—perhaps a worse sin in the eyes of researchers than disapproval.[9]

Evaluation findings provide politicians and policymakers with only one source of "evidence" for deciding which social programs or policies to support or oppose. Henry J. Aaron cites opinion studies that show that governmental officials are more likely to trust their intuitions and common-sense beliefs about social problems than empirical research results.[10] No doubt, personal values, religious beliefs, professional training and affiliations, and prior research experiences also play a role in how evaluation findings will be received and used by policymakers. David Greenberg and Marvin Mandell classify the factors that influence research utilization into two distinctive categories, namely, the qualities of the research and the qualities of the research environment. They maintain that a thorough understanding of why some evaluation studies are used while others are ignored requires an appreciation for the role played by both factors.

According to Greenberg and Mandell, the research qualities that increase the likelihood of use are its relevance, timeliness, communication and visibility, generalizability, and credibility.[11] It is rather obvious that research that is pertinent to the policy debate at hand has a better chance of being consulted than research that is out of sync with current policy issues and policy "windows." But as Larry Orr notes, some social experiments can have a relatively long shelf life, maintaining their relevance and timeliness because of the persistence and/or intractability of a problem.[12] The income maintenance and welfare-to-work studies conducted by MDRC in the 1970s and early 1980s are prime examples, exerting a significant impact on the deliberations that attended the passage of both the Family Support Act and PRWORA.

Nor is it surprising that research that is visible to the policy community and that is generalizable beyond a sample of individuals representative of a particular geographic location has greater influence on politicians than narrowly focused, unpublished, or embargoed research. These qualities, moreover, tend to be mutually reinforcing. Research that is made available to the popular press, scholarly journals, professional conferences, public interest groups, and policy working groups has a greater likelihood of reaching the status of new evidence for a larger audience. Wider exposure to study findings sets the stage for the possible advance of both science and punditry as the inevitable comparisons are made with other populations, settings, times, treatments, and outcomes.

Of the research qualities listed by Greenberg and Mandell, it is the credibility of the experiment's—or for that matter any research's—empirical findings that is most critical for its utilization by policymakers. This is not to say that assessments of "worthiness of belief" are simply responses to the scientific rigor of the research: namely, clear conceptual logic, reliable and valid measurement, appropriate and correctly specified statistical analyses, strong research design, and correctly implemented sampling. Orr, a veteran evaluator, observes that policymakers—and I would add a good many policy analysts—are generally not qualified to judge the scientific integrity of research and rely on "indirect indicators" of the reliability of research evidence, for example, the reputation of the researchers, whether the results are generally accepted within the research community, and whether the

results are internally consistent and consistent with the users' own preconceptions and other evidence at their disposal.[13]

The credibility of the research conducted for New Jersey's Family Cap
evaluation in the eyes of Washington policymakers and analysts was certainly colored by the reputation or, to put it more accurately, by the lack of
reputation of evaluation team members in executing large-scale welfare
reform experiments. Although each member of the Rutgers research team
had extensive experience with large data set and applied econometric analyses, none of us had the social experimentation track record of an MDRC,
Abt Associates, or Mathematica Policy Research (MPR), the so-called "Big-
Three" of social experiment evaluators. In the words of David Greenberg,
Mark Shroder, and Matthew Onstott, "By hiring a Big Three firm that has
previously conducted successful evaluations and has a known expertise in
the specific program area a funding agency is buying credentials from a firm
with a track record."[14]

When a social experiment's credibility is viewed by politicians, policy
analysts, and government officials as an amalgam of scientific rigor, reputation, and acceptability, the lines between qualities of the research and
qualities of the research environment begin to blur. This is because, as Carol
Weiss asserts, policymakers are more likely to receive "information" about
the research than they are "knowledge" of the experiment's actual conduct
and content. This is no small distinction. For Weiss, "Knowledge . . . often
communicates a sense of accuracy, rightness and validity, whereas information has a tentative enough aura to contain partial, biased or invalid
understandings.[15] How this information is used, moreover, depends on how
consistent it is with two other elements of the policy environment: active
ideologies and current interests. Weiss defines ideology as philosophy, principles, values, and political orientation and interests as self-interest, that is,
reelection, enhanced career paths, relevance.[16]

The information-ideology-interests framework is a helpful one to keep in
mind as the reader seeks to understand the policymaker response to New
Jersey's Family Cap experiment. Information that both seeped and then
flowed from our research was, by turns, palatable and distasteful to politicians, government bureaucrats, advocacy groups, and "think tanks." In
addition, the findings did not support fully any of the ideological positions
carved out by principal welfare reform protagonists. Orr comments that
political actors tend to be suspicious of evidence that requires a complicated[17] explanation and our explanation of Family Cap impact presented a
bit of a tangle for true believers on both sides of the economic rehabilitation
versus family reconstruction, illegitimacy versus abortion and, and egali-
tarianism versus racism debates. What is more, a good deal of the information emanating from the evaluation proved to be incongruous with the
interests of state officials, who sought the prestige that accompanies leadership in successful welfare reform, lawyers at the American Civil Liberties Union (ACLU) and the National Organization of Women (NOW) who

opposed welfare rule changes, and some university administrators at Rutgers, who may have feared state reprisals for unflattering findings.

Pushing for Results

The contract to evaluate New Jersey's Family Development Program began in mid October of 1993. An interim report on impacts from the panel analysis of the caseload was due at the end of December 1995; another interim report on impact from the social experiment was to follow in mid April 1996.[18] The pressures of a court case, impending changes to the Family Support Act and AFDC, and national interest in America's first Family Cap, however, compelled the incoming governor Christine Todd Whitman, and the continuing commissioner of human services, William Waldman, to look for answers sooner. As Waldman conveyed to a *New York Times* reporter, "We got a little burned with some of the early numbers so we've been reticent to give them out."[19]

The study conducted by June O'Neill, commissioned by the state to bolster its defense of the Family Cap in *C. K. v. Shalala*, was greeted with a good deal of skepticism by welfare reform critics. Adam Zaretsky, an economist at the Federal Reserve Bank of St. Louis, questioned whether the roughly one year of post–Family Cap data employed by O'Neill was a long enough period to accurately measure birth effects.[20] Patricia Donovan from the Alan Guttmacher Institute was more provocative in her assessment: "A lag in reporting largely explains the whopping 29 percent decline in births for the first 10 months of the New Jersey Cap found in a 1994 study. The study was conducted by June O'Neill of Baruch College, who was subsequently appointed director of the Congressional Budget Office at the request of the State of New Jersey.... State officials say the analysis comparing the evaluation groups to the control group ... had only about five months of reliable data on births."[21] The Goertzel and Young paean to Family Cap success also made state officials a bit uneasy, no doubt reflecting on the confusion and anxiety that simple trend analyses originating from the governor's and commissioner's offices was having on wannabe Family Cappers across the country. Here was yet another estimate of birth declines without a legitimate counterfactual.[22]

In December 1994, the Division of Family Development in NJDHS asked my colleagues and me to replicate the O'Neill report using the same sample of 3,691 ongoing cases provided to June O'Neill. A preliminary analysis with an "approximated" sample did not reveal any statistically significant birth effects;[23] neither did an assessment of births from August 1993 through July 1994 in which all the ongoing cases in the evaluation sample were used. I communicated these very preliminary results to the Division of Family Development and NJDHS on June 14, 1995, in a two-page letter that emphasized our findings were based on "only one full year of post-program data [for ongoing cases] with data on new application cases...too incomplete to include."[24] In an environment that had been imbued with nothing but success stories I was quite uncertain how this news would be treated.

Within a week's time, my letter was leaked to the *Washington Post* in an article entitled "N. J. Welfare 'Cap' Has No Effect on Births...."[25] While the reporting did make mention of my caveats, the principal theme was one of conflict—conflict between different research findings and conflict between Family Cap supporters and detractors. This theme was accentuated in subsequent news accounts, which were printed in other state and national news outlets. In a *Time* magazine piece, Michael Kramer observed how policy analysts like Charles Murray of the American Enterprise Institute and Robert Rector of the Heritage Foundation had "glowingly accepted" New Jersey's early reports of success and were now backing away from the O'Neill report.[26] Kramer went on to quote Sheldon Danziger, a public policy professor at the University of Michigan and one of the chief architects of the Center on Budget and Policy Priorities 11/94 entreaty against the spread of Family Caps, who said that O'Neill's work contradicted everything that had come before and that the Rutgers' results were more in line with what social science would expect.[27]

State reports on the June 14 letter focused on the political and legal fallout. Susan Kraham, a staff attorney with the National Organization for Women involved in the state constitutional challenge to the Family Cap, said that "the Rutgers study shows the policy is ineffective. The only result is to deny already poor families needed income."[28] Regina Purcell, associate director of social concerns for the New Jersey Catholic Conference, remarked, "Although still preliminary this data directly contradicts claims from proponents of the law that it resulted in substantial reduction in births." [29] The politicians most responsible for enacting New Jersey's Family Cap retorted that the press had gotten it wrong—the Cap was not about lowering birthrates at all. Former governor Jim Florio stated that "changes in the state's welfare rules were never specifically designed to lower birth rates." He continued that we did not move in this direction because we think women had children to get $64. "The law was passed to send a message to welfare mothers that they have to take responsibility for the consequences of their actions like all women are required to do." [30] Wayne Bryant reiterated Florio's response, noting that he simply wanted to place welfare mothers under the same economic limits as working parents. "This policy was a values policy" according to Bryant.[31] And in a direct swipe at the Rutgers evaluation Bryant intoned: "Studies being conducted on the Family Development Program's impact on births are not only incomplete and inconclusive.... They take a far too narrow view of the true intent of the law. The objective of this law is to link the acceptance of welfare benefits with the responsibility of working to support children."[32]

The primary protagonist in this alleged outing of the Family Cap was a senior program associate at the Annie E. Casey Foundation, Michael Laracy.

Prior to his joining the Casey Foundation in mid 1995, Laracy had spent some 17 years in New Jersey state government, most of it in NJDHS where he rose to assistant commissioner for policy planning and program evaluation. He had written two policy analyses of New Jersey's Cap, colorfully titled *The Jury Is Still Out* and *If It Seems Too Good to Be True, It Probably Is.*[33] In this latter document Laracy states that he was responsible for the design and implementation of the state's 1986 welfare reform program as well as for the federal waiver and evaluation design of the 1992 reform effort, the Family Development Program.[34] It is readily apparent from Laracy's writings, however, that he had turned sour on the Family Cap and he keenly wanted others to feel his passion.

Laracy's approach to the controversy over our evaluation findings was to urge temperance but avoid its actual practice. He was especially intent on calling attention to the misuse of data by Florio and Bryant. In an interview that appeared in the newsletter "Welfare to Work" Laracy opined that "some very powerful people went out on limbs with very little to support them ... now those limbs are broken off and they must be very embarrassed." Laracy concluded the interview with this prediction: "This [Rutgers Evaluation findings] is an authoritative conclusion but it's still too early to be decisive. I'd be really surprised if a year or more down the road the data shows that the law has a major effect."[35]

Laracy was among the very first to point up the serious, unintended consequences a Family Cap would be expected to have on the poor. In *The Jury Is Still Out* he warned that "in order to modestly reduce birth rates, the state of New Jersey may be significantly increasing the probability that many of the sanctioned infants will be neglected or will experience health problems or arrested development." [36] He castigated the state government for a failure to address the "misinformation and fear" that may be causing mothers to delay or not report births.[37] When interviewed by the *New York Times*, Laracy noted that no one had measured adverse effects of the Family Cap, "like how many families had become homeless."[38] In *If It Seems Too Good ...* he advised policymakers who were thinking of enacting a Family Cap not to be taken in by the earlier erroneous analyses and claims about impacts in New Jersey.[39]

In this bleak policy landscape, however, Michael Laracy caught a glimmer of hope in the form of Governor Christine Todd Whitman. He applauded the governor for her resoluteness in refusing to rush to judgment about the effect of the Family Cap until the Rutgers evaluation was farther along.[40] Laracy also praised Whitman for approving the U.S. Department of Health and Human Services (USDHHS) request to augment the Rutgers experiment with a panel analysis of the welfare caseload and for her help in bringing resources from the Kaiser Family Foundation into the evaluation. No one else, it would seem, was more pleased to have Governor Whitman handling the implementation of New Jersey's Family Cap than Michael Laracy, no one perhaps except Michael Laracy's wife, who served as the governor's chief of policy.[41]

In the days and months following the leak of the June 14 letter, I was contacted by the many national, state, and even international media outlets for comment on "the apparent failure of the Family Cap." My message, whether on the *MacNeil/Lehrer Newshour*,[42] CNBC,[43] or with print reporters from the *Washington Post, New York Times*, and state newspapers was to stress that these findings were very preliminary and only applied to approximately one-half of the sample, that is, to ongoing cases and even here after only about one year of treatment. I also attempted to make this message clear to organizations like the Alan Guttmacher Institute, the Family Research Council, the Center for Law and Social Policy (CLASP), and the American Enterprise Institute (AEI).

My June 14 letter, coming on the heels of earlier reports of Family Cap success in New Jersey, frustrated some policymakers in Washington who were trying hard to include a Family Cap in a welfare reform bill. Ron Haskins, then the majority staff director, U.S. House Committee on Ways and Means, told me that the research in New Jersey was presenting a "complicated picture" to Congress and that this was "not helping matters at all."[44] The House had passed its version of welfare reform in March 1995, which included a Family Cap, but the Senate could not agree with provisions aimed at nonmarital birth prevention.[45] This deadlock continued over the summer but the Senate planned to take up welfare reform once again in September.

One organization with an intense interest in the shape of welfare reform was the AEI, the conservative-leaning "think tank" located in Washington, which boasted among its resident scholars Robert Bork, Dinesh D'Souza, Irving Kristol, and Charles Murray. The Institute sponsored a conference in early September entitled "Addressing Illegitimacy: Welfare Reform Options for Congress." The conference organizer, Douglas Besharov, was clearly in the camp of policy experts who defined "births out-of-wedlock" as the central issue of welfare reform.[46] Besharov asked if I would participate in a session focused on the New Jersey Family Cap with Rudolph Myers, Division of Family Development, NJDHS, and Peter Rossi, the noted evaluator, serving as discussants. Other sessions on the issue of illegitimacy and its amelioration were to be presented by such welfare reform experts as Rebecca Maynard, Judith Gueron, Ron Haskins, Robert Rector, and Isabel Sawhill.

Only three months had passed since my June 14 letter and the additional data that had been collected did nothing to change our preliminary findings: for example, for ongoing cases, the decreases in birthrates form pre-Family Cap to post-Family Cap were not statistically different for experimental and control cases.[47] The conference, however, offered me an opportunity to hypothesize a little about why this was occurring, and I offered five conceivable reasons:

1. There actually is *no* effect of the Family Cap on births.
2. The treatment (Family Cap) was not applied to the correct target group, that is, the experimental group, leading to contamination of

results. We believe that this may not be a real issue in this case since the application of the Family Cap in the form of benefit loss came after the birth has occurred and hence could not have affected a woman's decision to get pregnant.

3. The FDP program elements, particularly the Family Cap element, were not fully understood by the program participants.
4. The program administrators' understanding of FDP program's rules and regulations, in particular, the Family Cap rule, may not be uniform across counties or the rules may not be understood by program administrators uniformly within the same county.
5. Not enough time has elapsed since FDP program implementation for real changes in participants' behavior to occur.[48]

Three of the possibilities I mentioned pinpointed treatment contamination—the "bleeding" alluded to in the Arkansas experiment—as reasons for the similar behavior exhibited by treatment and control women. Improper treatment delivery, sometimes referred to as "treatment wandering"[49] or "crossover effect"[50] was viewed by the evaluation team as highly unlikely since a control case could not receive the $102 or $64 child exclusion until after the child had been born and hence, the actual sanction could not have motivated the behavior. Moreover, monthly computer edits in the FDP data management system minimized the probability that any incorrect payment sanction would be continued long enough to affect a control woman's decision to have a subsequent birth.

Much more likely in a social experiment where the policy contains a message or threat of some future application is contamination arising from the experiment's failure to insulate controls from misinformation and misperceptions concerning their true experimental status and the type of treatment they can expect to receive. I like to think of this as contamination from "wondering." Guided by incomplete, conflicting, or erroneous information from the general media, other welfare recipients, or agency staff, control women might behave as though they have some nonzero probability of being "Capped." Serious contamination of the experiment's environment context, then, could be expected to attenuate any measured treatment versus control group differences to the point where real differences cannot be observed.[51]

Both Myers and Rossi raised the issue of contamination in their reviews of the Rutgers evaluation design. Myers was unequivocal in his stance stating, "The counterfactual condition thus created cannot represent the absence of the treatment, then, unless treatment is understood to mean simply the applicability of certain policy-related laws and regulations."[52] Peter Rossi, on the other hand, was a bit more circumspect, naming contamination of the information given to recipients as one of several possible reasons for our findings. He expressed doubt, however, that the experiment, even if properly implemented, would indicate any Family Cap impacts but added this perhaps not so tongue-in-cheek remark: "It doesn't matter what the experiment finds about Family Cap effects on fertility, the policy is the right thing to do. Too bad about the experiment, but full speed ahead on the policy."[53] I reprised a somewhat expanded version of these AEI remarks two weeks later at a Child Welfare League of America (CWLA) conference in Philadelphia, my last presentation in a professional or public forum until November 1998.

It appeared that my notoriety on the New Jersey evaluation was not being well received by some state officials and by Mary Davidson, the dean of the school of social work at Rutgers University. On May 22, 1995, around the time that I began receiving regular inquiries from the press about Family Cap impacts, I received a call from the director of the Division of Family Development asking if I could follow the "state model" for reporting project findings and deliverables. The "state model" as it was described to me was one "where work done by a Division Director, technical person, etc., can be released under a Commissioner's or Associate Commissioner's name."[54] Following this "state model" on the Rutgers evaluation project, I was told would ensure that the dean would be kept in the loop, since the dean would then be viewed as the project leader. In a June 8 meeting I was told by Dean Davidson that "I should listen to what the state was telling me." I replied that I thought the more appropriate model at a university like Rutgers was the "PI (Principal Investigator) in academic setting model," where the individual in charge of the actual conduct of the research should be named on reports, presentations, and other deliverables and the dean should be kept in the loop through a series of timely and ongoing briefing sessions.[55]

In September 1995, shortly after my presentations at AEI and CWLA I received another call from the Division of Family Development prohibiting me from any further direct contacts with the media, professional organizations, academic conferences, legal or advocacy groups without prior permission from Commissioner William Waldman. This policy remained in effect until November 1998 and directly contributed, I believe, to the confusion and misinformation that was to companion the evaluation over the next three years. I should also note over this same three-year period I made 17 requests to brief the dean on project process and reports but was not asked to give even one.[56]

Several days after the AEI conference, the U.S. Senate rejected the Family Cap in its newest bill on welfare reform.[57] In December, however, a House-Senate conference welfare reform bill put the Cap back in but allowed states to opt out of this restriction by enacting a Cap-specific proscription. In January, President Bill Clinton vetoed this bill, although the White House did not cite the inclusion of a Family Cap as a reason.[58] As the Congressional Record shows, research around the Family Cap, including our own, provided policymakers with little in the way of guidance in 1995.[59]

Using Surveys to Study Family Cap Effects

In early 1995, the evaluation team felt additional pressure from Governor Whitman's office and from the commissioner of NJDHS to provide some definitive results about Family Cap fertility impacts. The experimental results and those from the unbalanced panel of the entire caseload were taking too long to emerge from Trenton's viewpoint, in what was turning out to be a political-legal-media maelstrom. The state's answer to this situation was to strongly suggest that the evaluation team work with the Kaiser Family Foundation to conduct an opinion survey of welfare mothers and to get it done as soon as possible. Such a client survey was planned in the social experiment but here it was targeted for completion in mid 1998.[60]

The Henry J. Kaiser Family Foundation conducts policy research and public education programs primarily in the areas of health and healthcare financing policy. Its principal policy tool is the opinion survey and, in fact, the Foundation runs the largest public opinion research programs in the country on health issues. The president of this California-based Foundation, Drew Altman, had a special connection to New Jersey politics; he was the commissioner of NJDHS under Tom Kean, the Republican governor who had preceded the Democrat Jim Florio and he had ties to the Whitman administration. Michael Laracy, an advocate for the Kaiser-sponsored survey,[61] had worked on Altman's staff as an assistant commissioner when the REACH welfare reform was implemented in the mid-1980s. In effect, because of Altman's political connections with New Jersey government, we were being made an offer we couldn't refuse.

An opinion survey could certainly generate answers about fertility behavior more rapidly than waiting for behaviors to unfold in administrative data; however, the critical question is "Can survey responses on such a sensitive topic as childbearing be trusted?" The evaluation project team had its doubts, especially about the reporting of abortions influenced by the Family Cap—a topic of keen interest to the Kaiser Family Foundation.

The utility of opinion surveys in the study of highly personal or sensitive issues like income, crime victimization, or sexual behavior has been questioned repeatedly.[62] The dramatic underreporting of abortions in opinion surveys is especially well documented with only 35 percent to 65 percent of actual procedures being revealed by women.[63] Nonwhite and unmarried women, moreover, who predominate welfare populations, are significantly more likely than white women to underreport.[64] Women underreport abortions for many reasons including modesty about sexual behavior, psychologic repression and reaction to the survey methods being employed.[65] We discussed these issues with Kaiser staff who remained convinced that a survey, if implemented with their input and guidance, could yield reliable information on fertility behavior.

If a survey was to be conducted, however, NJDHS and the Rutgers evaluation team wanted it linked to the original experimental design as closely as possible so that results could be used as a baseline if and when the required 1998 client survey was undertaken. This called for a sample of 1,500 women—with equal numbers of both new and ongoing, and treatment and control group cases—responding to queries about individual responsibility, service delivery, family formation, employment, youth functioning, health, and health insurance in addition to fertility behavior.[66] Kaiser had much more circumscribed interests, wishing to focus on social/economic problems and fertility of Capped women. An agreement was reached and Kaiser reluctantly acquiesced to work within the framework of the social experiment. Altman, however, would not increase the size of his original grant award, which was $90,000.[67]

In May 1995, we drew a random sample of 3,570 cases from the 8,393 that comprised our experimental sample. This number, we believed, would net us over 1,500 survey respondents, assuming a 50 percent response rate and no ineligible households.[68] We also assumed that 90 percent of the survey interviews could be conducted by telephone with the remaining 10 percent done face-to-face. This would allow us to work within our $90,000 budget constraint at $60 per completed, 45-minute interview.[69] Using these specifications, we contracted with the nationally known survey research firm Schulman, Ronca and Bucuvalis (SRBI) to carry out the actual work. The assumption about working telephones, however, proved to be incorrect—the experimental sample was getting old, recipients were on the move, and many telephone numbers were outdated, and therefore more face-to-face interviews were required. In early January 1996 with 1,236 completed surveys—1,087 by telephone and 149 face-to-face—(a 41 percent response rate)—the Kaiser money exhausted and pressure mounting from the Foundation for results, I stopped the survey process with the approval of NJDHS and Kaiser.

When recipient attitudes toward the New Jersey Family Cap were tabulated, the answers surprised the evaluation team and seemed to astonish Altman and his staff. In our report to Kaiser we summarized these results in this way:

> With respect to the controversial Family Cap, recipients indicated what can only be termed as a positive response; 66.5 percent said the Family Cap, as they understood it, is a fair rule; 86.1 percent stated the Family Cap promotes individual responsibility; 71.5 percent believed the Family Cap helps women focus on job training and career; 69.8 percent thought the Family Cap stresses the financial responsibility of giving birth to a child; 50.0 percent said the Family Cap discourages out-of-wedlock births.[70]

Recipient reports on the impact that the Family Cap had on their pregnancy decisions were not as dramatic.

> 30.4 percent stated they avoided becoming pregnant; 30.2 percent noted that they began to use contraception methods more consis-

tently; 20.6 percent decided to have fewer children than they had expected; 6.1 percent said they had an abortion; 7.0 percent said they had advised a friend to have an abortion.[71]

The Kaiser Foundation reaction to an opinion survey that largely validated the contentions of former governor Jim Florio and (now) State Senator Wayne Bryant was less than enthusiastic. This demeanor can be seen clearly in the proposed title for a Kaiser press release drafted in April 1996 by Altman: "Many Say Family Cap Has Caused Them to 'Try Harder' to Get Off Welfare and Avoid Pregnancy, But For Those 'Capped' Also Makes It More Difficult to Provide Food, Clothing, and Other Necessities For Their Children; Seven Percent of Women in Study Cite Cap as Reason They Had an Abortion"[72] Then in early May, a Kaiser press conference in Washington where I would present survey findings was abruptly cancelled with no clear reason given for the cancellation.[73] The rationale for calling off the press conference was to be provided by Altman nearly three months later, however.

In a July 31, 1996, letter I was told by the Foundation that two independent researchers had raised serious concerns "about the response rate, representativeness of the sample and inconsistent responses of those surveyed."[74] Kaiser concluded that dissemination of the results would not inform the current debate on welfare reform in any positive way. Especially critical were the remarks of Harold Beebout, senior vice president at Mathematica, who asserted, "It is not clear that dissemination of such findings improves the information available to the policy community on such critical issues, and may provide misinformation."[75] Beebout had made his own calculation of our response rate at 20 percent and had boasted that in a survey environment similar to the one faced by Rutgers, with a long delay between sampling and surveying welfare respondents, MPR had achieved a 55 percent response rate. In point of fact, the MPR study Beebout refers to achieved a 43 percent response rate—not very different from what we obtained.[76] When I questioned Beebout about these response rates he replied in a memo that "the number I quoted in the review turned out to be a little high."[77] When I reported the errors in the Beebout review to Kaiser I was greeted with silence.

There is no question that a response rate of 41 percent, or for that matter 43 percent, can signal response pattern bias but, as Allen Rubin and Earl Babbie note, a demonstrated lack of response bias is far more important than a high response rate. In our final report to Kaiser and in an article that appeared in the American Journal of Public Health[78] it is clear that on most measured characteristics respondents and nonrespondents do not differ significantly. As table 5.1 shows, survey respondents closely reflected nonrespondents on treatment status, length of welfare receipt, marital status, mean age, number of children, employment, and county of residence, and

Table 5.1. Characteristics of Respondents and Nonrespondents to a Survey on the Impact of New Jersey's Family Development Program, July 1995– January 1996

Characteristic	Respondents Percent	Nonrespondents Percent
Experimental Status		
Experimental group	53.0	55.0
Control group	47.0	45.0
N	(1,223)	(1,782)
Welfare Use		
Long-term	53.2	55.2
Short-term	47.7	44.8
N	(1,223)	(1,782)
County of Residence		
Atlantic	5.2	6.1
Camden	14.4	13.0
Cumberland	6.2	4.8
Essex	22.7	25.7
Hudson	13.1	16.4
Mercer	6.0	6.1
Passaic	8.6	7.8
Union	7.4	7.2
All other	16.4	12.9
N	(1,223)	(1,782)
Education		
Less than high school	35.5	41.8
All other	64.5	58.2
N	(1,229)	(1,740)
Marital Status		
Never married	59.2	64.1
All other	40.8	35.9
N	(1,232)	(1,752)
Race		
White	22.8	18.0
Black	53.5	48.8
Hispanic	23.7	32.2
Other	0.0	1.0
N	(1,232)	(1,752)
Number of Abortions:	(1,233)	(1,782)
0	81.7	80.7
1	12.5	10.7
2	3.9	5.3
3	1.4	2.0
4	0.4	0.8
5	0.1	0.5
Average Number of AFDC-Eligible		
Children	1.8	1.8
N	(1,233)	(1,782)
Employed	29.7	28.9
N	(1,233)	(1,782)
Average Age of Respondent	32.2 yrs	31.4 yrs
N	(1,232)	(1,782)

Numbers here are somewhat lower than what appears in Kaiser Report due to list-wise missing values [Radha Jagannathan (2001) *American Journal of Public Health*].

even the number of reported abortions. The major difference between the groups was representation of Hispanics, with respondents having 8.5 percent less Hispanic representation than nonrespondents.

The Kaiser Foundation may have been correct to cancel its press conference even if their rationale may have been suspect. One reason for canceling may be viewed in table 5.2 where my colleague Radha Jagannathan compares the number of abortions admitted by women in the Kaiser-sponsored survey and the number that appear on Medicaid claims files used by the state to make reimbursements to physicians and hospitals for medical procedures. Here it is clear that women, especially black women, substantially underreport the number of abortions they receive. Overall, Jagannathan

Table 5.2.   Self-Reported vs. Actual Abortions, by Welfare Recipients' Characteristics and Survey Implementation Factors, July 1995–January 1996

Characteristic	N	Number of Abortions Reported	Number of Actual Abortions[a]	Percent of Actual Abortions Reported
Race				
White	281	17	24	71.0
Black	659	59	251	24.0
Hispanic	282	17	50	34.0
Age				
16–24	244	39	142	27.5
25–28	246	25	80	31.3
29–33	246	20	55	36.4
34–38	243	8	31	25.8
38+	246	1	17	5.9
Marital Status				
Married	127	5	16	31.3
Separated/ divorced	365	17	55	30.9
Never married	726	70	253	27.7
Education				
< High school	435	33	110	30.0
High school	564	39	137	28.5
> High school	194	21	72	29.2
Mode of Interview				
In person	143	4	40	10.0
Telephone	1,090	89	285	31.2
Interview Length				
Long	452	23	120	19.2
Short	780	70	205	34.1
Overall	1,233	93	325	29.0

[a]According to Medicaid claims files [Radha Jagannathan (2001) *American Journal of Public Health*].

reports that only about 29 percent of actual abortions were self-reported in the survey sample with many women reporting that their pregnancies ended in a birth when, in fact, the pregnancy was aborted.[79] The findings fit well with the existing literature on self-reported fertility behavior and appeared to justify our concerns about using surveys to study sensitive, sexual and reproductive issues—concerns we shared with Kaiser very early on.

In January 1997, John Harwood, a reporter for the *Wall Street Journal*, wrote a lengthy front-page piece on how social science research was being misused by liberal and conservative foundations and think tanks with each side seeking the upper hand in the welfare reform debate.[80] Harwood described how critics saw the Kaiser decision to reject the New Jersey survey as much more ideological than methodological. Especially troubling to the Foundation, these critics contend, were the rumors that were circulating about welfare recipients considering the Family Cap to be a fair rule. I was not one of those critics, of course, inasmuch as I was forbidden by NJDHS from speaking to anyone about the evaluation. It was not one of my finest moments when Harwood quoted me in his article saying, "If I talk to anybody, I'm in big trouble." Nevertheless, I believed state officials when they warned if I talked they would shut the evaluation down.

The recipient opinion survey had a number of unintended consequences, some good, others not so good, for both Kaiser and the evaluation team. Quoting Jane Austen on the first page of the final report we delivered to the Foundation, I only acknowledged the latter: "Surprises are foolish things. The pleasure is not enhanced and the inconvenience is often considerable."[81] The survey, however, was to prove very useful in addressing what would become the most serious attack on the credibility of our research methodology and findings.

Secret Research

In May 1996, and only a month behind schedule, we completed the first draft of our long anticipated Interim Report on the Impact of New Jersey's Family Development Program. After considerable input from NJDHS, the Division of Family Development, and ACF, a third and final draft was completed at the end of July combining what we knew from both the experiment and the caseload analysis thus far.[82] Chapter 6 of the Interim Report— "Program Impact: Births, Abortions and Family Planning"—particularly the abortion analysis, generated the most interest among state and federal officials. Reporting lags of four to six months on the public welfare and Medicaid claims administrative systems limited our assessment of fertility impacts to ongoing cases through July 1995.[83] Our findings were far from remarkable and, if anything, did not paint the Family Development Program or the Family Cap in an unfavorable light—or so I thought.

- There still were no statistically significant differences in the birth-rates of treatment and control cases;
- There were no significant differences in abortion rates between treatment and control cases;
- (Contraceptive) sterilization rates did not differ between the two groups;
- There was a statistically significant difference in family planning utilization with treatment cases about 4 percent more likely than controls to use professional counseling services;
- There was no significant difference between treatment and control cases in the use of contraceptive drugs and devices.[84]

But NJDHS responded to the Interim Report in a fashion that was truly remarkable, opting not to release the document to media or to the general public. Inasmuch as I was prohibited from distributing the report under the terms of the evaluation contract, and forbidden to speak to any outside entity about its content, the press, local politicians, and advocacy groups like NOW, the ACLU, the Catholic Bishop's Council, and others began to draw their own conclusions. Reporters, it seemed, never stopped calling about the whereabouts of the Rutgers evaluation report and my nonanswers to their queries only increased suspicions. I began to hear the phrases "state cover-up," "what does the state have to hide?" and "secret research" expressed with greater frequency.

While I was never given an explicit reason by NJDHS for its reluctance in releasing this report I am sure the policy environment at the time contributed. Welfare reform in the form of HR3734 was again making its way through Congress and Family Caps were as contentious as ever.[85] The report's less than definitive findings might only serve to add more confusion to a political landscape already cluttered with too many claims of Family Cap success and failure. There was also the prospect of more litigation. In August 1996 the Third Circuit Court had unanimously affirmed the federal district court's decision upholding the New Jersey Family Cap. But soon after this decision, NOW and the ACLU were already making plans to bring their suit to the state courts should they receive an adverse ruling.[86] Perhaps the report was seen as providing more fodder for the plaintiffs.

The question of research credibility also may have played a role in NJDHS hesitancy. Reports from the evaluation of the nation's second oldest Family Cap in Arkansas were questioning the feasibility of experimenting with a Family Cap. Carol Turturro, principal investigator, was now widely quoted as declaring "there's a lot of confusion" between experimentals and controls about who is really subject to a Cap.[87] And in both the Interim and Kaiser reports we presented a table, drawn from the recipient survey, which compared the actual assignment of cases discussed in chapter 4, with recipients' perceived experimental status; the simple cross-tabulation was not encouraging. Only 35 percent of the cases randomly assigned to the control group stated they were told they were in a control group. Among assigned treatment cases, 28 percent stated that they were told they were controls.[88] Kaiser's opting to cancel the recipient survey presentation due to alleged methodological flaws, despite the post hoc, ergo propter hoc logic this decision reflected, could also have contributed.

On September 11, 1997, over 14 months after its completion, NJDHS released the Interim Report to the public. At a press conference that no one from the evaluation team was allowed to attend, Governor Christine Whitman stressed that "the intent of the Family Cap was never to reduce the birth rate or to save money, the goal of this provision was to send a message of personal responsibility to families on welfare."[89] Human Services Commissioner William Waldman noted that since the birthrate had dropped as much in the control group as in the treatment group "it may be the responsibility message of the Family Cap rather than the provision itself that contributed to the birth rate decline."[90] He cautioned, however, that it is difficult to have a true control group when the women who are not Capped still may have read or seen news accounts about the Family Cap. On the whole, state officials seemed content with the Interim Report results—the welfare recipients survey had shown the Cap was perceived as a fair rule that promoted individual responsibility and self-sufficiency. The lack of an abortion effect was great news.

The press put its own spin on the contents of the Interim Report and it was not one of FDP and Family Cap success. Readers were greeted with headlines like these the day after the press conference:

> "Study Finds Family Cap Did Not Cut Rate of Births" (New York Times);[91] "N.J. Study Uncertain on the Value of Child Caps" (Philadelphia Inquirer);[92] "New Jersey Officials Say Birth Rate Drop Not Linked to Welfare Benefits Cap" (Washington Post);[93] "Welfare Cap Didn't Affect Birth Rates—Jersey Kept Rutgers Study a Secret" ([Newark] StarLedger);[94] "Report: Child Cap No Deterrent for Welfare Mothers" (The Trenton Times).[95]

These articles and many others like them made it clear why the NJDHS had finally chosen to release the report in September 1997—the state was forced to. When the ACLU and NOW filed against the constitutionality of the Family Cap in state district court on September 4, 1997, they also filed a Freedom of Information request compelling the release of the Interim Report.[96] For welfare rights groups the report was evidence that the Family Cap policy was a proven failure.

Misinforming the Policy Community

Among many in the welfare policy research community it was the New Jersey evaluation that was suspect, not the policy. David Greenberg and

Matthew Shroder in their influential *Digest of Social Experiments* saw information diffusion as a clear threat to the internal validity of the experiment. Their gloomy prediction is best left in their own words: "To determine the effects of the [Family Cap] innovation the state randomly selected a relatively small control sample of the welfare population for whom the Cap did not apply. However, the policy change had already been widely publicized and the state could not control the information that the control group received from sources other than program administrators. Subsequent studies have shown that the members of the control group believed that the Family Cap applied to themselves and the results of the experiment, when completed, are likely to prove anomalous."[97]

Control group contamination was also of paramount importance to Douglas Besharov and Peter Rossi at AEI. Besharov had recently founded The Welfare Reform Academy at the School of Public Affairs, University of Maryland. Among the Academy's charges is the critical, independent assessment of welfare reform evaluations by a "blue ribbon committee of experts in evaluation and related social science fields" to help policymakers "distinguish relevant and valid findings from those that are not."[98] This committee to review welfare reform studies lists Besharov and Rossi among its experts. In the Academy's initial publication, the authors call attention to New Jersey's Family Development Program: "It appears that many members of the control group believed that the Family Cap policy applied to them, probably because of the extensive statewide publicity this program received. Because this may have affected their behavior, it is unlikely that the impact of the demonstration can be determined by comparing the birth rates of the two groups."[99]

To the problem of contamination, another noted welfare reform researcher, Rebecca Maynard, and her colleagues appended a number of additional reasons why the New Jersey evaluation "would not be especially useful for guiding either state or national policy":[100] (1) the design does not measure any deterrent effect in the form of either delayed parenting or increased abortion rates; (2) differential attrition is not dealt with: those whose benefits are not increased as a result of a birth (those subject to a Cap) are less likely to report a birth to welfare officials than are those in the control group, from whom the reporting will trigger a benefit increase; (3) the actual financial consequences of the policy change are too small for the experiment to measure; and (4) the Family Cap is not the only component of the Family Development Program that can affect births.[101]

Maynard's first assertion, of course, is untrue and derives from a misreading of project proposals and reports. Her second point has the ring of plausibility but is indicative of a clear misunderstanding of the financial realities facing women on welfare. It is possible, in principle, that women in the treatment group who wish to have a birth are more likely to not report the birth or to leave welfare because the child will be excluded from the grant, and that therefore the experimental group will tend to have relatively lower birthrates. It is also possible, in principle, that there might be reporting biases involved if women subject to the Family Cap had no incentive to report the birth to the welfare system. In New Jersey, however, Capped cases received substantially more food stamp benefits and also were subject to a lower tax rate on earned income than controls. While the Family Cap could only affect the second or subsequent births on welfare, leaving welfare would result not only in the loss of AFDC, food stamp, and Medicaid benefits for the mother and enhanced food stamp benefits and Medicaid for the excluded child but also would disqualify all the other eligible children in the household from receiving benefits. Should the mother decide to stay on welfare but not report the birth, this would entail foregoing food stamp and Medicaid benefits for the child, where such benefits far outweigh the actual increase in the AFDC grant. Thus, failing to report a new birth or temporary exits from welfare would entail very high financial costs that Maynard and her colleagues fail to consider. I will have more to say about the issues of differential attrition, contamination, and multiple treatments a little later. Suffice it to say at this point that these criticisms are based on the conjecture of experts, earnestly extended, but conjecture all the same.

The year 1997 for project team members ended very much like those previous years with continual pressure to produce results and a sense of bewilderment regarding how these preliminary research findings were being utilized by policymakers, advocacy groups, researchers, and the press. We puzzled at how our tentative, incomplete analysis based on partial data could generate so many pronouncements of policy success or failure. We lamented that there were too few pieces like the one written by Melody Peterson in the *New York Times* cautioning that the final verdict on the New Jersey Family Cap was yet to be delivered.[102] Fortunately, the year 1998 would be different in one respect. Both our data and analyses were now sufficient to draw a number of conclusions about New Jersey's Family Development Program and the Family Cap.

6

Trying to Study the Family Cap

Introduction

While it is true that the politicians in New Jersey waffled over the true meaning of the Family Cap—whether it was about reducing births or increasing
self-determination—it was clear to these policy architects that the Family
Cap was never about abortions. As we have already seen, in the spring of
1995, when the state released some preliminary statistics on abortion rates for
welfare mothers, government officials were reluctant to link these rates to any
state or federal public policy. William Waldman, NJDHS commissioner, took
great care to argue that abortions fluctuate a good deal over time and that "it
was too early to conclude that the Family Cap law was responsible for an
apparent increase."[1] For state Senator Wayne Bryant, abortion was a "tough
decision" for women who cannot afford a pregnancy, but it was never the
intention of welfare reform in New Jersey to increase abortions among poor
women.[2]

Notwithstanding the protestations of these welfare reformers, Family Cap
rules had the potential for increasing the attractiveness of welfare in New
Jersey, even if the environment had generally turned more hostile. Jacob
Klerman, for example, points out that welfare reforms like the Family Cap
can only affect the behavior of pregnant women who would before reform
have chosen to remain on public assistance. For some women marriage, employment, or the generosity of relatives may become a more cost effective

option than welfare for raising the child. For others, not as fortunate perhaps, their option is to remain on welfare and either (a) contracept better, (b) bear the "excluded child," or (c) have an abortion. In Klerman's view, the choices made by these women on welfare will depend on which option each believes will increase the attractiveness of welfare the most.[3]

While the available research would appear to link welfare benefit generosity with recipient birthrates[4] there isn't much evidence that either the overall dollar amount of the welfare grant or the size of the dollar increment (decrement) has any influence on a woman's decision to abort. Studies by Stephen Mathews, David Ribar, and Mark Wilhelm,[5] Laura Argys, Susan Averett, and Daniel Rees,[6] and Ted Joyce and his colleagues,[7] all employing national samples, report that Aid to Families with Dependent Children/ Temporary Assistance for Needy Families (AFDC/TANF) welfare increment size has little effect on abortion decisions or rates. Rebecca Blank, Christine George, and Rebecca London[8] find much the same when they examine the influence of state maximum benefit levels.

The limitation of these studies is their failure to consider if the relationship between welfare benefits and abortions is contingent on the presence of other critical factors called moderators,[9] which work jointly with benefits to encourage recipient behavior. We are all familiar with medical and drug therapies where effectiveness depends not only on the dosage of the medication but on other indicators of lifestyle and life chances such as age, race, gender, smoking behavior, or weight. Similarly, Family Caps might increase the likelihood of a pregnant woman choosing an abortion over a birth, on or off welfare, if the economic and social conditions are favorable to do so. In New Jersey, Medicaid funding of abortions, which reduces the costs of abortion, may moderate the fertility effect of any welfare rules that seek to make births more expensive. Thus, what a Family Cap cannot accomplish alone, it can now do in the environment of Medicaid funding of abortions.

It is also possible for any joint effect of welfare reform and Medicaid policies on fertility behavior to be further moderated by welfare recipient characteristics that could signal differences in life chances. Two careful studies of Medicaid funding for abortion suggest that a prime candidate for the (additional) moderator role is race. In one of these analyses, Klerman looks at the effect of this funding on birth reductions among poor women from 1977 through 1992 and finds the reduction is over three times greater for black women than white women.[10] The quasi experiment conducted by S. Philip Morgan and Allan Parnell in North Carolina, discussed in chapter 3, finds that the number of pregnancies that would have been aborted if Medicaid funds were available to be nearly twice as high for black women.[11] These higher abortion rates for black women in response to Medicaid policy should not be surprising. As we have seen, poor black women have fewer prospects for marriage than do white women and their generally poorer education and concentration in impoverished communities limit their prospects for employment.[12] They, more than white or Hispanic women, could feel the pressures generated by the Family Cap most acutely—or so I began to believe as the evaluation data continued to accumulate.

Another feature of the welfare recipient's biography that could be expected to moderate any Family Cap effect on fertility behavior is the time the recipient has spent on welfare.[13] Indeed, the New Jersey experiment was constructed around this very idea with the distinction between new and on-going cases prominent in the sampling plan. It is readily conceivable that any racial differences in Family Cap impact may themselves be contingent on this additional factor. Black (white) women, for instance, with higher education and better job prospects would be expected to spend less time on welfare than other black (white) women. For them, fertility decisions might reflect considerations of opportunity cost as well as actual birth expenses and their choices could be different than those of other women of their race.

I'm certain this complicated picture of moderated moderators was not what state and federal policymakers had in mind when they asked the simple question "Does the Family Cap work?" I kept this in mind as my colleagues and I prepared our final evaluation reports for the New Jersey Department of Human Services (NJDHS), Administration for Children and Families (ACF), and the Assistant Secretary for Planning and Evaluation (ASPE) in the U.S. Department of Health and Human Services, and I minimized our discussions of racial differences, for the time being, assuming that by doing so we could increase the chances of report release by the state. I was wrong.

Family Cap and Abortions

In December 1997, I provided the New Jersey Division of Family Development and NJDHS with a draft of the final report from our panel analysis of the entire AFDC/TANF caseload for December 1990 through January 1997.[14] As can be seen in figure 6.1, the counterfactual in this design is the fertility rate of interest (i.e., birth, abortion, sterilization) projected from the data that were observed before the Family Cap was implemented (t). For all fertility measures except births, (t) corresponds to the actual implementation of the Cap in October 1992. Since only births conceived on welfare are subject to the Family Cap, the effective implementation date (t) for pregnancies brought to term was September 1993. The difference between the actual fertility behavior (Y_2) and the behavior one would project to observe (Y_1) in the absence of the Family Cap, from t to T, is the Family Cap effect.

Before launching into the report's results I offer a brief statistical excursus that may help the reader better understand the state's response to the findings. In the first draft of this final report we used ordinary least squares (OLS) regression to get estimates of Family Cap effects for four fertility outcomes, namely, births, abortions, contraceptive sterilizations, and family planning

Measure of Fertility (%)

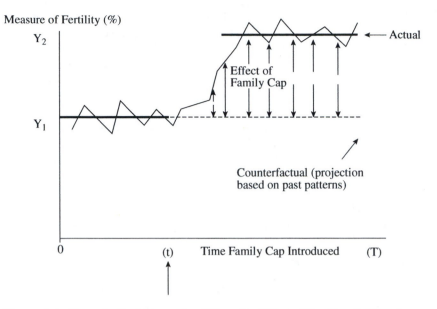

Figure 6.1. Hypothetical Example of How the Effect of the Family Development Program (FDP) Is Estimated Using Pre-Post Panel Design

visits. Our regression analyses of more than 305,000 welfare cases and over 2.8 million quarterly observations had this form:

$$P(Y_{it} = 1) = X_{it}\beta + \lambda_1 \text{ Family Cap}_{it} + \lambda_2 \text{ (Family Cap}_{it} \times \text{Time}_t) + \varepsilon_{it}$$

Equation 6.1

where i subscripts denote individuals, t subscripts denote calendar time from December 1990 through January 1997; Family Cap is an indicator variable equal to unity if the individual is subject to the Cap, and zero otherwise; time is a measure of linear time trend; and (Family Cap * Time) is the interaction term that allows for the possibility of change in treatment impact over time. The control variables included under X in equation 6.1 represent recipient characteristics (age, race, education, marital status, the number of AFDC children, earnings) and time-varying factors common to all individuals in the form of a simple time trend term and an indicator for calendar quarter to measure seasonal variation.[15] In order to control for changes in county job opportunities we also included county unemployment rates and JOBS program participations rates in the vector X, along with indicators for county of residence, which was intended to capture time-invariant factors shared by welfare recipients in the same county. The term ε in equation 6.1 designates an error term that is normally and identically and independently distributed (*iid*) across observations. Given the structure of our data these assumptions about the error term could be inappropriate because of the manner in which the outcome is measured and because in a panel, there are multiple observations per recipient. How inappropriate this is, of course, is ultimately an empirical issue that can be checked with specification tests and sensitivity analyses.

When an OLS regression is used to estimate a binary outcome like (1) having a birth or (0) not having a birth, the method is called a linear probability model (LPM). These LPM regressions have several advantages and several disadvantages when compared with other probability models such as logit and probit methods.[16] One potential disadvantage is that the error term may not have a normal distribution, but as Gujarati points out this issue diminishes as sample sizes become large.[17] The *iid* assumption is violated in LPM regression because the error terms vary systematically with the values of the independent variables. This assumption is also violated, in principle, by panel data since observations that repeat for the same case cannot by definition be independent. The problem can be obviated to a great extent through the computation of what are called heteroskedasticity-robust standard errors.[18] Finally LPM regression has a practical problem when it is used to predict the probabilities of events for individuals who have probabilities very close to either zero or one—sometimes these predictions exceed one or are less than zero—a somewhat absurd consequence of OLS that can be corrected by setting these out of range values to 0 or 1.

In head-to-head comparisons with other probability models, especially with very large samples and with outcomes that are not terribly skewed, LPM produces results that are quite similar to those of logit, probit, or poisson regression analyses.[19] For purposes of providing relatively easy to understand information to policymakers, LPM has some practical advantages as well. The marginal effect, that is, the impact of a predictor variable on an outcome, net of the influences of other predictor variables, is simply the regression coefficient (λ) associated with that variable in an LPM analysis. For example, a regression coefficient associated with a Family Cap of -0.089, in an analysis of births, indicates that the difference in birth probabilities between women covered by the rule or those who are not covered is about 9 percent lower for those covered.[20]

Another positive feature of LPM is the ease with which results can be used to simulate the number of events that could be expected to occur without and with a Family Cap over a time period of interest, in our case from October 1992 (or September 1993) through January 1997. Using the regression from equation 6.1 this difference can be calculated rather simply as

$$[\Sigma \; \text{Y-bar} + \beta(\text{Time}) \times 100{,}000] - [\Sigma \; \text{Y-bar} + \beta(\text{Time}) + \lambda_1(\text{Family Cap})$$
$$+ \lambda_2(\text{Family Cap} \times \text{Time}) \times 100{,}000]$$

where Y-bar is the mean quarterly probability of the event; β is the coefficient for time trend; λ_1 is the coefficient for Family Cap effect; λ_2 is the coefficient for the timepath of the Family Cap effect; TIME is the quarter number, 1 through 24; Family Cap is equal to 1, indicating exposure; and 100,000 is the approximate size of the quarterly AFDC/TANF population at risk in New Jersey over the study period.[21] By providing NJDHS and the federal agencies with Family Cap impacts in the form of both marginal effects and the actual numbers of events associated with them, we hoped to provide NJDHS, ACF, and ASPE with as clear an understanding as we could of the policy's workings.

The main message in this final draft report was that the Family Cap was indeed responsible for a decline in the birthrate among New Jersey's welfare population and that this decline was facilitated by increased family planning and more abortions. As might be expected, the rise in abortions, which we conservatively projected at 240 per year (and about 1,100 over the study period), was the center of attention in the governor's office, at NJDHS, and in the state Attorney General's office where a legal strategy was being formulated to defend the Family Cap in state court.

After a delay of several months, I received notification from the Division of Family Development that the draft final report would be reviewed by NJDHS, Office of Policy and Planning (OPP), and by staff at ACF and ASPE in Washington.[22] The OPP, which lacked the technical capacity to provide a rigorous internal review, retained the services of three outside experts and a statistical consultant. I recommended that the report be reviewed together with our draft final report on the experiment's results (which was nearly completed) inasmuch as this would give all the reviewers the benefits derived from our blended design strategy. The Commissioner's office rejected this proposal citing an immediate need to verify our nonexperimental design findings.

It was not just our regression-based impact analyses that troubled state officials; the descriptive presentation of birth and abortion temporal and spatial trends were not well received either. My colleagues and I did not focus our impact analysis on the moderating effect of race; rather, we simply controlled for any independent effect in our vector X of individual recipient characteristics. We did, however, believe it was necessary to show how fertility behaviors were distributed across the state's general and AFDC/TANF populations in order to provide the public and policymakers with a demographic context for assessing any Family Cap effects. Data presentation by race were particularly troubling to some state officials who felt we may have been helping to perpetuate a pernicious myth about welfare mothers.

Over the decade or so, a number of books and articles have been written that purport to explode the many myths that surround welfare recipients and the public welfare system. One myth that has been assailed often but refuses to go away is the belief that the typical welfare recipient is a young, black, never-married mother.[23] In his book, *Myth of the Welfare Queen*, for example, journalist David Zucchino declares that in Pennsylvania a majority of women on welfare are white and that the black women on the state's rolls show no inordinate propensity to have children.[24] Mark Rank, a social scientist who served as an expert witness for the plaintiffs in *C. K. v. Shalala*, also seeks to dispel the notion that most welfare recipients are minorities in his book *Living on the Edge*.[25] Using data from Wisconsin from 1980 through 1983 Rank finds the fertility rates for women on welfare in the state are considerably lower than those of national and Wisconsin populations. Zucchino's and Rank's work, along with other ethnographic accounts like those of Kathryn Edin and Laura Lein and Katherine Newman,[26] have certainly helped to humanize welfare recipients in the eyes of many Americans, but the capacity of these in- depth analyses to influence popular belief appears to have been minimal.

One reason why this particular myth about welfare is so resilient is that there are occasions when it is an accurate presentation of reality. As the philosopher Gilbert Ryle warns, a myth is not a fairy story; rather, it is a presentation of facts belonging to one category in the idiom appropriate to another.[27] Thus to characterize welfare as a black problem on a national scale is unrealistic since there are empirical data that confute this presentation of fact. So apparently is the case in both Pennsylvania and Wisconsin if the cited research is believed to be credible. But does the myth operate in Maryland, Illinois, or Georgia or from other fact-based reference points? In New Jersey, a state where black families compose over 50 percent of the welfare caseload, the typical welfare recipient is, indeed, a never-married black mother—a fact conceded by the Family Cap's author, Wayne Bryant.

The data presented in tables 6.1 and 6.2 caused the most difficulty. Here we see that both births and abortions are a much more common occurrence in New Jersey's welfare population than in the general population, and this is true for all races. If one averages the 24 quarterly rates for each column labeled "overall" births are at least 2.5 times higher while abortions are 6 to 7 times more common. Since the AFDC population counts are included in those of the general population, these differences are in fact even larger between welfare recipients and nonrecipients. And while it is true that births and abortions are decreasing in both the general and AFDC populations for the time period we show, the rate of decline is lower among welfare recipients.

If we combine the AFDC population rates from the two tables it becomes evident that black women on welfare in New Jersey differ dramatically from women of other races in two respects: namely, they have substantially more pregnancies (births plus abortions) than other women, and they receive far more abortions. While the abortion-to-birth ratio among white and Hispanic women averages about 0.47 and 0.56 respectively, the ratio is double, 1.2, for black women. We believed that by showing such disparate racial patterns in fertility behavior we could alert NJDHS to the possibility of differential Family Cap treatment effects. Instead, NJDHS-OPP found these descriptive data distracting, drawing attention away from the real intent of the report—the independent impact of the Family Cap. I became convinced from the series of protracted discussions that this final report (and the final

Table 6.1. New Jersey Quarterly Fertility Rates by Race/Ethnicity Total and AFDC Population (Births per 1,000 in Women 15–44 Years of Age)

Quarter Ending	General Population[a]				AFDC Population[b]			
	Overall	White	Black	Hispanic	Overall	White	Black	Hispanic
December 1990	14.1	12.5	18.6	20.0	36.0	31.8	38.3	35.4
March 1991	14.1	12.6	18.9	19.9	36.2	31.3	38.8	35.6
June 1991	14.6	13.3	18.0	20.8	35.4	32.1	36.0	37.3
September 1991	14.9	13.1	19.6	21.8	38.6	33.9	40.9	38.6
December 1991	13.9	12.1	18.4	20.9	34.9	31.7	36.4	36.2
March 1992	13.9	12.2	18.7	19.8	35.3	30.1	38.2	34.3
June 1992	14.5	13.1	18.1	19.3	34.3	32.0	36.2	33.5
September 1992	14.6	13.0	19.0	19.8	34.7	30.6	37.0	34.7
December 1992	13.9	12.1	18.2	19.8	33.4	30.8	35.0	32.7
March 1993	13.5	11.8	17.9	18.8	32.6	27.0	36.2	31.1
June 1993	14.2	12.8	17.7	19.4	31.5	28.6	33.8	30.4
September 1993	14.6	13.0	18.8	19.8	31.9	28.7	33.8	31.5
December 1993	13.3	11.6	17.6	18.5	28.1	25.8	29.3	28.0
March 1994	13.1	11.1	17.9	19.4	28.5	26.1	29.0	30.3
June 1994	13.5	12.0	16.9	19.0	27.7	28.7	27.3	28.1
September 1994	14.3	12.2	19.1	21.1	30.1	28.0	31.0	30.4
December 1994	13.2	11.1	17.9	20.2	28.5	26.4	29.1	29.6
March 1995	12.9	10.9	16.7	20.3	27.6	25.9	28.7	28.1
June 1995	13.6	12.0	15.8	20.4	25.1	23.2	25.0	27.6
September 1995	14.0	11.9	17.4	22.1	29.1	28.0	29.2	30.2
December 1995	12.7	10.6	15.6	19.8	25.3	24.4	24.8	27.2
March 1996	12.8	10.7	15.6	20.3	25.9	23.9	26.4	26.9
June 1996	13.1	11.4	14.7	20.0	24.3	22.0	24.6	26.5
September 1996	13.8	11.4	16.7	21.6	27.8	25.9	27.6	30.5
December 1996	12.9	10.4	15.7	21.4	28.0	27.6	28.7	27.3

[a]New Jersey Department of Health and Senior Services (NJDHSS), Birth Registration System. [b]New Jersey Department of Human Services—Division of Family Development, FAMIS.

Table 6.2.   New Jersey Quarterly Abortion Rates by Race/Ethnicity Total and
AFDC Population (Births per 1,000 in Women 15–44 Years of Age)

Quarter Ending	General Population[a]				AFDC Population[b]				
	Overall	White[c]	Black	Other	Overall	White	Black	Hispanic	Other
March 1991	5.1	2.5	14.4	20.5	30.3	16.1	36.7	18.6	14.5
June 1991	4.4	1.9	13	19.3	27.4	14.7	33.1	17.2	11.4
September 1991	4.2	1.8	12.1	17.9	26.1	14	31	16.1	14.1
December 1991	4.1	1.7	11.6	18.4	24.6	12.4	29.8	15.9	10.5
March 1992	4.9	2.2	13.9	20.9	28.5	13.9	34.8	18.9	11.2
June 1992	4.6	1.9	13.5	20	27.2	11.6	33.9	16.7	10
September 1992	4.5	1.9	13.1	19.1	26.9	11.7	33.6	16.1	14.4
December 1992	4.1	1.7	12.1	18.6	25.6	11.9	31.5	15.5	11.2
March 1993	4.7	2.1	14	16.3	29.8	13.6	37.3	17.5	6.4
June 1993	4.4	2.2	13.5	10.7	30	14.3	36.7	17.7	10.7
September 1993	4.2	2.1	13.1	7.3	28.3	12.5	35	16.1	8.6
December 1993	4.1	2	12.6	8.2	27.7	12.4	34.9	14.7	8.4
March 1994	4.5	1.9	13.5	16.2	30.2	14.8	37.3	16.3	8.9
June 1994	4	1.7	12.1	15.5	28.9	12.4	35.4	15.4	10.5
September 1994	3.8	1.7	11.3	12.9	26.2	10.3	31.7	14.6	6.9
December 1994	3.2	1.4	9	12.6	26.1	12	30.4	14.9	11.4
March 1995	4	1.8	11.9	14.3	30.7	13.7	34.9	16.8	8.8
June 1995	3.9	1.7	11.8	13.8	29.9	13.5	34.4	16.6	12.1
September 1995	3.8	1.6	11.5	12.9	28.9	13	32.4	15.3	11.6
December 1995	3.4	1.4	10.4	12.9	26.5	12.8	28.9	14.4	13
March 1996	4	1.7	11.7	15.4	30.2	13.6	32.7	15.7	9.4
June 1996	3.9	1.6	10.7	15.1	31.1	14.6	33.2	15.8	9.2
September 1996	3.7	1.6	10.7	12.1	29.1	12.7	30.2	14.7	10.8
December 1996	3.4	1.4	9.8	13.6	25.1	11.3	25.9	14.5	9.3

[a]New Jersey Department of Health and Senior Services (NJDHSS), Hospital/Abortion Facility Induced Pregnancy Termination Reports. [b]New Jersey Department of Human Services—Division of Medical Assistance and Health Services. [c]New Jersey Department of Health and Senior Services combines White and Hispanic women into one category.

report on the experiment) was not the forum where differences between the evaluation team and the state over the importance of race could be accommodated, so much of this material was moved to the appendix. A more realistic objective was to publish the results from these moderator analyses after the contract work was completed.

In early June 1997, about two months before we were scheduled to deliver a final report, revised to take into consideration the internal and external reviews of our draft, the draft final report of the caseload analysis found its way to the press. A spokesperson for NJDHS noted that the Attorney General's office had inadvertently shared the report with the NOW Legal Defense and Education Fund, the ACLU, representatives of the Catholic Church, and the press during a routine pretrial document exchange and were "simply unaware that it was a draft."[28] What made this claim suspicious was the simultaneous release of a May 14 document from the NJDHS–Division of Family Development (NJDHS–DFD), which attached the critical reviews of the draft from NJDHS, ACF, and ASPE.[29] This nine-page document pointed up numerous concerns with the report's statistical approach, analytic focus, and most of all, the "suggestions of causality."[30]

As they had done with the earlier Interim Report, NJDHS had once again succeeded in shooting itself in the foot. A story about increased abortions had metamorphosed into a major news event portraying a governmental agency intent on covering up unfavorable news. With my gag firmly in place I viewed the spectacle in silent amazement. The headlines printed in early June in newspapers across the state and the nation said it all:

> State Faults Welfare Overhaul Study's Abortion Link—But ACLU Says Officials Just Embarrassed ([Newark] Star-Ledger)[31]; Welfare Cap in N.J. Raised Abortion Rate, Study Finds—State Officials Reject Rutgers Data, Request Revision (Boston Globe)[32]; Study Finds N.J. Welfare Cap May Have Led to More Abortions—Officials Want More Analysis (Philadelphia Inquirer)[33]; Report Tying Abortion to Welfare Is Rejected: New Jersey Officials Question Its Validity (New York Times)[34]

For a three-week period I received constant inquiries from media outlets including Time magazine and U.S. News and World Report asking me to explain why NJDHS was reacting so negatively to this report. I refused to comment, noting only that a final report on the entire caseload impact would be completed very soon and would present the most comprehensive view possible of the effects of the Family Cap.[35] Many in the state were not willing to wait on our final work; apparently they had seen enough.

The plaintiffs in Sojourner v. NJDHS contended that the state's release of the report and letter was motivated more by political problems, not methodological ones. Martha Davis, a lawyer with NOW was blunt: "We think this is a final report that the state is trying to cover up by saying it is a draft. And we think the real reason for their objections is concern about what legislators will do if they see the conclusions the Rutgers researchers have drawn."[36] Sherry Leiwant, a senior attorney for NOW in Washington added that the report indicates the Family Cap policy "causes incredible suffering for families who are denied benefits" and that "these women are under pressure from their caseworkers to have abortions."[37] This identical point was made by Regina Purcell of the Catholic Conference of New Jersey: "We see it as a pretty serious report that we think should be the foundation to a repeal of this policy. . . . It is important to remember not only the number of babies that were aborted due to the Family Cap, but also the number of children born who were denied assistance. As of December [1997] more than 25,000 children in New Jersey have been denied cash benefits because of the Family Cap."[38] As to the report's methodological shortcomings, Lenora Lapidus, legal director of New Jersey ACLU, retorted "We showed the report to outside experts, including statisticians and economists, and they agree that it shows that the Family Cap is causing women to have abortions."[39]

The clamor generated by the report reverberated through the editorial pages, opinion columns and talk radio shows in the state and across the region with the Family Cap, Governor Whitman, and NJDHS receiving some very rough treatment. A [Newark] Star-Ledger editorial opined, "Keep going until you get the right answer. It doesn't matter what the facts are. The right answer is the one Trenton wants to hear. That's what the state seems to be telling the researchers it hired to study the effect New Jersey's welfare reform is having on the abortion rate."[40] Or this from the Philadelphia Inquirer: "Consider the children, the real innocents in this social engineering experiment. What are the long-term costs to society of poor children afforded less support and left out of society's plans from birth? Hopefully, Rutgers' researchers will take a close look at those results, presuming they are left alone by politicians and ideologues to do the research."[41]

Soon after, opinion pieces like these began appearing in newspapers across the country.[42]

The political ramifications from the mistaken release of our report were considerable. United States Congressman Chris Smith, a Republican, introduced a bill in the House of Representatives on June 16 (H.R. 4066) that prohibited states from implementing their own version of a Family Cap if they wished to receive a TANF block grant. His rationale for this legislation cited our research:

> Recently, my worst fears regarding abortion and the Family Cap were confirmed by a Rutgers University draft study prepared for the State of New Jersey which estimated that New Jersey's abortion rate increased by 240 abortions per year as a result of the state's Family Cap. . . . Thousands of other children have also been left to fend for themselves because their parents are not allowed to receive assistance on their behalf. I led a broad-based coalition of groups opposing the state's original request for a waiver in 1992 to implement a Family Cap policy because we knew that the Family Cap would only drive women into

greater depths of poverty and despair and consequently increase the likelihood that they would abort their child. Sadly, our concerns were confirmed by the Rutgers study.[43]

Governor Christine Whitman, another Republican, was beginning to have second thoughts on the utility of the Family Cap. The governor was quoted in an Associated Press interview as saying, "If there is clear proof that abortion rates are increasing as a result of our Family Cap, I will reconsider the law."[44] State Senator Wayne Bryant and former governor Jim Florio, both Democrats, remained silent throughout the entire press cycle.

Our report's abortion findings had the further effect of reinforcing the unlikely coalition of pro-life and pro-welfare rights groups in their opposition to the state's Family Cap. The conservative Catholic Conference and the liberal ACLU found common ground in a policy they believed was forcing women to choose abortions over birth. This "strange sorority of opponents" as Edwards referred to it in a *Time* piece,[45] had not escaped the attention of conservatives in several Washington think tanks either, where, as we have seen, illegitimacy trumps abortion as a preeminent family values issue. The evaluation team began to feel firsthand the tension between these think tanks, with their firm allegiance to individual rights and armchair social Darwinism, and anti-abortion conservatives seeking government intervention to enforce a valued social cause. Kenneth Neubeck and Noel Cazenave were not very far off the mark when they wrote "New Jersey's Family Cap research set off an early alarm about Family Cap provisions for religious conservatives and other pro-life groups who later broke with conservative political elites at the national level to oppose similar Family Cap provisions for PRWORA."[46] Any attempt to patch this fissure in the conservative (Republican) ranks over a Family Cap required that the abortion issue go away. What better way to begin the mending process than by discrediting the nation's only research that had alleged a Family Cap-abortion linkage.

What had been lost in the media frenzy of June 1998 was the fact that NJDHS, ACF, and ASPE did have several legitimate concerns about the methodology used in the pre-post report. Caveats needed to be placed in the report regarding the difficulty in establishing causal relationships in any panel design. Linear Probability Model regressions should not have been the only specifications presented in the report. The manner in which the pre-post design dealt with issues of entry effects and population composition changes needed to be more clearly explained. We took these criticisms very seriously and incorporated them in a series of sensitivity and specification tests that appeared in our final revised report.

In July we received the comments of the three experts retained by NJDHS and found that many of the concerns raised in the May 14 letter were repeated.[47] However, the expert reviews identified additional issues, some valid, others downright silly, that required our response, either in the final report or a rebuttal document. The use of LPM, the lack of independence between observations, the possibility of omitted controls, data quality, and alternative specification of the time path of the intervention were addressed and clarified in our revised report. We also presented a point-by-point response to each review in a September 9 document.[48]

The review submitted by one expert, which was especially harsh, was the only one to provide an overall assessment of the FDP evaluation, the verdict—"it was badly flawed to the point that the effects of FDP presented cannot be accepted."[49] What I, and other members of the evaluation team, was struck by in this critique was the aplomb with which it was written. For example, "ordinary least squares (LPM) is a mis-specification for binary dependent variables... " and "the effect of using observations that are correlated within individuals is to effectively reduce the sample size leading to upwardly biased standard errors."[50] And there is this imaginative (yet authoritative) process for reducing independence among observations: "An individual who gives birth in some quarter cannot give birth in the next three quarters, nor can that individual have had an abortion in the previous three quarters. An individual who has been sterilized in any quarter cannot be sterilized again.... Someone who has had an abortion in a quarter is not likely to have an abortion in the next quarter."[51] While it is true that women who have had a birth should be omitted for three subsequent quarters for any birth analysis it is clearly an incorrect use of dependent variables in reduced form regression equations to remove a case from a (abortion) risk pool because we know her fertility outcome. Also sterilizing operations are not 100 percent effective and a woman can be sterilized again, not to mention the fact that women in our data set did have abortions in contiguous quarters. Even experts can apparently get it wrong, or so it would seem.

By the end of July we completed our Final Report on the Impact of New Jersey's Family Development Program Results from a Pre-Post Analysis of AFDC Caseloads and submitted it to the state. Every effort was made to be responsive to the reviews we had received including alternative statistical specifications with logit and probit, adjusted risk pool analysis, specification tests, use of individual fixed effects and robust standard errors to adjust for observation dependence. The pattern of results was the same as in the draft report but the magnitude of the effects were, on average, larger. We concluded that

> between October 1992, the effective implementation of the Family Development Program (and the Family Cap), and the end of 1996, we estimate that there were 14,057 fewer births among AFDC female payees of childbearing age than would have occurred in the absence of the Family Development Program, about 3,500 per year; over this same period, we estimate that there were 1,429 more abortions among AFDC female payees than would have occurred in the absence of the Family Development Program, about 360 per year; following the implementation of the Family Development Program, there were 7,000

more family planning encounters per year than would have occurred in the absence of the Family Development Program, about 1,750 a year.[52]

We provided a series of caveats in the report but made it clear to NJDHS and the federal sponsors that

the estimates of birth, abortion, and other impacts provided above are somewhat conservative. The focus of this study was restricted to AFDC payees of childbearing age; the analysis did not include births, abortions, and other outcomes for daughters, siblings, and other non-payee women of childbearing age who reside in AFDC households and who are eligible for cash assistance. We also note that our analysis is restricted to the family formation behavior of women on AFDC. The Family Cap only applied to women on AFDC, and we cannot tell, from this analysis, whether the implementation of FDP and the Family Cap has any continuing effect on the childbearing decisions of AFDC recipients once they leave the rolls. Likewise, we do not know how the implementation of the Family Development Program and the Family Cap affects childbearing among women who are potentially eligible for AFDC/TANF, but who do not choose to apply.[53]

Notwithstanding these limitations we felt confident in our analyses and findings. Preliminary results from our analyses of the social experiment, moreover, undertaken with a complete set of new and ongoing cases in early 1998, were consistent with what we had found in the caseload panel. State officials met the final pre-post report with stony silence, providing no indication when it would be released to the public.

More Evidence of Family Cap Effect

Of course, the pre-post analysis was never considered by anyone on the evaluation team as furnishing the definitive, causal evidence of Family Cap effect. It was an important component in our blended design, but the primary purpose was to supplement inferences drawn from the social experiment while addressing the issues of internal and external validity inherent in social experimentation. The drama and media hype surrounding the pre-post report, however, diverted attention away from where we believed it should remain focused, namely, on the strongest evidence, on the experimental results. In April 1998 we had completed a final draft report on treatment versus control group differences for both new and ongoing cases. Comments from ACF and ASPE were forwarded the very next month but NJDHS deferred its review until the end of August. Apparently, after the fiasco that accompanied the release of the draft pre-post study, the last matter NJDHS wished to deal with was yet another Rutgers report.

The federal comments came from Howard Rolston, director of the Office of Planning, Research and Evaluation at ACF. Rolston expressed a major concern around the way we were handling the issue of case closings;

specifically, why we had not included an observation on each of the 8,393 cases for every quarter, from the time of sample entry through December 1996—even if the recipient had left welfare during some or all of those quarters. He remarked that if we failed to include observations on cases for the quarters they are not on welfare "the value of the random assignment is lost, the groups are no longer comparable and the evaluation becomes in effect a nonexperimental evaluation."[54] The remedy Rolston offered required keeping individuals in a risk pool and determining if women had births or abortions while off the rolls as well as while on welfare. About abortions he had this to say: "In the case of abortions we think it even more important to include events that occur while the case is off AFDC. Most persons concerned with abortion issues are concerned with total abortions, not just those to welfare recipients. It makes little difference to these persons whether or not the woman is receiving welfare at the time of the abortion. Here again we would urge that additional data concerning abortions in cases no longer receiving welfare be included."[55]

It is a bit of hyperbole to maintain that the value of random assignment is lost if cases are omitted from analysis for periods when they are unobserved. Such observations are obviously not receiving treatment and it is very difficult to attribute behavior to the intervention under study. In clinical trials it is relatively common practice to estimate treatment effects with and without these observations figured into the denominators for effect size (ES) computations.[56] The former calculation increases the statistical power of the analyses while the latter offers a more realistic portrayal of treatment dosage. The real issue here is treatment-correlated attrition or, as it is more often termed, differential attrition in the treatment and control groups.[57]

In an effort to determine if differential attrition influenced our estimates of Family Cap effects we conducted a number of descriptive and multivariate analyses on case closings, welfare spell lengths, and recycling in the draft final report. In the report we present analyses that show there were no statistically significant differences between treatment and controls on either the incidence of closing or the reasons for closing.[58] Experimentals were just as likely as controls to leave because of earned income, residence change, or other nonfinancial reasons. In only one instance, "failure to comply with AFDC regulations," did we find that experimentals were more likely to leave the rolls than controls—the 4 percent difference was statistically significant. Our analyses of differences in spell lengths and recycling incidence did not yield any statistically significant effects. Based on this evidence, we concluded, I believe correctly, that the magnitude of post-treatment bias in this experiment was reduced by the initial randomization and case stratification process, and that our decision to exclude unobserved cases did not compromise the experiment.[59]

The suggestion by Rolston to undertake simultaneous analyses of the fertility behavior of women both on and off welfare points up a serious misunderstanding at ACF regarding the kinds of comparisons that are legitimate in randomized experiments and those that are not. Larry Orr observes that it is not possible, for example, to derive experimental estimates of treatment impact on endogenously defined subgroups, that is, groups defined on the basis of the events that occur after random assignment. He goes on to state that a common question that cannot be answered in an experiment is the following: "What are the impacts of the treatment after participants left the program, as distinct from those impacts that occurred while they were in the program? Because length of stay in the program typically varies within the treatment group and the concept 'left the program' is not defined for the control group, there is no way to construct comparable time periods for treatment and control group members for the analysis of this question."[60]

Since leaving the welfare program can be affected by participation in FDP, the analysis Rolston proposes is endogenously defined and any estimates of fertility behavior differences could be biased. Needless to say, the remedy offered by Rolston indicating this rather basic misunderstanding of the limitations of experimental comparisons was disquieting inasmuch as it was ACF that was responsible for writing the terms and conditions of virtually all the experiments conducted under Section 1115.

The comments I received from NJDHS on the draft report on the social experiment were in large part a reiteration of the federal interests. Instead of hiring outside experts to review this report, NJDHS instead relied on the limited research expertise that was available at OPP and in the governor's office. It was quite evident from the tenor of the review that the state wanted the report couched heavily in the language of research limitations and reader caveats.[61] The demurrer statement "any opinions expressed in this report are those of the authors and do not necessarily represent the views of the State of New Jersey Department of Human Services" was required to be placed on the cover page of each final report. Initially, NJDHS asked that Rutgers University be included in this statement. I refused. The state critique ended on this dreary note: "Finally, the flaws in the design of the experiment seriously compromise our confidence in the results. Understanding that the Rutgers Team inherited this design as a required feature of the evaluation, it is nevertheless expected that the evaluators will fully explain the findings of this project in light of the limitations of both the logic and execution of the experiment at hand."[62] The most serious design flaw identified by NJDHS was evidence from our Kaiser sponsored survey of welfare recipients that appeared to indicate that both treatment and control group cases had received the same message about the application of the Family Cap; for example, subject contamination due to unsuccessful environment controls. I marveled at how such a "poorly designed survey" could provide such definitive information on control group contamination.

In early September 1998 we completed "A Final Report on the Impact of New Jersey's Family Development Program: Experimental-Control Group Analysis."[63] Our examination of the Family Cap's impact on fertility behavior was conducted using the same regression specification we had employed in our pre-post analyses (see equation 6.1). Outcome estimates were obtained from a series of parallel LPM, probit and logit regressions, using a variety of risk pool definitions, with both homoskedastic and heteroskedastic (robust) standard error assumptions. Of course, the counterfactual used to get the Family Cap effect identified in the social experiment was distinctive from what we had used in the pre-post study (figure 6.1); here it was the control group.[64] Simulations were conducted for each fertility outcome, using our regression coefficients, in the same fashion as in the pre-post analyses. In the experiment, however, the difference due to the Family Cap was simply

$$\lambda_1(\text{Family Cap}) + \lambda_2(\text{Family Cap} \times \text{Time}) \times 1,000$$

where 1,000 puts the difference in the form of a rate.

While this final report contained analyses of welfare recipiency, employment, and earnings, and recipient and case worker attitudes, the undeniable focal point was chapter 7: FDP Impacts on Births, Abortions and Family Planning. We looked at five distinctive outcomes in this chapter—births, abortions, and family planning visits—as we had in the caseload analysis, along with tubal sterilizations and contraceptive pill use. All of our analyses were conducted separately for new and ongoing cases. Of the former we had 20,868 person-quarter observations; for the latter we had 46,124, collected from October 1992 through December 1996. This was the first opportunity that state and federal officials had to review our new case analyses.

We summarized the principal findings as follows: For ongoing cases over the four-year observation period:

Members of the treatment group experienced a birthrate that was about nine percent lower than the control group birthrate.

Members of the treatment group utilized family planning services about 10 percent more often than the control group.

Members of the treatment group had about 28 percent more sterilizations than the control group.

There were no statistically significant differences between (ongoing) treatment and control group cases in abortions.

For new cases, the following Family Cap effects were observed:

Members of the treatment group experienced a birthrate that was 12 percent lower than the control group birthrate.

Members of the treatment group also experienced an abortion rate that was 14 percent higher than the control group abortion rate.

Members of the treatment group used contraception drugs and devices 21 percent more often than the control group.

There were no statistically significant difference between (new) treatment and control group cases in family planning utilization or sterilizations.[65]

With one exception, births for ongoing cases, these results were equivalent when the last observation carried forward (LOCF) denominator, suggested by Rolston, was replaced by the more conservative observed case (OC) denominator.[66] The use of an OC denominator in our ongoing case birth analyses did not reveal a statistically significant effect.

These findings were in large measure corroborated by what we had found in our pre-post caseload analyses. We were confident that a preponderance of the evidence uncovered in our blended research design pointed to a Family Cap–induced decrease in birthrates and to abortion as responsible for at least 10 percent of this decline and probably a good deal more.

Managing the Report Information

After thoroughly bungling the release of the Interim Report and the Draft Final Report from the pre-post analyses, the governor's office and NJDHS were now faced with the task of releasing the three final reports that marked the completion of the Rutgers evaluation.[67] The relationship between the state and the evaluation team had become increasingly estranged as the project trudged to conclusion and by the summer of 1998 we were incontrovertible adversaries. More reports meant simply more controversy around the Family Cap—a debate with which the Whitman administration had had its fill. Our research, once a minor irritant, was now the source of real alarm for defenders of the state's Family Cap policy.

In September 1998 state senators Diane Allen, a Republican, and Wynona Lipman, a Democrat, introduced a bill in the state Senate that would repeal the Family Cap. Both women had supported the passage of this legislation in 1992 but had a change of heart following the release of the Draft Report in June. Their legislation cited our report as providing data that "is profoundly disturbing and argues most persuasively for a repeal of this unequitable provision."[68] The bill was supported by the chairman of the Senate Human Services Committee, Louis Bassano, who said repealing the Family Cap "is the morally right thing to do."[69]

There was also a bipartisan effort in the State Assembly to rescind the Cap led by Assemblywomen Charlotte Vandervalk, a Republican, and Joan Quigley, a Democrat. In their bill, A-2398, our Draft Final Report was also cited as evidence of a policy gone terribly wrong, where the principal results were Capped children and forced abortions.[70] This bill and the state senate bill were supported by a broad coalition of religious and human rights groups including the Catholic and Lutheran churches, NOW, the

NOW Legal Defense and Education Fund, Legal Services of New Jersey, the American Civil Liberties Union, and the Association for Children of New Jersey.

Adding to this legislative pressure were new developments in the *Sojourner A. v. The New Jersey Department of Human Services* [*NJDHS*] lawsuit. In mid July, the ACLU and NOW filed a motion in state superior court charging that NJDHS had refused to give the plaintiffs our final pre-post and experimental-control reports, which they maintained were central to their arguments against the Family Cap.[71] The motion was a response to an earlier motion filed by the State Attorney General's office, which sought to dismiss the case. The ACLU attorneys accused the state of stonewalling and suggested that state officials "were not happy with the reports' conclusions," especially about abortions, "and were trying to change them."[72] The state response was that the reports were not yet in final form and required some revisions to "make sure the research we put out will contribute to the national debate."[73] Each side in this litigation had gotten it partially correct— the reports were not as readable as they could be nor as palatable as some thought they should be.

In July 1998 Governor Whitman replaced NJDHS Commissioner William Waldman with Michelle Guhl. What Guhl lacked in human services experience, I believed, was more than compensated for by her close relationship to the governor and by her independence from the pressures being exerted on the evaluation team by the dean at the University's School of Social Work. We had not had any direct contact with Commissioner Waldman or his staff since before the release of the Interim Report and I thought it was not the right time to mend our clearly broken communications and working relationship. On August 12, my Co-PI, Carol Harvey, and I proposed a meeting with the new commissioner where we could discuss three key issues: our input on any future state press releases in which our work was discussed, efforts undertaken by staff at NJDHS to impeach the credibility of our work, and future publication rights.[74] I had followed the NJDHS gag rule scrupulously but my colleagues and I had no intention of continuing this silence once we had completed our contractual obligations. There were now rumblings emanating from the Commissioner's Office that these rights arrogated to the state.[75]

With the help of the University's Media Relations Department, Harvey and I began drafting up press releases that I hoped NJDHS would take into consideration if and when a press conference took place. Any reference to our finding of increased abortions due to a Family Cap was met with instant resistance and open hostility. The Office of Public Information at NJDHS and the governor's press agent preferred to focus on a descriptive figure in the pre-post report (figure 6.2 a: Abortions per Thousand AFDC Payees by Quarter), which they contended showed abortions remained flat during the evaluation period.[76] The state's Information Office went so far as to alter the original scale we used in the figure to make the quarterly fluctuations appear more random than they really were.[77] So much for the voluntary attempt to produce a joint press release.

The problem of convincing the state to work cooperatively on a joint press release was made moot on October 2, 1998, when a superior court judge dismissed the state's bid to dismiss the *Sojourner A. v. NJDHS* lawsuit. In his opinion the judge granted class-action status to the more than 25,000 children who had been "Capped" under New Jersey's Family Cap, greatly increasing the financial stakes in the case. He also required the state to turn over Rutgers's final reports to the plaintiffs and to make the researchers available for information questioning at a press conference ordered to take place by November 2, 1998.[78] With a contempt citation in the offing, public information officials at both the governor's office and NJDHS began to take serious note of our concerns about what findings should receive emphasis and how these findings should be presented.

The press conference held on November 2, 1998, marked the first time since September 1995 that state officials and the project team jointly fielded questions about the New Jersey evaluation in a public forum. The state issued two press releases for the event: one from the governor's office, which paired our study with another on child poverty undertaken by Columbia University[79] and the second from NJDHS, which placed our work in the context of New Jersey's newest welfare reform, Work First New Jersey.[80] The release from the governor's office highlighted the positive responses of welfare clients demonstrated in the Kaiser-sponsored survey stating that "the Rutgers University research released today shows that the message of personal responsibility is working" and that participation in responsible family planning has increased, and the decrease in birthrates demonstrates that many welfare mothers have appropriately made the choice to not have additional children while on welfare because of their financial condition.[81] The only mention of abortion was to refer to the rescaled figure 6.2 a.

The NJDHS release was more faithful to actual content of the reports, choosing however to enmesh any abortion results in a tangle of cautions and limitations. With respect to both births and abortion Commissioner Guhl warned: "These findings indicate that the Family Cap may have been a factor in women's reproductive decisions. However, these are complicated, very personal decisions. To think that a woman decides to have a child or not have a child solely because of the small amount of money involved in the Family Cap trivializes a very complex issue. But I do think the Family Cap sends a message that people on welfare must face the same life decisions as everyone else. That is why I think it is an important element of welfare reform."[82]

The NJDHS press release contained a listing of our findings on births, abortions, family planning visits, and contraception use exactly as we presented them to the Office of Public Information. In an ostensible effort to soften the abortion results, NJDHS attached a copy of their display of figure 6.2 a.

The news accounts from the November 2 press conference described a set of Rutgers reports that gave both pro- and anti-Family Cap interests something to cheer about. Governor Whitman, a pro-choice Republican, told a *New York Times* reporter that the study's findings had persuaded her to maintain the state's Family Cap policy because of the decline in the number of births.[83] Whitman also noted correctly that while our research indicated an increase in abortions, more of these procedures occurred in the early years of Family Cap implementation with family planning visits and contraception exhibiting larger impacts after the Cap policy had become more established.[84] For Whitman and Commissioner Guhl the real message in our research was not abortion but increased personal responsibility.[85] Wayne Bryant described the abortion effects identified in our reports as "statistically insignificant."[86]

Opponents of the Family Cap also found a great deal in the reports to bolster their position. United States Representative Chris Smith claimed our research "adds significant impetus for reform." He added that "welfare is a necessary institution. The sooner you get off, the better. . . . But you don't use little babies as pawns."[87] Smith countered the Whitman argument that abortion rates had stabilized over the five-year study period with the question "Why is that good when abortion rates nationwide have been dropping?"[88]

State Senator Diane Allen thought the Rutgers studies would increase the chances for passage of her bill seeking repeal of the Cap[89] while Marie Tasy, director of legislative affairs for the New Jersey Right to Life Committee, believed the research would help the plaintiffs in *Sojourner A. v. NJDHS*. She observed that each report demonstrated that the Family Cap increases abortion and illustrated that "when you have a law that mandates taxpayer-funded abortion, as we have in New Jersey, and you combine that with a Family Cap law . . . the result is a lethal public policy that harms women and has been 100 percent fatal to children."[90] Editorial writers across the state and the country weighed in on the merits of the Family Cap, showing once again how divisive this policy had become.[91]

With the issue of the press conference behind us, I assumed our adversarial relationship with the state had come to an end. I was soon disabused of this notion through a series of actions undertaken by the state Attorney General's office, NJDHS, and NJDHS–DFD, which illustrated just how far apart our interests remained. Two weeks after the press event I was contacted by attorneys from the ACLU informing me that the Attorney General did not intend to call me, or for that matter, any of my project colleagues, to testify on behalf of the state in *Sojourner A. v. NJDHS*. The state had its experts, I was informed, Peter Rossi and Ted Goertzel, both vocal critics of the methodology and findings in our reports. In the weeks and months that followed I responded to interrogatories, requests for documents, requests for expert testimony, and threatened subpoenas, all initiated by the plaintiffs in this case.[92] The state Attorney General's office had apparently seen enough of our work and did not like what it saw.

The path to publication was a ride made as rough as possible by NJDHS. Staff at the University's Research and Sponsored Programs Office were informed by the NJDHS attorneys that our publication agreement dated January 27, 1993, was not binding and that a new agreement was required.[93] It was not until the end of March 1999 that a new memorandum of understanding regarding publication rights and data sharing was finalized.[94] This document provided NJDHS with 60 days to review and comment on all publications prepared for public dissemination.

The state took this review function very seriously and provided a great deal of feedback, most of it quite negative, on the form and substance of each manuscript we submitted. We, of course, made any changes that were shown to be factually incorrect but would not alter any analysis, interpretation, or discussion of results because of clashes with state opinion, interests, or ideology. The fact that our work was subsequently published in many peer-reviewed journals, including the *Journal of Economic Perspectives*, the *Journal of Labor Economics*, *Journal of Policy Analysis and Management*, the *American Journal of Public Health*, *Contemporary Economic Policy*, *Research in Labor Economics*, the *Journal of Marriage and Family*, the *American Journal of Evaluation*, the *Social Science Quarterly*, *Journal of Urban Affairs*, *Administration in Social Work*, the *Journal of Social Service Research*, and others, convinced me that the reviews told as much about the state reviewer motivations as they did about the content of our work.

The NJDHS—DFD made its contribution to the dissemination of Family Cap research by exercising its prerogative to recoup any equipment purchased by the Rutgers evaluation team to conduct work required under the contract. This action succeeded in slowing our research down for several months until new computers and printers could be purchased.

Our efforts to study New Jersey's Family Cap were proving to be an exhausting experience. The information we had provided in our reports could not possibly align with all the interests and ideologies that had formed around the implementation of a Family Cap. In November, I and the other members of the evaluation team received an "A" for academic integrity from the Center for the Analysis of Public Issues, a public policy institute located in Princeton, New Jersey. The accomplishment that garnered us this praise was "sticking to our original conclusion [in our reports] even after worried Human Services officials sent the reports back for reevaluation."[95]

7

Questioning the Family Cap Evidence

Introduction

Skepticism has been the steadfast companion of public welfare policies and programs from their very beginning. It has also dogged any evaluation research that has claimed success for these endeavors, however limited. These doubts about policy effectiveness are to be expected since the research is rooted in the scientific method where efforts to build proof occur through repeated attempts to refute any evidence offered as proof. The responsible researcher then is a skeptical researcher, one who, Paul Rosenbaum remarks, must defend his or her doubts as well as his or her findings through observation and verification.[1]

Over the past twenty years or so, this healthy skepticism concerning the means by which social policy research has been conducted (i.e., questions about measurement, data quality, sampling, design, and analysis) has become increasingly corrupted by a brand of cynicism that views results as tainted products in which the researcher and/or research sponsors have an ideological or emotional stake. Isabel Sawhill, an influential social scientist at The Urban Institute and Brookings Institution, laments, "Everyone wants to attach a political label to everything that comes out. There's no such thing as unbiased information or apolitical studies anymore."[2] Two factors in the policy environment have contributed to this expansion in the grounds for doubt: an extended period of highly partisan and divided government, especially in Washington, and the emergence of the dueling policy institutes, again primarily in Washington.

Once the exclusive province of social science progressives or liberals, today's policy institutes or "think tanks," as they are frequently called, provide haven for the agendas of both liberal policy analysts (Brookings Institution, The Urban Institute, Center for Budget and Policy Priorities, the Progressive Policy Institute) and conservatives (The CATO Institute, The Heritage Foundation, American Enterprise Institute, the Hudson Institute). This proliferation of policy institutes has raised concerns in some quarters, especially at research universities, that the checks and balances designed to ensure research objectivity remain underdeveloped, especially in the conservative think tank setting.[3] This charge, of course, presupposes that some analytic firewall separates objectivity and ideology in the public policy, economics, political science, and social work departments of universities and that the university appointments held by many scholars in the more liberal think tanks inoculate these individuals from the temptations of ideology. Both assumptions, however, have been challenged repeatedly, and not just by conservatives. Writers including David Stoesz, Terry Eagleton,[4] Russell Jacoby,[5] and Robert Lerner[6] document the liberal leanings of most university-based social science researchers. Moreover, as Pamela Winston demonstrates in her examination of the welfare reform debates around PRWORA, the ideological pressures inherent in the policy institute environment have a way of blurring the lines between policy research and analyses, on the one hand, and political activism and advocacy, on the other, as analysts seek to impress congressional committees or the White House with the importance of their work.[7]

Up until the completion of the final reports on Family Cap impacts in New Jersey, our research had been treated by the liberal and conservative policy institutes in Washington with a more or less muted curiosity. Yes, there was the brief dispute with the Kaiser Family Foundation but in this instance it was clear that the criticism was more pretense than substance, and focused on a peripheral part of the overall evaluation.[8] When the final reports were made public, however, the critical assessment of our research methods and findings began in earnest at several Washington-based think tanks. The most stinging critique of our work came from several scholar/researchers based at the American Enterprise Institute (AEI). It is through this critique that I gained an appreciation for the distinction between the tangible and the dismissive approaches to research criticism. Rosenbaum defines the former as a specific and plausible alternative interpretation of the available data that is itself capable of empirical investigation.[9] What the AEI reviews lacked in this sort of content they more than compensated for with the latter, which Rosenbaum describes using a quote from Sir Ronald Fisher's *The Design of Experiments*: "The [dismissive] type of criticism is usually made by what I might call a heavyweight authority. Prolonged experience, or at least the long possession of a scientific reputation, is almost a pre-requisite for developing successfully this line of attack. Technical details are seldom in evidence. The authoritative assertion: 'His controls are totally inadequate' must have temporarily discredited many a promising line of work; and such an authoritarian method of judgment must surely continue, human nature being what it is. . . ."[9] Dismissive criticism, as described by Fisher, does not typically lead to the development of new hypotheses or explanations but, as I show here, it can sometimes be tested to determine if there is any empirical basis to the doubts it seeks to raise.

National Scrutiny

Critiques of the Family Cap evaluation, whether conducted by New Jersey Department of Human Services—Office of Policy and Planning (NJDHS-OPP), New Jersey Department of Human Services—Division of Family Development (NJDHS-DFD), the governor's office, or by policy experts retained by the state, did not resonate at all well in New Jersey's media outlets, independent policy centers, and academic institutions. This had less to do with any careful assessment of evaluation study methodology than it did with a palpable mistrust of state government's capacity to provide honest answers to nettlesome welfare policy questions. It is a safe bet that many residents in the state agreed with this opinion that appeared in a [Newark] Star—Ledger editorial: "Maybe the brain trust in Trenton thinks it is better than the experts [at Rutgers] in calculating what is significant. Maybe it only wants studies that confirm the conclusions it wants to certify. Either way, the administration could save a lot of tax money by skipping the studies and spinning the tale it was planning to tell anyway."[10] A good many more individuals were confused about why the governor would reject a study that, for the most part, had provided evidence for the Family Cap's success. This editorial from the Asbury Park Press summarizes the sentiment: "State officials can't have it both ways. They condemn as simplistic and flawed an analysis of their policy's impact, but they continue to support the policy. If the payment cap is not intended to discourage births to welfare mothers and if state officials are not trying to send a moral message, then what are they trying to accomplish?"[11]

The credibility accorded Rutgers in any dispute with the New Jersey Department of Human Services (NJDHS) over research methodology or findings provides an excellent example of the operation of signaling theory. Research produced by a respected research university, prima facie, is given more credence than research or research criticism provided by a state organization not known for its prowess in the area. The controversy of our Family Cap research, in fact, may have engendered what George Borjas has called a perfectly separating signaling equilibrium[12] where virtually all Family Cap information generated by Rutgers was embraced and none of the criticisms introduced by state government were accepted. Such an equilibrium was not to prevail as our research received scrutiny in Washington by welfare policy experts—a good thing for the research and for a better understanding of the Family Cap policy as well. But as the political commentator Jim Hoagland observes, Washington is also the home of the politically and professionally snide who comprise "a self-regarding elite with an iron discipline of never being impressed by anything outside their own circle of cynicism."[13] Would the signaling pigeons come back to haunt the Rutgers evaluation in the Washington forum?

At the national level the bar of skepticism for a Family Cap effect was set exceedingly high from the policy's very beginning. When asked about the potential for a Family Cap to reduce births, Daniel Patrick Moynihan, New York senator and a renowned social scientist, responded "Nonsense . . . we really don't know what to do and anyone who thinks that cutting benefits can affect sexual behavior doesn't know human nature."[14] When June O'Neill presented her findings that the Family Cap had lowered births in New Jersey, Sheldon Danziger, the welfare policy expert from the University of Michigan, expressed incredulity: "Her work contradicted everything that had come before."[15] Peter Rossi, prior to his tenure as an expert witness for the state of New Jersey, is described in a *Wall Street Journal* article as a "skeptic of the overhaul [welfare] bill" capacity to affect social behavior.[16] There was also that statement circulated by the Center on Budget and Policy Priorities, signed by over 70 leading social science researchers, questioning the utility of any welfare policy in reducing out-of-wedlock childbearing.[17] The expert testimony in *C.K. v. Shalala* and in *Sojourner A. v. NJDHS*, some of which I cited in chapter 2, was also overwhelmingly of the opinion that a Family Cap could not reduce births and would only hurt Capped children.

It was not, however, the liberal-leaning social science establishment or their think tanks that presented the most serious challenge to the credibility of our Family Cap research. For example, a report issued by the Center for Law and Social Policy (CLASP), a progressive policy institute with close links to the Center for Budget and Policy Priorities, acknowledged what it saw as methodological issues in our reports but stopped well short of questioning the validity of the findings.[18] The main assault, instead, came from the right and here from that segment of the right that appeared to be very concerned by the effect our abortion findings were having on pro-life conservatives.

As we have seen, the Family Cap was a welfare reform policy that clearly divided conservatives into two camps, those for whom abortion was an acceptable response to an attempt to reduce out-of-wedlock births and those who found abortion to be a more repugnant form of moral corruption. Gwendolyn Mink, a friend of neither camp, had put it this way: "The welfare debate revealed that except the purest of abortion foes, the fact of illegitimacy is more morally freighted than the act of abortion. The need to teach those people not to reproduce unless they can afford it is more urgent than the call to protect the unborn; and the demand to reform welfare is more righteous than the struggle to preserve life."[19] Although Mink did not expressly identify the conservatives who wished "to teach those people not to reproduce" it is obvious she was referring to the libertarian and neoconservative elements of the right who have typically been viewed as weak on pro-life issues.[20] Charles Murray and a number of his colleagues at the American Enterprise Institute would find a place in this pantheon as would Newt Gingrich, at least in his congressional manifestation. So would the consummate neocon, William Kristol, editor of the *Weekly Standard*, who has stated, "we can't not reform welfare because it might lead to a few more abortions."[21]

Within weeks of conservative New Jersey Congressman Chris Smith's introduction of H.R. 4066, the bill that would deny Temporary Assistance for Needy Families (TANF) funds to any state employing a Family Cap, Ron Haskins, majority staff director for the U. S. House Committee on Ways and Means and close confidant of Newt Gingrich, requested that the Congressional Research Service (CRS) conduct an analysis of the New Jersey evaluation reports. The memo asked CRS to focus explicitly on the findings that purported to link Family Cap to increased abortions.[22] One strategy available for conservatives who sought to ensure that all on the right kept their eyes on the problem of out-of-wedlock births, the real objective of welfare reform, was to vigorously dispute any claim of a Family Cap abortion effect through an ostensibly rigorous reanalysis of our data.

The six-page CRS report examines our abortion results in light of the methodological approaches and statistical analyses employed in both the social experiment and pre-post caseload analyses. Inexplicably, however, Gene Falk and Christine Devere, the critique's authors, choose to compare the findings from the Interim analysis of experimental-control group differences (completed in July 1996) with the final analyses of pre-post differences (completed in 1998).[23] The Interim Report, of course, was hardly an accurate assessment of Family Cap impact inasmuch as data on the new cases subsample were too incomplete to report. This rather obvious comparison of "apples and oranges" did not deter the CRS researchers who offered this conclusion to Haskins and his committee. "We have analyzed two reports currently available on the New Jersey FDP [Family Development Program] completed by a team of researchers from Rutgers University. These two reports reach conflicting conclusions. The first report, based on evidence from a randomized experiment, found that the Family Cap had no effect on abortions. The second report, a statistical analysis of trends in abortions among the state's welfare population found a statistical relationship between implementation of the Family Cap and abortions. Specifically, this report concluded that abortions were higher than expected after implementing the Family Cap."[24] Falk and Devere discuss a number of methodological problems that they believed may have contributed to the difference in outcomes. Receiving prominent mention is the possibility of contamination in the experiment and omitted variable bias in the pre-post analyses. What is left unexpressed in their critique, however, is any acknowledgment of the considerable confusion that can be created by a comparison rooted more in expediency than in thoughtful scientific method. Regardless, Haskins and the House Ways and Means Committee had the assessment they needed.

Within weeks the CRS review began making the rounds through the policy institutes and media outlets in Washington. The editor of the *Weekly Standard*, William Kristol, chided Chris Smith for introducing legislation to repeal the Family Cap that was based on a "flawed Rutgers University study."[25] Kristol goes on to recount the "array of technical problems" uncovered in our report by CRS and alerts conservatives to Smith's unholy alliance with the National Organization of Women (NOW) and the American Civil Liberties Union (ACLU). In the November 1998 issue of *Welfare-to-Work*, an article headline on New Jersey's Family Cap and our study blared "N.J. Family Cap Study Showing Birth Drop, Abortion Rise May Be Flawed."[26] This piece cites Michael Kharfen, a U. S. Department of Health and Human Services—Administration for Children and Families (USDHHS-ACF) spokesman, who offers his own view of the CRS critique: "A regression analysis done by the university researchers also indicated that something may be wrong with the study when the results of that test contrasted sharply with other findings already reached. We have reservations that there are sufficient flaws in the methodology that puts the results into question."[27] My research colleagues and I were deeply troubled that an official from the very governmental agency that was funding the evaluation appeared unaware that he was parroting an invidious comparison between Interim experimental and Final pre-post analysis. In Washington, at least, the Rutgers Family Cap study was now quickly being transformed into the "flawed" Rutgers Family Cap study and there wasn't very much we could do about it. Simple time trend studies claiming to show that there never was a relationship between New Jersey's Family Cap and abortion were now receiving fresh acceptance. Among these were analyses by Robert Rector of the Heritage Foundation[28] and in New Jersey, by Ted Goertzel,[29] which found that Family Caps had been able to reduce births without apparently having any impact on abortions.

Family Cap Research at the Welfare Reform Academy

The most intense scrutiny of our research was to come from several welfare policy experts with affiliations at the American Enterprise Institute and the Welfare Reform Academy at the University of Maryland. The Academy, briefly described in chapter 5, was founded in 1999 by Douglas Besharov, a resident scholar at AEI and a professor at the University of Maryland School of Public Affairs. The idea for such an academy appears to have originated in the September 11, 1995, conference "Addressing Illegitimacy: Welfare Reform Options for Congress," sponsored by AEI. Whether donning an AEI or Welfare Academy hat, Besharov had shown a keen interest in New Jersey's Family Cap policy and our efforts to assess the policy's impact.

The principal tool that the Welfare Reform Academy planned to use in its "evaluation of welfare reform evaluations" was the Committee to Review Welfare Reform Research. In addition to Besharov and Peter Rossi, this committee included such leading policy analysts as Robert Boruch, James Heckman, Robinson Hollister, Christopher Jencks, Glenn Loury, Isabel Sawhill, Thomas Schelling, and James Q. Wilson. The charge of this group was to each year "assess the quality and relevance of the 10 to 25 most significant evaluation studies, identifying those findings that are sufficiently well-grounded to be regarded as credible."[30] A similar strategy for assessing welfare reform studies was proposed by two national poverty centers, the Institute for Research on Poverty at the University of Wisconsin and the Joint Center for Poverty Research (Northwestern University and the University of Chicago).[31] Indeed, the utilization of the expert panel as a mechanism for fusing science to public policy in a manner that is scientifically rigorous, balanced, and independent remains a common practice in the behavioral as well as the physical sciences.

This is not to say, however, that the use of expert panels has yielded an exemplary record in separating the light from the heat, especially when the research has focused on controversial social issues. Expert reaction to the Moynihan Report, captured in a volume by Lee Rainwater and William Yancey,[32] or the Coleman report, found in the book by Frederick Mosteller and Daniel Moynihan,[33] provides early cases of a swirl of interpretation and counterargument that bear the unmistakable mark of politics. The tumult surrounding reports on education, crime, and substance abuse, written by the social science experts who compose the federally sponsored Coalition for Evidence-Based Policy offers a current example.[34] So do the allegations of many in the scientific community that the Bush II Administration puts policy out in front of science when appointing expert panels and advisory committees.[35] If the observations of David Stoesz are correct, we are likely to see an escalation of these tensions as liberal and conservative policymakers attempt to control the means of analysis.[36]

The robustness of the expert panel review of politically charged research would appear to be enhanced a good deal if the points of view of individual members are adequately balanced and the review processes are sufficiently transparent to ensure any politics are identified and managed.[37] Sheila Jasanoff offers this compelling case for an inclusive expert panel: "Britain's long and painful struggle to manage the consequences of the BSE crisis ('mad cow disease') demonstrated the need to expose expert assessments of the probability of catastrophic events to wider technical and political scrutiny. In that case, a closed and narrowly constructed expert committee dismissed the likelihood of interspecies transfer of a poorly understood pathogenic agent as minimal; this judgment not only proved to be incorrect but caused enormous economic and political damage when it was found to be false."[38] Anthony Petrosino and his colleagues, moreover, find that study reviews that follow detailed, prospective protocols produce a transparency that, in turn, reduces relative judgments and "unknown and inexplicit" processes of reasoning.[39]

The blueprint on which the Welfare Reform Academy was established appeared to have the bases for the independent, scientific review of experts fully covered. In the preface to *Evaluating Welfare Reform: A Guide for Scholars and Practitioners*, Besharov, Rossi, and AEI staffer Peter Germanis listed seven criteria that would be employed for judging evaluations, namely:

1. Program Theory: Does the program or evaluation make sense in light of existing social science knowledge?
2. Research Design: Does the research design have both internal and external validity?
3. Program Implementation: How does the program actually operate?
4. Data Collection: Are the necessary data available and reliable?
5. Measurement: Are the key variables valid and can they be measured reliably?
6. Analytic Models: Are the data summarized and analyzed by means of appropriate statistical models?
7. Interpretation of Findings: Are the findings interpreted objectively and do they describe the limitations of the analyses and consider alternative interpretations? Are they placed in the proper policy or programmatic context?

Besharov, however, ends this listing with this disquieting codicil: "These criteria, of course, are not equally applicable to all evaluations."[40]

Nor apparently is each expert on the Academy's panel equally applicable to all evaluations. An examination of the many books, monographs, and papers produced in the nearly ten years of Academy operation reveals minimal to nonexistent involvement by most of the experts listed in *Evaluating Welfare Reform: A Guide*. The only experts on the Evaluation Review Committee roster to appear with regularity in these publications are Besharov and Rossi, a far more limited panel than was promised.

The Welfare Reform Academy's assessment of our New Jersey evaluation appeared in a 2000 publication entitled *Preventing Subsequent Births to Welfare Mothers*.[41] The principal critiques in the document were given by Douglas Besharov, Peter Rossi, and (in what appears to be his only review for the Academy) Glenn Loury, a former AEI Fellow. Additional heft was added to these reviews by the inclusion of the 1998 Congressional Research Service assessment conducted by Falk and Devere. Besharov, the publication editor, was perhaps unaware or unconcerned that the juxtaposition of the latter critique (which was based on an Interim report with incomplete data that did not reveal a Family Cap impact) and those of Rossi and Loury (which were based on a Final report with complete data showing a Family Cap impact) might yield some of the very confusion among policymakers, welfare practitioners, and the general public that the Welfare Academy had sworn to combat. Sloppy editing, however, was among the least of this volume's problems.

The assessments by Besharov, Loury, and Rossi were supplemented by briefer comments pieces from Michael Laracy, of the Annie E. Casey Foundation, and David Murray, an "itinerate cultural anthropologist turned statistics hound" who was at the time a consultant on the use of research by the media and public interest groups.[42] A comments response written by Rudolph Myers, NJDHS-DFD project manager for the evaluation, was not included in the publication for reasons that will soon be made apparent. After a great deal of rather unpleasant correspondence between Besharov and me, the Rutgers project team was also allowed to comment.

The manner in which the project team's comments on the Welfare Academy critique (really the Rossi critique) were solicited is in itself a rather interesting bit of theater. In early January 1999, Myers and Laracy received a copy of the Rossi assessment along with an invitation to respond by February 1.[43] My invitation was received on January 29 providing virtually no time for review and comment.[44] Respond we did, however, on February 4, in a letter that contained an eleven-page synopsis of what we believed were factual errors and evidence of unbalanced presentation in the Rossi critique.[45] In a series of attachments and actual computer output, moreover, we provided what we thought any objective observer would deem clear and convincing evidence for our assertions. So certain were we of the merits of our charges that we sent the contents of the February 4 response to the commissioner of NJDHS, the director of NJDHS–DFD, the director of Planning, Research and Evaluation at USDHS–ACF, the president of AEI, the University counsel at Rutgers, as well as to Besharov and Rossi.

Our contention that the Rossi critique was unbalanced to the extreme and therefore highly misleading may have fallen on deaf ears at AEI and the Welfare Reform Academy were it not for the observations on the Rossi paper circulated by the evaluation project manager at NJDHS–DFD, Rudolf Myers. In his January 28 correspondence to Besharov, Myers finds Rossi's "unusually acerbic critique more provocative than convincing."[46] Myers takes Rossi to task for what he viewed as an attempt to substitute authoritative pronouncement for useful, constructive appraisal and for his failure to accurately portray the research that was actually undertaken by the Rutgers team. Myers concludes the commentary with this:

> I find Professor Rossi's repeated representations of the Rutgers researchers as responsible for the design of this project, for soliciting a shift to non-experimental, pre-post design and for the failures in implementation of the Family Development Program confusing, disappointing, and ultimately inexcusable. The very documents he critiques contain clear narrative description of the facts, facts which differ markedly from his synoptic versions. It is very difficult for me to understand how this kind of scholarship advances either our understanding of the object of study (in this case the real consequences of the FDP) or

our refinement of the methods best used to reach that understanding when the ideal experimental situation does not materialize or long survive. In its present form, Professor Rossi's critique challenges our ethics more than our wits. I would hope that in its final form it will make a more positive contribution to the stated purpose of your proposed monograph.[47]

The Myers letter and the resultant buzz it created at NJDHS and ACF appeared to stimulate a recognition at the Welfare Reform Academy that the legitimacy of any critique of New Jersey's Family Cap evaluation might be enhanced by the inclusion of an evaluator's response. In April 1999, I was given a new deadline to provide a response to the Rossi critique (I was never shown those written by Besharov or Loury) that was suitable for publication in the Academy's forthcoming monograph. Suitability was clearly defined by Besharov and Germanis to be a piece that could not exceed 1,700 words.[48] I accepted the invitation on behalf of the evaluation team despite the restrictions believing that a limited opportunity for rebuttal was better than none at all. Besides, I never intended for the Welfare Reform Academy to be the final arbiter on the quality of our work.

Rossi's Design Flaw Search

The centerpiece of the Welfare Academy's monograph *Preventing Subsequent Births to Welfare Mothers* is the chapter written by Peter Rossi entitled "New Jersey's Family Development Program: An Overview and Critique of the Rutgers Evaluation."[49] Rossi, a past president of the American Sociological Association and the S. A. Rice Professor Emeritus at the University of Massachusetts, is considered by many to be one of the nation's leading evaluation theorists and practitioners.[50] His textbook, *Evaluation: A Systematic Approach*, written with Mark Lipsey and Howard Freeman, is one of the most popular in the field with over 90,000 copies sold.[51] Rossi, more than anyone else listed in the monograph, exemplifies the Academy's definition of expert—an individual whose work is widely known and respected.

Over the five decades that he has been plying his trade, Peter Rossi has become especially well known for a skepticism borne out of his innumerable evaluation experiences. It was Rossi after all who is credited with proposing the "Iron Law of Evaluation and other Metallic Rules." In a series of publications in the 1980s Rossi identified what he believed were the principal reasons why so many of the evaluations of government programs to help the poor, the disadvantaged, and the needy uncovered such limited effects. At the top of the list were poor conceptualization of both the problems being addressed and the solutions being sought, along with poor policy or program implementation.[52] These programmatic problems, of course, were typically passed on to the evaluator. In a 1987 article Rossi crystallized his growing skepticism into a series of laws regarding the practice of program evaluation:

The Iron Law—The expected value of any net impact assessment of any social program is zero.

The Stainless Steel Law—The better designed the impact assessment of a social program, the more likely is the net effect to be zero.

The Brass Law—The more social programs are designed to change individuals, the more likely the net impact of the program will be zero.

The Zinc Law—Only those programs that are likely to fail are evaluated.[53]

The Rossi critique of the New Jersey Family Cap evaluation concluded that the Family Development Program, and specifically the Family Cap, may have had an impact on fertility behavior but that deficiencies in program implementation and in our research methods cast strong doubts on the validity of our findings. The reasons for this assertion in Rossi's own words are these:

- The statistical models used to estimate the net effects of FDP are not appropriate, given the characteristics of the data. The use of linear multiple regression (OLS) with binary dependent variables is simply incorrect. Indeed, it is surprising that the researchers present OLS results and appear to regard them as valid. Although logit and probit regressions are designed for use with binary dependent variables, the likely presence of statistical dependencies within observations made on individual welfare recipients means that the resultant standard errors of effect coefficients are underestimated. Consequently, some or all of the effect coefficients that were marked as statistically significant in the reports may not be so had those dependencies been taken into account. If such corrections had been made, however, it is unlikely that the signs of coefficients would have changed.
- The implementation of the FDP experiment was flawed sufficiently to undermine the resulting data. Little evidence indicates that members of the experimental and control groups knew the particular AFDC and FDP rules to which they were subject. According to the survey of families (the Kaiser-sponsored survey) in the experiment, both experimental and control groups believed overwhelmingly that they were subject to the Family Cap, a finding so strong that it overcomes the survey's poor response rate. Although analysis of the data showed some FDP effects, the deficiencies in analysis methods must be taken into consideration. In addition, the omission of fertility events occurring while families were not enrolled in AFDC means that the analyses cannot be regarded as taking advantage of the randomized experimental design.
- The pre-post analysis is an evaluation research design that cannot support definitive estimates of the effects of a program. In particular, that design cannot take into account the effects of time or other

events that might affect outcomes. Some evidence shows that changes in the AFDC population occurred during the same period in which FDP was enacted and implemented. The effects estimated by the pre-post analysis are likely confounded with those changes.[54]

So strongly did Rossi believe in this conclusion that he felt compelled to use our evaluation as an exemplar in the sixth edition of his classic text *Evaluation: A Systematic Approach*. In fact, the evaluation became the model for "A Compromised Impact Assessment," one from which "the randomized experiment was judged to have failed" and "no impact estimates could be made."[55]

The Rossi critique was met with a chorus of agreement in *Preventing Subsequent Births to Welfare Mothers*. Michael Laracy, author of *If It Seems Too Good to Be True, It Probably Is* and *The Jury Is Still Out* found Rossi's conclusions to be reasonable and "his assessment to be fair, balanced and warranted."[56] He blamed the evaluation's failings squarely on the lack of commitment shown by the Florio administration. Laracy contended that the governor was actively opposed to rigorous evaluation of FDP and that a state budget crisis at the time resulted in the selection of the "cheapest proposal." Laracy exclaims, "Frankly, the resulting evaluation was a bargain-basement job...the state got what it paid for."[57]

In "Capping Families: What Do We Know?" David Murray is even less sanguine than Laracy in the hope of finding any redeeming qualities in our research. He inquires, "What do we know with certainty about the New Jersey outcome? Unfortunately, little, by the minimal criteria outlined above, the New Jersey experiment was deficient in nearly every regard."[58] So concerned is Murray about the spread of our findings in light of the Rossi critique that he invokes Wittgenstein's remonstrance from the Tractatus "Whereof one cannot speak, thereof one must be silent."[59] To the warning I can only respond as would Wittgenstein, "DaB es mir—oder Allen-so scheint, daraus folgt nicht, daB es so est."[60]

While Besharov in his commentary merely reprises the criticism leveled by Rossi in *Preventing Subsequent Births*, Glenn Loury, however, extends the Rossi claim of contamination in the social experiment to the process of random assignment itself. As evidence he draws upon a survey of case managers and income maintenance workers we conducted early on in the evaluation to help examine the FDP implementation. From his reading of the survey results, which were published in our Interim Report, Loury concludes: "The New Jersey FDP had similar [to Arkansas] implementation problems. The main duties of the caseworkers were to determine AFDC eligibility and to calculate benefit levels. About half of the workers were responsible for assigning new applicants to experimental or control groups for the purposes of the family-cap demonstration. This assignment process was supposed to be random; yet more than one quarter of the workers freely admitted to evaluation researchers that they used discretion in making assignments."[61] As I noted earlier, the evaluation team was never given a draft of the Loury critique in advance of its publication; had we been given such an opportunity Loury and his readers might have been awarded a better understanding of how the random assignment was actually conducted. As our Interim Report unambiguously outlines, questionnaires were received from 1,095 caseworkers (96 percent response rate) belonging to four distinct groups: income maintenance intake workers (N = 236), income maintenance ongoing caseworkers (N = 640), JTPA jobs counselor caseworkers (N = 58), and FDP family caseworkers (N = 161). Only intake workers, about 22 percent of these caseworkers (not the 50 percent as Loury asserts), obtained information, including Social Security numbers, demographic and budget data, from new applicants. And while it is true that about half of the 236 IM *intake* caseworkers reported some responsibility for assigning cases to the experiment, only 28 workers (about 11 percent of intake workers and 2.5 percent of all workers) stated they used substantial amounts of discretion when assigning cases. Loury simply misreads the tables in the report.[62] Did the use of discretion claimed by these workers really corrupt the random assignment as Loury asserts? Whether the reader wishes to use Loury's 25 percent or the actual 11 percent really doesn't matter; the answer is no. As I report in chapter 4 only 13 of the over 8,300 cases were ever misassigned, this according to state and federal reviews of the case allocation process.

Of course, the real issue here is not whether others agree with Peter Rossi's critique of our evaluation, it is the quality of the evidence used by Rossi himself. Excepting Loury's doubts about random assignment, the commentary in *Preventing Subsequent Births* is largely derivative, a recapitulation of the main themes. This perhaps is to be expected since critics like Besharov, Murray, and Laracy do not possess the statistical and econometric training that would support an independent methodological critique of the work. But just how strong is this evidence for a deeply flawed evaluation?

In our approximately 1,700-word piece, "The Evaluator's Reply," we briefly addressed the three major criticisms Peter Rossi offered as compelling evidence for our "deeply flawed" evaluation. The space limitations imposed upon us, however, did not allow for the depth of response that would have shown the Academy's criticism to be at the same time much more than the exercise of healthy scientific skepticism. We were also mindful that the suitability criterion imposed by the monograph's editors could destine much of our response for the cutting-room floor.

Let me now address each of the three major evaluation problems that Rossi identifies as evidence. The charge of inappropriate statistical models and our apparent ignorance of what they reveal about the data show Peter Rossi at his very best and worst.

As I have noted earlier, linear probability model (LPM) or ordinary least squares (OLS) with binary dependent variables, much more often than not, gives results very similar to those generated by probit, logit, and even Poisson regression methods. The limitations of the LPM method are often outweighed by the ease with which marginal effects can be calculated. When LPM models are estimated along with logit and probit models, as we did in our reports, it does not reveal an inability "to choose definitely among alternative statistical models," as Rossi contends[63]; it is indicative of the sound econometric practice of specification checking and sensitivity analysis.[64] In our Evaluator's Reply we show that whether LPM, logit, or probit, with or without heteroskedastic error assumptions, the birth and abortion effects of the Family Cap remain.[65]

Rossi's insistence "that the use of OLS with binary dependent variables is simply incorrect" had always struck me and members of the evaluation team as excessive, even a bit disingenuous. Harvey, Jagannathan, Killingsworth, and I had all taught a number of statistics and econometrics courses and knew that LPM had been utilized with binary dependent variables by many seasoned researchers with minimal ill effects. One of these seasoned veterans, in fact, was Peter Rossi himself.

In *Evaluation: A Systematic Approach*, sixth edition, the same volume in which the Family Cap evaluation is exhibited as an exemplar of compromised research, Rossi presents "Exhibit 8–E: Analysis of Randomized Experiments: The Baltimore LIFE Program,"[66] an evaluation conducted by Rossi, Richard Berk, and Kenneth Lenihan.[67] This experiment was designed to determine if financial aid given to newly released prisoners would ease their transition into the community and reduce rearrest; many of the dependent variables used by Rossi are binary. In the Exhibit Rossi shows table 8–E2 entitled "Multiple Regression Analysis of Arrests for Theft Crimes," a title that does not convey the actual statistical modeling that was used to generate the regression coefficients. What is remarkable here is that these coefficients are identical to those appearing in the source document "Money, Work and Crime" (table 2.4), where the table is entitled "Baltimore LIFE Experiment: Regression of Theft Arrest Dummy Variable on Financial Aid and Other Selected Variables" and where the text admits that OLS with a binary dependent variable was used.[68] Rossi and his colleagues provide this rationale for the use of LPM in the evaluation's many analyses in a footnote: "Because a dichotomous dependent variable necessarily yields heteroskedastic errors under ordinary least squares, the regression coefficients are inefficient and the standard errors and thus t-tests are biased. Yet, since the distribution on the dependent variable is not badly skewed, the results are not likely to be misleading. Equally important, Mallar and Thornton (in a separate analysis) obtained almost identical results using a probit model that is not subject to the problems associated with the linear probability approach."[69] Nowhere in Exhibit 8–E does Rossi warn the reader that the marginal effects discussed there are "simply incorrect." Rossi also applies LPM modeling in his analysis of the Texas and Georgia Transitional Aid to Released Prisoners (TARP) evaluation, which appears at Exhibit 8-G in his text; however, in these instances, no corroborating probit estimates are alluded to.[70]

When I wrote to Professor Rossi, asking why LPM modeling was legitimate for use by him and his colleagues but not by our evaluation team, I did not receive an answer.[71] I did notice however that Exhibit 8–H "A Compromised Impact Assessment: The New Jersey Family Cap Experiment" had been expurgated from the seventh edition of *Evaluation: A Systematic Approach*. I guess the point had been made after all.

By far the most serious charge leveled in the Rossi critique is one of severe contamination, gleaned from responses of 1,232 welfare recipients to the Kaiser Family Foundation–sponsored survey. We asked two questions on the survey, both of which appear in table 7.1, to help gauge the quality of the FDP implementation process from the perspective of the recipient. As I have noted, the team openly discussed the response patterns appearing in table 7.1 in our Interim and Final Reports. We have always contended that any implementation assessment using a one-point-in-time survey with a low response rate and two single item measures was of limited utility for assessing contamination in either the delivery of the treatment or the management of the environmental context. Rossi, on the other hand, believes that these questions, despite being "poorly worded,"[72] provide compelling evidence for such contamination. His position is strongly supported by Besharov, Loury, Murray, and Laracy in *Preventing Subsequent Births*.

Table 7.1. Recipient Survey Items Used by Rossi to Determine the Quality of the FDP Implementation Process

1. Have you been told that you are included in a control group of welfare recipients who receive welfare benefits under the old welfare rules that are called Reach or JOBS? No ☐ Yes ☐ Not Sure ☐

Membership Based on Question Response	Actual Assigned Membership	
	Treatment (n = 653)	Control (n = 579)
Experimental	65%	55%
Control	28%	39%
Not sure	6%	6%

2. If you were to remain on welfare and have a baby one year from now, what, if any, additional benefits would your child receive? (Check all that apply.)

	Treatment (n = 653) Percent Answering "Yes"	Control (n = 579) Percent Answering "Yes"
Additional food stamps	26.6	27.6
Additional cash benefits	4.4	6.9
Additional Medicaid	37.6	40.6
No additional benefits of any kind	35.5	34.5

The type of evidence Rossi and his fellow experts at the Welfare Academy have employed to identify what they believe are crippling levels of contamination in New Jersey's Family Cap experiment could have considerable implications for the field of evaluation and policy research if adopted widely. The threat of contamination is present in all research designs, for example, natural experiments, observational studies, and other quasi-experimental designs as well as randomized experiments.[73] But the Rossi approach to contamination appears to emphasize measures used to explain outcomes much more than the outcomes themselves, no matter that these explanations may derive from "poorly worded" measures, surveys with low response rates, or other less than optimal indicators of contamination. Moreover, since Rossi provides no criterion, statistical or otherwise, to identify when an explanation is insufficient to rule out contamination, impurity, no matter how impure, has the potential to trump measured treatment effects.

To provide the reader with some context with which to assess Rossi's contamination charges I contrast the responses to questions about recipient understanding of experiment status in four large Section 1115 waiver studies of Family Caps, including ours (table 7.2).[74] The other three evaluations were conducted by Abt Associates, widely regarded as one of the leaders in the field of social program evaluation. As in our case, Abt collected recipient responses using telephone surveys, supplemented by face-to-face interviews, but unlike the New Jersey evaluation, Abt committed sufficient resources and received response rates in the 70 percent range.

As you can see in table 7.2 sizable proportions of the control group in each study reported that they believed they were subject to the Family Cap

Table 7.2.   Survey Responses of Welfare Recipients to Questions about the Applicability of a Family Cap from Four Large Section 1115 Waiver Evaluations

Evaluation		Percent Responding Yes That Family Cap Applied to Them	
		Treatments	Controls
Better Chance Welfare Reform Program (Delaware)[a]	Abt Associates	62.5	37.5
Indiana Welfare Reform Program[b]	Abt Associates	55.5	35.6
New Jersey Family Development Program	Rutgers	65.0	55.0
Arizona Empowerment Demonstration[c]	Abt Associates	42.7	45.3

[a]Fein and Karweit (1997); [b]Fein, Beecroft, Hamilton, and Lee (1998); [c]Mills et al. (1999). See note 74.

policies; obversely, a significant proportion of the treatment group volunteered that they thought they were not covered. In the Arizona Empower Demonstration apparently more controls than treatment group members believed they were receiving welfare services under Family Cap rules.[75] Nor are the Abt results atypical, when recipients are asked about their experimental status in welfare reform studies the responses very often follow the general pattern shown in table 7.2.[76]

The approach typically taken by evaluators in welfare reform demonstrations and by program evaluators in general is to acknowledge that experimental subject confusion is present and that it serves to place a lower bound on true treatment versus control group differences.[77] David Fein and Jennifer Karweit sum up this position in their evaluation of Delaware's Family Cap: "It is also likely that the measured impacts understate ABC's full effects even during this early period. The client survey found some control group members mistakenly believed—or at least said they believed—that they were subject to ABC policies. This is not surprising given the extensive publicity surrounding welfare reform in Delaware and at the national level. Nonetheless, it means that control group behaviors and outcomes probably differ from what would have occurred in a pure pre-ABC policy environment. This effect cannot be measured, but argues that observed impacts are a conservative estimate of true effect."[78] As does Rossi, these researchers do not present actual analysis to support their conjecture on the role recipient misperception of experimental status plays on estimates of treatment impacts. If, however, the role is similar to what has been observed in the crossover literature, misperception would be expected to attenuate the absolute size of treatment versus control group differences like Fein and Karweit propose and not invalidate them as Rossi asserts.[79]

Putting Rossi's Contamination Thesis to Test

When reading the critique of our research in *Preventing Subsequent Births* I was struck by the extraordinary level of assuredness with which Rossi and fellow critics from the Welfare Reform Academy expressed themselves on the contamination issue. Perhaps an Abt Associates or Manpower Demonstration Research Corporation could shrug such criticism off; after all, their long history in the evaluation field provided a deal of credibility for contentions like "contamination begets attenuation." The Rutgers team was not in the same position to make pronouncements and, besides, the Academy was not reviewing any Family Cap studies being conducted by evaluation's "Big Three." We decided to put Rossi's assertion to empirical test using what has been termed the Rubin framework or Rubin Causal Model.[80] The key ideas in this approach are to deal with misperception as a form of noncompliance to an assigned treatment, to treat noncompliance as a potential outcome itself, and to classify and analyze respondents by their joint values on these compliance-dependent outcomes. The Rubin approach is especially well suited to settings where the assignment to a binary treatment can be ignored, but compliance with the assignment is not perfect so the receipt of actual treatment cannot be ignored. In this way both outcomes and "explanations" for those outcomes are modeled. The Rubin Causal Model (RCM) provides a framework within which the policy analyst can make inferences about overall treatment effectiveness based on treatment group assignment, and about efficacy where the focus is on the type of treatment provided, including considerations of treatment purity.

We applied the RCM to test the influence of misperception on abortion outcomes using our survey subsample of 1,233 respondents in an analysis that appeared in the *Journal of Policy Analysis and Management*.[81] The measure of abortion we use, abortions billed to Medicaid, is identical to that used in the full sample analyses described earlier. Abortions were selected from the fertility behaviors reported because findings in this instance have generated the most controversy and criticism.

Three estimation equations were fitted. The first examines the role of actual assignment to either the treatment or control group, and is specified as follows:

$$P(Abortion)_{it} = a + B(E_a)_i + e_{it}$$

Equation 7.1

Where $P(Abortion)_{it}$ refers to the probability that an abortion occurred for case i in time t; $(E_a)_i$ is actual experimental status for case i:

$E_a = 1$ for cases assigned to the treatment group
$E_a = 0$ for cases assigned to the control group

e_{it} is an error term. a, B are estimated model coefficients. This model, where treatment is given but may or may not be accepted by all is the "intention to treat" estimate.

The second specification tests for a relationship between an abortion outcome and perceived experimental status among the study sample, as revealed by their survey responses. Model 2 is specified as follows:

$$P(Abortion)_{it} = a + B(E_p)_i + e_{it}$$

Equation 7.2

where $(E_p)_i$ is perceived experimental status for case i;

$E_p = 1$ for cases that perceived themselves to be assigned
  to the treatment group;
$E_p = 0$ for cases that perceived themselves to be assigned
  to the control group.

This model directly examines the misperception explanation for the obser-ved experimental-control differences in abortions offered by Rossi.

Finally, in the third model specification, both actual and perceived exper-imental status are included as independent influences on abortion outcomes, in an attempt to discern the relative influence of each on the probability of an abortion. Specifically,

$$P(\text{Abortion})_{it} = a + B_1(E_{ap})_i + B_2(E_aC_p)_i + B_3(C_aE_p)_i + e_{it}$$

Equation 7.3

where $(E_{ap})_i = 1$ if case i is both an actual and perceived treatment case; $(E_{ap})_i = 0$ otherwise.
$(E_aC_p)_i = 1$ if case i is an actual treatment case, but a perceived control case; $(E_aC_p)_i = 0$ otherwise.
$(C_aE_p)_i = 1$ if case i is an actual control case, but a perceived treatment case; $(C_aE_p)_i = 0$ otherwise.

The above three groups are compared to the reference group

$(C_{ap})_i = 1$ if the case i is both an actual and perceived control case;
$(C_{ap})_i = 0$ otherwise.

a, B_1, B_2, and B_3 are estimated model coefficients.

If assigned status performs equally well for both "pure" and "impure" cases in model 3 it cannot act as a good instrumental variable within the Rubin framework.

Medicaid claims data were pooled for all cases for each quarter a treatment or a control group case in the sample received welfare benefits. Statistical models were estimated using logistic regression, and Huber-corrected stan-dard errors are computed to adjust for the possibility of clustering effects. The results from these analyses are presented separately for new and ongoing cases in table 7.3.

For new cases, actual assignment to treatment and control groups (model 1) yields a significant, positive treatment effect for survey respondents. That is, those survey respondents who were assigned at random to the treatment group and thus subject to the Family Cap were more likely to abort a preg-nancy over the observation period than their control group counterparts. Findings are quite different in model 2, where no significant effect was found if the respondents' perceptions of their experimental group assign-ment were used.

Model 3 shows that "pure" treatments, that is, subjects in the assigned treatment group who also correctly perceived their treatment status (E_{ap}), exhibit the expected positive abortion effect, compared with "pure" control group subjects (C_{ap}). The abortion effect is also positive and significant for assigned treatment group subjects who thought that they were control subjects and not subject to the FDP Family Cap (E_aC_p). Control group subjects who misperceived their status (C_aE_p) did not experience abortions at a significantly higher level than "pure controls." These findings would appear to confirm results we reported for the entire evaluation sample. Within the context of the RCM, the patterning of results for new cases in table 7.3 with E_{ap}, $E_aC_p > C_aE_p$, C_{ap} indicates that actual assignment does matter. If assigned status served merely as an instrument with the treatment effect conditioned solely on client perception then E_{ap}, $C_aE_p > E_aC_p$, C_{ap} would be expected.

Another way to examine relative difference between pure and impure cases is to perform subgroup analyses separately for pure and impure treatments and controls and compare impact differences in effect. If the estimated program difference is smaller for impure treatment-controls than it is for treatment-controls who "got it right" (i.e., pure treatments and controls), this would suggest that the measured contamination caused the overall

Table 7.3. Logistic Regressions for Probability of an Abortion for New and Ongoing Cases Using Actual and Perceived Group Assignment Predictors

Variable	New Cases			Ongoing Cases		
	Model 1	Model 2	Model 3[a]	Model 1	Model 2	Model 3[a]
Assigned treatment	0.559* (0.171)			0.202 (0.121)		
Perceived treatment		−0.141 (0.170)			0.001 (0.123)	
Assigned and perceived treatment (E_{ap})			0.932* (0.284)			0.121 (0.157)
Assigned treatment but perceived control (E_aC_p)			1.283* (0.306)			0.206 (0.178)
Assigned control but perceived treatment (C_aE_p)			0.596 (0.317)			−0.124 (0.172)
Intercept	−4.074 (0.144)	−3.614 (0.142)	−4.050 (0.259)	−3.708 (0.092)	−3.551 (0.093)	−3.591 (0.116)

*indicates significance at ≤ 0.05. [a]omitted category is assigned and perceived controls, i.e., "pure controls" (C_{ap}). Note: Robust standard errors are in parenthesis.

treatment-control difference to underestimate the magnitude of the treatment effect. The results of these bivariate logistic regressions are $b = 0.761$ (stan- (standard error $= 0.236$) for the subgroup analysis of pure cases and $b = 0.687$ (standard error $= 0.312$) for impure cases.

A similar analysis of the sample of ongoing case abortions shows no treatment effect associated with assigned treatment-control group status. Our analysis also shows no difference in abortion levels when perceived status is analyzed alone (model 2) or in concert with actual group assignment (model 3). These findings are consistent with full sample evaluation findings, which indicates that ongoing cases (who tended to be older and to have more children than new applicants) did not respond with an increase in abortion rates (or a downturn in births) to the implementation of FDP and its Family Cap.

There is no evidence from this examination of new or ongoing cases to suggest that contamination from misperception resulted in spurious treatment effects. When similar analyses are conducted for births and contraception, moreover, the conclusion to be drawn is also similar.

Possibly the poor showing of perceived treatment status in table 7.3 is due to the omission of respondent selection factors, other than actual assignment, that could be correlated to abortion outcomes. To test this possibility, Heckman selection models were estimated separately for new and ongoing cases using the set of covariates employed in our full sample analyses. These results indicate also that abortion outcomes are not subject to a selection mechanism that is based on misperceptions of self-reported experimental status.[82]

An empirical analysis of contamination provides stronger evidence for the attenuation hypothesis than it does the spurious hypothesis offered up by Rossi and the Welfare Academy. If implementation of New Jersey's Family Cap had proceeded more smoothly, the birth and abortion effects we had uncovered would most probably have been even larger.

The issue remains as to where recipients get the information they choose to act upon. For some, it no doubt comes from the news media; for others, from other recipients. When a recipient is seeking to determine the consequences for her welfare grant amount of a conception, adoption, or change in living arrangement, however, her caseworker is a likely outlet. Myers has referred to this process as a person-by-person indemnification from the proscribed treatment.[83] While not perfect, the process continues through a variety of recipient-worker interactions: namely, adding a baby, service referrals, redetermination of eligibility, change of address, reporting of income, sanctioning, and recoupment. Hence, incomplete, conflicting, or erroneous information need not be a permanent basis for action, and evidence from our analysis indicates that it is not. This is not to say that contamination cannot present a legitimate concern in evaluation research, only that the measures used by Rossi are inadequate to gauge its level and impact in the New Jersey evaluation.

I shared our contamination analysis with Rossi and Besharov but never received a response.[84] As was the case with the contention of improper statistical modeling, the Welfare Academy's charge of crippling contamination proved groundless.

Signals in the Washington Echo Chamber

Rossi's third criticism focused on our use of the unbalanced panel to provide "definitive estimates" of Family Cap treatment effects. Refutation of this supposed flaw, of course, does not require additional analyses; rather, it only calls for a careful reading of our contracts with NJDHS, USDHHS-ACF, and the Assistant Secretary for Planning and Evaluation (ASPE). The proposal to undertake a pre-post analysis was clearly labeled an "augmentation" effort, not an experimental replacement endeavor. Project managers at the state and federal levels saw value in our blended-design strategy, which is why both the experimental and nonexperimental studies were funded to completion.

The use of blended design, as I have described in chapter 4, calls for a critique that, at minimum, is open to the possibility of corroborating results under differing methodological assumptions. In our reports and in a comparative analysis of experimental and nonexperimental estimates of Family Cap, which appeared in the American Journal of Evaluation, we show a consistency of impact that Rossi chooses to ignore.[85] Yet in light of this consistency, the issues of entry effect and population heterogeneity have taken on a much duller hue than Rossi would have his readers believe.

One issue with our evaluation to which Rossi gives only brief attention but which has resonated with a number of other critics is the fact that the Family Cap was only one of several treatments that were implemented as part of FDP. These critics, which include Michael Laracy, Rebecca Maynard and her colleagues, and Jeffrey Grogger maintain that it is virtually impossible to disentangle the Family Cap effect on fertility from the effect of economic opportunities made available through most welfare reforms.[86] This is another form of the argument of the relative importance of rehabilitation versus punishment.

David Fein has identified four research strategies that have been employed to understand the specific policy component effects of a welfare reform that has been implemented as a package: namely, (1) document recipient exposure levels to each provision, (2) identify the unique goals that a component may have for recipients, (3) conduct cross-state comparisons if components vary among states, and (4) perform experiments with multiple treatments set up within a factorial framework.[87]

In the New Jersey experiment it could reasonably be conjectured that a Family Cap effect on fertility behavior is the result of a confounding with an aggressive Job Opportunities and Basic Skills Training (JOBS) program.

Although this contention of the influence of a second strong provision cannot be tested for the entire ten-county experimental sample, it can be studied in the seven counties in which enhanced JOBS and the Medicaid extension were phased in after the Family Cap was put into effect. While the Family Cap was initiated in all counties beginning October 1, 1992, enhanced JOBS began in Atlantic, Cumberland, Mercer, Passaic, and Union counties on October 1, 1993, and in Middlesex and Monmouth counties on December 1, 1994.[88] Inasmuch as the three largest welfare counties are excluded, any analysis of the remaining seven trades a test for component specificity for a decided diminution in statistical power. In this experimental context, however, the analysis is admissible since the county treatment phase-in schedules were not defined on the basis of any events that occurred after random assignment, that is, the schedules are exogenous.[89]

Using the same pooled-data analytic approach I have described in equation 6.1 and in the contamination analysis discussed earlier, I estimated two distinctive models separately for new and ongoing cases:

$$P(\text{Fertility Outcome}_{it}) = X_{it}B + \lambda_1 FDP_{it} + \lambda_2 (FDP_{it} \times Time_t) + e_{it}$$

Equation 7.4

$$P(\text{Fertility Outcome}_{it}) = X_{it}B + \lambda_1 \text{Family Cap}_{it} + B_2 \text{ JOBS(1)}_{it}$$
$$+ B_3 \text{ JOBS(2)}_{it} + \lambda_2 (\text{Family Cap}_{it} \times Time_t) + e_{it}$$

Equation 7.5

where i subscripts denote individuals and t subscripts denote calendar time from October 1992 through January 1997.[90]

In equation 7.4 the coefficient λ_1 estimates the composite effect of the Family Cap and enhanced JOBS while in equation 7.5 λ_1 provides an estimate of the Family Cap that is independent of the impact of JOBS. Here B_2 measures recipient exposure to JOBS in Atlantic, Cumberland, Mercer, Passaic, and Union counties and B_3 measures this program effect for Middlesex and Mercer counties. The vector XB, as before, provides estimates for individual and aggregate-level covariates.

Table 7.4 presents the Poisson regression estimates of the bundled and unbundled Family Cap impact for new case women. One sees from the table coefficients that the Family Cap estimate is significant in the birth, abortion, and contraception models and further that this effect is not diminished by the addition of enhanced JOBS exposure. With respect to births, the treatment group experiences a 15.4 percent ($e^{-.166} - 1 * 100$) lower birthrate than controls; abortions, on the other hand, are 27 percent ($e^{.242} - 1 * 100$) higher. The findings closely parallel those reported for the full sample of new cases where the fertility effects were attributed to the Family Cap. When ongoing cases are examined no Family Cap effect on births or abortions are found—once again replicating the full sample analysis. It would appear that the fertility impact of the FDP program emanates primarily from the Family Cap provision and not from JOBS, an indication that penalty is a more important motivational factor than any revised life priorities that recipients may have developed when they are linked to new skills and occupational opportunities. I present a fuller examination of the unbundled Family Cap effect in a 2004 issue of *Contemporary Economic Policy*.[91]

The sociologist Walter Wallace has written that "in science, as in everyday life, things must be believed to be seen, as well as seen to be believed."[92] At the state level, information from the state research university is more highly regarded by the public, media, and local politicians than any evidence offered by state government or its paid experts. In Washington, however, the signals do not usually favor the state university. Lacking political access, reputation, and the organization necessary for impression management the state university is forced to rely on the professional conference and peer-reviewed journal to make the case for the credibility of its research. While this undoubtedly makes for better research than that produced by ideologically driven think tanks, the process can be too slow to win the hearts and minds of national policymakers—at least in the short run.

In a politically charged environment like the one surrounding the Family Cap, the mere allegation of research flaws can play the same role in shaping perceptions as actual empirical evidence of any flaws. As I believe I have shown here, a great deal of the criticism leveled at the New Jersey Family Cap evaluation—by the Welfare Reform Academy and others—simply doesn't pass the test of empirical scrutiny. Experimental contamination did not lead to spurious results, we did not abandon the experimental design, nor did we employ statistical models and error term specifications that invalidated our work. Moreover, statements made by Rossi and other members of the Welfare Reform Academy about our failures to follow what are endogenously defined subgroups off welfare and to unbundled Family Cap treatment effects illustrate some basic misunderstandings about the strengths and weaknesses of experiments and blended designs. Nevertheless, these criticisms were successful in planting doubt, creating confusion and limiting the influence of potentially damaging research. The Welfare Reform Academy, with its close linkage to AEI, the Heritage Foundation, and many right-leaning politicians and policy experts, had succeeded in placing a fog around our research—a fog we have been trying to lift ever since.

In September 2001, the U. S. General Accounting Office (GAO) issued a report that reviewed several studies, including our work, that had examined the relationship between Family Caps and out-of-wedlock births.[93] Once again the principal assertions in Rossi's critique—experimental contamination and improper statistical models—were repeated. In this instance, however, the report's authors did not completely dismiss our findings, concluding instead that there was some evidence here, albeit "weak evidence,"

Table 7.4. Poisson Regressions for the Probability of Fertility Events for New Case Women

Predictors	Birth		Abortion		Contraception Use		Contraceptive Sterilization	
	(1)	(2)	(3)	(4)	(5)	(6)	(7)	(8)
FDP	-0.168*	–	0.246*	–	0.288**	–	-0.174	–
	(0.098)	–	(0.141)	–	(0.144)	–	(0.264)	–
Family Cap	–	-0.166*	–	0.242*	–	0.282**	–	-0.177
	–	(0.098)	–	(0.140)	–	(0.143)	–	(0.263)
Enhanced JOBS (1)	–	-0.072	–	-0.101	–	0.025	–	0.494
	–	(0.162)	–	(0.225)	–	(0.186)	–	(0.466)
Enhanced JOBS (2)	–	-0.137	–	0.248	–	0.547**	–	0.428
	–	(0.217)	–	(0.255)	–	(0.198)	–	(0.619)
Time trend	-0.065	-0.062	0.029	0.024	-0.010	-0.018	-0.072	-0.077
	(0.019)	(0.019)	(0.022)	(0.023)	(0.018)	(0.018)	(0.058)	(0.059)
June	0.199	0.187	-0.165	-0.162	-0.052	-0.032	0.257	0.309
	(0.156)	(0.157)	(0.167)	(0.170)	(0.078)	(0.078)	(0.373)	(0.375)
September	0.332	0.302	-0.377	-0.370	-0.282	-0.232	0.217	0.370
	(0.195)	(0.200)	(0.183)	(0.189)	(0.103)	(0.106)	(0.451)	(0.460)
December	0.177	0.158	-0.367	-0.344	-0.338	-0.279	-0.282	-0.216
	(0.187)	(0.190)	(0.185)	(0.187)	(0.096)	(0.097)	(0.488)	(0.495)
Black	0.165	0.169	0.356	0.357	-0.448	-0.458	-0.058	-0.072
	(0.131)	(0.131)	(0.199)	(0.201)	(0.173)	(0.173)	(0.348)	(0.349)
Hispanic	0.031	0.037	0.086	0.093	-0.278	-0.284	-0.043	-0.070
	(0.153)	(0.153)	(0.234)	(0.236)	(0.184)	(0.185)	(0.366)	(0.365)
High school dropout	0.069	0.069	0.471	0.469	-0.061	-0.054	0.529	0.541
	(0.201)	(0.201)	(0.329)	(0.328)	(0.281)	(0.281)	(0.563)	(0.564)

(continued)

137

Table 7.4. (*continued*)

Predictors	Birth		Abortion		Contraception Use		Contraceptive Sterilization	
	(1)	(2)	(3)	(4)	(5)	(6)	(7)	(8)
High school graduate	0.003	0.004	0.433	0.427	0.209	0.206	0.599	0.606
	(0.205)	(0.205)	(0.342)	(0.341)	(0.263)	(0.263)	(0.583)	(0.583)
Some college	0.135	0.137	0.637	0.631	0.474	-0.470	0.529	0.531
	(0.247)	(0.247)	(0.417)	(0.416)	(0.316)	(0.316)	(0.729)	(0.729)
Never married	0.073	0.074	0.315	0.316	0.202	0.202	-0.058	-0.060
	(0.131)	(0.131)	(0.201)	(0.200)	(0.182)	(0.182)	(0.324)	(0.325)
Age of mother	-0.072	-0.073	-0.084	-0.084	-0.026	-0.026	-0.031	-0.031
	(0.010)	(0.010)	(0.013)	(0.013)	(0.011)	(0.011)	(0.023)	(0.023)
Children on welfare	-0.035	-0.037	0.052	0.053	-0.142	-0.136	0.291	0.295
	(0.062)	(0.062)	(0.074)	(0.074)	(0.095)	(0.095)	(0.097)	(0.097)
County unemployment rate	0.140	0.119	-0.063	-0.063	-0.158	-0.127	-0.063	0.052
	(0.112)	(0.120)	(0.141)	(0.139)	(0.091)	(0.090)	(0.280)	(0.302)
County JOBS participation rate	-0.005	-0.004	0.010	-0.009	-0.001	-0.001	-0.010	-0.019
	(0.011)	(0.012)	(0.011)	(0.011)	(0.009)	(0.009)	(0.030)	(0.034)
Intercept	-2.09	-1.93	-2.22	-2.10	-0.479	-0.637	-4.43	-5.41
	(1.08)	(1.12)	(1.28)	(1.28)	(0.963)	(0.961)	(2.64)	(2.91)

*Significant at 10%; ** Significant at 5%. Notes: Robust standard errors in parenthesis. Analysis is conducted with 9601 person-quarter observations. All regressions include county fixed effects.

138

for a link between Family Caps and fertility behavior. The GAO recommended that USDHHS conduct additional research on TANF Family Caps to gain
a better understanding of how such policies might prevent and reduce births.
While I agree that additional research is needed in this area, I believe a good
deal can be learned from the limited amount that is available.

8

Testing Family Cap Theory

Introduction

All social interventions, the Family Cap included, comprise a theory, that is, a set of more or less logically connected statements that tells us why and how specific human behaviors occur or can be expected to occur. As Abraham Kaplan writes, theory sets forth some idea of the rules of nature's game and makes the moves in this game intelligible to us.[1] The theories that underpin social policies and programs may be implicit or explicit, transparent or opaque, simple or quite elaborate, but their structure is rarely accidental. Behind every operational program theory sits a group of stakeholders who possess the political power, financial resources, and information access to put their vision of "nature's game" into practice.

In figure 8.1.a, I show a program theory that captures the intentions of the New Jersey politicians and policy analysts who fashioned the state's Family Cap law in 1992. The rendering is antediluvian, that is, before the flood of publicity and controversy that engulfed Florio, Bryant, Waldman, and other Family Cap architects and spokesmen in early 1993. As we have seen, once debate over the policy's mechanisms and intentions became heated, nonmarital birth reduction virtually disappeared from the official discussions of policy design and from the promulgated flowgraph as well. Even the federal government began to back away from birth reduction as the key component of Family Cap policies. The following response from the U.S. Department of Health and Human Services—Administration for Children and Families

(A)

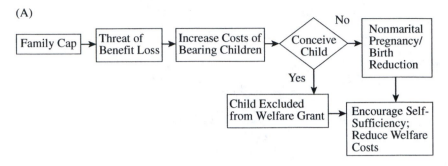

Figure 8.1.a. Family Cap Program Impact Theory: Stakeholder Professed

(USDHS–ACF) to a General Accounting Office (GAO) report on Family Cap research sums this up well:

> The focus of GAO's report is on the effect of State Family Caps on out-of-wedlock pregnancies among welfare recipients. The report carries an implicit assumption that Family Caps were put in place to reduce out-of-wedlock childbearing. It should be noted, however, that some States adopted Family Cap policies in order to achieve greater equity between welfare and working poor families, who do not get raises in their wages when additional children are born. The broader intent of treating aided families like working families was to further the message that self-sufficiency requires families to assume responsibilities. Therefore Family Caps were intended to impact not only out-of-wedlock births, but dependency as well.[2]

A policy built primarily on excluding children from benefits, however, is not what the original framers had in mind, at least in liberal New Jersey; if it had been, the policy would have never been signed into law.

While all program theories do not necessarily emanate from social science theory,[3] the Family Cap as it appears in figure 8.1.a is well rooted in conceptualizations of economic choice behavior. The flowgraph depicts a policy process built around price sensitivity where welfare mothers weigh the costs and benefits of having a child (or children) under the expectation of Family Cap sanction. The model entertains the possibility that some women will not make the "rational," pecuniary choice and instead will opt to bear a child (or children) she cannot support financially. These women will "learn the hard way," through economic hardship, what working women have always known—having children carries substantial economic cost. Either way, by the excluded child path or by births foregone (or at least postponed) the Family Cap, so the theory flows, teaches a life lesson in budgeting for children while receiving welfare benefits.

As pictured in figure 8.1.a, the mechanics of the Family Cap appear eminently egalitarian—all women on welfare are assumed to be faced with

more or less the same decision criteria. This is a program logic that plays
well in political circles but is poorly fashioned to handle real-world contingencies and the unanticipated behavioral outcomes they produce.[4] Gary
Becker, the economist most readily identified with the conceptualization
of fertility as a function of rational choice, recognized that the choice sets
available to individuals are also subject to preferences and tastes, which are
transmitted by ethnic groups, classes, and families.[5] Differing sex ratios and
marriage market conditions across racial groups, as we have seen, can exert
a substantial influence on the decision to bear children outside of marriage.

In figure 8.1.b, three "contingencies," which social scientists have identified as critical to a more thorough understanding of nonmarital births while
on welfare, are made explicit, namely, the racial composition of the welfare
caseload, the racial concentration of welfare recipients in communities, and
Medicaid funding for abortion. Our interest here, however, is not in any independent effects these factors may exert on the preference for a birth but in
their capacity to moderate or condition the impact of a Family Cap on the
birth decision.[6] In chapter 6, I briefly discussed the possible role that moderating variables might play in the conflicting research findings around the
relationship between welfare generosity, on the one hand, and births and especially abortions, on the other. Our findings of a Family Cap effect in New
Jersey could also be subject to a set of limiting conditions, particularly those

(B)

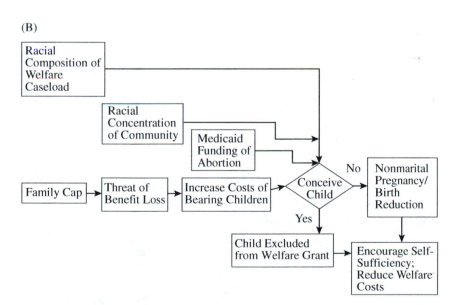

Figure 8.1.b. Family Cap Program Impact Theory: Social Science Informed
           Conception

shown in figure 8.1.b, which work synergistically with the Family Cap to focus its potency.

Notwithstanding the fact that a Family Cap has been adopted by more than half of the states in the nation, there are some very good reasons to conjecture that the policy will not work in all states as it has in New Jersey. If, for example, Joe Soss and his colleagues,[7] Richard Fording,[8] and other political scientists are correct in their assessments of the Family Cap (and welfare reform, in general) as a population control mechanism aimed at minorities, especially blacks, such policies would be expected to be more effectively implemented in states where the welfare population is predominately minority and mostly black. New Jersey fits this profile; Massachusetts, another Family Cap state, does not. Additionally, if Charles Murray's notion of a contravening culture, operating in concentrations of poor, minority women, is to be believed,[9] then any Family Cap effects would be expected to be dampened or weakened to the point of nonsignificance in states where the minorities compose a majority of the caseload and most of these individuals live in high-density, underclass locations. As we have seen, the Family Cap in New Jersey has minimal impact on chronic welfare cases, larger proportions of whom reside in the impoverished urban centers of Essex (Newark), Camden (Camden City), and Hudson (Jersey City) counties. Following Murray, to the extent these centers concentrate poor blacks with long-term welfare histories, the Family Cap effect would be anticipated to diminish to zero. It follows, then, that states that do not have minority welfare populations concentrated in very large cities, for example, Delaware or Tennessee, could experience larger Family Cap fertility effects than states that do.

The third contingency shown in figure 8.1.b, Medicaid funding for abortion, provides women on welfare with access to a technology that, in turn, could influence their decision to bring a pregnancy to term. Akerlof's Technological Shock explanation for nonmarital births asserts that abortion availability lowers the cost of abortion relative to the costs of childbearing for both women and their male partners.[10] A similar point has been made by Phillip Levine and Douglas Staiger.[11] Faced with a Family Cap—which further increases the cost of a birth—New Jersey's funding of abortion by Medicaid could encourage women to increase risky sexual behavior leading to more abortions and smaller reductions in nonmarital births. States like Arkansas and Wisconsin, which have adopted Family Caps but do not provide Medicaid funding for abortions, would not be expected to experience a Cap effect on births if virtually all of the decline in births is due to the availability of a low-cost abortion option.

The specification of moderators in figure 8.1.b does not so much weaken the experimental evidence of a Family Cap impact in New Jersey as it does, to use Mervyn Susser's term, "qualify"[12] the finding. Moderators are variables that precede the random assignment of recipients to treatment and therefore do not technically bias average treatment or intention-to-treat effects.[13] In essence, if racial composition, racial concentration, Medicaid funding for abortion, and length of time on welfare (not shown in the figure) are true moderators of Family Cap fertility effects, they simply stipulate the conditions under which the policy is most likely to succeed or fail. Moderator analysis, or exogenously defined subgroup analysis as it has been termed in the social experiment literature,[14] can provide unbiased estimates of "the effect of the treatment on the treated,"[15] an important research subject if one believes the treatment effect is influenced by welfare population heterogeneity.

In both the social experiment and pre-post analysis of the welfare caseload the extent of our moderator investigation was limited to subgroup analyses of new and ongoing case types. The expectation that any Family Cap impact could vary by the recipients' prior welfare spell lengths was built into the very architecture of the research design. Uncovering differences in Family Cap effect between the two groups had important programming implications and was politically innocuous. With respect to the three possible Family Cap modifiers presented in figure 8.1.b, however, our reports were largely silent.

Any discussion on our part of the moderating effect of Medicaid funding for abortion on the Family Cap-birth (or abortion) relationship was limited to pure conjecture. As Hubert Blalock pointed out many years ago, to empirically test an interaction X_1 (Family Cap) and X_2 (Medicaid funding) must be both present *and* absent for some segment of the population under study.[16] In New Jersey, Medicaid funding for abortion had been made available to all welfare recipients without any interruption in coverage since 1977; said differently, we had no variation in X_2. Nor could we bolster our suspicions, and those of many religious conservatives, of an X_1X_2 interactive effect by citing the research on cross-state comparisons. While a number of these studies had examined the influence of a Family Cap as an independent influence on fertility behavior, none had included Medicaid as a potential moderating factor.

With respect to racial composition and concentration effects we could have said a good deal more in our final reports to the state and federal governments but instead opted to limit our analyses to simple descriptive displays and appendix materials. The decision was a strategic one, which is an artful way of characterizing our concern about how the New Jersey Department of Human Services (NJDHS) would view any analyses that tilted away from an evaluation of average treatment effects toward racial disparities in Family Cap response. Although we were never directed to limit such analyses, I believe caution, indeed solicitude, was warranted given a project history of report embargoes, gag orders, paid experts, and the calls for seemingly endless edits and demurrer statements. In the eyes of the New Jersey politicians and policymakers who steadfastly supported the Family Cap, the evaluation team had become a source of ammunition for media criticism, litigation, and legislative challenges. Research that highlighted racial differences in Family Cap impact could only exacerbate what seemed to be an ever-growing adversarial relationship, possibly resulting in even more report-release delays, embargoes, and gag orders. Moreover, since we had always viewed our final reports more as launching points for further analyses than as the definitive, final word, and inasmuch as our racial analyses were still more suggestive than conclusive when we issued these reports, delaying the chronicling of racial moderator effects was a prudent course of action at the time.

It was clear, however, even from our descriptive data that black, white, and Hispanic women, who composed approximately 51, 16, and 33 percent of the New Jersey caseload in any given study year, were not exhibiting anything like an egalitarian response to the Cap. Some of the media, those diligent enough to read through report appendix charts and graphs, picked up on this subtext. A report in the *Boston Globe* reported that the Rutgers Study "suggests that black women have been more affected by the law than other racial groups. Abortions among black women on welfare exceeded births from March 1993 until at least September of 1996, while the abortion rate for white and Hispanic women increased only slightly."[17] The apparent racial disparities in response to the policy were not lost on the attorneys representing the plaintiffs in *Sojourner A. v. NJDHS* either. In December 1998, I was deposed by lawyers from the National Organization of Women (NOW) Legal Defense and Education Fund and the American Civil Liberties Union (ACLU) who were seeking clarification regarding analyses and findings in our final reports. This exchange between Sherry Leiwant, an attorney with NOW, and myself illustrate both the plaintiffs' interest in race effects and our reasoning for their elision:

LEIWANT: Let me ask you a little bit about the racial data in the reports. In terms of birth rates and abortion rates, did you look separately at how the Cap or FDP was impacting African-American women?

CAMASSO: Not separately, no. In some of the drafts we did some work but in the final reports we did not. They [racial variables] are used as control variables for compositional effects.

LEIWANT: I see. Why is it in the originals and not in the final?

CAMASSO: We went in that direction, in fact, we went in a number of directions to take a look at these effects, but I think once we did the pre-post, to get our focus straight on the treatment itself, we used these as compositional variables. It didn't mean they're not important variables and there could be other effects, it's just that we tried to keep our focus clearly on the overall impact of the Family Cap because that question was asked over and over and that's what we try to answer here [in our reports].

LEIWANT: Did anybody suggest to you that it's something that you could . . . you didn't have to do, that if you were going to eliminate something, you might as well eliminate that?

CAMASSO: No, and we wouldn't . . . even if somebody suggested that we wouldn't do it.[18]

With our reports released and an agreement between NJDHS and the University memorializing our publication rights, we began work on Family Cap moderators in earnest.

Testing for Racial Synergies

Although the racial analyses in our final reports was limited to controlling for compositional effects, the independent influence of these variables always proved to be significant. In the social experiment, for example, the marginal effect for black, new case, women was about 6 per 1,000 observations for births and nearly 9 per 1,000 for abortions.[19] In the pre-post these marginal effects for births and abortions were 4 and 10 per 1,000 for black women in the caseload.[20] No matter what statistical model specification we employed black women on the New Jersey welfare rolls exhibited higher birth and abortion rates than white women and therefore higher rates of pregnancy.

In table 8.1 I provide a description of the social experiment's new and ongoing case samples by experimental status for white, black, and Hispanic women. The most dramatic racial difference outlined in the table is marital status. Over three-quarters of the new case black women had never been married, compared with about 42 percent of white women and 52 percent of Hispanic women. Hispanic women were the least likely to have reported working or to have completed high school.

Using address and zip code data reported in the welfare data system, it was determined that women of different races were typically residing in communities with differing socioeconomic structures. The family income in areas where most white women on welfare lived averaged $40,012, whereas the family incomes where most black women and Hispanic women resided averaged $32,405 and $30,254, respectively. Moreover, the average percentage of white families who lived below the poverty level in predominately white areas was 5.2; this percentage was three times higher for black and Hispanic families who lived in predominately black and Hispanic areas. Because the differences in racial/ethnic densities in geographic areas mirror socioeconomic differences, inferences about racial concentration must take into consideration the potentially confounding influences of economic opportunity.

The analytic methods used to test for the moderating influence of race for women in the social experiment closely parallel those discussed in chapter 7. The pooled analyses included observations of women while they were active on the New Jersey welfare for the 17 quarters between September 1992 through December 1996. Here, however, Poisson regression is used instead of linear probability model (LPM), logit or probit. Poisson regression with multi-period data (i.e., observations in person quarters), while not yielding estimates of Family Cap impact very different from these other procedures, takes right-censoring of observations into account in the same manner that

Table 8.1. Sample Characteristics by Race, Experimental Status, and Case Type

Characteristic	Whites		Blacks		Hispanics	
	Experimental	Control	Experimental	Control	Experimental	Control
New Cases						
Percentage						
Education						
Less than high school	34.02	32.33	28.74	28.33	34.81	34.75
High school graduate	48.17	45.11	52.28	50.76	34.05	33.90
Some college	10.73	16.17	15.73	17.87	9.92	9.60
Other	0.23	0.75	0.54	1.14	0.15	0.28
Marital status						
Never married	41.82	34.57	73.82	74.40	52.01	51.10
Married	23.86	26.77	5.66	3.53	15.95	13.46
Widowed	0.45	0.37	0.64	0.37	0.60	0.55
Separated/divorced	33.87	38.29	19.88	21.70	31.44	34.89
Employed	21.36	23.79	19.87	21.15	17.59	15.11
Mean (Standard deviation)						
Age	31.26 (7.49)	32.22 (8.47)	30.33 (8.57)	30.27 (8.02)	31.74 (9.24)	31.48 (8.92)
Number of eligible children	1.72 (1.01)	1.67 (0.89)	1.59 (0.96)	1.74 (0.96)	1.73 (1.00)	1.82 (1.05)
Earned income averaged over entire sample	176.76 (390.61)	193.82 (390.90)	207.02 (391.96)	206.14 (412.98)	164.80 (326.17)	151.25 (314.81)
Those working	827.39 (526.15)	814.66 (528.49)	1041.8 (564.37)	974.63 (545.57)	937.15 (422.40)	1001.00 (426.21)
Number of cases	440	269	936	539	671	364

Ongoing Cases

Percentage

Education						
Less than high school	36.83	37.85	42.42	41.65	37.45	38.72
High school graduate	48.61	44.22	43.75	43.64	28.61	26.99
Some college	7.49	7.97	9.72	9.98	8.75	9.73
Other	0.64	1.59	0.44	0.75	0.86	0.22
Marital status						
Never married	44.77	45.24	77.40	80.74	53.38	56.10
Married	17.57	13.89	3.67	3.59	7.97	7.49
Widowed	0.84	1.19	0.92	1.08	1.11	0.21
Separated/divorced	36.82	39.68	18.01	14.59	37.54	36.20
Employed	21.55	23.02	17.17	16.75	17.15	15.85

Mean (Standard deviation)

Age	34.02 (7.25)	34.54 (8.29)	32.39 (8.05)	32.72 (8.23)	34.73 (8.74)	35.14 (9.46)
Number of eligible children	1.65 (0.94)	1.90 (1.08)	1.88 (1.22)	1.98 (1.20)	1.85 (1.14)	1.90 (1.06)
Earned income averaged over						
Entire sample	191.32 (432.29)	187.25 (413.95)	152.79 (336.03)	162.12 (373.01)	156.74 (331.49)	143.59 (317.01)
Those working	887.86 (594.08)	813.59 (544.04)	890.11 (431.44)	968.08 (428.10)	914.17 (409.53)	906.15 (422.79)
Number of cases	478	252	1,637	836	1,079	467

The totals by race/ethnicity differ slightly from the total ongoing cases shown because of missing values for the race/ethnicity variable or because the cases were coded as "Other" race/ethnicity.

a discrete-time hazard model does.[21] The regression coefficients (B) for any significant Family Cap treatment effect can readily be converted into a marginal effect by calculating $e^{(B)}$ at (X-bar), where $e^{(B)}$ can be interpreted as an incidence rate ratio and X-bar is the overall rate for the fertility outcome of interest. To convert this incidence rate into a percentage Blossfeld and his colleagues suggest the formula $(e^B - 1) * 100$.[22] This is the same statistical method I used in the unbundling analysis.

In table 8.2, I show the regression results for the Family Cap effect on births separately for white, black, and Hispanic women. Panel A of the table

Table 8.2.   Family Cap Effect on Births—Poisson Regression Results

	Whites	Blacks	Hispanics
(A) Ongoing Cases			
Regressor	Coefficient (SE)	Coefficient (SE)	Coefficient (SE)
Family Cap	−0.1894	−0.0442	0.0715
	(0.2115)	(0.0886)	(0.135)
Time	−0.0575	−0.0405*	−0.0486
	(0.0373)	(0.0173)	(0.0324)
Constant	−1.8074	−0.5056	−0.1323
	(1.9519)	(0.8221)	(1.3534)
Number of observations	5839	24209	13830
(B) New Cases			
Regressor	Whites Coefficient (SE)	Blacks Coefficient (SE)	Hispanics Coefficient (SE)
Family Cap	0.0931	−0.2325*	−0.1226
	(0.1839)	(0.0918)	(0.1410)
Time	−0.0463	−0.0651*	−0.1143*
	(0.0323)	(0.019)	(0.0200)
Constant	−2.2422	−3.1234*	−2.7555
	(1.8422)	(1.0432)	(0.1445)
Number of observations	3657	10073	6111

Number of observations are given in person-quarters. Robust, Huber-corrected standard errors are reported. All regressions include age, marital status, education, number of children, county fixed effects, county employment rate, and JOBS program participation rate.

Inasmuch as the Family Cap * Time interaction was not significant in these birth models, the regressions were re-estimated without the term. *p < .05.

gives the coefficients (standard errors) for the ongoing case sample while panel B does the same for new cases. Only the coefficients for Family Cap and time are shown in the table; coefficients for the control variables (the identical set used in the analyses presented in chapter 7) are not included for the sake of brevity. The interaction term (Family Cap×Time), meant to capture any differences in the time path over which the policy might unfold was not statistically significant and these models were reestimated without this interaction. Time is measured as elapsed time (number of quarters) since a recipient's assignment to the experiment.

Rather than present the moderating effect of racial composition on the Family Cap—fertility relationship as a multiplicative term in the regression models (e.g., using a white×Family Cap or black×Family Cap term), as it is usually done, I examine the racial influence in a separate (race-specific) regression context. I have sacrificed some statistical power here for, what I believe, is a certain clarity in the presentation of marginal effects. To test for significant differences in the treatment coefficients between groups I conduct simple z-tests.[23]

Panel A of table 8.2 shows that the Family Cap does not exert a statistically significant impact on any racial group in the ongoing case sample. For new cases, however, we see that the black birthrate is 21 percent, that is, $((e^{-.2325}-1)*100)$ lower in the experimental group while there isn't any Family Cap effect for whites and Hispanics. When z-tests are used to determine if the difference between black women, on the one hand, and whites and Hispanics, on the other, is significant across regressions, I find that they are.

To determine if any racial differences in Family Cap impact are not due simply to composition but to racial concentration as is contended in the contravening culture literature, Radha Jagannathan and I estimated 18 separate regression models in an article that appears in the *Journal of Marriage and Family* that were both race and racial density specific.[24] Once again, z tests are used to determine the significance of any between community differences. I summarize the results for both the within- and between-community differences in treatment and control birthrates in table 8.3.[25] Panels A and C of the table show that there aren't any significant within- or between-community treatment effects for white and Hispanic women. For black women, classified as new cases, however, we see that the Family Cap has a birth impact only when these women reside in predominately nonblack residential areas. When I compare this Family Cap effect with that estimated for black women who reside in predominately black residential areas I find the z test for between-community difference to be statistically significant. The results in table 8.3 suggest that the moderating effect of racial density may not simply be a reflection of socioeconomic difference. If this was indeed the case we would expect to see little difference in the response of black and Hispanic women to the Family Cap, conditioned on racial density.

In table 8.4, I present the results from the race-specific regression models for Family Cap impact on abortions. We can see from panel A that the only

Table 8.3.   Family Cap Effect on Births for Racial Groups Based
on Residence (n)

(A) Whites		
	Ongoing	*New*
(1) Residence in predominantly White community	ns (1,410)	ns (702)
(2) Residence in predominantly non-White community	ns (4,630)	ns (3,116)
(3) Z-test for between-community difference (1)–(2)	ns	ns

(B) Blacks		
	Ongoing	*New*
(1) Residence in predominantly Black community	ns (15,885)	ns (5,847)
(2) Residence in predominantly non-Black community	ns (9,418)	* (4,621)
(3) Z-test for between-community difference (1)–(2)	ns	*

(C) Hispanics		
	Ongoing	*New*
(1) Residence in predominantly Hispanic community	ns (5,271)	ns (2,201)
(2) Residence in predominantly non-Hispanic community	ns (9,148)	ns (4,152)
(3) Z-test for between-community difference (1)–(2)	ns	ns

Full regression includes covariates on age, education, marital status, number of children, county fixed effects, county employment rate, and JOBS program participation rate. Observations are in parentheses. $p < .05$.

statistically significant effect is the Family Cap×Time interaction for Hispanics. Abortions appear to have declined initially in the treatment group but over time this effect turns positive and contributes to an overall slightly lower abortion rate among Hispanics in the ongoing case sample (2.9%). In panel B, the new case sample, both black and Hispanic women in the treatment group experience significant Family Cap impacts. For black women, the Family Cap increases abortions by about 32 percent ($(e^{.279} - 1) * 100$), for Hispanic women the effect is 50 percent ($(e^{.403} - 1) * 100$) higher than among controls. The z tests reveal statistically significant intergroup difference in their abortion response to the Family Cap.

Table 8.4.   Family Cap Effect on Abortions—Poisson Regression Results

(A) Ongoing Cases

	Whites	Blacks	Hispanics
Regressor	Coefficient (SE)	Coefficient (SE)	Coefficient (SE)
Family Cap	−0.0320 (0.2597)	−0.0067 (0.0869)	−0.1791 (0.3105)
Time	−0.0176 (0.0443)	−0.0633* (0.0176)	−0.0669† (0.0403)
Family Cap * time	See note	See note	0.0566† (0.0333)
Constant	−2.763 (2.4665)	0.3157 (0.7715)	−0.3087 (1.4323)
Number of observations	5,839	24,209	13,830

(B) New Cases

	Whites	Blacks	Hispanics
Regressor	Coefficient (SE)	Coefficient (SE)	Coefficient (SE)
Family Cap	0.0963 (0.2360)	0.2796* (0.1076)	0.4032* (0.1873)
Time	0.0118 (0.0497)	0.0212 (0.0181)	−0.0312 (0.0382)
Constant	−3.9890 (0.1890)	−3.4589 (0.0902)	−4.1029 (0.1601)
Number of observations	3,657	10,073.0	6,111.0

Number of observations are given in person-quarters. Robust, Huber-corrected standard errors are reported. All regressions include age, marital status, education, number of children, county fixed effects, county employment rate, and JOBS program participation rate. Observations are in parentheses.

Inasmuch as the Family Cap * Time interaction term was not significant in five out the six abortion models (the exception is for Ongoing Case Hispanics) the regressions were re-estimated without the term. †$p<.10$, *$p<.05$.

In table 8.5 I summarize the Family Cap effects on births and abortions and present these effects both as a percentage change calculated from the Poisson regressions and the actual change in the mean rate that is implied by the percentages, that is, the marginal effect. The mean outcome rate presented here is that of the control group; this is the rate that would have been observed in the absence of the Family Cap. In panel A, the overall effects of the Family Cap are too small in any racial group to result in a substantial

Table 8.5. Family Cap Effects as Estimated Increase (Decrease) in the Rate of Fertility Events and as a Percentage Increase (Decrease) of the Control Group Rate

(A) Ongoing Cases

Outcome	Whites			Blacks			Hispanics		
	Mean per 1,000 obs	% Change	Estimated Change per 1,000 obs	Mean per 1,000 obs	% Change	Estimated Change per 1,000 obs	Mean per 1,000 obs	% Change	Estimated Change per 1,000 obs
Births	19.00	−17.0	−3.2	24.00	−4.3	−1.0	17.00	7.4	1.3
Abortions	16.00	−3.1	−0.5	38.00	−0.01	−0.3	18.00	−16.4	−2.9

(B) New Cases

Outcome	Whites			Blacks			Hispanics		
	Mean per 1,000 obs	% Change	Estimated Change per 1,000 obs	Mean per 1,000 obs	% Change	Estimated Change per 1,000 obs	Mean per 1,000 obs	% Change	Estimated Change per 1,000 obs
Births	29.00	9.8	2.8	42.00	−21.00	−8.80*	34.00	−11.5	−3.9
Abortions	19.00	10.1	1.9	31.00	32.00	9.90*	17.00	50.00	8.50*

*p < .05.

change of either birth or abortion rates over the experimental period. In the new case sample, the 21 percent decline in births and 32 percent increase in abortions yield marginal effects of 8.8 (per 1,000 observations) fewer births and 9.9 (per 1,000 observations) more abortions among black women over the evaluation period. For Hispanic women the 50 percent change in abortions found in the Family Cap group yields a marginal effect of 8.5 more abortions (per 1,000 observations).

In these tests of a racial moderator, the experimental evidence indicates that the New Jersey Family Cap effect on both birth and abortion decisions is conditioned by a women's racial/ethnic status. Both the racial composition of the caseload and the racial concentration of recipients (of color) appear to influence the policy's impact. However, as was the case in the original average treatment effect analyses, only new cases are affected in these moderator analyses.

While white women, no matter their new or ongoing case status, did not have a significant birth or abortion response to the Family Cap, length of welfare dependency implied in new or ongoing case status did matter for minority women. It was only new case black women who responded to the Family Cap with lower birthrates and higher abortion rates and it was only new case Hispanic women who had more abortions. For both groups this would appear to indicate that the Family Cap has not done a very good job in limiting pregnancies.

While these findings provide strong evidence for the moderating influence of race, the overall patterning of results does not fit neatly within any one of the theoretical frameworks I discussed in chapter 3. If, for example, racism and the population control mechanism suggested by the explanation were the driving forces behind the Family Cap why do ongoing, black and Hispanic women escape the policy's influence so remarkably well? Such women, with their more established dependence on welfare, would be expected to be the primary targets of a Family Cap implemented solely by means of prejudice or statistical discrimination. Of course, the data indicate something quite different.

As I have discussed earlier, women in the new and ongoing case samples differ not just in their welfare use and dependence but on a number of demographic factors. As shown in table 8.1, these differences can be found in each racial/ethnic group with black women demonstrating some of the largest cross-sample dissimilarities. Most striking, perhaps is the large difference in education between black ongoing and black new case women—a difference not as nearly pronounced in the white or Hispanic samples. Whereas about 28 percent of black women who were new cases had not completed high school, 42 percent of those in the ongoing case sample had not graduated. For white women this difference was about 4 percent and for Hispanic women only 3 percent. This large education difference among black women could indicate that new case women have a higher market value for their time and are more responsive to a Family Cap as these women substitute the enhancement of employment skills for childbearing. Such behavior would seem to fall in line with opportunity structure explanations like that proposed by William J. Wilson, with the racial concentration effects further bolstering this argument.[26] After all, black women residing in higher income, predominately white communities are less likely to be isolated in job-poor environments.

Before attributing the Family Cap effect to the moderating influence of divergent opportunity structures masquerading as racial differences, it is useful to reprise some of the basic tenets of this theory. First of all, its advocates tend to heavily discount the influence that welfare benefit levels can have on fertility behavior. Recall the statement circulated by the Center on Budget and Policy Priorities.[27] There is also the premise that racial/ethnic differences can be explained away by class difference, an idea that has gained great currency in the social science community at least since Wilson published his book *The Declining Significance of Race* in 1978.[28] And then there is the considerable mismatch between the theory's prediction and the evaluation results. Setting aside the fact that the Family Cap has an effect on fertility, there is the ostensive anomaly that black women—but not white or Hispanic women—living in predominately white communities, are affected. If the Family Cap impact is conditional on life chances or economic class, the behavior of women on welfare regardless of race should be influenced by this policy. Obversely, if the opportunity costs are different for different racial groups on welfare in more affluent (or more impoverished) areas the economic opportunity conceptualization leaves us wondering why.

A somewhat more persuasive explanation for the data can be found in the work on contravening culture advanced by Charles Murray and others.[29] The finding that the Family Cap birth effect is confined to black women living in predominately white areas is expected as are the results that show that racial concentration is not a factor in white and Hispanic fertility decisions. For Murray what distinguishes these racial responses is not different opportunity structures but cultural differences in the acceptability of nonmarital births and of welfare as a tolerable vehicle for raising children. Murray singles out high-density black neighborhoods as purveyors of nonmainstream proximate culture, a culture not present to the same extent in poor white (and Hispanic) concentrations. It follows then that black women on welfare who are able to extricate themselves from this countervailing culture would be more likely to adopt values common to the larger society, and these would include the norms promulgated by the Family Cap. Where the countervailing culture explanation comes up very short is in the fertility responses of white women. Inasmuch as these women remain linked to the larger culture, regardless of the racial concentration in which they reside, the Family Cap would be expected to exert its most consistent influence here. Neither our experimental nor pre-post data bear this prediction out.

There are some results from this examination of racial composition and racial concentration modifiers that also suggest that the Family Cap impact on fertility is subject to more than just cultural preferences or economic opportunities. As I have noted, the findings for black and Hispanic women of abortion rate increases that are greater than birth reductions imply that pregnancies increased. Although the 1115 waiver guidance is vague on the subject it is clear from the Personal Responsibility and Work Opportunity Reconciliation Act (PRWORA) legislation that Family Caps were designed to reduce births *without* increasing the abortion rate, anticipating that conceptions and pregnancies would decline through abstinence and better contraception use.[30] In fact, the original legislation offered a $20 million "Illegitimacy Bonus" to states that had the largest declines in the illegitimacy ratio coupled with an abortion to live birth ratio that was lower than 1995 levels.[31]

This rise in pregnancies in an environment of child exclusion would, at first blush, look to be a grand exercise in irrational behavior. This might perhaps be true if it were not for a safety mechanism operating in New Jersey (and some other states) that makes abortion accessible to welfare recipients without restriction. The Akerlof model predicts that lower-cost abortion availability could be expected to increase a woman's willingness to engage in sexual activity without the prospect of marriage while lowering the financial and psychological barriers of many women to an abortion.[32] The results of lower cost abortion, then, are increased pregnancies, increased abortions and an uncertain impact on nonmarital births. Akerlof and his colleagues paint scenarios where nonmarital births may decrease slightly, not at all, or could in fact increase depending upon the proportions of women who feel the barriers to abortion have been lowered sufficiently. This variation in nonmarital birth response was actually observed in the New Jersey experiment with increased abortions yielding lower birthrates for black women but not for Hispanic women. The difference may be more a function of differences in unwanted pregnancies rather than any differences in stigma thresholds between these two groups. In a low-cost abortion environment, the Family Cap—a policy never designed to thwart pregnancies—could be anticipated to further decrease both the financial and psychic cost of an abortion relative to a birth. This may be especially true for poor black women who, despite strong religious beliefs, face a highly unfavorable marriage market.[33]

This interplay between Medicaid, race, and the Family Cap in exacerbating an abortion dynamic without fully addressing nonmarital births is, of course, a conjecture from the New Jersey data. Since all women, whether treatment or control, pre– or post–Family Cap, were exposed to Medicaid reimbursement, empirical estimates of any Medicaid moderator effect cannot be educed. To test this kind of moderator relationship fertility rates (or choices) must be tracked over time as both Medicaid and Family Cap policies change, subjecting individuals within or across areas to differing policy mixes. Using a national database that facilitates such cross-area comparisons I explore if, indeed, the Family Cap effects observed in New Jersey can be explained by the complex interaction of race, low-cost abortion, and child exclusion.

The Inadvertent Policy Mix

A very common strategy in policy research when experimental data are limited or unavailable is to exploit so-called natural experiments. As Bruce Meyer notes, the term inappropriately suggests that such studies are experiments and moreover that they are spontaneous.[34] Natural experiments, also referred to as observational studies[35] and quasi-experimental designs,[36] like controlled experiments, attempt to determine if a policy, program, or treatment causes some behavior but unlike experiments, do not establish a counterfactual condition through random assignment of subjects. Instead subjects are sorted "naturally" into treatment or comparison groups through such ostensibly exogenous sources of variation as natural disasters, macroeconomic and demographic dislocations, and political processes. A widely cited example of a natural experiment is the cross-state comparison of different minimum wage levels on the employment of low-income workers conducted by David Card and Alan Krueger.[37] Federal legislation has given states considerable discretion in setting a minimum wage level for their workforce so long as this level does not dip below the federal standard. A transparent source of exogenous variation emerges as states do their own thing, some choosing the federal standard, others opting to be more generous.

How close natural experiment estimators of treatment effect approximate controlled experiment estimators depends on the extent to which the source of variation in the policy, program, or other treatment type is truly exogenous. In the minimum wage research, for example, if the states that choose to fund a higher minimum wage than the federal requirement are also the states that have relatively high demand for low-income workers to begin with, then outcomes like unemployment rates for poor workers may have more to do with the structure of the low-wage market in a state than the minimum wage level. As I have written elsewhere, the strength of the impact evidence found in observational studies is contingent on how clear the assignment rules are, the extent to which these rules are correlated with the outcome of interest in the absence of any actual treatment and, of equal importance, if the selection process itself can be modeled and a counterfactual inference made.[38] Treatment estimates obtained from observational studies and quasi-experimental designs may or may not approximate those secured through random assignment experiments. For example, in studies of supported work demonstrations by Robert Lalonde and welfare-to-work programs by Daniel Friedlander and Philip Robins, a variety of nonrandom comparison groups constructed from readily available national samples, statistical matching, or cross-state program data provides earnings and employment impacts that can be far different from available experimental data.[39] Comparative studies like those conducted by Lalonde and Friedlander and Robins have divided economists and other policy researchers into those who view experiments as the only way to cut through what they see as the fog engendered by econometric specification testing and those who claim this to be so much hyperbole.[40] Of course, in the absence of more blended designs this debate is most likely to continue indefinitely.

Most of the research conducted on the fertility impacts of a Family Cap has been observational studies using state policy difference as their source of exogenous variation. This is to be expected given the dearth of experiments on a subject of considerable interest to politicians and policymakers. Researchers have taken advantage of existing data from vital statistics, Current Population Surveys (CPS), or from longitudinal surveys such as the Panel Study of Income Dynamics (PSID), the Survey of Income and Program Participation (SIPP), and the National Longitudinal Survey of Youth (NLSY) to construct balanced or unbalanced panels of welfare recipients and/or poor women, with or without time and state fixed effects.[41] It is also important to distinguish studies in this literature that directly measure an operating Family Cap from those that make inferences about Family Cap effects from state difference in welfare benefits levels or increments but that do not actually observe any implemented Family Caps. These latter studies require us to use our imagination and apply the behavioral lessons learned from the typically positive changes in welfare benefits to a policy that produces benefit decrements. Some of these studies, like those conducted by Laura Argys, Susan Averett, and Daniel Rees, by Philip Robins and Philip Fronstin, and by Elizabeth Powers, find enough evidence to suggest that if a Family Cap was implemented nonmarital births would be discouraged.[42] Others, by Jeff Grogger and Stephen Bronars, and Robert Fairlie and Rebecca London find such speculation to be unwarranted.[43]

Drawing conclusions about Family Cap impact from studies of Aid to Families with Dependent Children (AFDC) or Temporary Assistance for Needy Families (TANF) benefit levels or benefit changes is not as straightforward as some researchers make it appear. Benefit levels may be endogenous, that is, they may be the consequence of birth or abortion rates and not their cause. Benefit levels in states also tend to be highly correlated with marginal benefit levels in those same states, making it difficult to determine which component is truly driving any fertility effect. Cross-state comparisons are also subject to unobserved differences that may cause benefit levels and fertility to covary across states irrespective of any welfare policy changes.[44] The assumption of approximately constant unmeasured differences across states, if incorrect, could mask real differences in policies, family structure, or welfare recipient attitudes that might be correlated with other benefit levels and fertility behavior.[45]

Cross-state observational studies that actually examine an implemented Family Cap would appear to circumvent a number of these issues. Assuming for the moment that the endogeneity, simultaneity, and selection problems just described are obviated by a policy introduced deus ex machina, natural experiments often fall prey to errors of omission, the most common of which are omitted variables; that is, events, other than the policy of interest that provide alternative explanations for results and omitted interactions, that is, policies with effects that are conditioned by omitted or measured variables.[46] Bruce Meyer warns that the exclusion of these interactions is a common identifying assumption in the designs of too many natural experiments.[47]

Inasmuch as the results from several cross-state observational studies have been used by some think tanks and policy analysts to refute findings from the New Jersey experiment and blended design, the quality of this evidence deserves a careful review. I begin with the analysis undertaken by Wendy Dyer and Robert Fairlie of the Family Caps instituted in Arkansas, Georgia, Indiana, New Jersey, and Virginia.[48] These researchers use CPS data from 1989 to 1999 to examine the impact of Family Cap policies on birthrates of single, less-educated women with children, aged 15–45[49] and find negative but nonsignificant policy coefficients for New Jersey, Indiana, and Virginia and nonsignificant coefficients for Arkansas and Georgia. Notwithstanding the numerous model specification checks used by Dyer and Fairlie, the construction of the comparison group in this study is puzzling and could very well influence the findings. With a stated goal of focusing "on the effect of Family Cap policies implemented as waivers under the former AFDC programs" Dyer and Fairlie proceed to identify the comparison groups with "28 non-Family Cap states" a number of which actually instituted Family Cap, either under Section 1115 (Connecticut [1/96], Maryland [3/96], and Massachusetts [11/95]) or PRWORA (North Carolina, Oklahoma, South Carolina, Tennessee, and Idaho) sometime during the study period. The counterfactual also included states that never instituted a Family Cap.[50] If for the sake of argument we assume the Family Cap did have a modest fertility effect, it is quite possible that any treatment effect would be differenced-out, or at the very least would be attenuated, by a design that includes some Family Cap states as treatment cases and others as nontreatment cases.

A rather widely quoted study by Melissa Schettini-Kearney, which appears on a number of think tank Web pages, utilizes vital statistics to examine the Family Cap-birth relationship for all women aged 15–34.[51] Pooling data from 1989 to 1998 for all 50 states, Schettini-Kearney reports that there is no statistically significant evidence that Family Caps lower fertility in regression models estimated for all women, married women, and unmarried women that control for welfare benefit levels, time limit and work exemption policies, time and state fixed effects. Of course, one wouldn't expect to find strong negative Family Cap coefficients in analysis of all women aged 15–34 or married women since these groupings are not the focus of a Family Cap.

Schettini-Kearney does, however, find several statistically significant coefficients that suggest that Family Caps actually *increase* births to unmarried women. For example, Schettini-Kearney reports a significant, positive birth effect of the Family Cap for unmarried, black, high school dropouts aged 20 to 24. The author also finds significant, positive effects for black teens aged 15 to 19, for white, unmarried high school dropouts aged 20–24, and for all ages if the Family Cap indicator incorporates a 12-month lag. Throughout the discussion of her work, the author uses such expressions as "curiously statistically significant," "surprising findings," and "counter-intuitive" and remarks "these estimates stand in stark contrast to the find-ings of Camasso et al. in the case of New Jersey's Family Cap."[52] This latter observation is quite true.

Neeraj Kaushal and Robert Kaestner investigate the impact of a Family Cap on the birth decisions of a sample of "less educated, unmarried women" drawn from the CPS March 1995–1999 series.[53] To construct comparison groups these researchers draw samples of married women with high school or less education and unmarried women with an associate degree from the same CPS series. After warning that the efficacy of difference-in-difference[54] methodol-ogy depends critically on the appropriateness of the comparison groups, Kaushal and Kaestner appear to have serious misgivings about those that they selected. Although most of the fertility estimates they present are not statis-tically significant, the ones that are significant are always in the wrong direc-tion with women in non-Family Cap states exhibiting lower births and those on Family Cap states demonstrating higher fertility. Kaushal and Kaestner admit that the pattern of their results "counter almost all theory."[55]

Ted Joyce and his colleagues extend their cross-state comparison of Fam-ily Cap impact to include abortions as well as births and is the first study to do so.[56] Their use of within state comparison groups is also an important advance in methodological approach. Like Schettini-Kearney, this team of researchers restrict their analyses to women 15 to 34 but limit their sample to low-income, unmarried women. Birth information is gleaned from vital statistics while abortions information was obtained from state termination of pregnancy (ITOP) files with the help of the Alan Guttmacher Institute. Both the birth and abortion analyses were restricted to the 18 states that collected data from 1992 through 2000 on mother's age, race, marital status, completed schooling, parity, gestation age of the fetus, and year of abortion. The authors conclude that there has been no major reproductive response, that is, births or abortions, due to the Family Cap.

Joyce and his colleagues are a bit modest, however, when summarizing their results. Like Schettini-Kearney, Kaushal and Kaestner, and Dyer and Fairlie, they too find that the Family Cap has a statistically significant *pos-itive* relationship to births. This effect is present in the regression-adjusted analyses of the entire sample and in the separate regression-adjusted ana-lyses of white and black women. These investigators offer a number of rea-sons for what appears to be a commonplace, counterintuitive result in cross-state studies of the Family Cap but fail to mention an obvious one, namely, imprecise measurement of the Family Cap treatment. In an analysis lim-ited by the availability of data, Joyce et al. identify Family Cap treatment with seven relatively low-population, southern, and northwestern states: Arkansas, Idaho, Mississippi, North Carolina, North Dakota, South Carolina, and Virginia. If the Family Cap effect is confined to larger, industrial, northeastern or north-central states with generally more liberal social policy agendas, including Medicaid funding for abortions, that is, states like

New Jersey, Maryland, and Illinois, the conclusions drawn by Joyce and his colleagues could be quite different.

Not all of the cross-state comparisons of the Family Cap have led to counterintuitive findings. Ann Horvath-Rose and H. Elizabeth Peters, using vital statistics from 1984 through 1996, report declines in the nonmarital birth ratios for women aged 20–49 that are 9–12 percent lower in Family Cap states.[57] Traci Mach also finds a statistically significant negative impact of the Family Cap on births in the sample of women aged 18–44 drawn from the 1989–1998 March Supplement of the CPS.[58] When Mach performs separate analyses for welfare users and nonusers, she finds that the Family Cap effect is restricted to the former group where births declined by 10 percent.

Accounting for such incongruous findings has been a longstanding issue in the literature on welfare benefits and fertility. The studies conducted by Dyer and Fairlie, Joyce et al., Schettini-Kearney, and Kaushal and Kaestner employ samples of women, many of whom have never experienced public assistance and are unlikely to respond to a Family Cap. This lack of welfare participation data is often viewed as an inoculation against welfare caseload dynamics[59] but this protection can come at the cost of realism. As Mach points out, living in a state that has a Family Cap is not synonymous with being affected by a state's Family Cap. She provides this example of a third or higher parity birth in New Jersey: "Suppose that Mother A is currently receiving benefits while Mother B is not. If both mothers gave birth to an additional [third] child the maximum benefit available to Mother A is $424 because she conceived the child while receiving benefits while Mother B is eligible for the maximum benefit of $488."[60] Schettini-Kearney attempts to address this problem by applying zero marginal benefits to births six months (and twelve months) subsequent to a state's implementation of a Family Cap. Effects like this, while imaginative, can only provide a crude approximation of a woman's exposure to public welfare.

I believe a far more serious contribution to the mixed results in this research area is not simply the gradations of realism—as critical as these might be—but failures in articulating the policy context that could mean the difference between the policy's success and failure. Clear conceptualization and measurement of this "policy space" may not be essential in experiments where, as William Shadish, Thomas Cook, and Donald Campbell explain, the causal structure is less ambitious but its understanding is highly attainable.[61] In observational studies, where our manipulation of cause is more uncertain, we do not have the same luxury of neglect.

In their comments on the insignificant and surprising effects found in studies of welfare reform, Gregory Acs, Katherin Phillips, and Sandi Nelson point to the importance of the larger welfare reform climate containing bundles of separate policies.[62] They warn that welfare recipients may change their behavior in response to a synergy among these components and not to a specific initiative. Most of the studies I have reviewed here do control for time limits[63] but counterintuitive, that is, wrong sign, regression coefficients, very often a diagnostic for omitted variable bias, indicate this might be insufficient. The exception here is the research of Horvath-Rose and Peters who model seven additional welfare waivers including time limits, modified work, strengthened child support, and expanded income disregards. What sets this study apart, however, is that Horvath-Rose and Peters are alone in attempting to control for state abortion policy when examining the Family Cap-fertility relationship.

Some National Evidence

In an effort to better understand why the evidence of Family Cap impact in New Jersey runs counter to so much of what has been found in cross-state comparisons, I conducted an observational study that tests explicitly for the racial and Medicaid conditioning of the policy. The study differs from the previous state level research described in this chapter in three significant ways. First, the scope of the examination is broader than anything else done to date and includes observations on all states and the District of Columbia from 1980 through 2000. Second, multiple measures of fertility are used including the nonmarital birthrate, illegitimacy ratio, abortion rate, abortion to birth ratio, and the general fertility rate. This last measure especially is viewed here as a nonequivalent outcome variable that one would not expect to change as significantly as the others because of a welfare reform intervention.[64] In this respect it serves as a type of counterfactual check. Last, the econometric modeling is conceptually guided, drawing upon the five theoretical frameworks reviewed in chapter 3.

To aid the reader in navigating the statistical analyses that follow, I provide a typology of states that, I believe, captures the principal ideological anchoring points employed by political stakeholders to explain why a Family Cap can or cannot work (figure 8.2). This typology differs from other taxonomies in the welfare reform literature where the goal appears to be the conceptual or empirical classification of states on such dimensions as policy flexibility, stringency, or complexity.[63] The "Lesser of Two Evils" typology, as I term it, in figure 8.2, and its extension to racial difference, links policy to expected outcome. Since the ideological positions depicted in the typology dovetail with particular economic or sociological theories of personal choice, the empirical tests of relative effectiveness also help to shed light on the accuracy of competing theoretical predictions.

For states like New Jersey, Illinois, Maryland, and Massachusetts, the implementation of a Family Cap in a welfare policy environment where Medicaid is used to pay for the abortions of poor women, virtually without restriction (medically necessary abortions), clearly signals an interest in the reduction of illegitimacy by all available means. Proponents of a Family cap conditioned on readily available abortions, as we have seen, are an odd alliance of neoconservatives (William Kristol), conservative pragmatists

Figure 8.2.   Reproductive Policies for Women on Welfare within the
"Lesser of Two Evils" Typology

		Family Cap	
		Yes	*No*
Medicaid Funding for Medically Necessary Abortions	Yes	Illegitimacy Evil Paramount Policy Mechanisms: Family Cap, penalty, abortion, contraception States: New Jersey, Illinois, Maryland, Massachusetts, and three others Proponents: Libertarians, neo-conservatives, realists on the political left	No Evils Policy Mechanisms: employment, child support, child care, abortion States: Minnesota, New York, Oregon, Washington, and ten others Proponents: welfare rights advocates, reproductive rights advocates, unrepentant liberals
	No	Illegitimacy and Abortoin as Twin Evils Policy Mechanisms: Family Cap, penalty, abstinence, contraception, personal responsibility States: Arkansas, Florida, Georgia, Virginia, and twelve others Proponents: morality legislators, welfare residualists	Abortion Evil Paramount Policy Mechanisms: abstinence, child support, child care States: Michigan, Ohio, Pennsylvania, Texas, and fifteen others Proponents: conservative Christians, pro-lifers

(Newt Gingrich), and libertarians (Charles Murray), and liberal realists like New Jersey's Wayne Bryant who view abortion as just another choice.[66] The fact that virtually all the governments that have adopted this policy configuration are inveterate blue states indicates that supporters from the political left may actually be in the majority here.

Most states that have adopted a Family Cap, however, have done so without countenancing a role for abortion. Labeled "morality legislators" and welfare residualists by their detractors,[67] legislators in Family Cap, restrictive Medicaid funding states follow the lead of national policymakers (Phil Gramm, Dick Armey) and policy analysts (Gary Bauer) who view illegitimacy and abortion as dual signs of moral decay.[68] From this perspective a Family Cap by itself possesses sufficient capacity to promote individual responsibility. Nearly all of the state legislatures that have implemented a Family Cap with limited Medicaid funding for abortion can be classified as southern blue states.[69]

Both groups of Family Cap states embrace positions on nonmarital births that are consistent with rational utility theory. Increasing the cost of bearing and raising a child (or children) would be expected to reduce pregnancies and, consequently, births. For those Family Cap supporters, however, who do not have faith that pregnancy reduction alone will reduce births sufficiently, low-cost abortion provides the woman with another decision point to do the "responsible thing." In effect the neoconservatives and political realists propose illegitimacy reduction through a combined fetal and pregnancy control program. If they are correct, an empirical assessment should reveal a statistically significant joint effect of a Family Cap and Medicaid funding for abortion (Family Cap × Medicaid) on lowering nonmarital births and raising abortions. If, on the other hand, proponents of the stand-alone Family Cap are right only the main effect of this policy is necessary to significantly reduce nonmarital births. Abortions among women on welfare from this vantage point should not increase as a result of implementing a Family Cap because the cost is kept high.

In New York, Minnesota, Oregon, Washington, and six other predominately blue states the legacy of public assistance and welfare reform as a rehabilitative and JOBS program was evident in waivers sought under Section 1115 and in work requirement legislation introduced under PRWORA.[70] Here the Family Cap is viewed simply as punishing the poor, unlikely to achieve any real impact on births except to further impoverish thousands of excluded children.[71] This perspective of an effete policy resonates quite harmoniously with the thesis advanced by William Julius Wilson and a large segment of mainstream social science that a better way to reduce nonmarital births to women on public assistance is to increase the market value of these women through education, job training, and job placement opportunities.[72] Empirical analysis would be anticipated to result in a zero impact of a Family Cap, irrespective of the availability of Medicaid abortion funding for the medically needy.

The final group of 19 states classified in the typology, many in the nation's west and midwest, have also rejected Family Caps as a moral and practical solution to illegitimacy. Responsive to the arguments offered by pro-life groups like National Right to Life, the Conference of Catholic Bishops, and articulate national spokesmen such as U.S. Representative Chris Smith (R-NJ),[73] legislators in states like Pennsylvania, Ohio, Michigan, Missouri, and Texas have taken seriously the prospect of Family Cap-induced abortion. Not surprisingly, in many of these same states strong pro-life advocacy has either blocked or forced the repeal of any legislation permitting medically necessary abortions through the state's Medicaid program.[74] Like neoconservatives and realists from the political left, Christian conservatives and their allies agree that the synergy between Family Caps and no- or low-cost abortion will influence fertility behavior but unlike proponents of a

Family Cap the belief here is that the impact on abortion will be substantial while the reduction in nonmarital births is negligible. It is a position that finds social science support in the technological shock explanation for illegitimacy offered by Akerlof and his colleagues.[75]

The typology in figure 8.2 can be extended to entertain the notion that Family Cap and Medicaid policies are targeted at specific racial/ethnic groups. A number of welfare scholars including Jill Quadagno and Martin Gilens have maintained that states that adopt punitive welfare measure and low benefit levels are responding to the public's hostility to public assistance qua a program for minorities.[76] Such contentions would appear to be borne out in studies by Richard Fording and Joe Soss and his colleagues, which have found that states with larger proportions of blacks on AFDC/TANF tend to adopt stricter work requirements, shorter time limits, more punitive sanctions, tougher child support enforcement, and Family Caps than their counterparts.[77] Granting that racially motivated policy has behavioral consequences, empirical research would expect to uncover a Family Cap impact on fertility behavior that is much more pronounced in states with large populations of poor black and (perhaps) Hispanic women. The evidence for this joint effect would be manifest in a statistically significant coefficient for the interaction between (Family Cap × Proportion black population). This same significant interaction would be consistent with Murray's permissive (countervailing) culture exegesis except the overall effect would be hypothesized to reduce illegitimacy most in states with smaller concentrations of black women on the welfare caseload.[78]

The racial hostility argument can, in principle, be extended to states with large minority caseloads that have enacted both a Family Cap and Medicaid funding for abortion. In these cases, however, the caricature of the punitive welfare state managed by uncaring conservatives becomes more difficult to draw. States like Connecticut, Massachusetts, New Jersey, California, and others in the upper left corner of the "Lesser of Two Evils" typology have long been sensitive to the reproductive rights of women and also provide some of the most generous AFDC/TANF benefits in the country. The recognition that a Family Cap can be more effective in controlling the birthrates of poor black women in concert with low-cost abortion (i.e., Family Cap × Medicaid × Black) than as a stand alone (Family Cap × Black) requires an admission by welfare rights advocates that racially targeted population control is not the sole purview of conservatives. This demands a break with ideological orthodoxy few appear willing to make.[79] It is New Jersey, after all, a liberal state with a large, black, welfare population and not a state that Wendy Chavkin, Diana Romero, and Paul Wise describe as "discouraging both abortion and carrying a pregnancy to term—circumscribing reproductive choice in both directions"[80] that is responsible for the Family Cap impacts that we have observed.

To test the relative impacts of independent and jointly operating Family Caps on nonmarital births and abortions nationally, I estimated a series of regression models with the following OLS specification:

$$Y_{st} = B_1 W_{st} + B_2 P_{st} + B_3 A_{st} + B_4 X_{st} + \lambda_1 \text{Family Caps}_s + \lambda_2 (\text{Family Cap} \\ \times \text{Medicaid}) + \lambda_3 (\text{Family Cap} \times \text{Black}_{st}) + \lambda_4 (\text{Family Cap} \times \text{Medicaid} \\ \times \text{Black}_{st}) + \gamma (\text{Medicaid} \times \text{Black}_{st}) + \sigma_s + \acute\omega_t + e_{st}$$

Equation 8.1

where W is a vector of welfare policy variables that includes whether or not a state had work requirements or time limits under Section 1115 and/or instituted more stringent work requirements on shorter time limits under PRWORA in year t.[81] The vector also includes a measure of whether or not a state paid for medically necessary abortions under Medicaid in year t. P represents a vector of political climate variables that measure the political affiliation of state governors and legislators in year t; A is a set of variables that captures a state's AFDC/TANF caseload size and composition at the baseline (1980); and X is a vector of state- and year-specific economic and demographic variables. σ represents a vector of state fixed effects; ώ a vector of year-specific fixed effects covering 1980–2000; and e is a random error term that varies by state and year. To adjust for the possibility of confounding from within state time trends due to the length of the panel, time was modeled using both linear and quadratic terms. The focal variable in the model, of course, is the main effect of the Family Cap along with its suspected conditional impacts derived from the theoretical and ideological arguments discussed earlier. Y, as noted earlier, is measured as year- and state-specific birth and abortion rates (or ratios). I estimated a parallel set of regressions testing for the impact of Family Caps on Hispanics. A detailed description of each of the variables used in the analysis, together with data sources, is provided in table 8.6.

The specification of the W, P, A, and X variable vectors draws upon models employed in the Mach, Horvath-Rose and Peters, Joyce et al., Schettini-Kearny, and Dyer and Fairlie research already discussed. The political and economic controls were also gleaned from abortion analyses conducted by Rebecca Blank et al., Phillip Levine et al., and Stephen Matthews, David Ribar, and Mark Wilhelm.[82] The coding of welfare time limits and work requirements follows from the research of Fording, Soss et al., and Schettini-Kearny.[83] The incorporation of Medicaid funding for abortion in both birth and abortion analyses was influenced by the work of Argys et al., Medoff and Mathews and others.[84]

The distributions of the study variables for the 50 states and the District of Columbia over the 21-year study period are provided in table 8.7. The means for the qualitative independent variables like Family Cap and Medicaid (funding) for abortion represent the proportion of state-years in which this policy is observed. The values shown for AFDC caseload size, composition, and for benefit levels reflect 1980 statistics. Because interpolations are used for years in which data was unavailable or uncollected there are no

Table 8.6. Description of the Data Sources Used in the National Analysis of Family Cap Impact

Variable Name	Source and Measurement
Outcomes	
General fertility rate	Live Births/Female Population 15–44 years * 1000 Data for the numerator from National Center for Health Statistics. Vital Statistics of the United States 1980–2000. Volume 1. Data for the Denominator from U.S. Census Bureau Population and Housing Unit 1980, 1990, 2000 intervening years from Current Population Survey (CPS) population estimate.
Nonmarital birth rate	Live Births to Unmarried Women/Unmarried Female Population 15–44 years * 1000 Data for the numerator from National Center for Health Statistics. Nonmarital childbearing in the United States, 1940–199 Vol 48. No. 16, 2000 and National Vital Report Vol. 50 No. 5, 2002. Data for the Denominator from U.S. Census Bureau Population and Housing Unit 1980, 1990, 2000 intervening years calculated from intercensal population estimate.
Illegitimacy ratio	Live Births to Unmarried Women / Total Live Births * 100.
Abortion rate	Number of abortions / Female Population 15–44 years * 1000. Data for numerator from the Alan Guttmacher Institute through regular surveys of abortion providers, 1980–2000. Data interpolated for 1983, 1986, 1989, 1990, 1993, 1994, 1997, 1998, years when surveys were not conducted.
Abortion ratio	Number of abortions / Number of Live Births * 100. Ratio is calculated in the manner used by Center for Disease Control. Surveillance Summaries Vol.52/NoSS-12 (2003). This differs from the abortion ratio = abortions/(abortions + live births) used in Alan Guttmacher analyses. See abortion Incidence and Services in the United States in 2000. Perspectives on Sexual and Reproductive Health. 35(1): 6–15.

Welfare policies

Family Cap
Time limits
Work requirements /
Enhanced JOBs

Coded 1 if policy operating in the state and year, else coded 0: Data for Pre-PRWORA, i.e., 111S Waiver implementation from USDHSS,ASPE: Setting the Baseline on State Welfare Waivers, 1997; http:// 158.70.177.60/hsp/isp/waiver2/title.htm. Data on PRWORA policies through 2000 from Urban Institute: Assessing the New Federation. State TANF Policies as of July 1999, Welfare Rules Databook, 2000: Council of Economic Advisers. Technical Report: The Effects of Welfare Policy and the Economic Expansion on Welfare Caseload, 1997; and more stringent time limits and work requirements than PRWORA from American Public Welfare Association: Survey Notes 1. 1997 and 2000 update.

Medicaid pays for abortion

Medically necessary abortions are coded 1 if policy operating in the state and year, else coded 0. Data from Alan Guttmacher Institute. Public Funding Reports in 1980, 1981, 1984, 1986, 1991, 1993, 1996, 1998, 1999, 2000; National Abortion and Reproductive Rights Action League Foundation (NARAL); Who Decides State by State Reports 1992–2000.

Political climate

State governor republican
Republican-controlled
State Senate
Republican-controlled
State House

Coded 1 if Republican, else Coded 0 : Data from National Governors Association. The Book of States 1979–2000; National Gay and Lesbian Task Force, 1996–2000. http://www.ngltf.org/ Statelocal/Legend.htm.

AFDC/TANF information

Maximum welfare benefit

AFDC/TANF Payment for 3-person families in dollars. Data from USDHHS, ACF (ACF-1346, Streamlined Plan for AFDC; Green Books for 1981, 1982, 1985, 1987, 1989, 1990, 1991, 1992, 1993, 1994, 1996, 1998, 2000; USDHSS, ACF Third Annual Report to Congress, 2000.

(continued)

169

Table 8.6 (*continued*)

Variable Name	Source and Measurement
AFDC/TANF population	Number of Recipients on state caseload. Data from AFDC/TANF Recipients. Tabulations provided by ACF to author.
Percent AFDC/TANF families with children 0–2 years	Data from ACF Characteristics and Financial Circumstances of AFDC Recipients, 1979, 1983, 1986–1994 from www.acf.dhhs.gov/programs/OFA/Character for 1994–2000.
Percent AFDC/TANF families black	
Percent AFDC/TANF families Hispanic	
Economic and Demographic data	
Unemployment rate	Ratio for states and years from USDOL Bureau of Labor Statistics, Employment and Earnings,
Women in labor force	1980–2000; Number of women for state and year from USDOL. Geographic Profile of Employment
Unmarried women to all women ratio	and Unemployment 1980–2000;
	Data for numerator and denominator from U.S. Census Bureau with intervening years calculated from
	intercensal population estimate;
Percent female population black	Population females, aged 15–44 by race for state and year. Data from U.S. Census Bureau. Population
Percent female population white	and Housing Unit Counts 1980, 1990, 2000 with intervening years from Current Population Reports.
Percent female population Hispanic	

Table 8.7.   Distribution of the National Study Variables across State-Year
Observations. (Observations = 1071)

Variable	Mean	Standard Deviation	Minimum	Maximum
General fertility rate	66.54	9.23	49.09	123.66
Nonmarital birth rate	38.12	10.91	3.25	69.75
Illegitimacy ratio	26.16	9.29	2.33	69.58
Abortion rate	22.97	18.63	0.96	175.49
Abortion/birth ratio	0.35	0.31	0.02	3.37
Family Cap	0.12	0.32	0	1
Time limits	0.13	0.36	0	1
Work requirements	0.16	0.37	0	1
Medicaid for abortions	0.30	0.46	0	1
Governor Republican	0.46	0.49	0	1
State senate Republican	0.34	0.48	0	1
State house Republican	0.31	0.46	0	1
Maximum welfare benefit (1980)	294.70	104.94	96	492
Welfare caseload (1980)	204,427	269,506	6848	1,400,000
Percent AFDC with child 0–2 years (1980)	35.80	4.72	24.60	53.11
Percent AFDC black (1980)	34.88	29.28	0	98.0
Percent AFDC Hispanic (1980)	4.42	8.86	0	37.22
Unemployment rate	6.17	2.19	2.20	18.10
Women in labor force	1,112,549	1,204,592	80,100	7,776,000
Unmarried/all-women ratio	0.45	0.05	0.34	0.72
Percent female population black	10.50	11.93	0.22	69.74
Percent female population Hispanic	5.71	7.59	0.45	42.10

missing cases in the analyses. To illustrate the considerable variability in racial composition and reproductive outcomes among the 23 Family Cap states I also provide table 8.8. It would appear that, contrary to the impression given in the welfare racism literature, not all states have enacted Family Caps to punish majority black or Hispanic welfare caseloads; in fact, over one-third of these states do not have combined black and Hispanic proportions that approach 50 percent. If statistical discrimination is the motivation for enacting such legislation, size doesn't matter or so it would appear. Family Cap states also reflect a gamut of nonmarital birth and abortion rates (ratios), some well above the national average, others considerably below. The ratio of black women on welfare to black women in the population, which in most cases is about 3.5 to 1, mirrors that of non-Cap states and is reflective of the greater difficulties black women have had in escaping public assistance under welfare reform. On the whole, Family Cap states as a group do not look remarkably different from other states. Data "eyeballing" especially when the data is generated from nonexperimental designs can be very misleading, however, and is especially poor in identifying complex variable interactions—the type of interactions that I believe are operating in some Family Cap states.

In tables 8.9 through 8.13 I present the results for the regression-adjusted marginal effects of state Family Caps on fertility behavior.[85] While the coefficients are the product of simple OLS regression, the standard errors are adjusted to account for any heteroskedasticity that might be introduced through the repetition of states over time.[86] For each fertility outcome I provide four model specifications, namely, (1) the simple difference effect of a Family Cap with fixed effects for time and states, (2) the previous model with controls for other welfare policies (except Medicaid funding for abortion), political climate, AFDC/TANF information and economic and demographic factors, (3) model 2 with Medicaid funding for abortion added, and (4) a model that includes all model 3 variables along with the hypothesized conditioning effects of Medicaid funding and proportion of female population black on any Family Cap–fertility relationship.[87] This model sequencing is designed specifically to determine the extent to which omitted variable bias, in the form of Medicaid funding for abortion and omitted interaction term bias due to the exclusion of Medicaid × Family Cap, Black × Family Cap and Medicaid × Black × Family Cap could be influencing the often "surprising" Family Cap effects found in the studies I have made mention of above.

Results from the analyses of the nonmarital birthrate (per 1,000 women of childbearing age) are shown in table 8.9. Models 1 through 3 show an expected and consistently negative relationship between a state's implementation of a Family Cap and the decline in nonmarital birthrate. The regression coefficients (and marginal effects) indicate that the stand-alone effect of the Family Cap, even after adjusting for the effects of covariates, state, and time fixed effects and Medicaid funding for abortion, is about

Table 8.8. A Demographic and Reproductive Outcomes Profile of States with Family Cap Policies, December 1996

State	Family Cap Implementation Date	Percent Female Population Aged 15–44		Percent AFDC–TANF Population Aged 15–44		Nonmarital Birth Rate	Illegitimacy Ratio	Abortion Rate	Abortion Ratio
		Black	Hispanic	Black	Hispanic				
Arizona	November 95	3.00	22.70	8.10	39.70	62.90	39.00	19.50	0.26
Arkansas	July 94	15.70	2.30	58.10	0.50	52.40	34.30	11.30	0.17
California	August 97	6.80	29.80	16.80	37.90	48.10	31.50	32.30	0.44
Connecticut	January 96	8.60	8.20	31.40	36.00	38.40	31.00	21.70	0.36
Delaware	October 95	18.20	3.80	70.00	3.90	43.00	36.00	24.10	0.41
Florida	October 96	14.10	14.90	47.20	17.70	46.90	35.80	31.20	0.49
Georgia	January 94	27.90	3.90	72.30	1.10	47.80	36.30	20.70	0.34
Idaho	July 97	0.40	6.80	1.00	11.30	37.60	20.90	6.20	0.08
Illinois	December 95	14.90	10.50	57.80	12.80	46.50	34.30	25.60	0.38
Indiana	May 95	8.30	2.80	39.50	3.50	44.60	32.10	11.40	0.18
Maryland	March 96	26.60	3.60	73.90	1.40	41.10	33.30	26.00	0.43
Massachusetts	November 95	5.00	5.90	17.20	28.70	26.90	25.60	29.30	0.51
Mississippi	October 95	35.90	1.10	86.20	0.20	59.80	45.00	7.20	0.11
Nebraska	November 95	3.80	4.20	26.00	6.50	35.50	25.10	12.30	0.19
New Jersey	October 92	13.30	11.80	52.50	27.90	36.80	29.10	34.90	0.57
North Carolina	July 96	21.70	3.30	63.40	1.80	44.20	33.40	19.70	0.33
North Dakota	July 98	0.58	1.00	1.20	0.30	33.90	25.10	9.40	0.15
Oklahoma	October 96	7.50	4.20	28.90	2.30	46.00	31.00	11.60	0.18
South Carolina	October 96	29.60	1.80	72.50	0.70	46.70	37.40	11.40	0.19
Tennessee	September 96	16.20	1.60	55.20	0.60	45.10	33.30	14.90	0.24
Virginia	July 95	19.20	3.90	65.00	2.00	37.50	28.90	18.60	0.32
Wisconsin	January 96	5.40	2.90	44.20	6.80	34.00	27.40	12.80	0.21
Wyoming	February 97	0.78	6.10	4.20	12.90	38.20	27.00	2.70	0.04

Table 8.9.   Fixed Effects Regression Results for Nonmarital Birth Rate

Regressors	Model 1 Coefficient (Std. Error)	Model 2 Coefficient (Std. Error)	Model 3 Coefficient (Std. Error)	Model 4 Coefficient (Std. Error)
Family Cap	−1.3117 (0.9690)	−1.8588* (0.9703)	−1.9306* (0.9517)	−0.8726 (1.0582)
Medicaid pays for abortion			−1.7089 (1.2238)	0.0118 (1.1572)
Female population black		1.51739 (0.8200)	1.6232* (0.7975)	1.6489* (0.8335)
Medicaid *Family Cap				−4.2521* (2.1315)
Female population black *Family Cap				−3.2384* (1.0666)
Female population black *Medicaid				−3.6509 (2.7807)
Medicaid *Family Cap * female population black				2.4995 (2.5209)
Constant	23.1787* (0.6426)	26.0667* (10.1263)	26.766* (9.7105)	30.7474* (9.4864)
R-squared	0.2734	0.3050	0.3109	0.2832
Number of observations	1,071	1,071	1,071	1,071

Standard errors are robust, adjusting for state clustering;   *indicates statistical significance at p ≤ .05.

2 fewer births for 1,000. When the regression model is respecified, however, to include the hypothesized conditioning influences of race and Medicaid funding the main effect of the Family Cap diminishes to nonsignificance.

The interpretation of a relatively complex set of hierarchical difference-in difference estimators can be challenging and for this reason I compute the point estimate, standard error and t-statistic for the joint effect of $\lambda_1 + \lambda_2 + \lambda_3 + \lambda_4$ as presented in equation 8.1 using STATA's Lincom procedure.[88] The regression coefficient for the Family Cap joint effect is −4.11 with a standard error of 1.51 (t = −2.72), indicating that Family Caps lower non-marital birthrates by nearly 4 per 1,000 in states that have higher than average proportions of black women in the population and that pay for abortion through Medicaid than in states without these qualifying conditions. The statistical significance of the joint effect points out that regression models that specify the Family Cap impact on nonmarital births as an independent, main effect can be misleading by failing to pinpoint when and where these policy effects can be expected to occur.

In table 8.10, I repeat the same model sequence for the ratio of nonmarital births per 100 live births with much the same results. As a main effect the Family Cap lowers this illegitimacy ratio by about 1.8 percent but this effect becomes nonsignificant when the hypothesized interactions are incorporated (model 4). The overall conditional effect $(\lambda_1 + \lambda_2 + \lambda_3 + \lambda_4)$ is -5.41 with a standard error of .777 (t $= -6.96$), or 5 percent fewer nonmarital births in states with Family Caps, Medicaid Funding, and higher proportions of black women.

The Family Cap impact on abortions is provided in tables 8.11 and 8.12. In models for the abortion rate per 1,000 women of childbearing age a significant, positive independent effect of a little more than 2 abortions per 1,000 is found in specifications with controls for Medicaid and other covariates. When the joint effect of the Family Cap on abortion rate is computed using the coefficients in model 4, the joint effect is 6.12 (standard error 1.5,

Table 8.10.   Fixed Effects Regression Results for Illegitimacy Ratio

Regressors	Model 1 Coefficient (Std. Error)	Model 2 Coefficient (Std. Error)	Model 3 Coefficient (Std. Error)	Model 4 Coefficient (Std. Error)
Family Cap	−1.6433* (0.5760)	−1.7704* (0.6084)	−1.7926* (0.6043)	0.1312 (0.5214)
Medicaid pays for abortion			−0.5269 (0.4925)	−0.2149 (0.4818)
Female population black		1.8047* (0.4670)	1.8374* (0.4606)	1.8364* (0.4079)
Medicaid *family cap				−2.9390* (0.7578)
Female population black *Family Cap				1.4749* (0.4605)
Female population black *Medicaid				−0.0216 (1.097)
Medicaid *Family Cap *female population black				−1.1340 (1.0997)
Constant	14.8031* (0.4062)	−6.5593 (5.5365)	−6.3436 (5.6551)	−3.2610 (5.2854)
R-squared	0.3386	0.6089	0.6050	0.5900
Number of observations	1,071	1,071	1,071	1,071

Standard errors are robust, adjusting for state clustering; *indicates statistical significance at p ≤ .05.

Table 8.11.   Fixed Effects Regression Results for Abortion Rate

Regressors	Model 1 Coefficient (Std. Error)	Model 2 Coefficient (Std. Error)	Model 3 Coefficient (Std. Error)	Model 4 Coefficient (Std. Error)
Family Cap	3.0569* (1.6936)	0.2348* (0.9425)	2.2076* (0.9291)	1.1171 (1.2878)
Medicaid pays for abortion			−0.6466 (1.3739)	1.7432* (0.8744)
Population female black		−0.8958 (0.8163)	−0.8558 (0.8353)	−0.6552 (0.8197)
Medicaid *Family Cap				1.4243 (2.8936)
Female population black *Family Cap				0.6189 (1.6035)
Female population black *Medicaid				6.2967* (3.1823)
Medicaid *Family Cap *female population black				2.9844 (2.7065)
Constant	26.2336* (0.5917)	17.343* (6.8002)	17.6084* (6.727)	15.883* (6.9286)
R-Squared	0.0249	0.0440	0.0940	0.1377
Number of observations	1,071	1,071	1,071	1,071

Standard errors are robust, adjusting for state clustering; *indicates statistical significance at p ≤ .05.

$t = 4.08$) indicating a statistically significant impact of about 6 abortions per 1,000 more in states that have higher than average proportions of black women and that pay for abortion through Medicaid. The marginal and joint effects of the Family Cap on the abortion-to-birth ratio, however, are not statistically significant, indicating that Caps do not influence this indicator of abortions.

In table 8.13 the regression results from what I have called the nonequivalent outcome, general fertility rate (GFR), are shown. Here, as in the Joyce et al., Schettini-Kearny, and Kaushal and Kaestner studies cited above, positive, "nonintuitive" relationships between Family Cap implementation and general birthrates are revealed.[89] However, when the conceptually guided interaction set is incorporated into the specification, as was done in model 4, the stand-alone effect of the Family Cap disappears. When the overall joint effect of the Family Cap is computed as a function of $(\lambda_1 + \lambda_2 + \lambda_3 + \lambda_4)$, the coefficient once again indicates a significant *positive* relationship. Inasmuch as the Family Cap was designed to influence a very explicit birth behavior, nonmarital births, with an incidence that is concentrated among women on

Table 8.12. Fixed Effects Regression Results for Abortion-to-Birth Ratio

Regressors	Model 1 Coefficient (Std. Error)	Model 2 Coefficient (Std. Error)	Model 3 Coefficient (Std. Error)	Model 4 Coefficient (Std. Error)
Family Cap	0.0359 (0.0248)	0.01808 (0.0125)	0.0195 (0.0127)	0.0145 (0.0209)
Medicaid pays for abortion			0.0360 (0.2183)	0.0245 (0.0157)
Female population black		−0.0094 (0.0095)	−0.0116 (0.0095)	−0.0124 (0.0093)
Medicaid * Family Cap				0.0025 (0.0364)
Female population black * Family Cap				0.0066 (0.0239)
Female population black * Medicaid				0.0273 (0.0387)
Medicaid * family Cap * female population black				−0.0017 (0.0412)
Constant	0.4190* (0.0211)	0.5181 (0.3298)	0.5034 (0.3118)	0.4970 (0.3061)
R-squared	0.0171	0.0431	0.0074	0.0072
Number of observations	1,071	1,071	1,071	1,071

Standard errors are robust, adjusting for state clustering; *indicates statistical significance at $p \leq .05$.

welfare, the GFR would not appear to be the measure of choice to capture the effects of policies driven by welfare reform.

The overall pattern of results from this national analyses of Family Cap impact supports the contention that the policy works and that conditions under which it works best are Medicaid funding for abortion and higher than average numbers of black women in the state population. These conditions were present in New Jersey where the experimental evidence for a Family Cap effect on fertility was strong; they were not present in Arkansas where the Family Cap was determined to exert little effect on either births or abortions. The failure of previous cross-state studies to incorporate relevant policy variables that condition how Family Caps affect behavior (Schettini-Kearny, Joyce et al.), their omission of states where these joint effects are operative (Dyer and Fairlie, Joyce et al.), or their employment of outcome measures with low proportions of predictable variance (Kaushal and Kaestner, Schettini-Kearney) could be responsible for the many "surprising" and confusing findings that appear in the literature.

As was the case with the findings from the New Jersey experiment and blended design, the results from the national analyses of Family Cap impact do not fit tidily within the predictions of a particular theoretical framework. Welfare racism, for example, with its focus firmly on welfare reform as punishment for the poor, is hard pressed to explain why Family Caps are more effective in states like New Jersey, Maryland, California, Illinois, Massachusetts, and Connecticut with more liberal benefit packages and well-developed social safety nets. These are not the states, moreover, that would be expected to exhibit the largest declines in black nonmarital birthrates or illegitimacy ratios if Charles Murray's racial density thesis is accepted.[90] Black concentrations are smaller in Family Cap states like Arizona, Indiana, Tennessee, Wisconsin, Delaware, and Wyoming yet Family Cap effects are also much smaller. Of course, the Family Cap effect we are seeing may be originating from lower-density areas outside large cities such as Chicago, Baltimore, or Los Angeles; this was the pattern after all observed in the New Jersey experiment. Still this very limited scope of effect is a puzzling finding, poorly explained by contravening culture. It is plausible that changes in economic opportunity could also be driving the birth declines observed in New Jersey and other states classified where illegitimacy is the primary evil. Here again the evidence is weak. There is no evidence, for example, in the patterns of 21 years of unemployment rates or women's labor force participation rates that would indicate these states have consistently outperformed neighboring states in their regions in creating jobs for poor men and women,[91] a sine qua non in William J. Wilson's calculus for reducing out-of-wedlock births.

The importance of abortion availability for understanding the prevalence of nonmarital births is anticipated in the "technological shock" theory of George Akerlof and his colleagues. The finding from the cross-state analyses like those from the New Jersey experiment that the declines in nonmarital births are less than the increases in abortions would appear to signal an increase in pregnancies. This could indicate that the Family Cap is achieving limited success in raising either the costs or the level of stigma associated with bearing a child outside of marriage, a critical element in both the Akerlof and Murray formulations. It could also reflect the policy's impotence in increasing the stigma of abortion.

In table 8.14, I show a side-by-side comparison from the national data of the joint effects of Family Caps, Medicaid, and racial composition for black and Hispanic women, the two groups exhibiting birth and abortion impacts. What is most striking in these results is the distinctive role played by racial composition in the fertility responses of these women. For black women it is only with the inclusion of racial composition that the synergistic effect of Family Cap × Medicaid funding is significant for nonmarital birth and abortion rates. The former decrease by about 4 per 1,000 while the latter increases by 6 per 1,000. The illegitimacy ratio also indicates a sensitivity to racial composition with higher proportions of black women raising the

Table 8.13.   Fixed Effects Regression Results for General Fertility Rate

Regressors	Model 1 Coefficient (Std. Error)	Model 2 Coefficient (Std. Error)	Model 3 Coefficient (Std. Error)	Model 4 Coefficient (Std. Error)
Family Cap	2.4669* (0.9798)	2.4648* (1.1661)	2.3698* (1.1543)	0.0915 (1.943)
Medicaid pays for abortion			−2.2588 (1.3850)	2.7516 (1.0524)
Female population black		−0.9102 (2.9299)	−0.7703 (2.9030)	−0.4888 (2.8426)
Medicaid * Family Cap				2.7516 (3.4311)
Female population black * Family Cap				2.0833 (1.9645)
Female population black * Medicaid				−7.3612* (2.4201)
Medicaid * Family Cap * female population black				3.0160 (3.7007)
Constant	69.693* (1.3345)	84.7507* (18.8443)	85.6750* (18.2809)	82.4145* (16.5938)
R-squared	0.0495	0.0566	0.0707	0.0806
Number of observations	1,071	1,071	1,071	1,071

Standard errors are robust, adjusting for state clustering; *indicates statistical significance at p ≤ .05.

Family Cap × Medicaid effect from 2.8 fewer nonmarital births per 100 live births to 5 per 100.

For Hispanic women the inclusion of ethnic composition weakens the effect of Family Cap × Medicaid funding on fertility outcomes. A statistically significant nonmarital birth effect (−6.6 per 1,000) drops to a nonsignificant effect (−3.0 per 1,000) as does significant abortion effect—from 6.5 per 1,000 to 4.6 per 1,000. The illegitimacy ratio impact, too, follows this pattern, decreasing from a more potent −7.0 per 100 to −3.2 per 100, although the effect remains statistically significant.

The differential impact of black and Hispanic group composition and the concentration effects it may signal on black and Hispanic fertility behavior should not come as a complete surprise. It is after all black concentration that sets up the unbalanced marriage markets identified by Robert Willis, Daniel Lichter, and others[92] and Murray's urban underclass.[93] Moreover, Hispanics do not appear to experience the extreme residential segregation, which Massey and Denton term hypersegregation, that black Americans

Table 8.14.   Comparison of the Joint Effects of Medical Funding for Abortion and Racial Composition on the Relationship between Family Cap and Fertility Behavior for Blacks and Hispanics. Fixed Effect Regression Coefficients (Heteroskedastic Standard Errors)

	Fertility Measures			
Joint Effect[†]	Nonmarital Birth Rate	Illegitimacy Ratio	Abortion Rate	Abortion-to-Birth Ratio
Blacks				
Family Cap × Medicaid	−3.3795 (2.1062)	−2.8077* (0.8064)	2.5415 (3.1396)	0.0172 (0.0376)
Family Cap × Medicaid × female population —black	−4.1184* (0.5171)	−5.4167* (0.7777)	6.1249* (1.508)	0.0221 (0.0171)
Hispanics				
Family Cap × Medicaid	−6.6237* (0.7978)	−7.0051* (0.4238)	6.5109* (1.1413)	0.0572* (0.0159)
Family Cap × Medicaid × female population —Hispanic	−3.0936 (1.8249)	−3.2018* (0.7254)	4.6813 (3.8147)	0.0449 (0.0465)

[†]Tests of Black and Hispanic Joint Effects were conducted in separate regressions. Female Population Black and Female Population Hispanic are used as covariates in all regressions with Female Population White serving as the reference category.   *Significant at $p \leq .05$.

do.[94] Hence, any diminution of Family Cap × Medicaid funding effect in this instance would simply resonate the inclusion of a superfluous factor in a regression analysis.

Nor is it surprising from this analysis that the significant decline in nonmarital birthrates for black women is a result of the increase in abortions that take place in areas of high black composition. This would appear to contradict findings from the New Jersey experiment where nonmarital births declined in areas with lower concentrations of black women. However, here in this national analysis, the measure of concentration is much less precise, limiting direct comparisons between the experimental and cross-state analyses.

What is not expected from this comparison of the fertility behavior of black and Hispanic women is the influence that the Family Cap coupled with Medicaid funding for abortion has had on abortions among Hispanic women. James Q. Wilson's observation that Hispanic women have not responded in the same way to abortion availability as have black women— their utilization is much lower—would appear to need amendment in the environment of welfare reform.[95] As in the New Jersey experiment, Family Cap coupled with Medicaid funding increases abortions in a group that is not subject to an environment of too few marriageable men, extreme segregation, or contravening culture. Moreover, in these national data this abortion rise yields statistically significant declines in nonmarital birthrates and illegitimacy ratios.

The conclusion to be drawn from both the New Jersey experiment and from this national analysis is that the Family Cap has indeed impacted the "preference" for nonmarital childbearing. In a policy mix that includes Medicaid funding for abortion, Family Caps have succeeded in raising both the financial and psychological costs of nonmarital births in large measure through the lowering of both the financial and psychic costs of abortion. Perhaps reflecting the importance of cultural values and preferences, Family Caps exert their greatest impact on blacks when black community density is taken into consideration; this is not the case for Hispanics. Nevertheless, Hispanics also appear to have received the Family Cap message.

Without any real commitment to the rehabilitative potential of public welfare, it is easy to see why neoconservatives, libertarians, and similar welfare reformers aren't that concerned about a "few more abortions." Abortion provides a cost effective solution to the problem of out-of-wedlock births using some of the very machinery put in place by political liberals. It is an irony that has not been lost on more progressive welfare reformers who, through it all, show little appetite for undoing these Family Cap effects.

9

Sauntering to Reauthorization

Introduction

I believe this book illustrates that, perhaps now more than ever, welfare policy research is as much a social activity as it is a technical-statistical endeavor. Indeed, when perennial social issues of the day like racial disparity and abortion become a focus of an evaluation, technical quality concerns can recede far into the distance, just so much background noise. On the other hand, allegations of critical flaws in technical quality can on occasion become the evaluation story, entangling research findings in a web of controversy that serves to limit their influence. Journalists and advocacy groups are usually responsible for the diminution of technical discussion with think tank intellectuals and policy experts becoming increasingly complicitous in purposeful obfuscation. The New Jersey evaluation of the Family Cap has had more than its share of both.

In his book *Quixote's Ghost*, David Stoesz describes the politicization of quantitative research findings by liberal and conservative think tanks as the battle "to control the means of analyses."[1] Anna Kondratas of The Urban Institute makes the same point without the Marxian metaphor when she calls much of contemporary public policy debate as arguments where "everybody [believes themselves] entitled to his own statistics."[2] The effect has been to breathe new life into Hugh Hecho's lament of the lack of trustworthy, understandable information on the real impacts of welfare reform.[3]

The traditional litmus test of the high technical quality of an evaluation study has been acceptance of the research in peer-reviewed journals.[4] As I have shown in the references provided in the book, the research my colleagues and I have conducted on New Jersey's Family Cap has met this standard many times over. Yet we get a vastly different picture of the evaluation's technical quality from the widely disseminated, in-house publications produced by policy centers like the American Enterprise Institute–linked Welfare Reform Academy and the Alan Guttmacher Institute.[5] Which sources should be believed? I trust that the analyses and arguments I have presented in these pages will convince readers to be cautious of think tank analysts making claims for value neutral, nonpartisan research.

Results from the New Jersey Family Cap evaluation provide a fine example of the misalignment of empirical information with political interests and ideological positions. The principal research finding of a policy engendering a decline in births through abortion is a difficult outcome for devotees of the Family Cap to support—at least publicly. David Greenberg and Matthew Shroder repeat the old joke that some people use research the way a drunk uses a lamppost—not for illumination, but for support.[6] My colleagues and I, it would appear, were not able to provide a suitable lamppost for either purpose. On the other hand, we offer a veritable smorgasbord of reasons to galvanize opponents.

I believe that the likelihood of achieving any internal consistency among these research findings and the current interests and ideologies that have driven welfare reform over the past 25 years will remain quite low. I base this observation on two features of the current welfare reform environment that serve to restrict rigorous, open, research-grounded debate. The first of these is the rise of the passionate policy expert, with a unique blend of moral earnestness and analytic skills who filters research for policymaker and politician consumption. The second is the pervasive belief in the feasibility of human capital formation, independent of family supports.

Interested Policy Experts

The inchoate form of today's social policy expert appeared on the Washington political scene during Franklin Roosevelt's first New Deal in 1933–1934. Names like Harry Hopkins, Rexford Tugwell, and Harold Ickes, key members of FDR's brain trust, would undoubtedly be enshrined in any liberal-progressive's welfare policy hall of fame.[7] The plethora of social programs generated by the New Deal and its aftermath increased the need for additional policy experts, notes David Ricci, as Congress and legislative staffs required more and more specialized knowledge to perform their oversight functions.[8] Lyndon Johnson's War on Poverty owed a heavy intellectual debt to individuals like Michael Harrington, John Kenneth Galbraith, and Arthur Schlesinger Jr., social theorists and commentators with impeccable liberal-progressive credentials. The influence of opportunity theory as advanced by Richard Cloward and Lloyd Ohlin was especially important to the rehabilitative thrust that continues in all welfare reform legislation through the Personal Responsibility and Work Opportunity Reconciliation Act (PRWORA).[9] This utter dominance of the liberal policy expert in Washington political circles ended in the mid-1970s when conservative experts began to emerge in significant numbers from think tanks, media organizations, and advocacy groups.[10]

We owe a debt to liberal- and conservative-leaning policy experts for their role in providing the press and general public with a crush of position papers, briefing reports, and fact sheets containing information and opinion that once found its way only to academics, legislative staffers, and interested politicians. Unfortunately, for the policy establishment, this proliferation of easily accessible documents has also increased the public's awareness of the foibles and pratfalls that have befallen the policy assessment process with regularity. This has also proven to be unfortunate for consumers who are left with confusion and diminished confidence.

Social welfare policy experts often use what they believe to be relevant information to predict or forecast how a program or course of action will perform in the near and distant future. They also use their expertise to distinguish real-time trends from short-term fads and whimsy. Here are a few predictions with relevance to the subject matter covered in this book.

Michael Katz in his book *The Undeserving Poor* provides this 1989 obituary for Charles Murray: "Murray ascended into the policy universe with the speed of a rocket, but his tenure was brief. No administration can persuade Congress to dismantle the welfare state or pretend that the attendant misery, chaos and potential violence should be endured as a prelude to progress."[11] To paraphrase Mark Twain, reports of Charles Murray's death have been greatly exaggerated.[12]

Henry Aaron, writing in 1978, commented on the legacy of the early debates between the adherents of the cultural and environmental views of poverty: "In retrospect, the debate between [these] views of poverty seems to have vanished without leaving significant intellectual residue. The reason may be the failure of either side in the debate to formulate the issues precisely, the lack of evidence and the unwillingness of participants to suggest the kinds of tests or information that would resolve the debate."[13] The major provisions of PRWORA, together with the spirited discussion that led to their adoption, suggest that Aaron may merely have been looking in the wrong places. Also in 1978, William Julius Wilson published his book *The Declining Significance of Race*.[14] His thesis of opportunity determined primarily by class membership and not skin color is contradicted by a host of social indicators and opinion studies.[15]

Some of the predictions made by social policy experts have been breathtaking in their inaccuracy. Arthur Schlesinger, in a 1986 book, forecast a third renaissance of progressive social values to take hold of the country in the 1990s. This resurgence he intones would be of the same scale as Roosevelt's New Deal and Johnson's Great Society.[16] Of course, what we actually got was a rollback of progressive welfare policy under President Bill Clinton on a scale few policy analysts and pundits ever imagined.

After PRWORA was passed, dire predictions of irreparable harm to families and children began to circulate in Washington's policy centers and beyond. One of the most prominent came in a 1996 report issued by Sheila Zedlewski and her colleagues at The Urban Institute. Here the authors prophesied that 1.1 million children would be thrown into poverty[17] as a result of the legislation. To date, no such calamity has occurred and little or no harm to children can be traced directly to welfare reform.[18]

One of the most significant forecasting stumbles by a social scientist can be found in the prognostications of Daniel Bell, one of the original neoconservatives, on the emergence of the new social policy and planning elite. What makes Bell's predictions emerge as naive is not the presence of a technical decision-making class; in fact, since the publication of Bell's influential books, *The End of Ideology* (1960) and *The Coming of Post-Industrial Society* (1973) this class has grown in both numbers and in influence. It is his misapprehension of how this knowledge would function within the political system where Bell's vision becomes blurred. In *The End of Ideology*, the author observes that technical decision making is calculating and instrumental and that it is diametrically opposed to ideological problem solving, which is emotional and expressive.[19] His theme in *The Coming of Post-Industrial Society* is that with the waning of ideology, the political process will become increasingly dependent on technical knowledge and its procedures.[20] Simply put, people would begin listening to reason. What I believe Bell underestimated was the level of cross-fertilization between ideology and fact that would continue to infect public policy debate.[21]

An arena where the blending of stubbornly held belief and empirically derived fact is most visible to the public is the high-profile court case where scientists and policy experts serve as expert witnesses. David Faigman, a law professor at the University of California, describes the current expert witness environment as one where the expert very quickly becomes a strategist for the side that retains his/her services.[22] It is also an environment that tolerates the expert's broad experience as a substitute for actual data and analyses. Faigman advocates turning over the selection of experts from the prosecution and defense to the bench. The Court Appointed Scientific Experts project of the American Association for the Advancement of Science may be an important first step in the process.

Inaccurate predictions of complicated social outcomes and policy impacts are quite understandable even if they are disconcerting. The knowledge base in such policy areas as child welfare, mental health, delinquency prevention, and welfare reform is thinner than perhaps it should be and mistakes are inevitable. It is the reactions of policy experts to the disconfirmation of their assessments and predictions that should give the public real pause.

Philip Tetlock in an analysis of how political scientists cope with evidence that runs counter to their predictions and assessments uncovers what he terms "the pervasiveness of double standards," where lower levels of procedural rigor and data quality are applied to findings that are consistent with ideological preconceptions. He observes this normative pattern across the dozen or so experiments he and other researchers have performed. "Experts switched on the high-intensity search light of skepticism only for dissonant results. Whether we trace the problem to excessive skepticism toward dissonant data or insufficient skepticism toward consonant data, counterfactual beliefs often appear self-perpetuating, effectively insulated from disconfirming evidence by a protective belt of defensive maneuvers and further reinforced by an understandable disinclination to attribute confirming evidence to either methodological sloppiness or to partisan bias."[23] The general reluctance of policy experts in the social and behavioral sciences to admit mistakes appears to be a growing problem, exacerbated by the increasingly adversarial environment in which they find themselves.[24]

The exercise of ideology in the social policy sciences is in no better view than in the exercise of myth busting. As I noted in chapter 6, any number of welfare policy experts have denounced the myth that the majority of women receiving Aid to Families with Dependent Children/Temporary Assistance for Needy Families (AFDC/TANF) are black. In 1995, for example, the Joint Center for Political and Economic Studies, a Washington policy center that conducts research on issues of special concern to black Americans published this myth and fact about the racial composition of the AFDC caseload nationally

> Myth: Most families on welfare are black.
> Fact: Of the 4.9 million families on AFDC, 39% are white, 37% are black, and 17% are Hispanic. The proportion of the AFDC population that is black has been dropping.[25]

The problem with this particular myth-fact pairing is that it is inconsistent with the empirical facts. From 1983 through 2001, with the exception of 1992 and 1993, the proportion of black families on welfare has exceeded that of whites, and the number of black children on welfare has surpassed the number of white children in every year in this time series.[26] The claim that the proportion of black families has been dropping since 1973 is pure fiction;[27] if anything it has risen since 1994.

Another myth that has been exposed in the welfare policy literature is that welfare benefits provide an incentive for women to bear additional children.[28] Here again we encounter the myth about myth. In a 1995 report issued by the National Center for Health Statistics[29] and in a 1998 report published by the National Research Council[30] the consensus of the available research indicates a statistically significant negative relationship between births among poor women and AFDC/TANF benefit levels. Chapter 3 also provides a listing of many of these studies and, of course, there are the findings for the New Jersey and national analyses presented in these pages.

Finally, many welfare policy experts seek to dispel the myth that welfare recipients are somehow different from other individuals in our country. Mark Rank summarizes the general misperception in this way: "[The] book attempts to convey the realities, not the myths, of welfare recipiency.... This book presents those facts. It seeks neither to glorify nor to demean those who turn to public assistance but rather to provide an objective and clear accounting of the experience of living on welfare.... Perhaps the main theme running throughout the book is that the welfare recipient is not that different from you or me—no better, no worse."[31]

While the goal of Rank's book, *Living on the Edge*, and others of the genre are laudable, the author is guilty of replacing an old myth with a newer, potentially more damaging one: that of the down-on-their-luck, plucky-spirited survivor in need of understanding and a heavy dose of human capital infusion. The characterization deemphasizes the fertility, educational, and family formation choices and behaviors that distinguish the average welfare recipient from his/her counterpart in the working and middle classes. In so doing, it trivializes the disruption, danger, stress, and disorganization that attends individuals with exceedingly low levels of family and other social capital. A logical welfare policy outcome of the new myth is time limits.

Lawrence Mead has described a public policy elite in Washington who have been largely isolated from the dynamic welfare reform that has taken place at the state and local levels. He notes, "In the case of welfare, the public has proven wiser than most experts."[32] Mead may be correct but as the research on New Jersey's Family Cap demonstrates, more isolation need not lead to the abatement of forecasts that do not predict, mistakes that go unacknowledged, or myths that beget more myths. And surely the isolation of these elites does not increase the likelihood that counterfactual findings from the hinterlands will gain acceptance.

The Ideology of Human Capital

One subject on which progressive and conservative welfare reformers can agree is that welfare recipients need to improve the stocks of human capital that are available to the them. Human capital as it is defined by Gary Becker, an originator of the concept, is the sum total of an individual's skills, knowledge, health, and values that give that person the capacity to act in new and productive ways.[33] As we have seen, conservatives favor a strategy for human capital improvement that relies heavily on job search and more immediate labor force attachment, fueled by rugged individuals and other stalwart American values, while liberals advocate longer-term investments in vocational training and postsecondary education. Both PRWORA and the reauthorization of TANF by Congress under the Deficit Reduction Act of 2005, which stresses job search over education and training as the welfare recipient's principle route to economic self-sufficiency,[34] indicate that the conservative vision is now firmly in place.

Ron Haskins, now a fellow at the Brookings Institution in Washington, has declared the last decade of welfare reform to be an unequivocal success.[35] In the 10-year period from 1996 through 2005 the number of TANF recipients has declined nationally from over 12.6 million to about 4.7 million—a 63 percent decline. In New Jersey the number of recipients decreased from 288,000 to about 107,000, almost a 63 percent decline.[36] Figures available from USDHHS-ACF for 2006 indicate the decline is continuing.

Concomitant with the unprecedented exodus from AFDC/TANF is the number of (former) recipients who have entered the job market and who have full- or part-time employment. In its *Sixth Annual Report to Congress* on the status of the TANF program, the Administration for Children and Families (ACF) recounted the "remarkable achievement" of welfare reform in putting even the most unskilled and uneducated women into the workforce.[37] For women earning less than 200 percent of the federal poverty level, that is, about $30,000 a year for a family of three, employment rose from 51 percent in 1996 to 59 percent in 2002, after reaching nearly 61 percent in 2000. For the lowest 20 percent of earners, wages increased from an annual average of $1,823 in 1996 to $2,368 in 2002, a 30 percent improvement. For women whose annual earnings placed them in the 21 to 40 percent category of earners, income from working rose from an average of $5,310 per year in 1996 to $10,570 or a 99 percent increase.[38] If 1993 is used as the base rate the wage increases for these two groups, which contain nearly all women on welfare or who have left welfare, the income increase is even more dramatic.[39] The employment and earning experiences of welfare reform in New Jersey have been equally impressive. A five-year evaluation of the state's Work First New Jersey program conducted by Mathematica Policy Research found that a sample of approximately 1,600 families experienced a pattern of substantial economic progress from 1998 through 2003. Income from wages increased on average from $14,184 at the study baseline to $19,753 at the study's end. Average hourly wages also exhibited a steady rise from $8.05 an hour on the first survey to $9.73 five years later when the last survey was administered.[40]

The Mathematica study also revealed what is readily evident from national ACF data but not given prominent attention: namely, the vast majority of these families are not earning anything like 200 percent of the poverty level, an amount considered necessary to make ends meet.[41] Indeed, the surveys of former Work First New Jersey recipients revealed that the percentage of families living below the poverty level ($15,670 for a family of three) ranged from a high of 65 percent in 1999 to 46 percent in 2003.[42] Of course, this is a vast improvement over the income most of these families would have received if they had remained on welfare since the combination of cash benefit and in-kind assistances offered in most states ensures an income well below the poverty level.

It is unlikely, moreover, that this employment and earnings profile of (former) welfare recipients would change a great deal if PRWORA and Work First New Jersey had placed a greater emphasis on education and training. Three- and five-year follow-up studies of multiple welfare-to-work sites conducted by Manpower Demonstration Research Corporation (MDRC) find that educational and training investments did not yield added economic benefits relative to a labor force attachment approach.[43] In their review of 20 programs in which random assignment was used, Charles Michalopoulous and Christine Schwartz report an impact of between $400–$600 per year for both types of programs. Gayle Hamilton and her colleagues find much the same when comparing the five-year earnings impacts of labor force attachment, educational investment, and mixed strategies used in 11 mandatory welfare-to-work programs. In our own analysis of the Family Development Program we discovered that the welfare recipients from New Jersey counties that emphasized labor force attachment earned on average about $165 per year (and $650 over four years) more than recipients from counties offering a more education and skills enhancement approach.[44]

With the welfare reform goal of moving millions of poorly educated, husbandless mothers with young children off welfare largely achieved, the complementary goal of economic self-sufficiency appears to be a work in progress. The Bush administration and many conservatives believe that the act of working, in and of itself, is the very essence of self-determination. This position was expressed by Wade Horn, assistant secretary at ACF in testimony given before the Ways and Means Committee in the U.S. House of Representatives: "The architects of welfare reform believed that welfare recipients were capable of work. They did not consider welfare recipients to be helpless clients forever in need of government assistance. Rather, they believed that welfare recipients could compete in the labor market and succeed."[45] According to Robert Rector of the Heritage Foundation, the reauthorization of TANF can be expected to tie the knot between work and self-sufficiency even tighter.[46]

Liberal and progressive policy analysts, as might be expected, do not view the possession of $7 to $9 an hour jobs as the premise for economic self-determination. As Mark Greenberg of the Center for Law and Policy maintains, retention and advancement are affected by wages and other aspects of initial job placement such as health benefits, child care, and travel time.[47] Greenberg calls on the federal and state government to adopt a more balanced employment approach that focuses on skill building and job quality in addition to job search. His point may be valid. The study of Work First New Jersey, for example, shows that the economic gains for (former) recipients come in the years immediately after they entered the program; the pace of their progress slowed substantially after these early successes. In addition, three-quarters of recipients were out of work at some time during the study follow-up period with, on average, a nine-month hiatus between jobs. Also during the follow-up period 40 percent of those who exited TANF returned to public assistance for some period of time.[48] Low wage growth and lapses in employment and benefits coverage have also been reported in national studies for nonwhite and poorly educated women.[49] The reauthorization of TANF in the view of liberal think tanks like the Center on Budget and Policy Priorities and the Center for Law and Social Policy is seen as providing few new resources to move substantial numbers of recipients out of poverty-level jobs to employment that allows them to make ends meet.[50]

There appear to be real limits on the potential for human capital acquisition by many former and current welfare recipients. We caught a glimpse of this threshold effect in the MDRC studies cited above—if one is willing to entertain the notion that the trivial differences in earnings generated by labor force attachment and educational investment programs are not due to poor program implementation or too short follow-up periods. In a more recent examination of the earnings potential of women who have moved out of welfare and into work at low wage jobs, Janet Currie concludes that we can't expect to see enough growth to greatly change the economic situations in these households.[51] The analysis conducted by Pedro Carneiro and James Heckman are especially sobering in this regard.[52] Based on their own extensive research and that of other labor economists they find the rate of return for most job training programs is far below 10 percent. The poorest rates of return, moreover, occur for programs that target the least skilled and poorly educated. Job Corps, long considered to be one of the most successful government-sponsored training programs, for example, can only be found successful, according to Carneiro and Heckman, if one is willing to assume that benefits last indefinitely and the social costs of taxation are negligible. Absent those assumptions the program impact is about $3 per week or about $624 over a four-year follow-up period, an impact that is not statistically significant.[53] Carneiro and Heckman conclude that more efficiency in public spending for human capital would be achieved by diverting monies to preschool and schooling programs for adolescents and away from job training for low-skilled adults.

Conservatives, notwithstanding their exhortations of "work will make recipients free," have recognized that in both PRWORA and in the 2005 reauthorization of TANF that the human capital stocks of welfare recipients are likely to peak at rather low thresholds if reform relied solely on the improvement of personal skills and education. In PRWORA this realization is expressed in the goals of out-of-wedlock pregnancy reduction and two-parent family formation. In the reauthorization it takes its form in the healthy marriage initiative. Without employing the term, the legislation is an acknowledgment that human capital can also be enhanced by an improvement in the quality of one's social relationships, that is, through increases in social capital.

The most extensive discussion of social capital can be found in the work of James Coleman. In his *Foundations of Social Theory* he defines the concept in this way: "Social capital is a set of resources that inheres in family relations and in community social organization and that is useful for the cognitive and social development of a child or young person. These resources differ for different persons and can constitute an important advantage for children and adolescents in the development of their human capital."[54] Social capital, according to Coleman, manifests itself in a variety of forms that include the creation of sets of obligations and expectations, the potential for information acquisition, responsibility and authority relationships, and the formation of norms and sanctions, behavioral rewards and punishments. Like personal human capital, the rate of return on investment in social capital appears to be highest for children and adolescents and lowest for adults. However, also like the investment return for personal skill building there are instances when the social capital of adults can be improved significantly with marriage being one of those events.

Coleman was one of the first social scientists to document the importance the home environment provided by parents and family resources in promoting readiness for academic achievement of children.[55] As Carneiro and Heckman point out, the accumulated research on human capital formation continues to point up the negative impact that adverse family environments, for example, homes of poor, single-parent, poorly educated families, have on children's knowledge and skill development. The damage seems to extend even deeper to the development of noncognitive skills like self-discipline, persistence, reliability, trustworthiness, and dependability.[56]

The family creation policy of welfare reform appears to make good social science and political sense. There are, however, several obstacles to this initiative that vitiate the rise in the social capital stocks of black women, at least in the short run. The most fundamental of these is the condition of the current marriage market. In 1965, Daniel Patrick Moynihan noted that "the unemployment among (male) Negroes outside the south has persisted at catastrophic levels since the first statistics were gathered in 1930."[57] After some employment gains in the mid 1960s through the early 1970s, black males experienced significant increases in unemployment and in time spent out of the labor force.[58] John Bound and Richard Freeman show that the retreat from labor force participation has been most pronounced for younger black males.[59] Charles Murray presents data that show the percentage of black males, aged 16–24, not enrolled in school, who are not actively looking for work, rose from about 9 percent in 1964 to nearly 25 percent in 1997.[60] Poor employment records are frequently coupled with criminal records. In 2002 about 40 percent of the adults in prison, local jail, on probation or parole— nearly 1.1 million individuals—were black males, the vast majority aged

18–35. Like young black unemployment and labor force dropout rates, young black correctional supervision rates continue to climb.[61]

Promoting marriage in disadvantaged populations generally is a very challenging endeavor, setting aside for the moment the sex ratio imbalances in poor black communities. Low-income unmarried couples have been characterized as "fragile families," often expressing their intention to wed, but seldom doing so. When married most of these unions do not last very long.[62] The obstacles to healthy, long-term marriages facing low-income couples, regardless of race, are considerable and include spells of unemployment and underemployment, housing availability, increases in family and household sizes, and a variety of other macro- and micro-level stresses.[63]

In the evaluation of the Family Development Program the vast majority of the women we studied (over 75 percent) were essentially raising their children by themselves, married couples were few, and new marriages were an extreme rarity. The evaluation of Work First New Jersey, conducted by Mathematica, paints much the same portrait for former and cycling welfare cases. Robert Wood and his colleagues sum up the involvement of fathers in this way: "Fewer than one in five children of clients lived with their biological fathers at the end of the followup period. Older children and African American children were the least likely to live with their fathers. Among children not living with their fathers, more than half had not seen their fathers at all in the past three months. In addition, two-thirds had received no financial support from their fathers in the past month."[64] The marriage focus of PRWORA and the reauthorization of TANF have stimulated the creation of a number of programs designed to promote the benefits of a stable marriage. The centerpiece of these initiatives is the marriage class and the marriage curriculum, which provide skills and information believed necessary to create a successful relationship. As M. Robin Dion explains, however, this curricula has been designed primarily for well-educated, middle-class couples who are engaged or already married.[65] In order to determine if marriage education can succeed with low-income couples, USDHHS-ACF is sponsoring three large, long-term evaluations—for example, Building Strong Families, Supporting Healthy Marriage, and the Community Healthy Marriage Initiative—that focus on the feasibility of inculcating and restoring the norms and values for the institution of marriage.[66]

The success of marriage promotion programs in increasing the social capital of current and former public welfare recipients remains very much an open question.

Thomas Sowell warns the adoption of new sets of norms and values, what he calls "cultural capital," may or may not be successful and can be modified or altered to take forms never anticipated by the introducing agent.[67] In other words, social capital may not always be fungible. There are, however, other ways to increase the social capital of welfare recipients outside of marriage, the principal one involves placing limitations on the number of dependent children. The nearly universally held belief among social scientists, backed by a great deal of empirical evidence, holds that the resources, attention, and interest of parents in each of child (or children) is inversely related to the number of dependent children.[68]

The importance of small family size for social capital and by extension for human capital accumulation is discussed by social scientists in two seemingly unrelated fashions. The first takes the perspective of the parent and introduces such imagery as the unintended or unwanted pregnancy or birth. Here we are told, and the evidence appears to bear this out, unintended children are at higher risk for suffering infant mortality, growing up with a single parent, experiencing poverty, doing poorly in school, and committing a crime in adolescence.[69] A second and more shrill way of addressing the issue found in the economics literature is through the concept of the poor or "low-quality" child.[70] Recognizing that such ascription is bound to be controversial, Gary Becker takes great pains to clarify the term's meaning.

> A family must determine not only how many children it has but also the amount to spend on them—whether it should provide separate bedrooms, send them to nursery school and private colleges, give them dance or music lessons and so forth. I will call more expensive children higher quality children, just as Cadillacs are called higher quality cars than Chevrolets. To avoid any misunderstanding, let me hasten to add that "higher quality" does not mean morally better. If more is voluntarily spent on one child than on another, it is because the parents obtain additional utility from the additional expenditure and it is this additional utility which we call higher quality.[71]

As Willis points out, low-quality children are more likely to be produced through out-of-wedlock births than through marriage and the same can be said of unwanted or unintended births.[72] Stocks of social capital, already at minimal levels in single-parent households, become further diluted; in this way the unwanted infant is metamorphosed into a low-quality toddler and adolescent.

Family size can be limited in a variety of ways: namely, through abstinence, effective contraception use, foster home placement, offering a child (or children) for adoption, institutionalization and, of course, through abortion. Since an estimated 75 percent of unwanted births are aborted[73] and abortion rates are double for women at or below 200 percent of poverty,[74] abortion can be an effective mechanism to prevent the additional drain of social capital in poor and minority populations. By targeting such groups some researchers and policy analysts have claimed that substantial societal benefits also occur. This is the contention, for example, of John Donohue and Steven Levitt in a study they conducted on the impact of legalizing abortion on crime.[75] These researchers credit Roe v. Wade with lowering murders, violent crimes, and property crimes in the 1990s by between 15 and 25 percent and providing a social savings on the order of $30 billion annually in reduced crime. Donohue and Levitt conclude that the reason abortion and crime are so closely linked is that "abortion has a disproportionate effect on the births of those who are most at risk of engaging in criminal behavior."[76]

Donohue and Levitt report that they find an especially strong relationship between the much higher rates of abortion for black women and the reduction in crime among black youth. They provide this example regarding homicides.

> Fertility declines for black women [due to abortions] are three times greater than for whites (12 percent compared with 4 percent). Given that homicide rates of black youth are roughly nine times higher than those of white youth, racial differences in the fertility effects of abortion are likely to translate into greater homicide reductions. Under the assumption that those black and white births eliminated by legalized abortion would have experienced the average criminal propensities of their respective races, then the predicted reduction in homicide is 8.9 percent. In other words taking into account differential abortion rates by race raises the predicted impact of abortion legalization on homicide from 5.4 percent to 8.9 percent.[77]

William Bennett, the well-known conservative pundit and writer created a firestorm when he drew upon this research and uttered, "If you wanted to reduce crime, you could—if that were your sole purpose—you could abort every black baby in this country and your crime rate would go down."[78]

The Donohue and Levitt research and Bennett's remarks are illustrative of two arguments that, in the spirit of social capital accumulation, are making abortion for black and Hispanic women increasingly palatable among many conservatives as well as liberals. The first of these is the "marriage is for white people" justification. I have addressed the impact that low male to female sex ratios in marriage age cohorts is having on marriage rates for black men and women. Joy Jones reports the marriage rate for blacks has been dropping since the 1960s and today blacks have the lowest marriage rate of any racial group in the United States. Citing 2001 U.S. Census data, Jones provides these sobering statistics: "43.3 percent of black men and 41.9 percent of black women in America have never been married, in contrast to 27.4 percent and 20.7 percent respectively for whites. African American women are the least likely in our society to marry. In the period between 1970 and 2001, the overall marriage rate in the United States declined by 17 percent, but for blacks it fell by 34 percent."[79] Jones traces the reasons that have made marriage for black women seem unnecessary or unattainable to the prevalence of mores for love, sex, and childbearing outside of marriage and an increasingly unappealing appraisal of black men by black women. In her words, "In an era of brothers on the 'down low,' the spread of sexually transmitted diseases and the decline of the stable blue-collar jobs that black men used to hold, linking one's fate to a man makes marriage a risky business for a black woman."[80] Peggy O'Crowley, citing the work of William Julius Wilson and Stephanie Coontz, makes much the same case when she questions whether marriage for black women on welfare will improve their life chances. She reports that this is very unlikely if both men and women in the marriage pool have few skills, poor education, and meager prospects.[81]

Corollary to the "won't marry" argument is the "won't parent" charge given voice by actor Bill Cosby. Decrying the crime, illiteracy, teen pregnancy, and other self-destructive behaviors that plague inner-city youth, Cosby places blame squarely on the shoulders of poor black parents, most of whom are women. In a 2004 speech given at the NAACP's commemoration of the 50th anniversary of *Brown v. Board of Education*, Cosby's outrage was visible: "The lower economic and lower middle class economic people are not holding their end in this deal. In the neighborhood that most of us grew up in, parenting is not going on. . . . I'm talking about people who cry when their son is standing there in an orange suit. Where were you when he was 2? Where were you when he was 12? And where were you when he was 18 and how come you don't know he had a pistol?"[82] Employing less colorful language, James Heckman, Nobel Laureate in Economics, makes much the same point. He cites the considerable research that shows that cognitive and noncognitive deficits in children emerge early, before schooling, and if left uncorrected create low-skill adults who lack the self-discipline, dependability, and trustworthiness that are highly valued in a work setting.[83] Absent successful rehabilitation and marriage strategies, abortion provides a third way to help black and Hispanic women accumulate social and human capital, while simultaneously appealing to liberals' passion for reproductive freedom and many conservatives' sense of social pragmatism.

While I am certain that most liberal and conservative politicians and policy analysts would deny that an abortion approach to social and human capital formation is in operation, there are several indications that hint it may already be well in motion. The Alan Guttmacher Institute, for example, reports that while the abortion rate continues to decrease and even plummet for some groups, the rates for poor and minority women continue to rise. During the frenzy days of welfare reform, from 1994 through 2000, women 20 years old and older and living at less than 200 percent of the poverty level experienced a 27 percent increase in abortions.[84] For women on Medicaid the increase was also large—19 percent. More recent reports by Guttmacher appear to indicate that this increase is continuing at a time when increased restrictions to delay abortions such as waiting periods and parental notifications have also been on the rise.[85] Cross-classify these data with information Guttmacher provides on unintended pregnancies and contraception failure and the evidence points to the most significant rise in abortion occurring among poor, black women.

Absent the job training and opportunities, which many progressives see lacking, and the marriage prospects, which many conservatives imagine emerging, what will economic self-sufficiency look like under welfare reform's family size limitation strategy? I believe Katherine Newman in her book *No Shame in My Game* provides one likely possibility in the form of Kyesha:

The difference between Kyesha and her less successful friends can be credited to Burger Barn's citadel of the low-paid hamburger flipper, the one place most Americans would not think to look for positive inspirations, role models or any other source of salvation for a poor girl from Harlem's housing projects. Working every day after school, Kyesha developed the kind of discipline and sense of order in her life that she had utterly lacked before she started earning a living....Her mother, a longtime welfare recipient, encouraged the progress from the sidelines. It was Dana who insisted that Kyesha get two abortions and finish school.[86]

While Kyesha's story is inspiring, she is unlikely to become anyone's poster woman for what welfare reform has to offer.

Policy and Evidence—Some Final Thoughts

A great many Americans would agree with Ron Haskins's assessment that welfare reform has been a striking success.[87] Welfare caseloads have dropped dramatically without any clearly perceptible rises in overall poverty, child poverty, or child hunger.[88] Neither the physical well-being, mental health, nor educational adjustment of children appears to have been harmed in any substantial way by mothers leaving welfare for work.[89] The same can also be said of the Family Cap. A 2001 report issued by the General Accounting Office calculated that about 108,000 families each month nationally had one or more children excluded from welfare payments, here again, however, harm to the mother or child is supported only by what GAO terms "weak evidence."[90] Legislation at the national level like the Kucinich provision (2003) and bills sponsored by Representatives Chris Smith and Patsy Mink (2001) that would have penalized states that imposed a Family Cap remain unsupported and largely forgotten.[91] Only one state, Illinois, has enacted legislation that would rescind its Family Cap. The Family Cap, it appears, is here to stay at least for the time being.

The evaluation of the New Jersey Family Cap shows, if it illustrates anything about policy research, that the relationship between research and politics, between evidence and policy, is complex and changing. Gary Henry and Melvin Mark note that an evaluation can influence collective actions in a variety of ways, most especially by agenda setting through media reports, by policy-oriented learning from advocacy group action, policy change initiations through legislative and legal processes, and by the diffusion of research findings to other jurisdictions.[92] All of these mechanisms were in play throughout the evaluation of New Jersey's Family Cap and its aftermath, as were the interest and ideologies that sought to block or limit these pathways. By fits and turns, the work of my colleagues and I was put to what Carol Weiss, Erin Murphy-Graham, and Sarah Birkeland would call political, instrumental, and conceptual uses. There were even attempts to put our findings to imposed use by some politicians and policymakers.[93] These efforts at utilization were challenged by other interests touting evidence of faulty analysis, contamination, and a variety of other methodological flaws. Other evidence used to reject our findings is a series of studies that report that the Family Cap does not reduce births but actually leads to their increase! The latter part of this message has yet to make it to Web sites of the think tanks and policy institutes that trumpet such studies.

While most Americans would not oppose a Family Cap for women on welfare, fewer, I believe, would approve of the manner in which it achieves its policy objective. A 2002 article in *The Nation* called it "New Jersey's dirty little secret."[94] Race-specific, population control is never likely to become popular among liberals who frame abortion for the poor as a women's rights issue nor conservatives who see it as an issue of moral rights. The melding of declining marriage rates, higher incarceration rates, and lower labor force participation rates in the black community, however, provide the near-perfect confluence of factors to trigger a Family Cap abortion response among poor black women. Moreover, even without these factors present in the Hispanic community, the combination of Family Cap and Medicaid funding is found to raise abortion rates.

Citing the failures of human capital investment programs for the poor and disadvantaged through schools and manpower development initiatives, James Heckman calls for a renewed emphasis on family policy—"intervening early and actively in failing families."[95] Obviously, abortion is one such intervention, but are there others? Here are a few "back of the envelope" program possibilities that I feel would cut right to the heart of the social and human capital issue.

- Expanding mentoring and tutoring opportunities for poor black, and Hispanic children sponsored by business, industry, and other private-sector individuals and organizations. The Bridge-to-Employment (BTE) program sponsored by Johnson & Johnson is a good example of public-private partnership using these opportunities to increase minority participation in science and healthcare careers. Bridge-to-Employment and programs like Big Brothers Big Sisters could mitigate the cognitive and noncognitive deficits that are found too frequently among disadvantaged and minority children. These programs have also been shown to place disadvantaged children in direct contact with adults who have established successful careers in our competitive society.
- Facilitating interracial adoption. This initiative would reduce our reliance on the less than optimal foster placement system while placing children in more stable family environments. The focus of this initiative should be placed on the adoption of black boys, who by most accounts tend to languish in foster care for the longest periods.
- Fundamental restructuring of inner city schools. The sociologist Orlando Patterson is on target, I believe, when he makes a plea for more school involvement in the lives of poor minority children as an

antidote for too much unsupervised (street) time.[96] Longer school days, structured after school programs, greatly reduced summer vacations and curriculum that stresses hard (personal capital) and soft (social capital) skills could remove some of the socialization burden being placed on single parent households while at the same time helping to prepare poor children for productive futures.
- Promoting interracial marriage. Interracial marriage has remained very low in this country. Perhaps it is time for a faith-based initiative that is designed explicitly to cross this color barrier.

These proposals, the first two rather modest and the latter two quite a bit more radical, could be undertaken in concert with, or in lieu of, the rehabilitative and marriage initiatives that government has pursued, is currently following and, in all likelihood, will follow in the near future—initiatives that have done very little to halt the crumbling of the black family in poor communities.

. . . .

Several years ago Peter Edelman noted that "conversations with anyone involved in the Family Cap debate—activists, lawyers, think-tankers and even the General Accounting Office—all wend their way around to the 'Rutgers Study'. . . commissioned by the state and written by Michael Camasso and a team of Rutgers University professors."[97] This notoriety was accompanied by considerable costs, however. Shortly after I finished my contract work with the state of New Jersey and when I began presenting the research at professional conferences and in academic journals, my office was moved by Dean Davidson away from faculty and staff at the School of Social Work to a room, several miles away from the School, co-located with staff from property management and physical plant. This move coincided closely with the dean's presentation of the School's first Public Policy Leadership Award to State Senator Wayne Bryant for his work "on authorizing the Family Cap legislation"[98] and with the dean's offer of a faculty position to William Waldman, the former commissioner of human services, who presided over much of the Family Cap implementation controversy. Waldman, an ardent supporter of the policy,[99] accepted the position of adjunct professor and executive in residence in 2001. Bryant, too, became a Rutgers faculty member shortly afterward, accepting the position of distinguished adjunct professor of law and public affairs.[100] A clever wag could educe that politics had trumped research once again; not being so clever I continued to press on—from a distance.

Notes

Chapter 1

1. Stark, Shelly, and Levin-Epstein, Jodi (1999). *Excluded Children: Family Cap in a New Era*. Washington, DC: Center for Law and Public Policy (CLASP). The Center lists Family Cap states and dates of implementation as NJ, October 92; GA, January 94; AR, July 94; IN, May 95; VA, July 95; DE, October 95; MS, October 95; AZ, November 95; MA, November 95; NE, November 95; IL, December 95; CT, January 96; WI, January 96; MD, March 96; NC, July 96; TN, September 96; FL, October 96; OK, October 96; SC, October 96; WY, February 97; ID, July 97; CA, August 97; ND, July 98.

2. Harvey, Carol, Camasso, Michael J., and Jagannathan, Radha (2000). Evaluating Welfare Reform Waivers Under Section 1115. *Journal of Economic Perspectives, 14*, pp. 165–188.

3. Ibid.

4. U.S. House of Representatives, Committee on Ways and Means. *1996 Green Book*. Washington, DC: U.S. Government Printing Office.

5. Fording, Richard C. (2003). Laboratories of Democracy or Symbolic Politics? The Racial Origins of Welfare Reform. In Sanford F. Schram, Joe Soss, and Richard C. Fording (Eds.), *Race and the Politics of Welfare Reform* (pp. 72–97). Ann Arbor: University of Michigan Press. See especially pp. 81–88; and Mink, Gwendolyn (1999). *Welfare's End*. Ithaca, NY: Cornell University Press, p. 98.

6. Noble, Charles (1997). *Welfare As We Knew It: A Political History of the American Welfare State*. New York: Oxford University Press; and Balz, Dan,

and Brownstein, Ronald (1996). *Storming the Gates: Protest Politics and the Republican Revival.* Boston: Little, Brown.

7. Roberts, Dorothy (1997). *Killing the Black Body: Race, Reproduction and the Meaning of Liberty.* New York: Pantheon.

8. Cross, Theodore (Ed.). Black Out-of-Wedlock Births: The Deception That Put Welfare Reform over the Top. *Journal of Blacks in Higher Education*, *13*, p. 13. Also see Roberts, Dorothy, ibid.; Winston, Pamela (2002). *Welfare Policymaking in the United States*; and Neubeck, Kenneth J., and Cazenave, Noel A. (2001). *Welfare Racism: Playing the Race Card against America's Poor.* New York: Routledge.

9. Haskins, Ron (2002). Looking to the Future: Commentary 2. The Future of Children. *The Journal*, *12*, pp. 192–195. See especially p. 194.

10. Haskins, R., Sawhill, J., and Weaver, Kent (2001). Welfare Reform: An Overview of Effects to Date. Policy Brief No. 1. *Welfare Reform and Beyond.* Washington, DC: Brookings Institution.

11. Bauer, Gary, and Gramm, Phil (1995, August 30). Why Pro-Lifers Should Support Welfare Reform. *The Wall Street Journal*, p. 10.

12. Murray, Charles (1993, October 29). The Coming White Underclass. *The Wall Street Journal*, p. A14.

13. Reardon, David C. (1995). Trading in Lives: Thoughts on Welfare Reform. *The Post Abortion Review*, *3*, pp. 1–8; U.S. Catholic Bishops' Council (1995). *Moral Principles and Priorities for Welfare Reform.* Chicago: Archdiocese of Chicago; and Kelly, James R. (1995, December 30). Why Republican and New Democrat Welfare Changes Need Legal Abortion. *America*, *173*, pp. 7–11.

14. Roberts, Dorothy (1997). Killing the Black Body; and Neubeck, Kenneth J., and Cazenave, Noel A. (2001). *Welfare Racism.*

15. Hecho, Hugh (2001). The Politics of Welfare Reform. In Rebecca Blank and Ron Haskins (Eds.), *The New World of Welfare* (pp. 169–200). Washington, DC: Brookings Institution. See especially p. 196.

16. Mead, Laurence M. (2001). The Politics of Conservative Welfare Reform. In Rebecca Blank and Ron Haskins (Eds.), *The New World of Welfare* (pp. 201–220). Washington, DC: Brookings Institution. See especially p. 214.

17. For classic definitions see Becker, Gary S. (1993). *Human Capital: A Theoretical and Empirical Analysis with Special Reference to Education.* Chicago: University of Chicago Press; and Coleman, James S. (1990). *Foundations of Social Theory.* Cambridge, MA: Harvard University Press.

18. Hecho, Hugh (2001). The Politics of Welfare Reform.

19. Grogger, Jeffrey, Karoly, Lynn A., and Klerman, Jacob A. (2002). *Consequences of Welfare Reform: A Research Synthesis. RAND/DRU–2676–DHHS.* Santa Monica, CA: RAND.

20. Rainwater, Lee, and Yancey, William L. (1967). *The Moynihan Report and the Politics of Controversy.* Cambridge, MA: MIT Press.

21. Rose, Nancy E. (1995). *Workfare or Fair Work: Women, Welfare and Government Work Programs.* New Brunswick, NJ: Rutgers University Press.

22. For more details on this rule see Gilens, Martin (1999). *Why Americans Hate Welfare: Race, Media, and the Politics of Antipoverty Policy.*

Chicago: University of Chicago Press; and Piven, Francis F., and Cloward, Richard A. (1971). *Regulating the Poor: The Functions of Public Welfare.* New York: Pantheon.

23. U.S. House of Representatives, Committee on Ways and Means. *1996 Green Book.*

24. For example, see Rose, Nancy E. (1995). *Workfare or Fair Work*; Winston, Pamela (2002). *Welfare Policymaking in the United States*; Noble, Charles (1997). *Welfare As Knew It*; and Mink, Gwendolyn (1998). *Welfare's End.*

25. Rose, Nancy E. (1995). *Workfare or Fair Work*; and Winston, Pamela (2002). *Welfare Policymaking in the United States.*

26. Gueron, Judith M., and Pauly, Edward (1991). *From Welfare to Work.* New York: Russell Sage Foundation.

27. U.S. House of Representatives Committee on Ways and Means. *General Explanation of the Family Support Act of 1988.* Washington, DC: U.S. Government Printing Office.

28. Bane, Mary Jo, and Ellwood, David T. (1994). *Welfare Realities: From Rhetoric to Reform.* Cambridge, MA: Harvard University Press.

29. Winston, Pamela (2002). *Welfare Policymaking in the United States.*

30. U.S. House of Representatives Committee on Ways and Means (1988). *General Explanation of the Family Support Act of 1988.*

31. U.S. House of Representatives Committee on Ways and Means (1998). *1998 Green Book.* Washington DC: U.S. Government Printing Office.

32. Bell, Stephen H., and Douglas, T. (2000). Making Sure of Where We Started: State Employment and Training Systems for Welfare Recipients on the Eve of Federal Reform. Occasional Paper Number 37. Washington, DC: The Urban Institute; U.S. General Accounting Office (1999). Welfare Reform: States' Implementation and Effects on the Workforce Development System— Statement of Cynthia M. Fagnone (GAO/T-HEHS-99–190). Washington, DC: U.S. General Accounting Office; and U.S. General Accounting Office (1994). Welfare to Work: Current AFDC Program Not Sufficiently Focused on Employment (GAO/HEHS-95–28). Washington, DC: U.S. General Accounting Office.

33. Gilens, Martin (1999). *Why Americans Hate Welfare*, p. 8.

34. Lieberman, Robert C. (1998). *Shifting the Color Line: Race and the American Welfare State.* Cambridge, MA: Harvard University Press, p. 151.

35. Piven, Francis F., and Cloward, Richard A. (1971). *Regulating the Poor*; and Mink, Gwendolyn (1998). *Welfare's End.*

36. U.S. House of Representatives Committee on Ways and Means (1998). *1998 Green Book.*

37. Mink, Gwendolyn (1998). *Welfare's End.*

38. McLanahan, Sara, and Garfunkel, Irwin (1993). Single Motherhood in the United States: Growth, Problems and Policies. In Joe Hudson and Burt Galaway (Eds.), *Single Parent Families: Perspectives in Research and Policy* (pp. 15–29). Toronto: Thompson.

39. Bell, Winifred (1965). *Aid to Dependent Children.* New York: Columbia University Press.

40. U.S. House of Representatives Committee on Ways and Means. *General Explanation of the Family Support Act of 1988*, p. 7.

41. Bane, Mary Jo, and Ellwood, David T. (1994). *Welfare Realities*, pp. 23–27.

42. U.S. House of Representatives, Committee on Ways and Means (1996). *1996 Green Book*.

43. U.S. House of Representatives (1996). *Personal Responsibility and Work Opportunity Reconciliation Act of 1996: Conference Report*. Washington, DC: U.S. Government Printing Office.

44. Tabulations are available at http://www.acf.hhs.gov/programs/ofa/.

45. Nightingale, Demetra S. (2002). Work Opportunities for People Leaving Welfare. In Alan Weil and Kenneth Finegold (Eds.), *Welfare Reform: The Next Act*, pp. 103–120. Washington, DC: The Urban Institute.

46. Winston, Pamela (2002). *Welfare Policymaking in the United States*. See also Lopest, Pamela (2001). *How Are Families That Left Welfare Doing? A Comparison of Early and Recent Welfare Leavers, Policy Brief B–36*. Washington, DC: The Urban Institute.

47. U.S. House of Representatives (1996). *Personal Responsibility and Work Opportunity Reconciliation Act of 1996*.

48. U.S. House of Representatives, Committee on Ways and Means (1996). *1996 Green Book*.

49. U.S. House of Representatives (1996). *Personal Responsibility and Work Opportunity Reconciliation Act of 1996*.

50. See, for example, Piven, Francis F., and Cloward, Richard A. (1971). *Regulating the Poor*; Lieberman, Robert C. (1998). *Shifting the Color Line*; and Quadagno, Jill (1994). *The Color of Welfare: How Racism Undermined the War on Poverty*. New York: Oxford University Press.

51. Lieberman, Robert C. (1998). *Shifting the Color Line*.

52. U.S. House of Representatives Committee on Ways and Means (1998). *1998 Green Book*.

53. Lieberman, Robert C. (1998). *Shifting the Color Line*.

54. Winston, Pamela (2002). *Welfare Policymaking in the United States*; Weil, Alan (2001). Program Redesign by State in the Wake of Welfare Reform: Making Sense of the Effects of Devolution. In Greg Duncan and P. Lindsay Chase-Lansdale (Eds.), *For Better or For Worse: Welfare Reform and the Wellbeing of Children and Families* (pp. 63–80). New York: Russell Sage Foundation; and Neubeck, Kenneth J., and Cazenave, Noel A. (2001). *Welfare Racism*.

55. U.S. House of Representatives, Committee on Ways and Means (1996). *1996 Green Book*.

56. Benefit calculations are available at http://www.acf.hhs.gov/programs/ofa/.

57. Piven, Francis F., and Cloward, Richard A. (1971). *Regulating the Poor*.

58. Bane, Mary Jo, and Ellwood, David T. (1994). *Welfare Realities*; and Neubeck, Kenneth J., and Cazenave, Noel A. (2001). *Welfare Racism*.

59. Piven, Francis F., and Cloward, Richard A. (1971). *Regulating the Poor*; and Rose, Nancy E. (1995). *Workfare or Fair Work*.

60. Piven, Francis F., and Cloward, Richard A. (1971). Ibid.; and Neubeck, Kenneth J., and Cazenave, Noel A. (2001). *Welfare Racism.*

61. Bane, Mary Jo, and Ellwood, David T. (1994). *Welfare Realities.*

62. Lieberman, Robert C. (1998). *Shifting the Color Line*; and Piven, Francis F., and Cloward, Richard A. (1971). *Regulating the Poor.*

63. Lieberman, Robert C. (1998). Ibid.

64. Winston, Pamela (2002). *Welfare Policymaking in the United States*, p. 7. See also Rose, Nancy E. (1995). *Workfare or Fair Work*; Mink, Gwendolyn (1998). *Welfare's End*; and Weil, Alan (2001). Program Redesign by State in the Wake of Welfare Reform. In Greg Duncan and P. Lindsay Chase-Lansdale (Eds.), *For Better or for Worse* (pp. 63–80). New York: Russell Sage Foundation.

65. Gueron, Judith M., and Pauly, Edward (1991). *From Welfare to Work*; and Greenberg, David, and Shroder, Mark (1997). *The Digest of Social Experiments.* 2nd ed. Washington, DC: The Urban Institute.

66. Harvey, Carol, Camasso, Michael J., and Jagannathan, Radha (2000). *Evaluating Welfare Reform Waivers.*

67. Riccio, John A., and Orenstein, Alan (1996). Understanding Best Practices for Operating Welfare-to-Work Programs. *Evaluation Review, 20*, pp. 3–28.

68. Hamilton, Gayle, Friedman, Stephen, Gennestian, Lisa, Michalopoulos, Charles, Walter, Johanna, Adams-Ciardullo, Diana et al. (2001). *How Effective Are Different Welfare-to-Work Approaches? Five-Year Adult and Child Impacts for Eleven Programs.* New York: Manpower Demonstration Research Corporation (MDRC).

69. Quoted in Gueron, Judith M., and Pauly, Edward (1991). *From Welfare to Work.*

70. U.S. House of Representatives, Committee on Ways and Means (1996). *1996 Green Book.*

71. U.S. House of Representatives (1996). *Personal Responsibility and Work Opportunity Reconciliation Act of 1996.*

72. Grogger, Jeffrey, Karoly, Lynn A., and Klerman, Jacob A. (2002). *Consequences of Welfare Reform*; and Moffitt, Robert A., and Ver Ploeg, Michele (Eds.). *Evaluating Welfare Reform in an Era of Transition.* Washington, DC: National Academy Press.

73. Pavetti, LaDonna, and Bloom, Dan (2001). State Sanctions and Time Limits. In Rebecca Blank and Ron Haskins (Eds.), *The New World of Welfare* (pp. 245–269). Washington, DC: Brookings Institution.

74. Weil, Alan (2001). Program Redesign by State in the Wake of Welfare Reform. In Greg Duncan and P. Lindsay Chase-Lansdale (Eds.), *For Better or for Worse: Welfare Reform and the Wellbeing of Children and Families* (pp. 63–80). New York: Russell Sage Foundation.

75. See, for example, Shiller, Bradley R. (1999). State Welfare-Reform Impacts: Content and Enforcement Effects. *Contemporary Economic Policy, 17*, pp. 210–222; Fording, Richard C. (2003). Laboratories of Democracy or Symbolic Politics? The Racial Origins of Welfare Reform. In Sanford F. Schram, Joe Soss, and Richard C. Fording (Eds.), *Race and the Politics of Welfare Reform* (pp. 72–97). Ann Arbor: University of Michigan Press; Soss,

Joe, Schram, Sanford F., Vartanian, Thomas P., and O'Brien, Erin (2001). Setting the Terms of Relief: Explaining State Policy Choices in the Devolution Revolution. *American Journal of Political Science 45*, pp. 378–395; and Council of Economic Advisers (1999). *Technical Report: The Effects of Welfare Policy and the Economic Expansion on Welfare Caseload: An Update*. Washington, DC: CEA.

Chapter 2

1. Three court decisions in particular stand out where racial differences were critical to the decision—(1) New Jersey Supreme Court: *Southern Burlington County NAACP v. Mount Laurel Township* (1975) reaffirmed in 1983. The Court established Mount Laurel Doctrine, that is, municipalities must use zoning in an affirmative manner to provide affordable housing to low- and moderate-income households; (2) New Jersey Supreme Court: *Abbott v. Burke* (1998). New Jersey Core Curriculum Content Standards were applied to determine if all districts were progressing equally. Those that were not were given additional funding and services to help catch up. The New Jersey Public School Education Act of 1975 was overturned; (3) New Jersey Supreme Court: *State of New Jersey v. Soto* (1996). Drug convictions of 17 drug dealers were thrown out because police were using race as the criterion to pull over drivers on the New Jersey Turnpike.

2. Brown, Michael K. (1999). *Race, Money, and the American Welfare State*. Ithaca, NY: Cornell University Press, p. 71.

3. Piven, Francis F., and Cloward, Richard A. (1971). *Regulating the Poor: The Functions of Public Welfare*. New York: Pantheon; Schram, Sanford E. (2003). Putting a Black Face on Welfare: The Good and the Bad. In Sanford Schram, Joe Soss, and Richard C. Fording (Eds.), *Race and the Politics of Welfare Reform* (pp. 196–222). Ann Arbor: University of Michigan Press; and U.S. Department of Health and Human Services, Administration for Children and Families. Characteristics and Financial Circumstances of AFDC Recipients, www.acf.dhhs.gov/programs/ofa/character.

4. Brown, Michael K. (1999). *Race, Money, and the American Welfare State*, pp. 366–367.

5. Lieberman, Robert C. (1998). *Shifting the Color Line: Race and the American Welfare State*. Cambridge, MA: Harvard University Press, p. 127.

6. Piven, Francis F., and Cloward, Richard A. (1971). *Regulating the Poor*. See also Rose, Nancy E. (1995). *Workfare or Fair Work: Women, Welfare and Government Work Programs*. New Brunswick, NJ: Rutgers University Press.

7. Quadagno, Jill (1994). *The Color of Welfare: How Racism Undermined the War on Poverty*. New York: Oxford University Press; and Key, V. O. Jr. (1949). *Southern Politics in the State and Nation*. New York: Knopf.

8. Fording, Richard C. (2003). Laboratories of Democracy or Symbolic Politics? The Racial Origins of Welfare Reform. In Sanford F. Schram, Joe Soss, and Richard C. Fording (Eds.) *Race and the Politics Welfare Reform* (pp. 72–97). Ann Arbor: University of Michigan Press.

9. Soss, Joe, Schram, Sanford F., Vartarian, Thomas P., and O'Brien, Erin (2001). Setting the Terms of Relief: Explaining State Policy Choices in the Devolution Revolution. *American Journal of Political Science*, *45*, pp. 378–395.

10. Chavkin, Wendy, Romero, Diana, and Wise, Paul H. (2002). What Do Sex and Reproduction Have to Do with Welfare? In Francis F. Piven, Joan Acker, Margaret Hallock, and Sandra Morgan (Eds.) *Work, Welfare and Politics* (pp. 95–112). Eugene: University of Oregon Press; Neubeck, Kenneth J., and Cazenave, Noel A. (2002). Welfare Racism and Its Consequences: The Demise of AFDC and the Return of the States' Rights Era. In Francis F. Piven, Joan Acker, Margaret Hallock, and Sandra Morgan (Eds.), *Work, Welfare and Politics* (pp. 35–53). Eugene: University of Oregon Press; and Roberts, Dorothy (1997). *Killing the Black Body: Race, Reproduction, and the Meaning of Liberty*. New York: Pantheon.

11. U.S. House of Representatives, Committee on Ways and Means. *1996 Green Book*. Washington, DC: U.S. Government Printing Office, p. 1330.

12. Rainwater, Lee, and Yancey, William L. (1967). *The Moynihan Report and the Politics of Controversy*. Cambridge, MA: MIT Press.

13. Murray, Charles (1984). *Losing Ground: American Social Policy 1950–1980*. New York: Basic; Murray, Charles (1993, October 29). The Coming White Underclass. *Wall Street Journal*, p. A14.

14. Murray, Charles (1993). Welfare and the Family: The U.S. Experience. *Journal of Labor Economics* 11:S224–S262.

15. Moffitt, Robert A. (1998). The Effect of Welfare on Marriage and Fertility. In Robert A. Moffitt (Ed.), *Welfare, the Family and Reproductive Behavior* (pp. 50–97). Washington, DC: National Academy Press.

16. Gilens, Martin (1999). *Why Americans Hate Welfare: Race, Media and the Politics of Antipoverty Policy*. Chicago: University of Chicago Press; Johnson, Martin (2003). Racial Context, Public Attitudes and Welfare Effort. In Sanford F. Schram, Joe Soss, and Richard C. Fording (Eds.), *Race and the Politics of Welfare Reform* (pp. 151–161). Ann Arbor: University of Michigan Press.

17. Roberts, Dorothy (1997). *Killing the Black Body*, p. 215.

18. Klerman, Jacob A. (1998). Welfare Reform and Abortion. In Robert A. Moffitt (Ed.), *Welfare, the Family and Reproductive Behavior* (pp. 98–133); and Chavkin, Wendy, Romero, Diana, and Wise, Paul H. (2002). What Do Sex and Reproduction Have to Do with Welfare? In Francis F. Piven, Joan Acker, Margaret Hallock, and Sandra Morgan (Eds.), *Work, Welfare and Politics* (pp. 95–112).

19. Neubeck, Kenneth J., and Cazenave, Noel A. (2002). Welfare Racism and Its Consequences. In Francis F. Piven, Joan Acker, Margaret Hallock, and Sandra Morgan (Eds.), *Work, Welfare and Politics* (pp. 35–53).

20. Schram, Sanford E. (2003). Putting a Black Face on Welfare. In Sanford Schram, Joe Soss, and Richard C. Fording (Eds.) *Race and the Politics of Welfare Reform*, 196–222. See especially p. 202.

21. Bane, Mary Jo, and Ellwood, David T. (1994). *Welfare Realities: From Rhetoric to Reform*. Cambridge, MA: Harvard University Press, p. 44; Finegold, Kenneth, and Staveteig, Sarah (2002). Race, Ethnicity, and Welfare

Reform. In Alan Weil and Kenneth Finegold (Eds.), *Welfare Reform: The Next Act* (pp. 203–223). Washington DC: The Urban Institute.

22. Finegold, Kenneth, and Staveteig, Sarah (2002). Race, Ethnicity, and Welfare Reform. In Alan Weil and Kenneth Finegold (Eds.), *Welfare Reform* (pp. 203–223).

23. Winston, Pamela (2002). *Welfare Policymaking in the United States: The Devil in Devolution*. Washington, DC: Georgetown University Press.

24. Lieberman, Robert C. (1998). *Shifting the Color Line*, p. 159.

25. Gilens, Martin (1999). *Why Americans Hate Welfare*; and Johnson, Martin (2003). Racial Context, Public Attitudes and Welfare Effort. In Sanford F. Schram, Joe Soss, and Richard C. Fording (Eds.), *Race and the Politics of Welfare Reform* (pp. 151–161). Ann Arbor: University of Michigan Press.

26. Perales, Nina (1995). A "Tangle of Pathology": Racial Myth and the New Jersey Family Development Act. In Martha A. Fineman and Isabel Karpin (Eds.), *Mothers in Law: Feminist Theory and the Legal Regulation of Motherhood* (pp. 250–269). New York: Columbia University Press. See especially p. 262.

27. Bryant, Wayne (1992, July, October). Testimony at Public Hearing before New Jersey State Assembly Health and Human Services Committee, p. 42.

28. Ibid., p. 45.

29. Goertzel, Ted G., and Hart, John (1995). New Jersey's $64 Question: Legislative Entrepreneurship and the Family Cap. In Donald F. Norris and Lyke Thompson (Eds.), *The Politics of Welfare Reform* (pp. 109–145). Thousand Oaks, CA: Sage. See especially p. 110.

30. Family Development Act. PL1991. Assembly Numbers 4700, 4701, 4702, 4703, 4704, 4705. New Jersey General Assembly. Trenton, NJ.

31. Waldman, William, and Reitz, Marion E. (1993). New Jersey Family Development Program. County Guidelines. Trenton, NJ: Department of Human Services.

32. Ibid., p. 4.

33. Family Development Act. PL1991. Assembly Numbers 4700, 4701, 4702, 4703, 4704, 4705. New Jersey General Assembly. Trenton, NJ.

34. Kroft, Steve (Writer) and Bonin, Richard (Director). (1994). The $64 Question. Bonin, Richard (Producer).

Goertzel, Ted G., and Hart, John (1995). New Jersey's $64 Question: Legislative Entrepreneurship and the Family Cap. In Donald F. Norris and Lyke Thompson (Eds.), *The Politics of Welfare Reform* (pp. 109–145). Thousand Oaks, CA: Sage.

35. For example, for an unCapped family in New Jersey, the birth of a second child will result in an increase of $102.00 in cash assistance but will reduce the maximum food stamp allotment for a family of three by $127.70 or 30 percent of cash assistance grant for a total combined benefit of [$322.00 + ($315.00 − 0.30 × $322.00)] or $540.40. For a Capped family the birth of a second child would result in a total combined cash assistance and food stamp benefit of ($162.00 + $315.00), or $477.00.

36. *C. K. v. Shalala*. 883 F. Supp 991 (D.NJ.1995).

37. Ibid.

38. Ibid.

39. For discussions of lawsuits brought in Indiana, California, and Nebraska see Stark, Shelly, and Levin-Epstein, Jodi (1999). *Excluded Children: Family Cap in a New Era*. Washington, DC: Center for Law and Public Policy; Welfare-to-Work (2001). *Lawsuits Take Aim at Family Cap 10*, 84–85. Washington, DC: MII; Gastley, Kelly (2005). Why Family Cap Laws Just Aren't Getting It Done. *William and Mary Law Review 46*, pp. 373–414.

40. Appleton, Susan F. (1996). When Welfare Reforms Promote Abortion: Personal Responsibility, Family Values, and the Right to Choose. *85*, pp. 155–190.

41. *Mahrer v. Roe*. 432 U.S. 464 (1977).

42. *Harris v. McRae*. 448 U.S. 297 (1980).

43. *Planned Parenthood of S. E. Pennsylvania v. Casey*. 112 U.S. 2791, 2811 (1992).

44. *Dandridge v. Williams*. 397 U.S. 471 (1970).

45. *C. K. v. Shalala*. 883 F. Supp. 991 (D.NJ.1995), p. 1014.

46. *C. K. v. Shalala*. 92 F.3d, 195 (3rd Cir. 1996).

47. *Sojourner, A. v. The New Jersey Department of Human Services*, No. 97–EXL–L10171 (D.NJ. 2000).

48. *Sojourner, A. v. The New Jersey Department of Human Services*, Exhibit Q.

49. New Jersey Department of Human Services, Office of Policy and Planning (1997) *Comparison of NJ's Old Welfare System and the New Work First NJ Program*. Trenton, New Jersey. Department of Human Services. Work First New Jersey incorporated virtually all of the waivers that the state had implemented under FDP. A notable exception was the "elimination of the marriage penalty" provision, which had encouraged very few marriages.

50. Goertzel, Ted, and Kucharski, Stephen (n.d.). Assessing the Impact of New Jersey's Welfare Reform: Scientific, Ethical and Legal Issues. New Brunswick, NJ: Rutgers University, Forum for Policy Research. Mimeo.

51. *Sojourner, A. v. The New Jersey Department of Human Services*, Exhibit J.

52. Ibid., Exhibit P.

53. Ibid., Exhibit L.

54. Ibid., Exhibit M.

55. Ibid., Exhibit O.

56. Ibid., p. 39.

57. Schuppue, Jonathan (2000, August 31). Judge Rejects Challenge to State's Welfare Cap. *The [Newark] Star-Ledger*, p. 25.

58. *Sojourner, A. v. The New Jersey Department of Human Services*. A–2787–00T5 (Appellate Division, April 5, 2002).

59. *Sojourner, A. v. The New Jersey Department of Human Services*. A–160–01 (Supreme Court of New Jersey, August 4, 2003).

60. Ibid., p. 26.

61. Ibid., p. 24.

62. Leusner, Donna (1993, November 9). Pregnancy Drop: Fewer Welfare Women Conceive in First Two Months of Benefit Cutoff. *[Newark] Star-Ledger*, p. 1.

63. Ibid.

64. O'Neill, June (1994). *Expert Testimony in* C. K. *v. Shalala.* U.S. District Court—New Jersey. Civil Action No. 93–5354.

65. Peterson, Iver (1995, May 17). Abortions Up Slightly for Welfare Mothers. *New York Times*, p. 14; and Havemann, Judith. (1995, May 17). Abortion Rate Increased under NJ Family Cap. *Washington Post*, p. 11.

66. Winston, Pamela (2002). *Welfare Policymaking in the United States*; Feddman, Linda (1995, August 9). Lawmakers Clash over Family Caps. *Christian Science Monitor*, p. 1.

67. Peterson, Iver (1995, May 17). Abortions Up Slightly for Welfare Mothers, p. 14.

68. Stout, Hilary (1995, March 17) So Far, Efforts to Discourage Women on Welfare from Having More Children Yield Mixed Results. *Wall Street Journal*, p. 14.

69. Dorning, Michael (1995, May 17). Abortions Up Slightly for N.J. Welfare Moms.Chicago Tribune, p. 3.

70. Goertzel, Ted G., and Young, Gary S. (1996). New Jersey's Experiment in Welfare Reform. *The Public Interest* 125, 72–80.

71. Klerman, Jacob A. (1999). U.S. Abortion Policy and Fertility. *American Economic Review*, *89*, 261–264.

72. Ruess, Michelle (1995, May 17). Abortions Rise as NJ Limits Welfare Payments. *The Bergen Record*, p. 1.

Chapter 3

1. Leusner, Donna (1993, December 2). Lawsuit Targets Jersey on Denial of Child Benefits to Welfare Moms. [*Newark*] *Star-Ledger*, p. 1.

2. New Jersey PL 1991, chapter 523. January 21, 1992.

3. Leusner, Donna (1995, October 11). Author of State's Welfare Reform Says GOP Plans Hurts Family Values. [*Newark*] *Star-Ledger*, p. 4.

4. Dorning, Michael (1995, March 12). Welfare Cap on Families Shows Signs of Success. *Chicago Tribune*, p. 12.

5. Haskins, Ron, Sawhill, Isabel, and Weaver, Kent (2001). Welfare Reform: An Overview of Effects to Date. Policy Brief No. 1. *Welfare Reform and Beyond*. Washington, DC: Brookings Institution.

6. Gingrich, Newt, Armey, Dick, and House Republicans (1994). The Contract with America. Washington, DC: The Republican National Committee.

7. Rector, Robert E. (1996). Yet Another Sham Welfare Reform: Examining the NGA Plan (Backgrounder # 1075). Washington, DC: The Heritage Foundation; Bauer, Gary, and Gramm, Phil (1995, August 30). Why Pro-Lifers Should Support Welfare Reform. *The Wall Street Journal*, p. 10.

8. Brownstein, Ronald (1994, May 26). Clinton Joins Backers of Family Cap on Welfare Benefits. *Los Angeles Times*, p. 3; Balz, Dan, and Brownstein, Ronald (1996). *Storming the Gates: Protest Politics and the Republican Revival.* Boston: Little, Brown.

9. Winston, Pamela (2002). *Welfare Policymaking in the United States: The Devil in Devolution*. Washington, DC: Georgetown University Press; Balz, Dan, and Brownstein, Ronald (1996). Ibid.

10. Kearney, Melissa S. (2004). Is There an Effect of Incremental Welfare Benefits on Fertility Behavior?: A Look at the Family Cap. *Journal of Human Resources*, *39*, pp. 295–325; McLanahan, Sara S. (1985). Charles Murray and the Family. In *Losing Ground: A Critique* (pp. 1–7). Institute for Research on Poverty Special Report Series (SR # 38). Madison: University of Wisconsin-Madison.

11. Murray, Charles (2001). Family Formation. In Rebecca Blank and Ron Haskins (Eds.), *The New World of Welfare* (pp. 137–168). Washington, DC: Brookings Institution. See especially pp. 148–152; Wilson, James Q. (2002). *The Marriage Problem*. New York: Harper Collins, p. 51.

12. Ventura, Stephanie J., Bachrach, Christine A., Hill, Laura, Kaye, Kelleen, Holcomb, Pamela, and Koff, Elisa (1995). *The Demography of Out-of-Wedlock Childbearing*. USDHHS, National Center for Health Statistics (Pub. No. [PHS-95–1257]). Washington, DC: U.S. Government Printing Office; Ventura, Stephanie J., and Bachrach, Christine A. (2000). Nonmarital Childbearing in the United States, 1940–1999. *National Vital Statistics Reports*, *48*(16). Washington, DC: NCHS, NVSS, National Vital Statistics System.

13. Murray, Charles (1993, October 29). The Coming White Underclass. *Wall Street Journal*, p. A14; Murray, Charles (1999). *The Underclass Revisited*. Washington, DC: American Enterprise Institute.

14. Haskins, Ron, Sawhill, Isabel, and Weaver, Kent (2001). Welfare Reform: An Overview of Effects to Date. Policy Brief No. 1. *Welfare Reform and Beyond*. Washington, DC: Brookings Institution, p. 4.

15. U.S. General Accounting Office (1994). *Families on Welfare: Sharp Rise in Never-Married Women Reflects Societal Trend. (GAO/HEHS–94–92)*. Washington, DC: GAO.

16. U.S. House of Representatives (1996). Personal Responsibility and Work Opportunity Act of 1996. *Conference Report to Accompany HR 3734*. Washington, DC: U.S. Government Printing Office.

17. McLanahan, Sara S. (1995). The Consequences of Nonmarital Childbearing for Women, Children and Society. In *Report to Congress on Out-of-Wedlock Childbearing* (pp. 229–239). USDHSS National Center for Health Statistics (Pub. No. [PHS–95–1257]). Washington, DC: U.S. Government Printing Office. See especially p. 234.

18. Jagannathan, Radha, Camasso, Michael J., and McLanahan, Sara S. (2005). Welfare Reform and Child Fostering: Pinpointing Affected Child Populations. *Social Science Quarterly 86*, pp. 1080–1103.

19. Neubeck, Kenneth J., and Cazenave, Noel A. (2001). *Welfare Racism: Playing the Race Card against America's Poor*. New York: Routledge; Roberts, Dorothy (1997). *Killing the Black Body: Race, Reproduction and the Meaning of Liberty*. New York: Pantheon.

20. Ryan, William (1967). Savage Discovery: The Moynihan Report. In Lee Rainwater and William Yancey (Eds.), *The Moynihan Report and the Politics of Controversy* (pp. 457–466). Cambridge, MA: MIT Press. See especially p. 464.

21. This is a marriage forced on the father by his family and/or the family of the mother because of a pregnancy, or in some cases an actual birth. It has also been termed a shotgun wedding.

22. Piven, Frances F. (2002). Welfare Policy and American Politics. In Frances F. Piven, Joan Acker, Margaret Hallock, and Sandra Morgan (Eds.), *Work, Welfare and Politics* (pp. 19–33). Eugene: University of Oregon Press.

23. Ibid., p. 25.

24. Coontz, Stephanie (1992). *The Way We Never Were: American Families and the Nostalgia Trap*. New York: Basic; Coontz, Stephanie (2005, May 9). Our Kids Are Not Doomed. *Los Angeles Times*. p.11.

25. Berger, Peter, and Luckmann, Thomas (1980). *The Social Construction of Reality*. New York: Irvington.

26. Smith, Robert C., and Seltzer, Richard (2000). *Contemporary Controversies and the American Racial Divide*. Boston: Rowan & Littlefield.

27. Ventura, Stephanie J., and Bachrach, Christine A. (2000). Nonmarital Childbearing in the United States, 1940–1999.28. Soss, Joe, Schram, Sanford F., Vartanian, Thomas P., and O'Brien, Erin (2001). Setting the Terms of Relief: Explaining State Policy Choices in the Devolution Revolution. *American Journal of Political Science, 45*, pp. 378–403; Fording, Richard C. (2003). Laboratories of Democracy or Symbolic Politics? The Racial Origins of Welfare Reform. In Sanford F. Schram, Joe Soss, and Richard C. Fording (Eds.), *Race and the Politics Welfare Reform* (pp. 72–97). Ann Arbor: University of Michigan Press; and Johnson, Martin (2003). Racial Context, Public Attitudes and Welfare Effort. In Sanford F. Schram, Joe Soss, and Richard C. Fording (Eds.), *Race and the Politics of Welfare Reform* (pp. 151–167). Ann Arbor: University of Michigan Press.

29. *Planned Parenthood of Southeastern Pennsylvania v. Casey*. U.S. 112 (1992); Roberts, Dorothy (1997). *Killing the Black Body: Race, Reproduction and the Meaning of Liberty*. New York: Pantheon; and Neubeck, Kenneth J., and Cazenave, Noel A. (2001). *Welfare Racism*.

30. Becker, Gary S. (1981). A Treatise on the Family. Cambridge, MA: Harvard University Press.

31. Becker, Gary S. (1973). On the Interaction between the Quantity and Quality of Children. *Journal of Political Economy, 81*, pp. S279–S288.

32. Becker, Gary S. (1976). The Economic Approach to Human Behavior. Chicago: The University of Chicago Press. See especially chapter 11.

33. Becker, Gary S. (1976). Ibid.

34. See, for example, Levine, Phillip B., and Staiger, Douglas (1999). Abortion Policy and the Economics of Fertility. *Final Report Submitted to the Henry J. Kaiser Family Foundation*. Menlo Park, CA: Henry J. Kaiser Family Foundation.

35. Homans, George C. (1961). *Social Behavior: Its Elementary Forms*. New York: Harcourt, Brace, p. 81.

36. Becker, Gary S. (1996). *Accounting for Tastes*. Cambridge, MA: Harvard University Press.

37. Ibid., p. 19.

38. Murray, Charles (1993, October 29). The Coming White Underclass, p. A14; and Mead, Lawrence (1992). *The New Politics of Poverty*. New York: Basic.

39. Auletta, Ken (1983). *The Underclass*. New York: Vintage; and Murray, Charles (1999). *The Underclass Revisited*.

40. Bane, Mary Jo, and Ellwood, David T. (1994). *Welfare Realities: From Rhetoric to Reform*. Cambridge, MA: Harvard University Press; and Zimmerman, Shirley L., and Gager, C. T. (1997). A Potential Case of Social Bankruptcy: States' AFDC Payments and Their Teen Birth Rates. *Policy Study Journal, 25*, pp. 109–123.

41. Akerlof, George A., Yellen, Janet L., and Katz, Michael L. (1996). An Analysis of Out-of-Wedlock Childbearing in the United States. *Quarterly Journal of Economics, 111*, pp. 277–317.

42. Lewis, Oscar (1966). The Culture of Poverty. *Scientific American 215*, pp. 19–25; and Katz, Michael B. (1989). *The Undeserving Poor: From the War on Poverty to the War on Welfare*. New York: Pantheon.

43. Rainwater, Lee, and Yancey, William L. (1967). *The Moynihan Report and the Politics of Controversy*.

44. Ibid.

45. Hecho, Hugh (2001). The Politics of Welfare Reform. In Rebecca Blank and Ron Haskins (Eds.), *The New World of Welfare* (p. 175).

46. Murray, Charles (1984). *Losing Ground: American Social Policy 1950–1980*. New York: Basic.

47. Murray, Charles (1993). *The Coming White Underclass*, p. A14; Murray, Charles (1999). *The Underclass Revisited*; Murray, Charles (2001). Family Formation. In Rebecca Blank and Ron Haskins (Eds.), *The New World of Welfare*.

48. Murray, Charles (1999) *The Underclass Revisited*, p. 2.

49. Katz, Michael B. (1989). *The Undeserving Poor*; and Bane, Mary Jo, and Ellwood, David T. (1994). *Welfare Realities*.

50. Mead, Lawrence (1992). *The New Politics of Poverty*, pp. 148–149.

51. Center on Budget and Policy Priorities (1994). *Welfare and Out-of-Wedlock Births: A Research Summary*. Washington, DC: CBPP.

52. Studies that find a relationship between welfare benefits and nonmarital births include Argys, Laura M., Averett, Susan L., and Rees, Daniel T. (2000). Welfare Generosity, Pregnancies and Abortions among Unmarried AFDC Recipients. *Journal of Population Economics, 13*, pp. 569–594; Brinig, Margaret F., and Buckley, F. H. (1999). The Price of Virtue. *Public Choice, 98*, pp. 111–129; Clarke, George R. G., and Strauss, Robert P. (1998). Children as Income-Producing Assets: The Case of Teen Illegitimacy and Government Transfers. *Southern Economic Journal, 64*, 827–856; Grogger, Jeff, and Bronars, Stephanie G. (2001). The Effect of Welfare Payments on the Marriage and Fertility Behavior of Unwed Mothers: Results from a Twins Experiment. *Journal of Political Economy, 109*, pp. 529–545; Hoffman, Saul D., and Foster, Michael E. (2000). AFDC Benefits and Nonmarital Births to Young Women. *Journal of Human Resources, 35*, pp. 376–391; Horvath-Rose, Ann, and Peters, Elizabeth H. (2001). Welfare Waivers and Nonmarital Childbearing. In Greg Duncan and P. Lindsay Chase-Lansdale (Eds.), *Welfare Waivers and the Well Being of Children and Families* (pp.222–244). New York: Russell Sage Foundation; Jackson, Catherine A., and Klerman, Jacob A. (1996). *Welfare and American Fertility*. Discussion

Paper. Santa Monica, CA: RAND; Lundberg, Shelly, and Plotnick, Robert (1995). Adolescent Premarital Childbearing: Do Economic Incentives Matter? *Journal of Labor Economics, 13*, pp. 177–200; Mach, Traci (2001). *Measuring the Impact of Family Caps on Childbearing Decisions.* Department of Economics Working Paper 00–04. Albany: University of Albany-SUNY; Murray, Charles (1993). Welfare and the Family: The U.S. Experience. *Journal of Labor Economics, 11*, pp. 224–262; Powers, Elizabeth (1994). *The Impact of the AFDC Benefit Schedule on Birth Decisions and Program Participation.* Cleveland, OH: Federal Reserve Bank of Cleveland; Robins, Philip K., and Fronstin, Paul (1996). Welfare Benefits and Birth Decisions of Never-Married Women. *Population Research and Policy Review, 15*, pp. 21–43; and Rosenzweig, Mark R. (1999). Welfare, Marital Prospects and Nonmarital Childbearing. *Journal of Political Economy, 107*, pp. S3–S32. More recent studies finding little effect of welfare benefits include Acs, Gregory (1996). The Impact of Welfare on Young Mothers' Subsequent Childbearing Decisions. *The Journal of Human Resources, 31*, pp. 898–915; Fairlie, Robert W., and London, Rebecca A. (1997). The Effect of Incremental Benefit Levels on Births to AFDC Recipients. *Journal of Policy Analysis and Management, 16*, pp. 575–597; and Hoynes, Hillary (1997). Does Welfare Play Any Role in Female Headship Decisions? *Journal of Public Economics, 65*, pp. 89–117.

53. Rosenzweig, Mark R. (1999). Ibid.

54. Hoffman, Saul D., and Foster, Michael E. (2000). AFDC Benefits and Nonmarital Births to Young Women.

55. Mach, Traci (2001). Measuring the Impact of Family Caps on Childbearing Decisions.

56. Moffitt, Robert A. (1998). The Effect of Welfare on Marriage and Fertility. In Robert A. Moffitt (Ed.), *Welfare, The Family and Reproductive Behavior* (pp. 50–91). Washington, DC: National Academy Press. See especially p. 50.

57. Murray, Charles (1993). The Coming White Underclass, p. A14; Murray, Charles (1999). *The Underclass Revisited;* and Murray, Charles (2001). Family Formation. In Rebecca Blank and Ron Haskins (Eds.), *The New World of Welfare.*

58. Bane, Mary Jo, and Ellwood, David T. (1994). *Welfare Realities;* and Zimmerman, Shirley L., and Gager, C. T. (1997). A Potential Case of Social Bankruptcy.

59. Akerlof, George A., Yellen, Janet L., and Katz, Michael L. (1996). An Analysis of Out-of-Wedlock Childbearing in the United States; and Wilson, James Q. (2002). *The Marriage Problem.* New York: Harper Collins.

60. Jagannathan, Radha, and Camasso, Michael J. (2003). Family Cap and Nonmarital Fertility: The Racial Conditioning of Policy Effects. *Journal of Marriage and Family, 65*, pp. 52–71.

61. Wilson, William J., and Neckerman, Kathryn M. (1991). Poverty and Family Structure: The Widening Gap between Evidence and Public Policy Issues. In Sheldon H. Danziger and David H. Weinberg (Eds.), *Fighting Poverty: What Works and What Doesn't* (pp. 232–259). Cambridge, MA: Harvard University Press. See especially p. 253.

62. Wilson, William J. (1987). *The Truly Disadvantaged*. Chicago: University of Chicago Press; and Wilson, William J. (1991). Public Policy Research and the Truly Disadvantaged. In Christopher Jencks and Paul E. Peterson (Eds.), *The Urban Underclass* (pp. 460–481). Washington, DC: Brookings Institution.

63. Willis, Robert J. (1999). A Theory of Out-of-Wedlock Childbearing. *Journal of Political Economy*, *107*, pp. S33–S64. See especially p. S55.

64. Ibid., p. S59.

65. Lichter, Daniel T., LeClere, Felicia B., and McLaughlin, Diane K. (1991). Local Marriage Markets and the Marital Behavior of Black and White Women. *American Journal of Sociology*, *96*, pp. 843–867. See especially p. 797; and Lichter, Daniel T., McLaughlin, Diane K., Kephart, George, and Landry, David J. (1992). Race and the Retreat from Marriage: A Shortage of Marriageable Men? *American Sociological Review*, *57*, pp. 781–799.

66. Lichter, Daniel T., McLaughlin, Diane K., and Ribar, David C. (1997). Welfare and the Rise in Female Headed Families. *American Journal of Sociology*, *103*, pp. 112–143.

67. Lichter, Daniel T., McLaughlin, Diane K., and Ribar, David C. (2002). Economic Restructuring and the Retreat from Marriage. *Social Science Research*, *31*, pp. 230–256. See also Blau, Francine D., Kahn, Lawrence M., and Waldfogel, Jane (2000). Understanding Young Women's Marriage Decisions: The Role of Labor and Marriage Market Conditions. *Industrial and Labor Relations Review*, *53*, pp. 624–647.

68. South, Scott J., and Lloyd, Kim M. (1992). Marriage Markets and Nonmarital Fertility in the United States. *Demography*, *29*, pp. 247–264.

69. Fossett, Mark A., and Kiecolt, K. Jill (1993). Mate Availability and Family Structure among African Americans in U.S. Metropolitan Areas. *Journal of Marriage and the Family*, *55*, pp. 288–302.

70. Neal, Derek (2004). The Relationship between Marriage Market Prospects and Never-Married Motherhood. *Journal of Human Resources*, *39*, pp. 938–957.

71. Ibid., p. 948.

72. Akerlof, George A., Yellen, Janet L., and Katz, Michael L. (1996). An Analysis of Out-of-Wedlock Childbearing in the United States.

73. Ibid., p. 281.

74. Ibid., p. 278.

75. Ibid., p. 308.

76. Wilson, James Q. (2002). *The Marriage Problem*. New York: Harper Collins.

77. U.S. House of Representatives, Committee on Ways and Means (1996). *1996 Green Book: Background on Material and Data on Programs Within the Jurisdiction of the Committee on Ways and Means*. Washington, DC: U.S. Government Printing Office.

78. *Harris v. McRae*. 448 U.S. 297 (1980).

79. Nash, Elizabeth (2001). Public Funding of Abortion for Poor Women: Where Things Stand. *The Guttmacher Report on Public Policy*, *4*, pp. 12–13; and Boonstra, Heather, and Sonfield, Adam (2000). Rights without Access:

Revisiting Public Funding of Abortion for Poor Women. *The Guttmacher Report on Public Policy*, *3*, pp. 8–11.

80. Jones, Rachel K., Darroch, Jacqueline E., and Henshaw, Stanley K. (2002). Patterns in the Socioeconomic Characteristics of Women Obtaining Abortions in 2000–2001. *Perspectives on Sexual and Reproductive Health*, *34*, pp. 226–235; Henshaw, Stanley K., and Kost, Kathryn (1996). Abortion Patients in 1994–1995: Characteristics and Contraception Use. *Family Planning Perspectives*, *28*, pp. 140–147; and Henshaw, Stanley K., and Silverman, Jane (1988). The Characteristics and Prior Contraception Use of U.S. Abortion Patients. *Family Planning Perspectives*, *20*, pp. 158–168.

81. These studies, which are used as the basis for some of the national analysis that are included in chapter 8, include Gold, R.B. (1980). Medicaid in FY78: States Fund Abortions, U.S. Covers Other Family Planning Services. *Family Planning/Population Reporter, 1980*, *9*(2), pp. 28–34; Gold, R.B. (1981). States Spent $74.7 Million for Family Planning Services under Medicaid Program in FY79. *Family Planning/Population Reporter, 1981*, *10*(2), pp. 32–38; Nestor, B., and Gold, R.B. (1982). Public Funding of Contraceptive, Sterilization and Abortion Services, 1982. *Family Planning Perspectives, 1984, 16*(3), pp. 128–133; Gold, R.B., and Macias, J. (1986). Public Funding of Contraceptive, Sterilization and Abortion Services, 1985, *Family Planning Perspectives, 1986, 18*(6), pp. 259–264; Gold, R.B., and Guardado, S. (1988). Public Funding of Family Planning, Sterilization and Abortion Services, 1987. *Family Planning Perspectives, 1988, 20*(5), pp. 228–233; Gold, R.B., and Daley, D. (1991). Public Funding for Contraception, Sterilization and Abortion Services, Fiscal 1990. *Family Planning Perspectives, 1991, 23*(5), pp. 204–211; Daley, D., and Gold, R.B. (1993). Public Funding of Contraceptive, Sterilization and Abortion Services, Fiscal Year 1992. *Family Planning Perspectives, 1993, 25*(6), pp. 244–251; Sollom, T., Gold, R.B., and Saul, R. (1996). Public Funding of Contraceptive, Sterilization and Abortion Services, 1994. *Family Planning Perspectives, 1996, 28*(4), pp. 166–173; Nash E. (2001). Public Funding of Abortion: Where Things Stand. *The Guttmacher Report on Public Policy*, *4*(1), p. 13. http://www.guttmacher .org/pubs/journals/gr040113.pdf; and Boonstra, H., and Sonfield, A. (2000). Rights without Access: Revisiting Public Funding of Abortion for Poor Women. *The Guttmacher Report on Public Policy*, *3*(2), 8–11. http://www .guttmacher.org/pubs/journals/gr030208.pdf.

82. Jones, Rachel K., Darroch, Jacqueline E., and Henshaw, Stanley K. (2002). Patterns in the Socioeconomic Characteristics of Women Obtaining Abortions in 2000–2001. *Perspectives on Sexual and Reproductive Health*, *34*, pp. 226–235.

83. Henshaw, Stanley K., and Kost, Kathryn (1996). Abortion Patients in 1994–1995: Characteristics and Contraception Use. *Family Planning Perspectives*, *28*, pp. 140–147.

84. Blank, Rebecca M., George, Christine C., and London, Rebecca (1996). State Abortion Rates: The Impact of Policy, Providers, Politics, Demographics and Economic Environment. *Journal of Health Economics*, *15*, pp. 513–553.

85. Cook, Philip J., Parnell, Allan M., Moore, Michael J., and Pagnini, Deanna (1999). The Effect of Short-Term Variation in Abortion Funding on Pregnancy Outcomes. *Journal of Health Economics, 18*, pp. 241–257.

86. Morgan, S. Philip, and Parnell, Allan M. (2002). Effects on Pregnancy Outcomes and Changes in the North Carolina State Abortion Fund. *Population Research and Policy Review, 21*, pp. 319–338.

87. Ibid., p. 335.

88. Levine, Philip B., Trainor, Amy B., and Zimmerman, David J. (1996). The Effect of Medicaid Abortion Funding on Abortions, Pregnancies and Births. *Journal of Health Economics, 15*, pp. 555–578.

Chapter 4

1. Harvey, Carol, Camasso, Michael J., and Jagannathan, Radha (2000). Evaluating Welfare Reform Waivers Under Section 1115. *Journal of Economic Perspectives, 14*, pp. 165–188.

2. Gueron, Judith M., and Pauly, Edward (1991). *From Welfare to Work.* New York: Russell Sage Foundation.

3. Winston, Pamela (2002). *Welfare Policymaking in the States: The Devil in Devolution.* Washington, DC: Georgetown University Press, p. 90.

4. Gueron, Judith M. (2002). The Politics of Random Assignment: Implementing Studies and Affecting Policy. In Frederick Mosteller and Robert Boruch (Eds.), *Evidence Matters* (pp. 15–49). Washington, DC: Brookings Institution. See especially p. 20.

5. Orr, Larry L. (1999). *Social Experiments: Evaluating Public Programs with Experimental Methods.* Thousand Oaks, CA: Sage and Friedlander, Daniel, and Robins, Philip K. (1995). Evaluating Program Evaluations: New Evidence on Commonly Used Nonexperimental Methods. *American Economic Review, 85*, pp. 923–937.

6. Gueron, Judith M. (2002). The Politics of Random Assignment: Implementing Studies and Affecting Policy.

7. Riccio, James A., Friedlander, Daniel, and Freedman, Stephen (1994). *GAIN: Benefits, Costs, and Three-Year Impacts of a Welfare-to-Work Program.* New York: Manpower Demonstration Research Corporation; and Riccio, James A., and Orenstein, Alan (1996). Understanding Best Practices for Operating Welfare-to-Work Programs. *Evaluation Review, 20*, pp. 3–28.

8. Riccio, James A. and Orenstein, Alan (1996). Ibid., p. 23.

9. Hamilton, Gayle (2002). *Moving People from Welfare to Work: Lessons from the National Evaluation of Welfare-to-Work Strategies.* New York: Manpower Demonstration Research Corporation (MDRC); and Michalopoulos, Charles, and Schwartz, Christine (2001). *What Works Best for Whom: Impacts of 20 Welfare-to-Work Programs by Subgroup.* New York: Manpower Demonstration Research Corporation (MDRC).

10. Petrosino, Anthony, Boruch, Robert F., Soydan, Haluk, Duggan, Lorna, and Sanchez-Meca, Julio (2001). Meeting the Challenges of Evidence-Based Policy: The Campbell Collaboration. *The Annals, 578*, pp. 14–34.

11. Boruch, Robert F. (2005). Better Evaluation for Evidence-Based Policy: Place Randomized Trials in Education, Criminology, Welfare and Health. *The Annals*, *599*, pp. 6–18.

12. Boruch, Robert F., DeMoya, Dorothy, and Snyder, Brooke (2002). The Importance of Randomized Field Trials in Education and Related Areas. In Frederick Mosteller and Robert Boruch (Eds.), *Evidence Matters* (pp. 50–79).

13. Agency for Healthcare Research and Quality (2002). *Systems to Rate the Strength of Scientific Evidence*. Evidence Report/Technology Assessment No. 47, 02.E016. Washington, DC: U.S. Department of Health and Human Services; Camasso, Michael J. (2004). Treatment Evidence in a Non-Experimenting Practice Environment. In Albert R. Roberts and Kenneth R. Yeager (Eds.), *Evidence-Based Practice Manual* (pp. 233–246). New York: Oxford University Press.

14. Petrosino, Anthony, Boruch, Robert F., Soydan, Haluk, Duggan, Lorna, and Sanchez-Meca, Julio (2001). Meeting the Challenges of Evidence-Based Policy: The Campbell Collaboration. *The Annals*, *578*, pp. 14–34; and Boruch, Robert F. (2005). Better Evaluation for Evidence-Based Policy: Place Randomized Trials in Education, Criminology, Welfare and Health. *The Annals*, *599*, pp. 6–18.

15. Boruch, Robert F., and Mosteller, Frederick (2002). Overview and New Directions. In Frederick Mosteller and Robert F. Boruch (Eds.), *Evidence Matters*; and U.S. Department of Education, Institute of Education Sciences (2003). *Identifying and Implementing Educational Practices Supported by Rigorous Evidence: A User Friendly Guide*. Washington, DC: The Council for Excellence in Government.

16. Cook, Thomas D., and Payne, Monique R. (2002). Objecting to the Objections to Using Random Assignment in Educational Research. In Frederick Mosteller and Robert Boruch (Eds.), *Evidence Matters*.

17. Orr, Larry L. (1999). *Social Experiments*.

18. Burtless, Gary (1995). The Case for Randomized Field Trials in Economic and Policy Research. *Journal of Economic Perspectives*, *9*, pp. 63–84; Shadish, William R., Cook, Thomas D., and Campbell, Donald T. (2002). *Experimental and Quasi-Experimental Designs for Generalized Causal Inference*. Boston: Houghton Mifflin; Campbell, Donald T., and Stanley, Julian C. (1966). *Experimental and Quasi-Experimental Designs for Research*. Chicago: Rand McNally; and Orr, Larry L. (1999). *Social Experiments*.

19. Heckman, James J., and Smith, Jeffery A. (1995). Assessing the Case for Social Experiments. *Journal of Economic Perspectives*, *9*, pp. 85–110; and Moffitt, Robert A. (1992). Evaluation Methods for Program Entry Effects: In Charles F. Manski and Irwin Garfinkel (Eds.), *Evaluating Welfare and Training Programs* (pp. 231–252). Cambridge, MA: Harvard University Press.

20. Nathan, Peter E., and Gorman, Jack M. (2002). Efficacy, Effectiveness and the Clinical Utility of Psychotherapy Research. In P. E. Nathan and J. M. Gorman (Eds.), *A Guide to Treatments That Work* (pp. 643–654). New York: Oxford University Press; Nathan, Peter E. (2004). The Clinical Utility of Therapy Research: Bridging the Gap between the Present and the Future. In A. R. Roberts and K. R. Yeager (Eds.), *Evidence-Based Practice Manual*

(pp. 949–960). New York: Oxford University Press; Rosenbaum, Paul R. (2002). *Observational Studies*, 2nd ed. New York: Springer; Sommer, A., and Zeger, Scott L. (1991). On Estimating Efficacy from Clinical Trials. *Statistics in Medicine*, *10*, pp. 45–52; and Flay, Brian R., and Collins, Linda M. (2005). Historical Review of School-Based Randomized Trials for Evaluating Problem Behavior Prevention Programs. *The Annals*, *599*, pp. 115–146.

21. Burtless, Gary (1995). The Case for Randomized Field Trials in Economic and Policy Research. *Journal of Economic Perspectives*, *9*, 63–84; and Moffitt, Robert A. (1992). Evaluation Methods for Program Entry Effects: In Charles F. Manski and Irwin Garfinkel (Eds.), *Evaluating Welfare and Training Programs* (pp. 231–252). Cambridge, MA: Harvard University Press.

22. Friedlander, Daniel, and Robins, Philip K. (1995). Evaluating Program Evaluations: New Evidence on Commonly Used Nonexperimental Methods. *American Economic Review*, *85*, pp. 923–937.

23. Lalonde, Robert (1986). Evaluating the Econometric Evaluations fo Training Programs with Experimental Data. *American Economic Review* 76:604–620; and Fraker, Thomas M., and Maynard, Rebecca (1987). The Adequacy of Comparison Group Designs for Evaluations of Employment-Related Programs. *Journal of Human Resources*, *22*, 194–227; and Burtless, Gary, and Orr, Larry L. (1986). Are Classical Experiments Needed for Manpower Policy? *Journal of Human Resources*, *21*, 606–639.

24. Grissmer, David, Flanagan, Ann, Kawata, Jennifer, and Williamson, Stephanie (2000). *Improving Student Achievement*. Santa Monica, CA: Rand Corp, p. 33.

25. Orr, Larry L. (1999). *Social Experiments*, p. xi; Cook, Thomas D., and Payne, Monique R. (2002). Objecting to the Objections to Using Random Assignment in Educational Research. In Frederick Mosteller and Robert Boruch (Eds.), *Evidence Matters*.

26. See, for example, Grinnell, Richard M. (1997). *Social Work Research and Evaluation*. Itasca, IL: F. E. Peacock; Greenberg, David, and Shroder, Matthew (1997). *The Digest of Social Experiments*, 2nd ed. Washington, DC: The Urban Institute; Cook, Thomas D., and Payne, Monique R. (2002). *Objecting to the Objections to Using Random Assignment in Educational Research*. In Frederick Mosteller and Robert Boruch (Eds.), *Evidence Matters*; and Shadish, William R., Cook, Thomas D., and Campbell, Donald T. (2002). *Experimental and Quasi-Experimental Designs for Generalized Causal Inference*.

27. Patton, Michael Q. (1978). *Utilization-Focused Evaluation*. Beverly Hills, CA: Sage, p. 207.

28. Stake, Robert E. (2004). *Standards-Based and Responsive Evaluation*. Thousand Oaks, CA: Sage, p. 30.

29. Lincoln, Yvonna S., and Guba, Egon G. (2004). The Roots of Fourth Generation Evaluation. In Marvin C. Alkin (Ed.), *Evaluation Roots: Tracing Theorists' Views and Influences* (pp. 225–241). Thousand Oaks, CA: Sage. See especially p. 239.

30. Lincoln, Yvonna S. (2004). Review of Scientific Research in Education and Evidence Matters. *Academe*, *90*, pp. 110–115; and Hartman, Ann (1990). Many Ways of Knowing [Editorial]. *Social Work*, *35*, pp. 3–4.

31. Cook, Thomas D., and Payne, Monique R. (2002). Objecting to the Objections to Using Random Assignment in Educational Research. In Frederick Mosteller and Robert Boruch (Eds.), *Evidence Matters*; Camasso, Michael J. (2004). Treatment Evidence in a Non-Experimenting Practice Environment: Some Recommendations for Increasing Supply and Demand. In Albert R. Roberts and Kenneth R. Yeager (Eds.), *Evidence-Based Practice Manual* (pp. 233–246). New York: Oxford University Press; and Shadish, William R., Cook, Thomas D., and Campbell, Donald T. (2002). *Experimental and Quasi-Experimental Designs for Generalized Causal Inference.*

32. Orr, Larry L. (1999). *Social Experime*nts; Weiss, Carol H. (1983). Ideology, Interests and Information: The Basis of Policy Positions. In Daniel Callahan and Bruce Jennings (Eds.) Ethics, The Social Sciences and Policy Analysis (pp. 213–245). New York: Plenum; and Greenberg, David H., and Mandell, Marvin B. (1991). Research Utilization in Policymaking: A Tale of Two Series of Experiments. *Journal of Policy Analysis and Management, 10,* pp. 633–656.

33. Harvey, Carol, Camasso, Michael J., and Jagannathan, Radha (2000). Evaluating Welfare Reform Waivers under Section 1115.

34. New Jersey Department of Human Services, Division of Family Development (1992). *DFD Instruction No. 92–9–9.* Procedures for Control and Treatment Groups. Trenton, NJ: NJ DHS; and Camasso, Michael J., and Harvey, Carol (1994). *Quarterly Progress Memorandum on FDP Evaluation.* New Brunswick, NJ: Rutgers University, School of Social Work.

35. Harvey, Carol, Camasso, Michael J., and Jagannathan, Radha (2000). Evaluating Welfare Reform Waivers under Section 1115.

36. Orr, Larry L. (1999). Social Experiments; and Mohr, Lawrence B. (1995). *Impact Analysis for Program Evaluation.* Thousand Oaks, CA: Sage.

37. Harvey, Carol, Camasso, Michael J., and Jagannathan, Radha (2000). Evaluating Welfare Reform Waivers under Section 1115.

38. Haveman, Robert (1997). Potentials and Problems of a Pre-Post Design for State-Based Evaluation of National Welfare Reform. In *Evaluating Comprehensive State Welfare Reforms: A Conference* (pp. 25–41). Madison, WI: IRP; Cain, Glen G. (1997). Controlled Experiments in Evaluating the New Welfare Programs. In *Evaluating Comprehensive State Welfare Reforms* (pp. 61–72).

39. Shadish, William R., Cook, Thomas D., and Campbell, Donald T. (2002). *Experimental and Quasi-Experimental Designs for Generalized Causal Inference*;Cook, Thomas D., and Campbell, Donald T. (1979). *Quasi-Experimentation: Design and Analysis Issues for Field Settings.* Chicago: Rand McNally; Mohr, Lawrence B. (1995). *Impact Analysis for Program Evaluation.* Thousand Oaks, CA: Sage; and Manski, Charles F. (1996). Learning about Treatment Effects from Experiments with Random Assignment of Treatments. *Journal of Human Resources, 31,* 709–733.

40. Moffitt, Robert A., and Ver Ploeg, Michele (Eds.) (1999). *Evaluating Welfare Reform: A Framework and Review of Current Work.* Washington, DC: National Academy; and Greenberg, David, and Shroder, Matthew (1997). *The Digest of Social Experiments,* 2nd ed. Washington, DC: The Urban Institute.

41. Flay, Brian R., and Collins, Linda M. (2005). Historical Review of School-Based Randomized Trials for Evaluating Problem Behavior Prevention Programs.

42. Heckman, James J. (1992). Randomization and Social Policy Evaluation. In Charles F. Manski and Irwin Garfinkel (Eds.), *Evaluating Welfare and Training Programs* (pp. 201–230). Cambridge, MA: Harvard University Press; and Heckman, James J., and Smith, Jeffery A. (1995). Assessing the Case for Social Experiments. *Journal of Economic Perspectives*, 9, pp. 85–110.

43. Heckman, James J., and Smith, Jeffery A. (1995). Ibid.; and Moffitt, Robert A., and Ver Ploeg, Michele (Eds.) (2001). *Evaluating Welfare Reform in an Era of Transition*. Washington, DC: National Academy.

44. Formally, expected (average) behavior while on welfare is the product of the probability of being on welfare, $\Pr(D=1)$, and the expected value of behavior Y while on welfare, $E(Y|D=1)$, that is,

$$\Pr(D=1)\ E(Y|D=1)$$

Policy changes can alter either or both of these, that is,

$$\Delta[\Pr(D=1)\ E\ (Y|D=1)] = [E(Y|D=1)][\Delta\Pr(D=1)] + [\Pr(D=1)][\Delta(E(Y|D=1))].$$

45. Garfinkel, Irwin, Manski, Charles F., and Michalopoulos, Charles (1992). Micro Experiments and Macro Effects. In Charles F. Manski and Irwin Garfinkel (Eds.), *Evaluating Welfare and Training Programs* (pp. 253–273). Cambridge, MA: Harvard University Press; and Cain, Glen G. (1997). Controlled Experiments in Evaluating the New Welfare Programs. In *Evaluating Comprehensive State Welfare Reforms: A Conference* (pp. 61–72). Madison, WI: IRP.

46. Moffitt, Robert A. (1992). Evaluation Methods for Program Entry Effects. In Charles F. Manski and Irwin Garfinkel (Eds.), *Evaluating Welfare and Training Programs*. Cambridge, MA: Harvard University Press, p. 241.

47. Garfinkel, Irwin, Manski, Charles F., and Michalopoulos, Charles (1992). Micro Experiments and Macro Effects.

48. Moffitt, Robert A. (1998). The Effect of Welfare on Marriage and Fertility. In R. A. Moffitt (Ed.), *Welfare, the Family and Reproductive Behavior* (pp. 50–97). Washington, DC: National Academy.

49. Manski, Charles F. (1997). The Mixing Problem in Programme Evaluations. *Review of Economic Studies*. 64, 537–553. and Pepper, John V. (2003). Using Experiments to Evaluate Performance Standards: What Do Welfare-to-Work Demonstrations Reveal to Welfare Reformers? *Journal of Human Resources*, 38, pp. 860–880.

50. Hotz, V. Joseph, Imbens, Guido W., and Mortimer, Julie H. (1999). *Predicting the Efficacy of Future Training Programs Using Past Experiences*. NBER–238. Cambridge, MA: National Bureau of Economic Research.

51. Friedlander, Daniel, and Robins, Philip K. (1995). Evaluating Program Evaluations: New Evidence on Commonly Used Nonexperimental Methods. *American Economic Review*, 85, pp. 923–937.

52. See, for example, Cook, Thomas D., and Campbell, Donald T. (1979). *Quasi-Experimentation.*

53. Rank, Mark R. (1983). Exiting from Welfare: A Life-Table Analysis. *Social Service Review, 59,* pp. 358–376; Moffitt, Robert A. (2002). Experience-Based Measures of Heterogeneity in the Welfare Caseload. In Michele Ver Ploeg, Robert A. Moffitt, and Constance F. Citro (Eds.), *Studies of Welfare Populations: Data Collection and Research Issues*; and Ellwood, David T., and Bane, Mary Jo (1994). Understanding Welfare Dynamics. In Mary Jo Bane and David T. Ellwood (Eds.), *Welfare Realities: From Rhetoric to Reform* (pp. 28–66). Cambridge, MA: Harvard University Press.

54. Robinson, T. M. (1987). *Fragments: A Text and Translation/Heraclitus.* Toronto: University of Toronto Press. p.27.

55. Moffitt, Robert A., and Ver Ploeg, Michele (Eds.) (2001). *Evaluating Welfare Reform in an Era of Transition*; Ver Ploeg, Michele (2002). Preexit Benefit Receipt and Employment Histories and Postexit Outcomes of Welfare Leavers. In Michele Ver Ploeg, Robert A. Moffitt, and Constance F. Citro (Eds.), *Studies of Welfare Populations: Data Collection and Research Issues* (pp. 415–472). Washington, DC: National Academy Press; and Stevens, D. (2002). Welfare, Employment, and Earnings. *Memorandum Proposal for the Panel on Data and Methods for Measuring the Effects of Changes in Social Welfare Programs.* Committee on National Statistics. Baltimore: University of Baltimore.

56. Cook, Thomas D., and Campbell, Donald T. (1979). *Quasi-Experimentation.* Chicago: Rand McNally; and Shadish, William R., Cook, Thomas D., and Campbell, Donald T. (2002). *Experimental and Quasi-Experimental Designs for Generalized Causal Inference.*

57. Moffitt, Robert A., and Ver Ploeg, Michele (Eds.) (2001). *Evaluating Welfare Reform in an Era of Transition*; and Moffitt, Robert A., and Ver Ploeg, Michele (Eds.) (1999). *Evaluating Welfare Reform: A Framework and Review of Current Work.* Washington, DC: National Academy.

58. Meyer, Bruce D. (1995). Natural and Quasi-Experiments in Economics. *Journal of Business and Economic Statistics, 13,* pp. 151–159. See especially p. 153.

59. Stock, J. H., and Watson, M. W. (2003). *Introduction to Econometrics.* Boston: Addison-Wesley; Orr, Larry L. (1999). *Social Experiments*; and Moffitt, Robert A. (1998). The Effect of Welfare on Marriage and Fertility. In R. A. Moffitt (Ed.), *Welfare, The Family and Reproductive Behavior* (pp. 50–97). Washington, DC: National Academy.

60. Meyer, Bruce D. (1995). Natural and Quasi-Experiments in Economics. *Journal of Business and Economic Statistics, 13,* pp. 151–159.

61. Orr, Larry L. (1999). *Social Experiments.*

62. Mohr, Lawrence B. (1995). *Impact Analysis for Program Evaluation*; Shadish, William R., Cook, Thomas D., and Campbell, Donald T. (2002). *Experimental and Quasi-Experimental Designs for Generalized Causal Inference.*

63. Moffitt, Robert A., and Ver Ploeg, Michele (Eds.) (2001). *Evaluating Welfare Reform in an Era of Transition,* p. 73.

64. Flay, Brian R., and Collins, Linda M. (2005). Historical Review of School-Based Randomized Trials for Evaluating Problem Behavior Prevention Programs.

65. Rosenbaum, Paul R. (2002). Observational Studies, 2nd ed. New York: Springer.

66. Harvey, Carol, Camasso, Michael J., and Jagannathan, Radha (2000). Evaluating Welfare Reform Waivers under Section 1115; Greenberg, David, and Shroder, Matthew (1997). The Digest of Social Experiments, 2nd ed. Washington, DC: The Urban Institute; and Moffitt, Robert A., and Ver Ploeg, Michele (Eds.) (2001). Evaluating Welfare Reform in an Era of Transition.

67. New Jersey Department of Treasury (1992). Family Development Program Evaluation for the Department of Human Services. T1281. Trenton, NJ: Department of Treasury.

68. Camasso, Michael J., and Harvey, Carol (1995). Proposal to Augment the Five-Year Evaluation of the Family Development Program, rev. New Brunswick, NJ: Rutgers University.

69. Baltagi, Badi H. (2001). Econometric Analysis of Panel Data. New York: John Wiley.

70. Harvey, Carol, Camasso, Michael J., and Jagannathan, Radha (2000). Evaluating Welfare Reform Waivers under Section 1115.

71. Turturro, Carolyn, Benda, Brent, and Turney, Howard (1997). Arkansas Welfare Waiver Demonstration Project. Little Rock: University of Arkansas at Little Rock, School of Social Work.

72. The counties are Atlantic, Camden, Cumberland, Essex, Hudson, Mercer, Middlesex, Monmouth, Passaic, and Union. We restricted our non-experimental caseload analyses to these same ten counties to help make the experimental and panel analysis as comparable as possible.

73. New Jersey Department of Treasury (1992). Family Development Program Evaluation for the Department of Human Services. T1281. Trenton, NJ: Department of Treasury.

74. Ibid.

75. Ellwood, David T., and Bane, Mary Jo (1994). Understanding Welfare Dynamics.

76. Moffitt, Robert A., and Ver Ploeg, Michele (Eds.) (2001). Evaluating Welfare Reform in an Era of Transition; and Moffitt, Robert A. (2002). Experienced-Based Measures of Heterogeneity in the Welfare Caseload. In Michele Ver Ploeg, Robert A. Moffitt, and Constance F. Citro (Eds.), Studies of Welfare Populations: Data Collection and Research Issues (pp. 473–499).

77. James Heckman has pointed up the issue faced by all experiments about when to randomize. Too early a stage or too narrow a time frame could yield a potential conflict between obtaining better estimates of a behavioral model and producing simple estimates of mean impacts that cannot be generalized. We find no difference in Family Cap impacts assessed using the opening cohort sample accrued through the planned sampling period (December 1993) and the actual opening cohort sample (that accrued through December 1994). Analyses presented here report on the actual sample appearing in table 4.1.

78. Manski, Charles F. (1996). Learning about Treatment Effects from Experiments with Random Assignment of Treatments. Journal of Human Resources, 31, pp. 709–733.

Manski asserts a great many social experiments, including the now-classic experiments conducted by MDRC, focus on the population fraction receiving treatment under a program. This often amounts to a comparison of welfare reform treatment and AFDC treatment (controls) without consideration of individuals who are not currently on the rolls. Hence, under the assumption of no entry effects, the experiment produces estimates of efficacy that are more descriptive of the "average effect of treatment on the treated" than "an average treatment effect."

79. Krueger, Alan B. (1999). Experimental Estimates of Education Production Functions. *Quarterly Journal of Economics, 114*, pp. 497–532; Orr, Larry L. (1999). *Social Experiments*; and Stock, J. H., and Watson, M. W. (2003). *Introduction to Econometrics*. Boston: Addison-Wesley. This method of pooling, however, needs to take into consideration the possibility that the exit rates between experimental and control group cases differ. There were no significant experimental-control differences in reasons for exit due to marriages, change in residence, or earned income; and a Cox regression analysis of experimental attrition found no significant differences between experimental and control group cases in the hazard of leaving AFDC/TANF. Further, no differences were found between the two groups in overall length of stay on welfare, recidivism, or continuous stay lengths (spells). See Radha Jagannathan, Michael J. Camasso, and Mark R. Killingsworth (2004). New Jersey's Family Cap Experiment: Do Fertility Impacts Differ by Racial Density? *Journal of Labor Economics, 22*, pp. 431–460.

80. Rank, Mark R. (1983). Exiting from Welfare: A Life-Table Analysis. *Social Service Review, 59*, pp. 358–376; and Ellwood, David T., and Bane, Mary Jo (1994). Understanding Welfare Dynamics.

81. Because all cases in the post-reform period (except for the control cases in the experimental sample) were subject to the Family Cap, I also computed mean and median spell lengths for experimental sample excluding the control cases. These mean and median spell lengths were virtually identical to those reported in table 4.5 for the experimental sample as a whole.

Chapter 5

1. Leusner, Donna (1993, November 9). Pregnancy Drop: Fewer Mothers Conceive in First Two Months of Benefit Cutoff. [*Newark*] *Star-Ledger*, p. 1; O'Neill, June (1994). Expert Testimony in *C. K. v. Shalala*, U.S. District Court—New Jersey Civil Action No. 93–5354; and Goertzel, Ted G., and Young, Gary S. (1996). New Jersey's Experiment in Welfare Reform. *The Public Interest, 125*, pp. 72–80.

2. Harvey, Carol, Camasso, Michael J., and Jagannathan, Radha (2000). Evaluating Welfare Reform Waivers under Section 1115. *Journal of Economic Perspectives, 14*, pp. 165–188; Wiseman, Michael (1996). State Strategies for Welfare Reform: The Wisconsin Story. *Journal of Policy Analysis and Management, 15*, pp. 515–546; and Quinn, Lois M., and Magill, Robert

S. (1994). Politics Versus Research in Social Policy. *Social Service Review*, *68*, pp. 503–520.

3. Quinn, Lois M., and Magill, Robert S. (1994). Ibid.

4. Ibid, p. 514.

5. Harvey, Carol, Camasso, Michael J., and Jagannathan, Radha (2000). Evaluating Welfare Reform Waivers under Section 1115. States were permitted, under certain conditions, to continue any Section 1115 waivers that were in effect at the time that the Personal Responsibility and Work Opportunity Reconciliation Act (PRWORA) was signed into law, although they were released from any evaluation requirements for these waivers. However, after the passage of this welfare reform legislation, Administration for Children and Families (ACF) continued to encourage evaluation and provided funding support on a competitive basis for self-initiated evaluations. Nine states received funding to continue previously initiated evaluations of their Section 1115–waivered experiments. These experiments were termed "Welfare Reform Waiver Studies," or "Track 1" evaluations.

Another group of states received funding to evaluated Section 1115–waivered programs that were significantly modified for implementation under Temporary Assistance for Needy Families (TANF). These evaluations ("Welfare Reform Modified Waiver Studies" or "Track 2" evaluations) consisted largely of process/implementation analyses. The process analysis is, in many instances, augmented by tracking studies of families who have left the welfare rolls.

It is no coincidence that most of the Track 2 evaluations were strictly process oriented, with no rigorous evaluation of programmatic impacts, costs, or benefits. Process analyses can identify operational problems or flaws, and programmatic elements and procedures can be adjusted to address these problems, and there are no potentially embarrassing judgments waiting in the wings about adverse program effects or whether the program is effective.

6. Rossi, Peter H., Freeman, Howard E., and Lipsey, Mark W. (1999). *Evaluation: A Systematic Approach*, 6th ed. Thousand Oaks, CA: Sage; Babbie, Earl (1992). *The Practice of Social Research*, 6th ed. Belmont, CA: Wadsworth; Weiss, Carol H. (1998). *Evaluation*, 2nd ed. Upper Saddle River, NJ: Prentice Hall; Monette, Duane R., Sullivan, Thomas J., and DeJong, Cornell R. (2002). *Applied Social Research*, 5th ed. New York: Harcourt.

7. Coleman, James S., Campbell, Ernest Q., Hobson, Carol J., McPartland, James, Mood, Alexander M., Weinfeld, Frederic D., and York, Robert (1966). *Equality of Educational Opportunity*. Washington, DC: U.S. Government Printing Office.

8. Coleman, James S., Kelly, Sara D., and Moore, John A. (1975). *Trends in School Integration*. Washington, DC: The Urban Institute.

9. Harvey, Carol, Camasso, Michael J., and Jagannathan, Radha (2000). Evaluating Welfare Reform Waivers under Section 1115; Greenberg, David H., and Robins, Philip K. (1986). The Changing Role of Social Experiments in Policy Analysis. *Journal of Policy Analysis and Management*, *5*, pp. 340–362; Greenberg, David H., and Mandell, Marvin B. (1991). Research Utilization Policymaking: A Tale of Two Series (of Social Experiments). *Journal of Policy Analysis and Management*, *10*, pp. 633–656. Perhaps George

Bernard Shaw said it best in his play *The Devil's Disciple* (1901 [Act 2]): The worst sin toward our fellow creatures is not to hate them but to be indifferent to them: that's the essence of inhumanity.

10. Aaron, Henry J. (1998). *Politics and the Professors: The Great Society in Perspective.* Washington, DC: Brookings Institution.

11. Greenberg, David H., and Mandell, Marvin B. (1991). Research Utilization Policymaking.

12. Orr, Larry L. (1999). *Social Experiments: Evaluating Public Programs with Experimental Methods.* Thousand Oaks, CA: Sage Press.

13. Ibid., p. 239.

14. Greenberg, David, Shroder, Mark, and Onstott, Matthew (1999). The Social Experiment Market. *Journal of Economic Perspective, 13,* pp. 157–172. See especially p. 167.

15. Weiss, Carol H. (1983). Ideology, Interest and Information. In Daniel Callahan and Bruce Jennings (Eds.), *Ethics, The Social Sciences and Policy Analysis* (pp. 231–245). New York: Plenum. See especially p. 225.

16. Ibid, p. 224.

17. Orr, Larry L. (1999). *Social Experiments.*

18. Camasso, Michael J. (1995). *Proposal to Augment the Five-Year Evaluation of the Family Developmental Program (Revised JAN-11).* New Brunswick, NJ: Rutgers University School of Social Work; and Myers, Rudolf (1993). *Revised Schedule of Due Dates for FDP Evaluation.* Trenton, NJ: Division of Family Development, NJDHS.

19. Henneberger, Melinda (1995, April 11). State Aid Is Capped, but to What Effect? *New York Times,* p. 18.

20. O'Neill, June (1994). Expert Testimony in *C. K. v. Shalala,* U.S. District Court—New Jersey Civil Action No. 93–5354; and Zaretsky, Adam M. (1995). *How Statistics Can Mislead: The Case of Family Caps in State Welfare Programs.* St. Louis: Federal Reserve Bank.

21. Donovan, Patricia (1995). The Family Cap: A Popular but Unproven Method of Welfare Reform. *Family Planning Perspectives, 27,* pp. 166–171. See especially p. 169.

22. Goertzel, Ted G., and Young, Gary S. (1996). New Jersey's Experiment in Welfare Reform. *The Public Interest, 125,* pp. 72–80. See especially p. 76.

23. We were never able to exactly replicate the analysis conducted by O'Neill in her report due to some rather odd and unfortunate circumstances that befell the Division of Family Development Data Center. The programmer who had supplied the sample of cases to Dr. O'Neill had died and the list of case identifiers he had used to supply the researcher with case extracts could not be found. What remains unexplained is why O'Neill was not given the entire sample of ongoing cases. After extensive analysis that ended in December 1995, we concluded that "while some difference in birth rates between the experimental and control cases did exist when all births were counted while the ongoing case sample was being populated, this difference diminished to a point where it is not statistically significant."

24. Michael J. Camasso (1996, April 25). Testing Family Cap Impact Using an O'Neill Approximated Sample (memo). New Brunswick, NJ:

Rutgers University School of Social Work.24. Camasso, Michael J. (1995). June 14 Letter to Rudolf Myers. New Brunswick, NJ: Rutgers University School of Social Work, p. 2.

25. Vobejda, Barbara (1995, June 21). NJ Welfare "Cap" Has No Effect on Births, Study Finds. *Washington Post*, p. 8.

26. Kramer, Michael (1995, July 5). The Myth about Welfare Moms. *Time*, p. 21.

27. Ibid.

28. Ruess, Michelle (1995, June 22). Welfare Reform Failing to Lower Birthrate in NJ, Study Finds. *The Bergen Record*, p. 3.

29. Carter, Kathy B. (1995, June 22). Study Finds Reduction in Welfare Benefits Hasn't Cut Birth Rates. [*Newark*] *Star-Ledger*, p. 3.

30. Ibid.

31. Ibid.

32. Ibid.

33. Laracy, Michael C. (1994). *The Jury Is Still Out: An Analysis of the Purported Impact of New Jersey's AFDC Child Exclusion (a.k.a., Family Cap) Law*. Washington, DC: Center For Law and Social Policy; Laracy, Michael C. (1995). *If It Seems Too Good to Be True, It Probably Is*. Baltimore: The Annie E. Casey Foundation.

34. Laracy, Michael C. (1995). *If It Seems Too Good to Be True, It Probably Is*, p. 11.

35. Morales, Cecilio (1995). *New Jersey Family Cap Has No Effect in First Year, New Data Show. Welfare-to-Work* (7-17-95). Washington, DC: MII Publications, p. 102.

36. Laracy, Michael C. (1994). *The Jury Is Still Out*, p. 6.

37. Ibid., p. 7.

38. Henneberger, Melinda (1995, April 11). State Aid Is Capped, but to What Effect? *New York Times*, p. 18.

39. Laracy, Michael C. (1995). *If It Seems Too Good to Be True, It Probably Is*, p. 8.

40. Ibid.

41. Laracy did note this connection to the Whitman administration several years later in a brief article, "Comments on Rossi," which appeared in Douglas J. Besharov and Peter Germanis (Eds.) (2000). *Preventing Subsequent Births to Welfare Mothers*. University of Maryland: School of Public Affairs.

42. *MacNeil/Lehrer News Hour*, 6/16/95.

43. *CNBC News*, 8/7/95.

44. Haskins, Ron. Personal communication.

45. Winston, Pamela (2002). *Welfare Policymaking in the States: The Devil in Devolution*. Washington, DC: Georgetown University Press.

46. Gibbs, Nancy (1994, June 20). The Vicious Cycle. *Time*, pp. 25–32.

47. Camasso, Michael J. (1995). New Jersey's Evaluation. In Douglas Besharov (Ed.), *Addressing Illegitimacy: Welfare Reform Options for Congress* (pp. 16–22). Washington, DC: American Enterprise Institute.

48. Camasso, Michael J. (1995). New Jersey's Evaluation. In Douglas Besharov (Ed.), *Addressing Illegitimacy*, p. 16.

49. Bernstein, Ilene N., Bohrnstedt, George W., and Borgatta, Edgar F. (1975). External Validity and Evaluation Research: A Codification of Problems. *Sociological Methods and Research, 4*, pp. 101–128.

50. Orr, Larry L. (1999). *Social Experiments.*

51. Mohr, Lawrence B. (1995). Impact Analysis for Program Evaluation. Thousand Oaks, CA: Sage; and Orr, Larry L. (1999). *Social Experiments.*

52. Myers, Rudolf (1995). *New Jersey's Family Cap: Measuring the Effects.* Trenton, NJ: Division of Family Development, NJDHS.

53. Rossi, Peter (1995). What the New Jersey Experiment Results Mean and Do Not Mean. In Douglas Besharov (Ed.), *Addressing Illegitimacy*, pp. 23–25. See especially p. 25.

54. Camasso, Michael J. (1995, June 8). Memo to Dean Mary Davidson. New Brunswick, NJ: Rutgers School of Social Work.

55. Ibid.

56. Camasso, Michael J. (1998). November 2 Briefing Meeting Packet to Dean Mary Davidson. New Brunswick, NJ: Rutgers School of Social Work.

57. Fletcher, Martin (1995, September 15). Senate Tempers U.S. Welfare Revolution. *London Times*, p. 1; and Winston, Pamela (2002). *Welfare Policymaking in the States.*

58. Rector, Robert E. (1996). *Yet Another Sham Welfare Reform: Examining the NGA Plan.* Backgrounder #1075. Washington, DC: The Heritage Foundation.

59. See, for example, Congressional Record, House, Wednesday, March 22, 1995; Congressional Record, Senate, Wednesday, September 13, 1995; and Congressional Record, House, Thursday, December 14, 1995.

60. New Jersey Department of Treasury (1992). *Family Development Evaluation for Department of Human Services* (T1281). Trenton, NJ: NJDT, p. 31.

61. Laracy, Michael C. (1995). *If It Seems Too Good to Be True, It Probably Is.*

62. Edin, Kathy, and Lein, Laura (1997). *Making Ends Meet: How Single Mothers Survive Welfare and Low-Wage Work.* New York: Russell Sage Foundation; Dillman, Donald A. (2000). *Mail and Telephone Surveys: The Total Design Method.* New York: John Wiley; and Turner, C. F., Ku, L., Rogers, S. M., Lindberg, L. D., Pleck, J. H., and Sonnerstein, F. L. (1998). Adolescent Sexual Behavior, Drug Use and Violence: Increased Reporting with Computer Survey Technology. *Science, 280*, pp. 867–873.

63. Jagannathan, Radha (2001). Relying on Surveys to Understand Abortion Behavior: Some Cautionary Evidence. *American Journal of Public Health, 91*, pp. 1825–1831.

64. Hammerslough, C. R. (1986). Correcting Survey-Based Contraceptive Failure Rates for Abortion Underreporting. (Doctoral Dissertation. Princeton University); and Jones, Elise F., and Forrest, Jacqueline D. (1992). Underreporting of Abortion in Surveys of U.S. Women, 1965–1982. *Demography, 22*, pp. 415–430.

65. Udry, Richard J., Gaughan, Monica, Schwingl, Pamela J., Van der Berg, Bea J. (1996). A Medical Record Linkage Analysis of Abortion Underreporting. *Family Planning Perspectives, 28*, 228–231.

66. New Jersey Department of Treasury (1992). *Family Development Evaluation for Department of Human Services* (T1281). Trenton, NJ: NJDT.

67. Altman, Drew E. (1994). *Grant Award Notice to Michael J. Camasso.* Menlo Park, CA: Kaiser Family Foundation.

68. Rubin, Allen, and Babbie, Earl (1989). *Research Methods for Social Work.* Belmont, CA: Wadsworth; and Dillman, Donald A. (2000). *Mail and Telephone Surveys: The Total Design Method.* New York: John Wiley. The denominator in our calculation of response rates, 3,018 recipients, removes households where a father, grandparent, aunt, or guardian indicated responsibility for the children.

69. Camasso, Michael J., Jagannathan, Radha, and Harvey, Carol (1996). *The Recipient's Perspective: Welfare Mothers Assess New Jersey's Family Development Program and the Family Cap.* Menlo Park, CA: The Henry J. Kaiser Foundation.The survey instruments used in the survey are available from the Kaiser Family Foundation.

70. Ibid., p. 5.

71. Ibid., p. 36.

72. Hoff, Tina (1996). Proposed Press Release for Survey of Women on Welfare in New Jersey. Menlo Park, CA: Kaiser Family Foundation.

73. Kaiser Family Foundation (1996). Updated Agenda for Family Cap Briefing. Menlo Park, CA: Kaiser Family Foundation.

74. Hoff, Tina (1996). Memorandum on Press Conference Cancellation. Menlo Park, CA: Kaiser Family Foundation.

75. Beebout, Harold (1996). Independent Review of Rutgers Family Development Program Evaluation. Washington, DC: Mathematics Policy Research, p. 3.

76. Thornton, Craig, and Hershey, Alan M. (1990). *REACH Welfare Initiative Program Evaluation (MPR Reference No. 7862–400).* Princeton, NJ: Mathematics Policy Research, p. 6.

77. Beebout, Harold (1996). *Memorandum to M. J. Camasso on New Jersey REACH Survey.* Washington, DC: Mathematics Policy Research.

78. Jagannathan, Radha (2001). Relying on Surveys to Understand Abortions: Some Cautionary Evidence. *American Journal of Public Health,* 91, pp. 1825–1831. See especially p. 1827.

79. Ibid.

80. Harwood, John (1997, January 30). Think Tanks Battle to Judge the Impact of Welfare Overhaul. *Wall Street Journa,.* 229, p. 1.

81. Austen, Jane (1992). *Emma* (David Monaghan, Ed.). New York: St. Martin's.

82. Camasso, Michael J., Harvey, Carol, Jagannathan, Radha, Killingsworth, Mark, Hall, Dawn, and Agodini, Roberto (1996). *An Interim Report on the Impact of New Jersey's Family Development Program,* rev. ed. Trenton, NJ: NJDHS.

83. Ibid., p. 83.

84. Ibid., p. 7.

85. Winston, Pamela (2002). *Welfare Policymaking in the States.*

86. Slobodzian, Joseph A. (1996, August 10). Appeals Court Upholds NJ Family Cap. *Philadelphia Inquirer,* p. B1; and Leusner, Donna (1996, August

10). New Welfare Reality Upheld: Newborn Won't Increase Aid. [*Newark*] *New Jersey Star-Ledger*, p. 1.

87. McCullough, Marie (1996, June 2). Effect of NJ Family Cap Is a Matter of Argument. *Philadelphia Inquirer*, p. B1.

88. Camasso, Michael J., Harvey, Carol, Jagannathan, Radha, Killingsworth, Mark, Hall, Dawn, and Agodini, Roberto (1996). An Interim Report on the Impact of New Jersey's Family Development Program, rev. ed., pp. 207–208.

89. *NJDHS Press Release*, September 11, 1997, p. 1.

90. Ibid., p. 3.

91. Peterson, Melody (1997, September 12). Study Finds Family Cap Did Not Cut Rate of Births. *New York Times*, p. 1.92. Ginsberg, Thomas (1997, September 12). NJ Study Uncertain on Value of Child Caps. *Philadelphia Inquirer*, p. 1.

93. Vobejda, Barbara (1997, September 12). New Jersey Officials Say Birth Rate Drop Not Linked to Welfare Benefits Cap, p. 22.

94. Leusner, Donna (1997, September 12). Welfare Cap Didn't Affect Birth Rates: Jersey Kept Rutgers Study a Secret. [*Newark*] *Star-Ledger*, p. 1.

95. Stiles, Charles (1997, September 12). Report: Child Cap No Deterrent for Welfare Mothers. *Trenton Times*, p. 1.

96. Leusner, Donna (1997, September 12). Welfare Cap Didn't Affect Birth Rates, p. 1; and Peterson, Melody (1997, September 12). Study Finds Family Cap Did Not Cut Rate of Births, p. 1.

97. Greenberg, David, and Shroder, Matthew (1997). *The Digest of Social Experiments*, 2nd ed. Washington, DC: The Urban Institute, p. 29.

98. Besharov, Douglas J., Germanis, Peter, and Rossi, Peter H. (1997). *Evaluating Welfare Reform: A Guide for Scholars and Practitioners*. College Park: University of Maryland, Welfare Reform Academy, pp. 36–37.

99. Ibid., p. 44.

100. Maynard, Rebecca, Boehnen, Elizabeth, Corbett, Tom, and Sandefur, Gary (1998). Changing Family Formation Behavior through Welfare Reform. In Robert Moffitt (Ed.), *Welfare, the Family and Reproductive Behavior*. Washington, DC: National Academy, p. 163.

101. Maynard, Rebecca, Boehnen, Elizabeth, Corbett, Tom, and Sandefur, Gary (1998). Ibid., pp. 163–164.

102. Peterson, Melody (1997, September 21). In a Report on Welfare, Trends but No Final Verdict. *New York Times*, p. 28.

Chapter 6

1. Peterson, Iver (1995, May 17). Abortions Up Slightly for Welfare Mothers. *New York Times*, p. 14.

2. Ruess, Michelle (1995, May 17). Abortions Rise as N.J. Limits Welfare Payments. *Bergen Record*, p. 1.

3. Klerman, Jacob A. (1998). Welfare Reform and Abortions. In Robert A. Moffitt (Ed.), *Welfare, the Family and Reproductive Behavior* (pp. 98–133). Washington, DC: National Academy.

4. Moffitt, Robert A. (1998). The Effect of Welfare on Marriage and Fertility. In Robert A. Moffitt (Ed.), *Welfare, the Family and Reproductive Behavior* (pp. 50–97).

5. Matthews, Stephen, Ribar, David, and Wilhelm, Mark (1997). The Effects of Economic Conditions and Access to Reproductive Health Services on State Abortion Rates and Birth Rates. *Family Planning Perspectives, 29,* pp. 52–60.

6. Argys, Laura M., Averett, Susan L., and Rees, Daniel I. (2000). Welfare Generosity, Pregnancies and Abortions among Unmarried AFDC Recipients. *Journal of Population Economics, 13,* pp. 569–594.

7. Joyce, Ted, Kaestner, Robert, Korenman, Sanders, and Henshaw, Stanley (2004). *Family Cap Provisions and Changes in Births and Abortions.* NBER Working Paper. (No. 10214), pp. 1–42. Cambridge, MA: National Bureau of Economic Research.

8. Blank, Rebecca M., George, Christine C., and London, Rebecca A. (1996). State Abortion Rates: The Impact of Policies, Providers, Politics, Demographics and Economic Environment. *Journal of Health Economics, 15,* pp. 513–553.

9. Kenny, David A., Calsyn, Robert J., Morse, Gary A., Kinkenberg, W. Dean, Winter, Joel P., and Trusty, Michael L. (2004). Evaluation of Treatment Programs for People with Severe Mental Illness: Moderator and Mediator Effects. *Evaluation Review, 28,* pp. 294–324; Judd, Charles M., and Kenny, David A. (1981). *Estimating the Effects of Social Interventions.* Cambridge: Cambridge University Press;and Meyer, Bruce D. (1995). Natural and Quasi-Experiments in Economies. *Journal of Business and Economic Statistics, 13,* pp. 151–161.

10. Klerman, Jacob A. (1999). U.S. Abortion Policy and Fertility. *American Economic Review, 89,* pp. 261–264.

11. Morgan, S. Philip, and Parnell, Allan A. (2002). Effects on Pregnancy Outcomes of Changes in the North Caroline State Abortion Fund. *Population and Policy Review, 21,* pp. 319–338.

12. Massey, Douglas S., and Denton, Nancy A. (1993). *American Apartheid.* Cambridge, MA: Harvard University Press; and Wilson, William J. (1987). *The Truly Disadvantaged.* Chicago: University of Chicago Press.

13. Ellwood, David T., and Bane, Mary J. (1994). Understanding Welfare Dynamics. In Mary J. Bane and David T. Ellwood (Eds.), *Welfare Realities: From Rhetoric to Reform* (pp. 28–66). Cambridge, MA: Harvard University Press.

14. Camasso, Michael J., Harvey, Carol, Jagannathan, Radha, and Killingsworth, Mark (1997). *A Draft Final Report on the Impact of New Jersey's Family Development Program: Results from a Pre-Post Analysis of AFDC Case Heads from 1990–1996.* New Brunswick, NJ: Rutgers University School of Social Work and Bureau of Economic Research.

15. Characteristics such as race and age are, of course, completely exogenous to the treatment, but other characteristics such as education, marital status, and the number of AFDC-eligible children are potentially endogenous, since the Family Cap could affect these variables. To avoid this endogeneity, we measure each of these variables for each case using the value

observed as of the last pre-Cap quarter. We also ran this model using in-dividual fixed effects in an attempt to control for unmeasured differences between recipients.

16. The specification of the functional form for the probability of a bi-nary event in the probit model is the normal cumulative distribution func-tion (CDF), while the logit model uses the logistic function. Specifically, for the probit

$$P(Y=1|X)= \int_{-\infty} 1/\sqrt{2\pi} \exp[-1/2 \times \mu^2]d\mu=\phi(X'a)$$

While for the logit

$$P(Y=1|X)= \exp(X'a)/[1+ \exp(X'a)]=\Lambda(X'a)$$

17. Gujarati, Damodar N. (2005). *Essentials of Econometrics*, 3rd ed. Boston: McGraw-Hill Irwin.

18. Stock, James H., and Watson, Mark W. (2003). *Introduction to Econometrics*. Boston: Addison-Wesley.

19. Heckman, James J., and McCurdy, Thomas (1985). A Simultaneous Equations Linear Probability Model. *Canadian Journal of Economics, 18*, pp. 28–37; Cleary, Paul D., and Angel, Ronald (1984). The Analysis of Re-lationships Involving Dichotomous Dependent Variables. *Journal of Health and Social Behavior, 25*, pp. 334–348; Swafford, Michael (1980). Three Parametric Techniques for Contingency Table Analysis: A Nontechnical Commentary. *American Sociology Review, 45*, pp. 664–690; and Caudill, Steven B. (1988). An Advantage of the Linear Probability Model over Probit or Logit. *Oxford Bulletin of Economics and Statistics, 50*, pp. 425–427.

20. Note: The marginal effect on the probability of an event for a probit, or logit is considerably more complicated. For the probit it is

$$\partial Prob(Y=1)/\partial X_i=\phi(\Sigma B_i X_i)B_i$$

Where ϕ indicates the standard normal probability density function. For the logit, the marginal effect on the probability of an event i

$$\partial Prob(Y=1)/\partial X_i=\{e^{(\Sigma B_i X_i)}/[1+\{e^{(\Sigma B_i X_i)}]\}B_i]=P(1-P)B_i$$

where e is the exponential function.

21. Simulations based on probit and logit are somewhat more compli-cated, requiring that individual probabilities of the event be computed for each recipient in the database. These probabilities are then averaged across all the individuals observed in each quarter under both the counterfactuals and Family Cap conditions.

22. Myers, Rudy (1998, February 26). *Communication on Submission of Draft, Pre-Post Report*. Trenton, NJ: NJDHS—Division of Family Development.

23. Franklin, Donna L. (1997). *Ensuring Inequality: The Structural Transformation of the African-American Family.* New York: Oxford University Press, pp. 196–198; Gilens, Martin (1999). *Why Americans Hate Welfare.* Chicago: University of Chicago Press, pp. 133–153; Piven, Francis F. (2002). Welfare Policy and American Politics Pages, pp. 19–34. In Francis F. Piven, Joan Acker, Margaret Hallock, and Sandra Morgen (Eds.), *Welfare, Work and Politics* (pp. 19–34). Eugene: University of Oregon Press; and Roberts, Dorothy (1997). *Killing the Black Body: Race, Reproduction and the Meaning of Liberty.* New York: Vintage, pp. 217–225.

24. Zucchino, David (1997). *Myth of the Welfare Queen.* New York: Scribner.

25. Rank, Mark R. (1994). *Living on the Edge: The Realities of Welfare in America.* New York: Columbia University Press.

26. Edin, Kathryn, and Lein, Laura (1997). *Marking Ends Meet.* New York: Russell Sage Foundation, pp. 213-218 and following; and Newman, Katherine (1999). *No Shame in My Game: The Working Poor in the Inner City.* New York: Russell Sage Foundation.

27. Ryle, Gilbert (1984). *The Concept of Mind.* Chicago: University of Chicago Press.

28. Lewin, Tamar (1998, June 6). Report Tying Abortion to Welfare Is Rejected. *New York Times*, p. 5.

29. Myers, Rudy (1998, May 14). Communication on Submission of Draft, Pre-Post Report. Trenton, NJ: NJDHS—Division of Family Development.

30. Ibid, p. 4.

31. Raphael, Michael (1998, June 9). State Faults Welfare Overhaul Study's Abortion Link — But ACLU Says Officials Just Embarrassed. [*Newark*] *Star-Ledger*, p. 11.

32. Fitzgerald, Barbara (1998, June 9). Welfare Cap in N.J. Raised Abortion Rate, Study Finds—State Officials Reject Rutgers Data, Request Revision. *Boston Globe*, p. 3.

33. Ginsberg, Thomas (1998, June 9). Study Finds N.J. Welfare Cap May Have Led to More Abortions — Officials Want More Analysis. *Philadelphia Inquirer*, p. 4.

34. Lewin, Tamar (1998, June 8). Report Tying Abortion to Welfare Is Rejected: New Jersey Officials Question Its Validity. *New York Times*, p. 3.

35. Ibid., p. 5.

36. Ibid.

37. Ginsberg, Thomas (1998, June 9). Study Finds N.J. Welfare Cap May Have Led to More Abortions, page 4.

38. Raphael, Michael (1998, June 9). State Faults Welfare Overhaul Study's Abortion Link, p. 11.

39. Lewin, Tamar (1998). Report Tying Abortion to Welfare Is Rejected, p. 3.

40. An Abortive Effort [Editorial] (1998, June 14). [*Newark*] *Star-Ledger*, p. 2.

41. Children's Welfare: Family Cap of Child Exclusion? [Editorial] (1998, June 14). *Philadelphia Inquirer*, p. E5.

42. See, for example, editorials run in the *Courier-News*, Bridgewater, NJ (June 10); *Asbury Park Press* (June 13); *Trenton Times* (June 14); *Virginian-Pilot* (June 15); *Times-Leader*, Martins-Ferry, OH (June 14); *San Jose* (CA) *Mercury News* (June 16); *Allston-Brighton Tabulator* (MA) (June 16); *Sunday Visitor*, Huntington, IN (June 21); *The Californian* (June 23); *Olean Times Herald* (NY) (June 25); and *Home News Tribune* (NJ) (June 25).

43. *To prohibit States from imposing a family cap under the program of temporary assistance to needy families*, HR 4066, 105th Cong., 2nd sess., *Congressional Record Extension* 144 (June 16, 1998).

44. Fitzgerald, Barbara (1998, June 9). Hike in Abortions among Poor. *Trenton Times*, p. 1; and Wiggins, Ovetta (1998, June 10). Whitman May Review Welfare Cap. *The Bergen Records*, p. 1.

45. Edwards, Tamala M. (1998, June 22). Incite to Abort: Is That the Effect of the Family Cap on Welfare?, *Time*, p. 32.

46. Neubeck, Kenneth J., Cazenave, Noel A. (2001). *Welfare Racism: Playing the Race Card against America's Poor*. New York: Routledge, pp. 161–162.

47. Myers, Rudy (1998, July 27). *Transmittal of External Review Letters*. Trenton, NJ: NJDHS—Division of Family Development.

48. Camasso, Michael J., and Carol Harvey (1998, September 9). Response to External Review.

49. Myers, Rudy (1998, July 27). *Transmittal of External Review Letters*, p. 9.

50. Ibid., p. 7.

51. Ibid.

52. Camasso, Michael J., Harvey, Carol, Jagannathan, Radha, and Killingsworth, Mark (1998). *A Final Report on the Impact of New Jersey's Family Development Program: Results from a Pre-Post Analysis of AFDC Case Heads from 1990–1996*. New Brunswick, NJ: Rutgers University School of Social Work and Bureau of Economic Research, pp. ii–iii.

53. Ibid., p. v.

54. Rolston, Howard (1998, May 19). *Comments on Draft Final Report on the Social Experiment*. Washington, DC: ACF-Office of Planning, Research and Evaluation, p. 1.

55. Ibid., p. 2.

56. The U.S. Food and Drug Administration (FDA) uses two methods to account for attrition in randomized clinical trials: last observation carried forward (LOCF) and observed cases (OC). In LOCF analysis, when a subject drops from a trial, the results of the last observation are carried forward to succeeding periods as if the subject had continued to the completion of the trial. In OC analysis the results are reported only for those subjects who are still participating at the end of the time period assessed. It is widely considered that LOCF analysis provides more conservative estimates of treatment effects, but this claim has been disputed since LOCF analysis artificially increases degrees of freedom and statistical power. See, for example, Kirsch, Irving, Moore, Thomas J, Scoboria, Alan, and Nicholls, Sarah S. (2002). The Emperor's New Drugs: An Analysis of Antidepressant Medication Data Submitted to the U.S. Food and Drug Administration. *Prevention and Treatment*, 5, pp. 1–10; and Khan, A., Warner, H. A., and Braun, W. A. (2000). Symptom

Reduction and Suicide Risk in Patients Treated with Placebo in Antidepressant Clinical Trials. *Archives of General Psychiatry, 57*, pp. 311–317.

57. Shadish, William R., Cook, Thomas, D., and Campbell, Donald T. (2002). *Experiment and Quasi-experiment Design for Generalized Causal Inference.* Boston: Houghton Mifflin; and Mohr, Lawrence B. (1995). *Impact Analysis for Program Evaluation.* Thousand Oaks, CA: Sage.

58. Camasso, Michael J., Harvey, Carol, Jagannathan, Radha, and Killingsworth, Mark (1998, April). A Draft Final Report on the Impact of New Jersey's Family Development Program: Experimental-Control Group Analysis. New Brunswick, NJ: Rutgers University School of Social Work and Bureau of Economic Research.

59. In our final report on the social experiment we did include all the "quarterly observations" on a case and found that the results did not differ substantially from analysis conducted with proper risk pool denominators— if anything, the inclusion of these quarters inflated our treatment effects. We noted our disagreement with ACF in the report

> In response to the federal and state critique of the first draft of this report submitted in April 1998, we have conducted our analyses of all the outcomes, including births and abortions, listed in Table 3.1 without removing cases that had exited AFDC from the quarterly risk pool. The use of such risk pool denominators, we believe, is not appropriate in the cases of birth or abortion outcomes where it is impractical to obtain matchable person-level data on births and abortions that occurred while women were not receiving AFDC payments. Obtaining such data also appears to us to be well beyond the scope of the promulgated FDP policy. Our acquiescence to the use of unadjusted denominators is based on our comparative analyses of these same outcomes with risk pool adjusted denominators. The denominator unadjusted and adjusted analyses produce very similar results. The difficulties in interpretation engendered by the use of unadjusted denominators can be seen in the Tables produced in the Appendix to Chapter 3 of this report. Note how the birth and abortion rates decline as a function of denominator stability and fail to reflect AFDC population rates after September 1994.

This statement appears as page 34, note 13, in a Final Report on the Impact of New Jersey's Family Development Program: Experimental—Control Group Analysis delivered in October 1998.

60. Orr, Larry (1999). *Social Experiments.* Thousand Oaks, CA: Sage, p. 52.

61. Highsmith, Karen (1998, August 21). *Comments on Draft Final Report. Experimental v. Control Analysis.* Trenton, NJ: NJDHS, Division of Family Development.

62. Ibid., p. 4.

63. Camasso, Michael J., Harvey, Carol, Jagannathan, Radha, and Killingsworth, Mark (1998). A Final Report on the Impact of New Jersey's Family Development Program.

64. For example, with a probit we define the latent variable I $_{it}$ as

$$I_{it}=X_{it}\beta+\lambda_1 \text{Family Cap}_{it} +\lambda_2(\text{Family Cap}_{it} \times \text{Time}_t)+e_{it}$$

Where i subscripts denote individuals, t subscripts denote calendar time (which runs from October 1992 to December 1996); X denotes a vector of variables pertaining to the individual at each date; Family Cap is an indicator variable equal to unity if the individual is subject to the Family Cap, and zero otherwise; Time is a time trend; and e is an identically and independently normally distributed error term, with mean zero and σ^2 (which may be normalized to unity without loss of generality). We assume that a fertility event occurs if and only if $I_{it} > 0$. Set the binary indicator variable D_{it} equal to unity (zero) if a birth occurs (does not occur) for individual i in quarter t. Then

$$\Pr\{D_{it} = 1|X_{it}, \text{Family Cap}_{it}, \text{Time}_t\} = \Pr\{I_{it} > 0|X_{it}, \text{Family Cap}_{it}, \text{Time}_t\}$$
$$= \Pr\{e_{it} > -Z_{it}|X_{it}, \text{Family Cap}_{it}, \text{Time}_t\}$$

where

$$Z_{it} = X_{it}\beta + \lambda_1 \text{Family Cap}_{it} + \lambda_2 (\text{Family Cap}_{it} \times \text{Time}_t)$$

Under the assumption that the error time e is normally distributed, the log likelihood of a sample of individuals' birth histories is given by

$$\text{Log} \, t = D_{it} \log(1 - \varphi(-Z_{it})) + (1 - D_{it}) \log(\varphi(-Z_{it}))$$

where ϕ is the standard normal density function.

65. Camasso, Michael J., Harvey, Carol, Jagannathan, Radha, and Killingsworth, Mark (1998). *A Final Report on the Impact of New Jersey's Family Development Program*, p. v.

66. See note 56 above.

67. In addition to the pre-post and experimental control analysis I have cited, we also produced a report on the benefits and costs of the Family Development Program. See Camasso, Michael J., Harvey, Carol, and Jagannathan, Radha. *Cost Benefit Analysis of New Jersey's Family Development Program: Final Report.* New Brunswick, NJ: Rutgers University, School of Social Work and Bureau of Economic Research.

68. Leusner, Donna (1998, September 4). Family Cap Fight Back in Spotlight. [*Newark*] *Star-Ledger*, p. 1.

69. Leusner, Donna (1998, September 29). Foes Join Forces for Welfare Bill. [*Newark*] *Star-Ledger*, p. 1.

70. Ibid.; Rudeman, Wendy (1998, September 29). Welfare Cap Law under Fire. *The Courier News*, p. 3.

71. Parillo, Nancy (1998, July 23). *NOW Seeks State Report on Welfare Caps. Bergen Record.* , p. 3. See also (1998, July 23). State Is Sued over Report on Effects of Welfare. *New York Times*, p. 38.

72. Raphael, Michael (1998, July 23). ACLU Prods State for Welfare Reports. [*Newark*] *Star-Ledger*, p. 1.

73. Ibid.

74. Camasso, Michael J., and Carol Harvey (1998, August 12). Communication to Commissioner Guhl on Relationship with NJDHS.

75. Guhl, Michele K. (1998, September 8). *Communication to Principal Investigations*. Trenton, NJ: NJDHS; Rudczynski, Andrew B. (1998, September 23). *ACLU Request to Depose Principal Investigators of Draft Report*. New Brunswick, NJ: Rutgers University, Vice President for Research Policy and Administrations. .

76. Tenza, Jacqueline (1998, November 2). Press Release. Trenton, NJ: NJDHS, Office of Public Information.

77. The figure in panel A appears in our Final Pre-Post Report while the one in panel B was rescaled by the NJDHS press office to show more fluctuations.

78. Livio, Susan K. (1998, October 2). Judge Orders Family Cap Law Heard in Court. *Asbury Park Press*, p. 1.

79. McDonough, Peter (1998). *Statement of NJ Governor Christie Whitman Regarding the Family Cap and Personal Responsibility*. Trenton, NJ: Office of the Governor.

80. Tenza, Jacqueline (1998, November 2). Press Release.

81. McDonough, Peter (1998). Statement of NJ Governor Christie Whitman Regarding the Family Cap and Personal Responsibility.

82. Tenza, Jacqueline (1998, November 2). Press Release.

83. Preston, Jennifer (1998, November 3). With New Jersey Family Cap, Births Fall and Abortions Rose. *New York Times*, p. 19.

84. Livio, Susan K. (1998, November 3). Whitman to Enforce Family Cap Law. *Asbury Park Press*, p. 1.

85. Healy, Melissa (1998, November 3). Welfare Cap Cuts Births, Study Says. *Los Angeles Times*, p. 4.

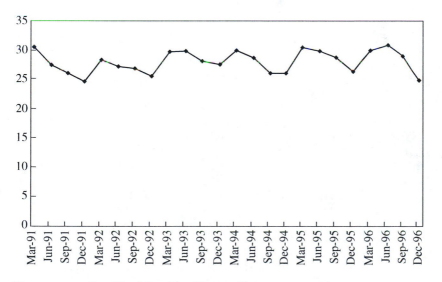

Figure 6.2.a. Our Final Pre-Post Report Chart

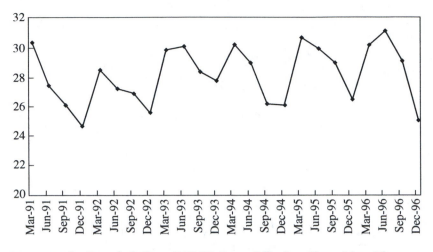

Figure 6.2.b. Rescaled Chart (NJDHS Press Office) to Show More Fluctuations

86. Leusner, Donna (1998, November 1). Welfare Births Down, Abortions Up Since Reform. [*Newark*] *Star-Ledger*, p. 1.

87. Ginsberg, Thomas (1998). Study of N.J. Family Cap Law Says Welfare Rule Led to More Abortions, page 1.

88. Wetzstein, Cheryl (1998, November 3). Welfare Policy Gets Credit for Reductions in Births. *Washington Times*, p. 1.

89. Preston, Jennifer (1998, November 3). With New Jersey Family Cap, Births Fall and Abortions Rose. *New York Times*, p. 19.

90. Wetzstein, Cheryl (1998, November 3). Welfare Policy Gets Credit for Reductions in Births. *Washington Times*, p. 1.

91. Once again the editorial pages ran black with ink. See, for example, *Atlantic City Press* (NJ), Nov. 14; *Richmond Times Dispatch* (VA), Nov. 18; *Asbury Park Press* (NJ), Nov. 14; and *Home News Tribune* East Brunswick (N.J.), Nov. 4.

92. Abel, Laura K. (1998, December 4). Communication to M. J. Camasso on schedule for disposition and/or subpoena in *Sojourner A. v. NJDHS*. Newark, NJ: Gibbons, Del Deo, Dolan, Griffinger and Vecchione. Also see Abel, Laura K. (1999, April 28). Communication to State Attorney General regarding M. J.Camasso Interrogatories and Request for Documents in *Sojourner A. v. NJDHS*. Newark, NJ: Gibbons, Del Deo, Dolan, Griffinger and Vecchione.

93. Rumbo, Daniel (1993). *Agreement on University Rights to Publish: Under Bid Proposal No. 93–X–27261*. New Brunswick, NJ: Rutgers University, Office of Research and Sponsored Programs.

94. Heins, David (1999, March 18). Memorandum of Understanding Regarding Family Development Program Data Sharing. Trenton, NJ: NDDHS—Division of Family Development.

95. Center for the Analysis of Public Issues (1998, November). Reporter Card on Dr. Michael J Camasso and His Rutgers Study Team. *New Jersey Reporter*, p. 4.

Chapter 7

1. Rosenbaum, Paul R. (2002). *Observational Studies*, 2nd ed. New York: Springer/Verlag.
2. Harwood, John (1997, January 30). Think Tanks Battle to Judge Impact of Welfare Overhaul, *Wall Street Journal*, p. 1.
3. Stoesz, David (2005). *Quixote's Ghost: The Right, The Liberati and the Future of Social Policy*. New York: Oxford University Press.
4. Eagleton, Terry (2003). *After Theory*. New York: Basic.
5. Jacoby, Russell (2000). *The Last Intellectual*. New York: Basic.
6. Lerner, Robert, Nagai, Althea K., and Rothman, Stanley (1996). *American Elites*. New Haven, CT: Yale University Press.
7. Winston, Pamela (2002). *Welfare Policymaking in the States: The Devil in Devolution*. Washington DC: Georgetown University Press.
8. Harwood, John (1997, January 30). Think Tanks Battle to Judge Impact of Welfare Overhaul, p. 1.
9. Rosenbaum, Paul R. (2002). *Observational Studies*, p. 9. Citing Ronald A. Fisher (1935) The Design of Experiments. Edinburgh: Oliver and Boyd. p. 2.
10. An Abortive Effort [Editorial] (1998, June 14). [*Newark*] *Star-Ledger* p. 20.
11. No Simple Answers [Editorial] (1998, June 13). *Asbury Park Press*, p. 10.
12. Borjas, George J. (1996). *Labor Economics*. New York: McGraw-Hill.
13. Hoagland, James (2004, October 31). A Campaign That Failed. *Washington Post*, p. B7.
14. Kramer, Michael (1995, July 5). The Myth about Welfare Moms. Time.
15. Ibid.
16. Harwood, John (1997, January 30). Think Tanks Battle to Judge Impact of Welfare Overhaul, p. 1.
17. Center on Budget and Policy Priorities (1994). *Welfare and Out of Wedlock Births. A Research Summary*. Washington, DC: CBPP.
18. Stark, Shelly, and Levin-Epstein, Jodie (1999). *Excluded Children: Family Cap in New Era*. Washington, DC: Center For Law and Social Policy.
19. Mink, Gwendolyn (1998). *Welfare's End*. Ithaca, NY: Cornell University Press. See also Popiel, Leslie A. (1994, July 22). Critics See Welfare Reform Increasing U.S. Abortion Rate. *Christian Science Monitor*, p. 3.
20. Wolfson, Adam (2004). Conservatives and Neoconservatives. *Public Interest, 154*, pp. 32–48.
21. Lewin, Tamar (1995, March 19). Abortion Foes Worry about Welfare Cutoffs. *New York Times*, p. 22.
22. Haskins Ron (1998). *A Memorandum to the Congressional Research Committee Requesting an Assessment of New Jersey's Family Cap Abortion*

Effect. Washington, DC: U.S. House of Representatives, Ways and Means Committee.

23. Falk, Gene, and Devere, Christine (1998). *Analysis of Evaluations of the New Jersey Family Development Program.* Washington, DC: Congressional Research Services.

24. Ibid., p. 1.

25. Doffing the Family Cap [Editorial]. (1998, August 3). *The Weekly Standard,* p. 2.

26. MII Publications, NJ. Family Cap Study Showing Birth Drop, Abortion Rise May Be Flawed. *Welfare-to-Work,* 7, pp. 172–173.

27. Ibid., p. 172.

28. Rector, Robert (1995). *The Impact of New Jersey's Family Cap on Out-of-Wedlock Births and Abortions.* Washington, DC: The Heritage Foundation.

29. Goertzel, Ted G. (2000, March). *Defending New Jersey's Family Cap Welfare Reform in the Courts.* Paper presented at the Seventieth Annual Meeting of the Eastern Sociological Society, Baltimore, MD.

30. Besharov, Douglas J., Germanis, Peter, and Rossi, Peter H. (1997). *Evaluating Welfare Reform: A Guide for Scholars and Practitioners.* College Park, MD: The Welfare Reform Academy, p. 37.

31. Corbett, Tom (1997). Informing the Welfare Debate: Introduction and Overview. In *Informing the Welfare Debate: Perspective on the Transformation of Social Policy* (pp. 1–24). Madison, WI: Institute for Research on Poverty.

32. Rainwater, Lee, and Yancey, William L. (1967). *The Moynihan Report and the Politics of Controversy.* Cambridge, MA: MIT Press.

33. Mosteller, Frederick, and Moynihan, Daniel P. (1972) (Eds). *On Equality of Educational Opportunity.* New York: Vintage.

34. Coalition for Evidence-Based Policy (2003). *Bringing Evidence-Driven Progress to Crime and Substance Abuse Policy: A Recommended Federal Strategy.* Princeton, NJ: Robert Wood Johnson Foundation; and Coalition for Evidence-Based Policy (2002). *Bringing Evidence-Driven Progress to Education: A Recommended Strategy for the U.S. Department of Education.* New York: William T. Grant Foundation.

35. Kennedy, Donald (2003). An Epidemic of Politics, *Science, 299,* p. 625.

36. Stoesz, David (2005). *Quixote's Ghost,* pp. 66–67.

37. Steinbrook Robert (2004). Science, Politics and Federal Advisory Committees. *New England Journal of Medicine, 356,* pp. 1454–1460; and Petrosino, Anthony, Boruch, Robert F., Soydan, Haluk, Duggan, Lorna, and Sanchez-Meca, Julio (2001). Meeting the Challenges of Evidence-Based Practice: The Campbell Collaboration. *The Annals, 578,* pp. 14–34.

38. Jasanoff, Sheila (2003). Accountability (No?) Accounting for Expertise. *Science and Public Policy, 30,* pp. 157–162. See especially p. 160.

39. Petrosino, Anthony, Boruch, Robert F., Soydan, Haluk, Duggan, Lorna, and Sanchez-Meca, Julio (2001). Meeting the Challenges of Evidence-Based Practice: The Campbell Collaboration. *The Annals, 578,* pp. 14–34.

40. Welfare Reform Academy (2006). *About the Welfare Reform Academy.* http://www.welfareacademy.org/whoweare; Besharov, Douglas J., Germanis, Peter, and Rossi, Peter (1997). *Evaluating Welfare Reform,* p. 37.

41. Besharov, Douglas J., Germanis, Peter (Eds.). (2000). *Preventing Subsequent Births to Welfare Mothers*. College Park, MD: The Welfare Reform Academy.

42. Lehrer, Eli (1999, March 1). Demystifying Statistics Is Murray's Number. *Insight on the News*.

43. Besharov, Douglas (1999, January). Personal Communication to Rudolf Myers, NJDHS-DFO, and to Michael Laracy, Anne E Casey Foundation.

44. Besharov, Douglas (1999, January 29). Personal Communication to author.

45. Camasso, Michael J (1999, February 4). Personal Communication to Douglas Besharov. The communication contained our response to Rossi's critique accompanied by several hundred pages of statistical output and annotations to which a response was never received.

46. Myers, Rudolf (1999, January 28). Response to Rossi's Critique of the New Jersey FDP Evaluation. Personal Communication to Douglas Besharov, p. 1.

47. Myers, Rudolf (1999). Ibid., p. 9.

48. Besharov, Douglas (1999, March 18). Personal Communication to author; Germanis, Peter (1999, April 8). Personal Communication to author; Germanis, Peter (1999, June 10). Personal Communication to author.

49. Rossi, Peter H. (2000). New Jersey's Family Development Program: An Overview and Critique of the Rutgers Evaluation. In Douglas J. Besharov and Peter Germanis (Eds.). *Preventing Subsequent Births to Welfare Mothers* (pp. 29–46).

50. Alkin, Marvin C. (2004). *Evaluation Roots: Tracing Theorist's Views and Influences*. Thousand Oaks, CA: Sage.

51. Rossi, Peter H., Lipsey, Mark W., and Freeman, Howard E. (2004). *Evaluation: A Systematic Approach*, 7th ed. Thousand Oaks, CA: Sage.

52. Ibid.; Rossi, Peter H., and Wright, James O. (1984). Evaluation Research: An Assessment. *Annual Review of Sociology, 10*, pp. 331–352.

53. Rossi, Peter H. (1981). The Iron Law of Evaluation and Other Metallic Rules. In Joanne H. Miller and Michael Lewis (Eds). *Research in Social Problems and Public Policy* (Vol. 4). Greenwich, CT: JAI.

54. Rossi, Peter H (2000). New Jersey's Family Development Program: An Overview and Critique of the Rutgers Evaluation. In Douglas J. Besharov and Peter Germanis (Eds.). *Preventing Subsequent Births to Welfare Mothers* (pp. 29–46). See especially p. 42.

55. Rossi, Peter H., Lipsey, Mark W., and Freeman, Howard E. (1999). *Evaluation: A Systematic Approach*, 6th ed. Thousand Oaks, CA: Sage, p. 304. A number of factual errors pointed out to the author of this exemplar, Peter Rossi, and to the publisher (Sage) by NJDHS-DFA and the evaluation team forced changes to any republication of Exhibit 8–H: A Compromised Impact Assessment: The New Jersey Family Cap Experience. The issue became moot when the publisher (Sage) decided to drop the Exhibit completely from future editions of the text.

56. Laracy, Michael C. (2000). Comments on Rossi. In Douglas Besharov and Peter Germanis (Eds). *Preventing Subsequent Births to Welfare Mothers* (pp. 47–49). See especially p. 47.

57. Laracy, Michael (2000). Comments on Rossi. In Douglas Besharov and Peter Germanis (Eds.). *Preventing Subsequent Births to Welfare Mothers* (pp. 47–49). See especially p. 48. Funds allocated for the Rutgers Evaluation totaled a little over $1.3 million, a rather substantial amount of money even by today's standards. Equating quality of product with money spent is unfortunately too common a practice in the field of human services delivery and evaluation. See, for example, Jay P. Greene, *Education Myths* (2004). Lanham, MA: Rowman & Littlefield. In fact, the evaluation was an even greater bargain once we returned over $150,000 to the state.

58. Murray, David (2000). Capping Families: What Do We Know? In Douglas Besharov and Peter Germanis (Eds.). *Preventing Subsequent Births to Welfare Mothers* (pp. 51–54). See especially p. 52.

59. Ibid., p. 53.

60. The English translation is "From its seeming to me—or to everyone—to be so, it doesn't follow that it is so." See G. E. M. Anscombe and G. H. Von Wright (Eds.). (1969). *Ludwig Wittgenstein: On Certainty*. New York: Harper & Ross, p. 2.

61. Loury, Glenn C. (2000). Preventing Subsequent Births to Welfare Recipients. In Douglas J. Besharov and Peter Germanis (Eds.). *Preventing Subsequent Births to Welfare Mothers* (pp. 13–28). See especially pp. 15 and 16.

62. Camasso, Michael J., Harvey, Carol, and Jagannathan, Radha (1996). *An Interim Report on the Impact of New Jersey's Family Development Program*. New Brunswick, NJ: Rutgers University, School of Social Work and Bureau of Economics Research. The reader is directed to p. 150, table 4.44, and its discussion in Camasso, Michael J., Harvey, Carol, Jagannathan, R., Killingsworth M., Hall, Dawn, and Agodini, Roberto (1996). An Interim Report on the Impact of New Jersey's Family Development Program. New Brunswick, NJ: Rutgers University, School of Social Work and Bureau of Economic Research.

63. Rossi, Peter H. (2000). New Jersey's Family Development Program: An Overview and Critique of the Rutgers Evaluation. In Douglas J. Besharov and Peter Germanis (Eds.). *Preventing Subsequent Births to Welfare Mothers* (pp. 29–46). See especially p. 36.

64. See, for example, Robert A. Moffit and Michele Ver Ploeg (Eds.). (2001). *Evaluating Welfare Reform in an Era of Transition*. Washington, DC: National Academy; and James H. Stock and Mark W. Watson (2003). *Introduction to Econometrics*. Boston: Addison-Wesley.

65. Camasso, Michael J., Harvey, Carol, Jagannathan, Radha, and Killingsworth, Mark R. (2000). The Evaluators Rely. In Douglas Besharov and Peter Germanis (Eds.). *Preventing Subsequent Births to Welfare Mothers* (pp. 43–46).

66. Rossi, Peter H., Lipsey, Mark W., and Freeman, Howard E. *Evaluation: A Systematic Approach*, 6th ed. Thousand Oaks, CA: Sage, pp. 294–295.

67. Rossi, Peter H., Berk, Richard A., and Lenihan, Kenneth J. (1980). *Money, Work and Crime: Experimental Evidence*. New York: Academic.

68. Ibid., p. 38.

69. Ibid., p. 39.

70. Rossi, Peter H., Lipsey, Mark W., and Freeman, Howard E. *Evaluation*, 6th ed., pp. 298–299.

71. Camasso, Michael J (2001, May 31). Personal Communication to Peter Rossi.

72. Rossi, Peter H. (2000). New Jersey's Family Development Program: An Overview and Critique of the Rutgers Evaluation. In Douglas J. Besharov and Peter Germanis (Eds.). *Preventing Subsequent Births to Welfare Mothers* (pp. 29–46). See especially p. 32.

73. Cook, Thomas D., and Campbell, Donald T. (1979). *Quasi-experimentation: Design and Analysis Issues for Field Settings.* Chicago: Rand McNally; and Rosenbaum, Paul R. (2002). *Observational Studies.*

74. Fein, David.J., Beecroft, Erik, Hamilton, William, and Lee, Wang S. (1998). *The Indiana Welfare Reform Evaluation: Program Implementation and Economic Impacts after Two Years.* Cambridge, MA: Abt Associates; Mills, Gregory, Kornfeld, Robert, Peck, Laura, Porcari, Diane, and others (1999). *Evaluation of the Arizona Empower Welfare Demonstration: Impact Study Interim Report.* Cambridge, MA: Abt Associates; and Fein, David J. (1999). *Will Welfare Reforms Influence Marriage and Fertility? Early Evidence from the ABC Demonstration.* Cambridge, MA: Abt Associates.

75. Mills, Gregory, Kornfeld, Robert, Peck, Laura, Porcari, Diane, and Others (1999). Ibid.

76. Bloom, Dan, Farrell, Mary, Kemple, James J., and Verma, Nandita (1999). *The Family Transition Program: Implementation and Three-Year Impacts of Florida's Initial Time-Limited Welfare Program.* Executive Summary. New York: Manpower Demonstration Research Corporation; Turturro, Carolyn, Benda, Brent, and Turney, Howard (1998). *Arkansas's Welfare Waiver Demonstration Project: Final Report.* Little Rock: University of Arkansas, School of Social Work; and Cherlin, Andrew, Angel, Ron, Brenton, Linda, Chase-Lansdale, Lindsey, Moffitt, Robert, and Wilson, William J. (2000, July 19). *Study Finds Welfare Recipients Understand Reform Rules Only Generally.* Headlines @ Hopkins News Release. Baltimore: Johns Hopkins University.

77. Orr, Larry L. (1999). *Social Experiments.* Thousand Oaks, CA: Sage; Lipsey, Mark W. (1990). Design Sensitivity: Statistical Power for Experimental Research. Thousand Oaks, CA: Sage; Cook, Thomas D., and Campbell, Donald T. (1979). *Quasi-experimentation*; Campbell and Cook note that if there is reason to believe that the average amount of exposure to the treatment is less for controls than experimental cases the researcher should continue to analyze the data as if from a pure experiment. Expect, however, that the detectable effect sizes will be reduced; Mills, Gregory, Kornfeld, Robert, Peck, Laura, Porcari, Diane, and Others (1999). *Evaluation of the Arizona Empower Welfare Demonstration*; Fein, David J., and Karweit, Jennifer A. (1997). *The ABC Evaluation: The Early Economic Impact of Delaware's A Better Chance Welfare Reform Program.* Cambridge, MA: Abt Associates; Fein, David J. (1999). *Will Welfare Reforms Influence Marriage and Fertility? Early Evidence from the ABC Demonstration.* Cambridge, MA: Abt Associates; and Bloom, Dan, Farrell, Mary, Kemple, James J., and Verma, Nandita (1999). *The Family Transition Program: Implementation and Three-Year Impacts of Florida's Initial Time-Limited Welfare Program Executive Summary.* New York: Manpower Demonstration Research Corporation.

78. Fein, David J., and Karweit, Jennifer A. (1997). *The ABC Evaluation: The Early Economic Impact of Delaware's A Better Chance Welfare Reform Program*. Cambridge, MA: Abt Associates, p. 45.

79. Cook, Thomas D., and Campbell, Donald T. (1979). *Quasi-experimentation*; Kemple, James J., Friedlander, Daniel, and Fellerath, V. (1995). *Florida's Project Independence: Benefits, Costs and Two-Year Impacts of Florida's JOBS Program*. New York: Manpower Demonstration Research Corporation; and Orr, Larry L. (1999). *Social Experiments*.

80. Angrist, Joshua D., Imbens, Guido W., Rubin, Donald B. (1996). Identification of Causal Effects Using Instrumental Variables. *Journal of the American Statistical Association, 91*, pp. 444–455; and Rubin, Donald B. (1974). Estimating Causal Effects of Treatments in Randomized and Nonrandomized Studies. *Journal of Educational Psychology, 66*, pp. 688–701.

81. Camasso, Michael J., Jagannathan, Radha, Harvey, Carol, and Killingsworth, Mark (2003). The Use of Client Surveys to Gauge the Threat of Contamination on Welfare Reform Experiments. *Journal of Policy Analysis and Management, 22*, pp. 207–223.

82. See ibid. for an extended discussion of this analysis.

83. Myers, Rudolf (1995). *New Jersey's Family Cap: Measuring the Effects*. Trenton, NJ: New Jersey Department of Human Services.

84. Camasso, Michael J. (2001, May 31). Personal Communication to Peter Rossi.

85. Jagannathan, Radha, Camasso, Michael J., and Killingsworth, Mark R. (2004). Do Family Caps on Welfare Affect Births among Welfare Recipients? Reconciling Efficacy and Effectiveness Estimate of Impact through a Blended Design Strategy. *American Journal of Evaluation, 25*, pp. 295–319.

86. Maynard, Rebecca, Boehnen, Elizabeth, Corbett, Tom, and Sandefur, Gary (1998). Changing Family Formation Behavior through Welfare Reform. In Robert A. Moffitt (Ed.). *Welfare, the Family and Reproductive Behavior* (pp. 134–175). Washington, DC: National Academy; Grogger, Jeffrey, Karoly, Lynn A., and Klerman, Jacob A. (2002). *Consequences of Welfare Reform: A Research Synthesis RAND/DRU–2676–DHHS*. Santa Monica, CA: Rand; and Laracy, Michael (2002). Comments on Rossi. In Douglas Besharov and Peter Germanis (Eds.). *Preventing Subsequent Births to Welfare Mothers* (pp. 47–49). See especially p. 48.

87. Fein, David (1994). Waiver Evaluations: The Pitfalls and the Opportunities. *Public Welfare, 52*, pp. 24–34.

88. In the three largest counties, Essex (Newark), Camden (Camden City), and Hudson (Jersey City) the JOBS program was initiated on the same date as Family Cap.

89. Orr, Larry L. (1999). *Social Experiments*.

90. The FDP × Time and Family Cap × Time coefficients in these models are always nonsignificant and are therefore dropped from further analysis.

91. Camasso, Michael J. (2000). Isolating the Family Cap Effect on Fertility Behavior: Evidence From New Jersey's Family Development Program Experiment. *Contemporary Economic Policy, 22*, pp. 453–467.

92. Wallace, Walter L. (1971). *The Logic of Science in Sociology*. Chicago: Aldine.

93. United States General Accounting Office (2001). *Welfare Reform: More Research Needed on TANF Family Caps and Other Policies for Reducing Out-of-Welfare Births (GAO–01–924).* Washington, DC: GAO.

Chapter 8

1. Kaplan, Abraham (1964). *The Conduct of Inquiry.* New York: Chandler, p. 302.

2. United State General Accounting Office (2001). *Welfare Reform: More Research Needed on TANF Family Caps and Other Policies for Reducing Out-of-Welfare Births (GAO–01–924).* Washington, DC: GAO, p. 37.

3. Weiss, Carol H. (1997). How Can Theory-Based Evaluation Make Greater Headway? *Evaluation Review* 21, pp. 501–524; and Rossi, Peter H., Lipsey, Mark W., and Freeman, Howard E. (2004). *Evaluation: A Systematic Approach,* 7th ed. Thousand Oaks, CA: Sage.

4. Weiss, Carol H. (1998). *Evaluation,* 2nd ed. Upper Saddle River, NJ: Prentice Hall.

5. Becker, Gary S. (1996). *Accounting for Tastes.* Cambridge, MA: Harvard University Press, p. 4. Becker uses preferences and tastes interchangeably, viewing them as relatively stable choices based on an individual's personal capital, that is, past consumption patterns, personal experiences, and capabilities, and social capital, that is, the influences of past actions by an individual's peers and others in their social network.

6. Susser, Mervyn (1973). *Causal Thinking in the Health Sciences.* New York: Oxford University Press; Kenny, David A., Calsyn, Robert J., Morse, Gary A., Keinkenberg, W. Dean, Winter, Joel P., and Trusty, Michael L. (2004). Evaluation of Treatment Programs for People with Severe Mental Illness: Moderator and Mediator Effects. *Evaluation Review, 28,* pp. 294–324.

7. Soss, Joe, Schram, Sanford F., Vartanian, Thomas P., and O'Brien, Erin (2001). Setting the Terms of Relief: Explaining State Policy Choices in the Devolution Revolution. *American Journal of Political Science, 45,* pp. 378–395.

8. Fording, Richard C. (2003). "Laboratories of Democracy or Symbolic Politics?" The Racial Origins of Welfare Reform. In Sanford F. Schram, Joe Soss, and Richard C. Fording (Eds.). *Race and the Politics of Welfare Reform* (pp. 72–97). Ann Arbor: University of Michigan Press.

9. Murray, Charles A. (1993). Welfare and the Family: The U.S. Experience. *Journal of Labor Economics,* 11, pp. 224–262.

10. Akerlof, George A., Yellen, Janet L., and Katz, Michael L. (1996). An Analysis of Out-of-Wedlock Childbearing in the United States. *Quarterly Journal of Economics, 111,* pp. 277–317. While Akerlof et al. limit their discussion to the expansion of abortion technology following *Roe v. Wade,* I believe their argument is equally apropos to the increase in the accessibility of abortion to poor women brought about by the public funding of medically necessary abortions.

11. Levine, Phillip B., and Staiger, Douglas (1999). *Abortion Policy and the Economics of Fertility. Final Report Submitted to the Henry J. Kaiser Family Foundation.* Menlo Park, CA: Henry J. Kaiser Foundation.

12. Susser, Mervyn (1973). *Causal Thinking in the Health Sciences*. New York: Oxford University Press, p. 124.

13. Shadish, William R., Cook, Thomas, D., and Campbell, Donald T. (2002). *Experimental and Quasi-experimental Design for Generalized Causal Inference*. Boston: Houghton Mifflin; and Manski, Charles F. (1997). Learning about Treatment Effects from Experiments with Random Assignment of Treatments. *Journal of Human Resources, 31*, pp. 709–733.

14. Orr, Larry L. (1999). *Social Experiments: Evaluating Public Programs with Experimental Data*. Thousand Oaks, CA: Sage.

15. Manski, Charles F. (1997). Learning about Treatment Effects from Experiments with Random Assignment of Treatments.

16. Blalock, Hubert W. (1965). Theory Building and the Statistical Concept of Interaction. *American Sociological Review, 30*, pp. 1–10; and Blalock, Hubert W. (1961). *Causal Inferences in Non-Experimental Research*. New York: Norton.

17. Study Finds New Welfare Policy Boosted NJ's Abortion Rate. (1998, June 18). *The Boston Globe*, p. 18.

18. Camasso, Michael J. (1998, December). Deposition of Michael J Camasso. RE *Sojourner, A. v. New Jersey Department of Human Services*. Docket No. Esx–L–10171–97.

19. Camasso, Michael J., Harvey, Carol, Jagannathan, Radha, and Killingsworth, Mark (1998). *A Final Report on the Impact of New Jersey's Family Development Program: Experimental-Control Group Analysis*. Trenton, NJ: New Jersey Department of Human Services, pp. 203–213.

20. Camasso, Michael J., Harvey, Carol, Jagannathan, Radha, and Killingsworth, Mark (1998). *A Final Report on the Impact of New Jersey's Family Development Program: Results from a Pre-Post Analysis of AFDC Case Heads from 1990–1996*. Trenton, NJ: New Jersey Department of Human Services, pp. 122–135.

21. Shumway, T. (2001). Forecasting Bankruptcy More Accurately: A Simple Hazard Model. *Journal of Business, 74*, pp. 210–222; Lancaster, Tony (1990). *The Econometric Analysis of Transition Data*. New York: Cambridge University Press. Right-censoring occurs in the data because we do not have fertility information on women for the periods that they are off the welfare rolls, a limitation that is consistent with the policymakers' intent to influence fertility behavior of women only while they are receiving public assistance. Such off-welfare periods and fertility information that extends beyond December 1996 need to be taken into consideration explicitly within the estimation procedure.

22. Blossfeld, Hans-Peter, Hamerle, Alfred, and Mayer, Karl U. (1989). *Event History Analysis*. Hillsdale, NJ: Lawrence Erlbaum. Because the number of birth or abortion events occurring in each quarter is unlikely to exceed one, the rate and probability of occurrence of these events coincide. Therefore probability models such as logit and probit yield estimates of impact virtually identical to Poisson models.

23. Stock, James H., and Watson, Mark W. (2003). *Introduction to Econometrics*. Boston: Addison-Wesley; and Aiken, Leona S., and West, Stephen G.

(1991). *Multiple Regression: Testing and Interpreting Interactions*. Thousand Oaks, CA: Sage.

24. Jagannathan, Radha, and Camasso, Michael J. (2003). Family Cap and Nonmarital Fertility: The Racial Conditioning of Policy Effects. *Journal of Marriage and Family, 65*, pp. 52–71. This article expands the analyses shown in tables 8.2 through 8.5.

25. For more detailed information on these regressions see Jagannathan, Radha, Camasso, Michael J., and Killingsworth, Mark (2004). New Jersey's Family Cap Experiment: Do Fertility Impacts Differ by Racial Density? *Journal of Labor Economics, 22*, pp. 431–460.

26. Wilson, William J. (1987). *The Truly Disadvantaged*. Chicago: University of Chicago Press.

27. Center on Budget and Policy Priorities (1994). *Welfare and Out-of-Wedlock Births: A Research Summary*. Washington, DC: CBPP.

28. Wilson, William J. (1978). *The Declining Significance of Race: Blacks and Changing American Institutions*. Chicago: University of Chicago Press.

29. Murray, Charles A. (1993). Welfare and the Family.

30. U.S. House of Representatives (1996). Personal Responsibility and Work Opportunity Reconciliation Act of 1996. *Conference Report to Accompany HR 3734*. Washington, DC: Government Printing Office.

31. Dye, Jane L., and Presser, Harriet B. (1999). The State Bonus to Reward a Decrease in "Illegitimacy": Flawed Methods and Questionable Effects. *Family Planning Perspectives, 31*, pp. 142–147; Korenman, Sanders, Joyce, Ted, Kaestner, Robert, and Walper, Jennifer (2005). *What Did the "Illegitimacy Bonus" Reward?* Unpublished manuscript, Baruch College.

32. Akerlof, George A., Yellen, Janet L., and Katz, Michael L. (1996). An Analysis of Out-of-Wedlock Childbearing in the United States.

33. Lichter, Daniel T., McLaughlin, Diane K., and Ribar, David C. (1998). *State Abortion Policy, Geographic Access to Abortion Providers and Changing Family Formation*. Paper Presented at the American Sociological Association meeting, San Francisco; and Albrecht, Carol M., Fossett, Mark A., and Cready, Cynthia M. (1997). Mate Availability, Women's Marriage Prevalence and Husband's Education. *Journal of Family Issues, 18*, pp. 429–452.

34. Meyer, Bruce D. (1995). Natural and Quasi-Experiments in Economics. *Journal of Business and Economic Statistics, 13*, pp. 151–161. See especially p. 152.

35. Rosenbaum, Paul R. (2002). Observational Studies, 2nd ed. New York: Springer/Verlag.

36. Cook, Thomas D., and Campbell, Donald T. (1979). *Quasi-Experimentation: Design and Analysis for Field Settings*. Chicago: Rand McNally; and Shadish, William R., Cook, Thomas, D., and Campbell, Donald T. (2002). *Experimental and Quasi-experimental Design for Generalized Causal Inference*.

37. Card, David, and Krueger, Alan B. (1995). *Myth and Measurement: The New Economics of the Minimum Wage*. Princeton, NJ: Princeton University Press.

38. Camasso, Michael J. (2004). Treatment Evidence in a Non-Experimenting Practice Environment: Some Recommendations for Increasing Supply and Demand. In Albert R. Roberts and Kenneth R. Yeager (Eds.). Evidence-Based Practice Manual (pp. 233–246). New York: Oxford University Press. See especially p. 234.

39. Friedlander, Daniel, and Robins, Philip K. (1995). Evaluating Program Evaluations: New Evidence on Commonly Used Non-experimental Methods. *American Economic Review, 85*, pp. 923–937; and Lalonde, Robert J. (1986). Evaluating the Econometric Evaluations of Training Programs with Experimental Data. *American Economic Review, 76*, pp. 604–620.

40. For the former position, see Burtless, Gary, and Orr, Larry L. (1986). Are Classical Experiments Needed for Manpower Policy? *Journal of Human Resources, 21*, pp. 606–639. For the latter position, see Heckman, James J., and Hotz, V. Joseph (1989). Choosing among Alternative Non-experimental Methods for Estimating the Impact of Social Programs: The Case of Manpower Training. *Journal of the American Statistical Association, 84*, pp. 862–874.

41. Nechyba, Thomas J. (2001). Social Approval, Values and AFDC: A Reexamination of the Illegitimacy Debate. *Journal of Political Economy, 109*, pp. 637–672; Jackson, Catherine A., and Klerman, Jacob A. (1996). *Welfare and American Fertility*. Santa Monica, CA: RAND; and Clark, George R. G., and Strauss, Robert P. (1998). Children as Income Producing Assets: The Case of Teen Illegitimacy and Government Transfers. *Southern Journal of Economics, 64*, pp. 827–856.

42. Argys, Laura M., Averett, Susan L., and Rees, Daniel I. (2000). Welfare Generosity, Pregnancies and Abortions among Unmarried AFDC Recipients. *Journal of Population Economics, 13*, pp. 569–594; Robins, Philip K., and Fronstin, Philip (1996). Welfare Benefits and Birth Decisions of Never-Married Women. *Population Research and Policy Review, 15*, pp. 21–43; and Powers, Elizabeth T. (1994). *The Impact of AFDC on Birth Decisions and Program Participation*. Federal Reserve Bank of Cleveland Working Paper. (No. 9408).

43. Fairlie, Robert W., and London, Rebecca A. (1997). The Effect of Incremental Benefit Levels on Births to AFDC Recipients. *Journal of Policy Analysis and Management, 16*, pp. 575–597; and Grogger, Jeff, and Bronars, Stephen G. (2001). The Effect of Welfare Payments on the Marriage and Fertility Behavior of Unwed Mothers. Results from a Twins Experiment. *Journal of Political Economy, 109*, pp. 529–545.

44. Nechyba, Thomas J. (2001). Social Approval, Values and AFDC: A Reexamination of the Illegitimacy Debate. *Journal of Political Economy, 109*, pp. 637–672.

45. Ellwood, David T., and Bane, Mary Jo (1994). Understanding Welfare Dynamics. In Mary Jo Bane and David T. Ellwood. *Welfare Realities: From Rhetoric to Reform* (pp. 28–66). Cambridge, MA: Harvard University Press; and Clark, George R. G., and Strauss, Robert P. (1998). Children as Income Producing Assets.

46. Cook, Thomas D., and Campbell, Donald T. (1979). Quasi-experimentation; and Shadish, William R., Cook, Thomas, D., and Camp-

bell, Donald T. (2002). *Experimental and Quasi-experimental Design for Generalized Causal Inference.*

47. Meyer, Bruce D. (1995). Natural and Quasi-Experiments in Economics. *Journal of Business and Economic Statistics, 13*, pp. 151–161. See especially p. 153.48. Dyer, Wendy T., and Fairlie, Robert W. (2004). Do Family Caps Reduce Out-of-Wedlock Births? Evidence from Arkansas, Georgia, Indiana, New Jersey and Virginia. *Population Research and Policy Review, 23*, pp. 441–473.

49. Ibid., p. 441.

50. For actual Family Cap implementation dates see L. Jerome Gallagher, Megan Gallagher, Kevin Perese, Susan Schreiber, and Keith Watson (1998). One Year after Federal Welfare Reform: A Description of State Temporary Assistance for Needy Families (TANF). Decisions as of October 1997. *Occasional Paper Number, 6.* Washington, DC: The Urban Institute.

51. Schettini-Kearney, Melissa S. (2004). Is There an Effect of Incremental Welfare Benefits on Fertility Behavior? A Look at the Family Cap. *Journal of Human Resources, 39*, pp. 295–325.

52. Ibid., p. 313.

53. Kaushal, Neeraj, and Kaestner, Robert (2001). From Welfare to Work: Has Welfare Reform Worked? *Journal of Policy Analysis and Management, 20*, pp. 699–719.

54. The treatment effect in a random experiment can be estimated by a difference estimator (β), which is simply ($Y_t - Y_c$) where Y_t is the mean for the treatment group on the outcome of interest and Y_c is the mean for the controls. However, if these data form a panel then a difference-in-difference estimator (DD) may be more efficient. In this instance (β) is equal to ($Y_{t,after} - Y_{t,before}$) − ($Y_{c,after} - Y_{c,before}$) where before and after refer to the time of treatment applications. It is also possible to calculate a difference-in-differences in differences estimator (DDD) if one believes another exogenous variable conditions the DD estimate. In a true experiment (D) (DD) and (DDD) all yield unbiased treatment impacts. This of course may not be the case in quasi-experiments or observational studies. See James Stock and Mark Watson, *Introduction to Econometrics* (2003). Boston: Addison-Wesley, especially chapter 11.

55. Kaushal, Neeraj, and Kaestner, Robert (2001). *From Welfare to Work,* p. 716.

56. Joyce, Ted, Kaestner, Robert, Korenman, Sanders, and Henshaw, Stanley (2004). Family Cap Provisions and Changes in Births and Abortions. *Population Research and Policy Review, 23*, pp. 475–511.

57. Horvath-Rose, Ann E., and Peters, Elizabeth H. (2001). Welfare Waivers and Non-Marital Childbearing. In Greg J. Duncan and P. L. Chase-Lansdale (Eds.). *For Better and for Worse: Welfare Reforms and the Wellbeing of Children and Families* (pp. 222–244). New York: Russell Sage Foundation.

58. Mach, Traci L. (2001). Measuring the Impact of Family Caps on Childbearing Decisions. Unpublished manuscript, State University of New York at Albany. Department of Economics.

59. See Dyer, Wendy T., and Fairlie, Robert W. (2004). Do Family Caps Reduce Out-of-Wedlock Births?; and Joyce, Ted, Kaestner, Robert, Korenman,

Sanders, and Henshaw, Stanley (2004). Family Cap Provisions and Changes in Births and Abortions.

60. Mach, Traci L. (2001). *Measuring the Impact of Family Caps on Childbearing Decisions.* Unpublished manuscript, State University of New York at Albany, Department of Economics, p. 3.

61. Shadish, William R., Cook, Thomas, D., and Campbell, Donald T. (2002). Experimental and Quasi-experimental Design for Generalized Causal Inference, p. 502.

62. Acs, Gregory, Phillips, Katherin R., and Nelson, Sandi (2005). The Road Not Taken? Changes in Welfare Entry During the 1990s. *Social Science Quarterly, 86,* pp. 1060–1079.

63. The studies by Dyer and Fairlie, and Joyce, Kaestner, Korenman, and Henshaw do not control for other components of welfare reform or other policies.

64. Camasso, Michael J. (2004). Treatment Evidence in a Non-Experimenting Practice Environment: Some Recommendations for Increasing Supply and Demand. In Albert R. Roberts and Kenneth R. Yeager (Eds.). *Evidence-Based Practice Manual* (pp. 233–246). New York: Oxford University Press. See especially p. 243. Studies of the fertility behavior of women on welfare are tantamount to studies of unmarried women. In the New Jersey experiment and caseload analysis approximately 93 percent of women were unmarried with 65 percent never married, 27 percent separated or divorced, and about 1 percent widowed. This, of course, is not the case in nonwelfare populations. It follows that studies that use live birthrate or general fertility rate as the outcome in welfare reform studies are measuring something quite different than nonmarital birthrates or ratios. One would expect the latter measures to be more sensitive to policy changes than the former.

65. Meyers, Marcia K., Gornick, Janet C., and Peck, Laura R. (2001). Packaging Support for Low-Income Families: Policy Variations across the United States. *Journal of Policy Analysis and Management, 20,* pp. 457–483; Pavetti, LaDonna, and Bloom, Dan (2001). State Sanctions and Time Limits. In Rebecca Blank and Ron Haskins (Eds.). *The New World of Welfare* (pp. 245–269). Washington, DC: Brooking Institution; and McKernan, Signe-Mary, Bernstein, Jen, and Fender, Lynne (2005). Taming the Beast: Categorizing State Welfare Policies: A Typology of Welfare Policies Affecting Recipient Job Entry. *Journal of Policy Analysis and Management, 24,* pp. 443–460.

66. See chapter 1, notes 9 and 12; chapter 2, note 72; and chapter 7, notes 20 and 21.

67. Mink, Gwendolyn (1998). *Welfare's End.* Ithaca, NY: Cornell University Press; Soss, Joe, Schram, Sanford F., Vartanian, Thomas P., and O'Brien, Erin (2001). Setting the Terms of Relief: Explaining State Policy Choices in the Devolution Revolution. *American Journal of Political Science 45,* pp. 378–395; and Katz, Michael B. (1989). *The Undeserving Poor.* New York: Pantheon.

68. See chapter 1, note 11.

69. States that more or less consistently implemented both a Family Cap and Medicaid abortion funding: CA, CT, ID, IL, MA, MD, NJ. States that have implemented a Family Cap but have not paid for abortions: AR, AZ,

DE, FL, GA, IN, MS, ND, NE, OK, SC, TN, VA, WI, WY. North Carolina also has a Family Cap but paid for medically necessary abortions when state funds were available. States without a Family Cap that pay for abortions: AK, HI, MN, MT, NY, OR, VT, WA, WV. The District of Columbia has paid for medically necessary abortions intermittently, depending on Washington's political climate. States that have not instituted a Family Cap or have paid for medically necessary abortions more or less consistently over the study period: AL, CO, IA, KS, KY, LA, ME, MI, MO, NH, NM, NV, OH, PA, RI, SD, TX, UT. Alaska stopped paying for medically necessary abortions in 1998 while New Mexico began the policy.

70. Rosewater, Ann (1997). Setting the Baseline: A Report on State Welfare Waivers. *A Report to the Assistant Secretary for Planning and Evaluation in the United States Department of Health and Human Services.* http://158.70.177.60/hsp/isp/waiver2/title.htm; and Rowe, Gretchen (2000). State TANF Policies as of July 1999: Welfare Rules Data Book. Assessing the New Federalism. Washington, DC: The Urban Institute.

71. Piven, Francis F. (2002). Welfare Policy and American Politics. In Francis F. Piven, Joan Acker, Margaret Hallock, and Sandra Morgen (Eds.). *Welfare, Work and Politics* (pp. 19–34). Eugene: University of Oregon Press; Roberts, Dorothy (1997). Killing the Black Body: Race, Reproduction and the Meaning of Liberty. New York: Vintage; and Soss, Joe, Schram, Sanford F., Vartanian, Thomas P., and O'Brien, Erin (2001). Setting the Terms of Relief: Explaining State Policy Choices in the Devolution Revolution. *American Journal of Political Science, 45,* pp. 378–395.

72. Wilson, William J. (1987). *The Truly Disadvantaged.* Chicago: University of Chicago Press.

73. Richard, John (1997). The Factors of Genuine Welfare Reform. *Origins, 24,* pp. 564–566; U.S. Catholic Bishop's Council (1995). *Moral Principles and Priorities for Welfare Reform.* Chicago, IL: Archdiocese of Chicago; and O'Steen, D. N. (1995). Welfare Reforms Pose Threat to Unborn Babies. *National Right to Life News, 22,* pp. 1, 4.

74. Schroedel, Jean K. (2000). *Is a Fetus a Person?* Ithaca, NY: Cornell University Press.

75. Akerlof, George A., Yellen, Janet L., and Katz, Michael L. (1996). An Analysis of Out-of-Wedlock Childbearing in the United States.

76. Gilens, Martin (1999). *Why Americans Hate Welfare.* Chicago: University of Chicago Press; and Quadagno, Jill (1994). *The Color of Welfare.* New York: Oxford University Press.

77. Soss, Joe, Schram, Sanford F., Vartanian, Thomas P., and O'Brien, Erin (2001). Setting the Terms of Relief: Explaining State Policy Choices in the Devolution Revolution. *American Journal of Political Science, 45,* pp. 378–395; and Fording, Richard C. (2003). "Laboratories of Democracy or Symbolic Politics?" The Racial Origins of Welfare Reform. In Sanford F. Schram, Joe Soss, and Richard C. Fording (Eds.). *Race and the Politics of Welfare Reform.*

78. Murray, Charles A. (1993). Welfare and the Family.

79. See, for example, Piven, Francis F. (2002). Welfare Policy and American Politics. In Francis F. Piven, Joan Acker, Margaret Hallock, and Sandra Morgen (Eds.). *Welfare, Work and Politics* (pp. 19–34). Eugene: University

of Oregon Press; Roberts, Dorothy (1997). Killing the Black Body; and Mink, Gwendolyn (1998). Welfare's End.

80. Chavkin, Wendy, Romero, Diana, and Wise, Paul H. (2002). What Do Sex and Reproduction Have to Do with Welfare? In Francis F. Piven, Joan Acker, Margaret Hallock, and Sandra Morgen (Eds.). *Welfare, Work and Politics* (pp. 95–112). Eugene: University of Oregon Press. See especially p. 107.

81. Under PRWORA states can establish time limits shorter than five years. Those that did so: AR, AZ, CT, DE, FL, GA, ID, IL, IN, LA, MA, NC, NE, NM, OH, OR, SC, TN, TX, UT, VA. States that adopted more stringent work requirements, for example, removed work exemptions based on age of child, and so forth: AR, AZ, CT, FL, GA, IA, ID, IL, MA, MI, MN, MT, NC, ND, NH, NM, NY, OK, OR, SD, TN, TX, UT, VA, WA, WI.

82. Blank, Rebecca M., George, Christine C., and London, Rebecca A. (1996). State Abortion Rates: The Impact of Policies, Providers, Politics, Demographics and Economic Environment. *Journal of Health Economics*, *15*, pp. 513–553; Levine, Phillip B., Trainer, Amy B., and Zimmerman, David J. (1996). The Effect of Medicaid Abortion Funding Restrictions on Abortions, Pregnancies and Births. *Journal of Health Economics*, *15*, pp. 555–578; and Matthews, Stephen, Ribar, David, and Wilhelm, Mark (1997). The Effects of Economic Conditions and Access to Reproductive Health Services on State Abortion Rates and Birth Rates. *Family Planning Perspectives*, *29*, pp. 52–60.

83. Fording, Richard C. (2003). "Laboratories of Democracy or Symbolic Politics?" The Racial Origins of Welfare Reform. In Sanford F. Schram, Joe Soss, and Richard C. Fordings (Eds.). *Race and the Politics of Welfare Reform*; Soss, Joe, Schram, Sanford F., Vartanian, Thomas P., and O'Brien, Erin (2001). Setting the Terms of Relief: Explaining State Policy Choices in the Devolution Revolution. *American Journal of Political Science*, *45*, pp. 378–395; and Schettini-Kearney, Melissa S. (2004). Is There an Effect of Incremental Welfare Benefits on Fertility Behavior?

84. Medoff, Marshall, H. (2002). The Determinants and Impact of State Abortion Restrictions. *American Journal of Economics and Sociology*, *61*, pp. 481–493; Argys, Laura M., Averett, Susan L., and Rees, Daniel I. (2000). Welfare Generosity, Pregnancies and Abortions among Unmarried AFDC Recipients. *Journal of Population Economics*, *13*, pp. 569–594; Matthews, Stephen, Ribar, David, and Wilhelm, Mark (1997). The Effects of Economic Conditions and Access to Reproductive Health Services on State Abortion Rates and Birth Rates. *Family Planning Perspective*, *29*, pp. 52–60. Matthews et al. utilize a number of measures for health input in their abortion and birth analyses including number of abortion providers, family planning clinics, and so forth. Such variables have been found to be endogenous with Medicaid benefits and restrictions and are therefore excluded from this national analysis. See, for example, Ted Joyce (1987). The Impact of Induced Abortion on Black and White Birth Outcomes in the United States. *Demography*, *24*, pp. 229–244; and Blank, Rebecca M., George, Christine C., and London, Rebecca A. (1996). State Abortion Rates: The Impact of Policies, Providers, Politics, Demographics and Economic Environment.

85. The full regressions, which include the coefficients for the welfare policy, political climate, AFDC caseload, economic and demographic controls appear in Camasso, Michael J., and Jagannathan, Radha. Why Family Caps Work: Evidence from a National Study. DAFRE Working Paper. Rutgers University, Cook College. The effects that appear in the tables are limited to the Family Cap and Medicaid funding for abortion difference (D) estimates, the Family Cap X Medicaid Funding, and Family Cap × Black difference in difference (DD) estimate, and the Family Cap × Medicaid × Black difference-in-differences-in differences (DDD) estimate.

86. For a discussion of clustering issues and their amelioration in difference-in-difference models see Bertrand, Marianne, Luttner, Erzo, and Mullainathan, Sendhil (2000). Network Effects and Welfare Cultures. *The Quarterly Journal of Economics, 115,* pp. 1019–1055. Robust standard errors are produced using Stata 9's cluster command, with states serving as the clustering units. See Stata Corporation (2005). Release 9. Longitudinal/Panel Data, XTREG.

87. Female population black was measured both as a continuous percentage and dichotomously as the percent above or below the mean percentage, that is, 10.5 (see table 8.7). Both measurement approaches produce similar results with the dichotomous coding providing a less cumbersome means of discussing Family Cap interactions and joint effects. Additional specification tests were conducted with (1) analysis limited for the years 1990–2000; (2) without a quadratic term for time; and (3) repeating the hypothesis tests done for blacks with Hispanics. I wish to thank Ted Joyce for suggesting several of these specification and sensitivity checks.

88. Stata Corporation. Stata Base Reference Manual Release 9 (Vol. 2) (2005). College Station, TX: Stata.

89. Joyce, Ted, Kaestner, Robert, Korenman, Sanders, and Henshaw, Stanley (2004). *Family Cap Provisions and Changes in Births and Abortions*; Kaushal, Neeraj, and Kaestner, Robert (2001). From Welfare to Work: Has Welfare Reform Worked? *Journal of Policy Analysis and Management, 20,* pp. 699–719; and Schettini-Kearney, Melissa S. (2004). Is There an Effect of Incremental Welfare Benefits on Fertility Behavior.

90. Murray, Charles (1993). Welfare and the Family.

91. For unemployment rates by state, see USDOL, Bureau of Labor Statistics, Employment and Earnings. For female participation in the labor force see USDOL Geographic Profile of Employment and Unemployment.

92. Willis, Robert J. (1999). A Theory of Out-of-Wedlock Childbearing. *Journal of Political Economy, 107,* pp. S33–S64; and Lichter, Daniel T., LeClere, Felicia B., and McLaughlin, Diane K. (1991). Local Marriage Markets and the Marital Behavior of Black and White Women. *American Journal of Sociology, 96,* pp. 843–867.

93. Murray, Charles (1999). *The Underclass Revisited.* Washington, DC: American Enterprise Institute.

94. Massey, Douglas S., and Denton, Nancy A. (1989). Hypersegregation in U.S. Metropolitan Areas: Black and Hispanic Segregation along Five Dimensions. *Demography, 26,* pp. 373–391; and Massey, Douglas S., and

Denton, Nancy A. (1993). *American Apartheid: Segregation and the Making of the Underclass*. Cambridge, MA: Harvard University Press.

95. Wilson, James Q. (2002). *The Marriage Problem*. New York: Harper Collins.

Chapter 9

1. Stoesz, David (2005). *Quixote's Ghost: The Right, The Liberati and the Future of Social Society*: New York: Oxford University Press, p. 66.

2. Harwood, John (1997, January 30). Think Tanks Battle to Judge Impact of Welfare Overhaul, *Wall Street Journal*, p. 1.

3. Hecho, Hugh (2001). The Politics of Welfare Reform In Rebecca Blank and Ron Haskins (Eds.). *The New World of Welfare* (pp. 169–200). Washington, DC: Brookings Institution.

4. Mark, Melvin M., and Henry, Gary T. (2004). The Mechanisms and Outcomes of Evaluation Influence. *Evaluation, 10*, pp. 1–10; and Henry, Gary T. (2003). Influential Evaluations. *American Journal of Evaluation, 24*, pp. 515–524.

5. There is this example from Stanley K. Henshaw, senior fellow at the Alan Guttmacher Institute writing in the Welfare Reform Academy publication entitled *Data Needs for Measuring Family and Fertility Change after Welfare Reform* (2004) Douglas Besharov (Ed.): "The Family Cap, for example, was found to have increased the abortion rate among Medicaid Recipients in New Jersey but limitations in New Jersey's abortion reporting, which captured only about 54 percent of the state's abortions in 1996, make the finding questionable. With the data currently available, it is difficult to know whether the abortion rate of low-income women increased in relation to that of higher income women after the new policies were adopted" (p. 58). Henshaw does not provide any rationale for why the Family Cap could be expected to influence higher-income women who are not on welfare and not subject to a Family Cap. Nor does he provide his reasoning behind the claim that because our research studied women who could be affected by the Family Cap, that is, poor women receiving Medicaid, that this leads to questionable findings. The criticism is especially odd because much of the data collected by Guttmacher on abortion finds that it is low-income women who are indeed experiencing the most significant rise in abortion.

6. Greenberg, David, and Shroder, Matthew (1997). The Digest of Social Experiments, 2nd ed. Washington, DC: The Urban Institute, p. 20.

7. Brown, Michael K. (1999). *Race, Money and the American Welfare State*. Ithaca, NY: Cornell University Press; and Noble, Charles (1997). Welfare As We Knew It: A Political History of the American Welfare State. New York: Oxford University Press.

8. Ricci, David (1993). *The Transformation of American Politics*. New Haven, CT: Yale University Press.

9. Katz, Michael B. (1989). *The Undeserving Poor*. New York: Pantheon.

10. Stoesz, David (2005). *Quixote's Ghost*.

11. Katz, Michael B. (1989). *The Undeserving Poor*, p. 156.

12. Clemens, Samuel (1897, June 2). Reports of Death. *New York Journal*, p. 2.

13. Aaron, Henry J. (1978). *Politics and the Professions*. Washington, DC: Brookings Institution, p. 22.

14. Wilson, William J. (1978). *The Declining Significance of Race: Blacks and Changing American Institutions*. Chicago: University of Chicago Press.

15. Henry J. Kaiser Family Foundation (2006). *African American Men Survey*. Menlo Park, CA: Kaiser Family Foundation; and Smith, Robert C., and Seltzer, Richard (2000). *Contemporary Controversies and the American Racial Divide*. Lanham, MD: Rowman & Littlefield.

16. Schlesinger, Arthur (1986). *The Cycles of American History*. Boston: Houghton Mifflin.

17. Zedlewski, Sheila, Clark, Sandra J., Meier, Eric, and Watson, Keith (1996). *Potential Effects of Congressional Welfare Reform Legislation on Family Incomes*. Report 406622. Washington, DC: The Urban Institute.

18. Chase-Lansdale, P. Lindsay, Moffitt, Robert A., Lohman, Brenda J., Cherlin, Andrew J., Coley, Rebekah L., Pittman, Laura, Roff, Jennifer, Votruba-Drzal, Elizabeth (2003). Mothers' Transitions from Welfare to Work and the Well-Being of Preschoolers and Adolescents. *Science, 299*, pp. 1548–1553; and Zaslow, Martha J., Moore, Kristin A., Brooks, Jennifer L., Morris, Pamela A., Taut, Kathryn, Redd, Zakia A., and Emig, Carol A. (2002). *Future of Children, 12*, pp. 79–95.

19. Bell, Daniel (1960). *The End of Ideology*. Glencoe, IL: Free, pp. 330–335.

20. Bell, Daniel (1973). *The Coming of Post-Industrial Society*. New York: Basic, p. 43.

21. See, for example, Skerry, Peter (2001, March 4). Dressing It Up As Science Can't Disguise The Politics. *Washington Post*, p. B5; and Mooney, Chris (2004, February 29). Beware "'Sound Science." It's Doublespeak for Trouble. *Washington Post*, p. B2.

22. Faigman, David L. (1999, August 22). Experts in the Courtroom: A Way to Sort Out Science from Spin. *Washington Post*, p. B3.

23. Tetlock, Philip E. (1999). Theory-Driven Reasoning about Plausible Pasts and Probable Futures in World Politics: Are We Prisoners of Our Preconceptions? *American Journal of Political Science, 43*, pp. 335–366. See especially p. 348.

24. See, for example, Cerf, Christopher B., and Navasky, Victor S. (1998). *The Experts Speak: The Definitive Compendium of Authoritative Information*. New York: Random House; Jacobs, Lawrence, and Shapiro, Robert Y. (1998, Summer). Is Washington Disconnected from Public Thinking about Social Security. *The Public Perspective*, pp. 54–57; Jasanoff, Sheila (2003). No Accounting for Expertise. *Science and Public Policy, 30*, pp. 157–162; and Steinbrook, Robert (2004). Science, Politics and Federal Advisory Committees. *New England Journal of Medicine, 350*, pp. 1454–1460.

25. McFate, Katherine (1995). *Making Welfare Work: The Principles of Constructive Welfare Reform*. Washington, DC: Joint Center for Political and Economic Studies.

26. The data can be found on the USDHHS–ACF Web site: www.acf.dhhs .gov/programs/OFA/CHARACTER. It is also reproduced from 1985 through

1999 in Sanford F. Schram. (2003). "Putting a Black Face on Welfare." In Sanford F. Schram, Joe Soss, and Richard Fording (Eds). *Race and the Politics of Welfare Reform* (pp. 196–221). Ann Arbor: University of Michigan Press.

27. Ibid., especially Schram's Presentation of PSID data.

28. Roberts, Dorothy (1997). *Killing the Black Body*. New York: Pantheon, pp. 217–225; Piven, Francis F., Acker, Joan, Hallock, Margaret, and Morgen, Sandra (Eds.). *Welfare, Work and Politics*. Eugene: University of Oregon Press; and Norris, Donald F., and Thompson, Lyke (1995). *The Politics of Welfare Reform*. Thousand Oaks, CA: Sage.

29. National Center For Health Statistics (1995). *Report to Congress on Out-of-Wedlock Childbearing (DHHS Pub No (PHS) 95–1257)*. Washington, DC: U.S. Government Printing Office; see especially Moffitt, Robert A. (1995). "The Effect of the Welfare System on Non-marital Childbearing." Pages 167–176 in this report.

30. Robert Moffitt (Ed.) (1998). Welfare, the Family and Reproductive Behavior. *National Research Council*. Washington, DC: National Academy.

31. Rank, Mark R. (1994). *Living on the Edge: The Realities of Welfare in America*. New York: Columbia University Press, p. 4.

32. Mead, Lawrence M. (2001). The Politics of Conservative Welfare Reform. In Rebecca Blank and Ron Haskins (Eds.). *The New World of Welfare*. Washington, DC: Brookings Institution, pp. 201–220. See especially p. 216.

33. Becker, Gary S. (1993). *Human Capital: A Theoretical and Empirical Analysis with Special Reference to Education*. Chicago: University of Chicago Press, p. 16.

34. USDHHS, ACF, Office of Public Affairs (2006). Welfare Reform Reauthorized. http://www.whitehouse.gov/news/releases/2006/02/20060208–8.

35. Haskins, Ron (2006). Welfare Reform Success or Failure? It Worked. *Policy and Practice, 64*, pp. 10–12.

36. USDHHS, ACF. (2006). Characteristics and Financial Circumstances of TANF Recipients. http://www.acf.hhs.gov.programs/OFA/.

37. USDHHS, ACF. (2006). Temporary Assistance for Needy Families. *Sixth Annual Report to Congress*. Washington, DC: ACF.

38. Ibid.

39. Haskins, Ron, Sawhill, Isabel, and Weaver, Kent (2001). Welfare Reform: An Overview of Effects to Date. *Policy Brief No. 1*. Washington, DC: Brookings Institution.

40. Wood, Robert G., Rangarajan, Anu, and Gordon, Anne (2004). *WFNJ Clients and Welfare Reform: A Final Look at an Early Group (MPR: 8575–325)*. Princeton, NJ: Mathematica Policy Research.

41. National Center for Children in Poverty (2004). State Policy Choices: Supports for Low-Income Working Families. New York: Columbia University, Mailman School of Public Health. The U.S. Census Bureau and USDHHS both record poverty statistics but each has its own calculations for poverty-level income. The census numbers are used to estimate the number of Americans living in poverty while the USDHHS figures are employed to determine financial eligibility for federal programs. The two sets of numbers do not differ dramatically. For example, the Census Bureau's poverty thresh-

old for a family of three persons in 2004 was $15,219; the USDHHS threshold of the same year was $15,670.

42. Wood, Robert G., Rangarajan, Anu, and Gordon, Anne (2004). *WFNJ Clients and Welfare Reform.*

43. Michalopoulos, Charles, and Schwartz, Christine (2000). *What Works Best for Whom: Impacts of 20 Welfare-to-Work Programs by Subgroup.* New York: MDRC; and Hamilton, Gayle (2002). *Moving People from Welfare to Work: Lessons from the National Evaluation of Welfare-to-Work Strategies.* New York: MDRC.

44. Jagannathan, Radha, and Camasso, Michael J. (2005). Beyond Intention to Treat Analysis in Welfare-to-Work Studies. *Journal of Social Service Research, 31*, pp. 43–60.

45. Horn, Wade F. (2005). July 14, 2005 Testimony before House Ways and Means Committee. http://www.hhs.gov/asl/testify/f050714.html, pp. 2–3.

46. Rector, Robert (2006). *Congress Re-Starts Welfare Reform. #991.* Washington, DC: The Heritage Foundation.

47. Greenberg, Mark (2006). Welfare Reform, Success or Failure: It Worked with Mixed Results. *Policy and Practice, 64*, pp.10–12. See especially p. 12.

48. Wood, Robert G., Rangarajan, Anu, and Gordon, Anne (2004). *WFNJ Clients and Welfare Reform*, pp. 15 and 16.

49. Acs, Gregory, and Loprest, Pamela (2005). Who Are Low Income Working Families? *Paper 1—Low Income Working Families.* Washington, DC: The Urban Institute; and Schochet, Peter, and Rangarajan, Anu (2004). *Characteristics of Low-Wage Workers and Their Labor Market Experiences: Evidence from the Mid to Late 1990s.* Washington, DC: Mathematica Policy Research.

50. Parrott, Sharon (2006). *Despite Inclusion of Marriage-Promotion Funding, Budget Bill Would Penalize States That Provide TANF Assistance to Poor Married Couples.* Washington, DC: Center on Budget and Policy Priorities; and Mezey, Jennifer, Parrott, Sharon, Greenberg, Mark, and Fremstad, Shawn (2005). *Reversing Direction on Welfare Reform.* Washington, DC: Center For Law and Social Policy.

51. Currie, Janet M. (2006). The Invisible Safety Net. Princeton, N.J.: Princeton University Press.

52. Carneiro, Pedro, and Heckman, James J. (2003). Human Capital Policy. In James J. Heckman and Alan B. Krueger (Eds.). *Inequality in America: What Role for Human Capital Policies?* (pp. 77–239). Cambridge, MA: MIT Press.

53. Ibid, p. 192.

54. Coleman, James S. (1990). *Foundations of Social Theory.* Cambridge, MA: Harvard University Press, p. 300.

55. Coleman, James S., Campbell, Ernest Q., Hobson, Carol J., McPartland, James, Mood, Alexander M., Weinfeld, Frederic D., and York, Robert L. (1966). *Equality of Educational Opportunity.* Washington, DC: U.S. Government Printing Office.

56. Carneiro, Pedro, and Heckman, James J. (2003). Human Capital Policy. In James J. Heckman and Alan B. Krueger (Eds.). *Inequality in America*, pp. 138–139.

57. Rainwater, Lee, and Yancey, William L. (1967). *The Moynihan Report and The Politics of Controversy.* Cambridge, MA: MIT Press, p. 66.

58. Farley, Reynolds (1988). Race to the Finish Line. *Demography, 25*, pp. 477–495; and Bound, John, and Freeman, Richard B. (1992). What Went Wrong? The Erosion of Relative Earnings and Employment among Young Black Men. *Quarterly Journal of Economics, 107*, pp. 201–233.

59. Bound, John, and Freeman, Richard B. (1992). Ibid.

60. Murray, Charles (1999). *The Underclass Revisited.* Washington, DC: American Enterprise Institute, p. 11.

61. U.S. Department of Justice, Bureau of Justice Statistics (2002). *Criminal Offenders Statistics.* http://www.ojp.usdoj.gov/bjs/.

62. Carlson, Marcia, McLanahan, Sara, and England, Paula (2004). Union Formation and Dissolution in Fragile Families. *Demography, 41*, pp. 237–262.

63. Fein, David (2004). *Married and Poor: Basic Characteristics of Economically Disadvantaged Married Couples in the U.S.* Working Paper. SHM 04–0. Bethesda, MD: Abt Associates.

64. Wood, Robert G., Rangarajan, Anu, and Gordon, Anne (2004). WFNJ Clients and Welfare Reform, p. 13. In their paper *The Continuing Good News about Welfare Reform* (2003), Robert Rector and Patrick F. Fagan of the Heritage Foundation claim that welfare reform is responsible for the decline in the share of black children living with single parents (47 percent to 43 percent) and the concomitant rise in those children living with married couples (34.8 percent to 38.9 percent). The study they cite as evidence is entitled *A Declining Share of Children Lived with Single Mothers in the Late 1990s* by Allen Dupree and Wendell Primus (2001) from the Center on Budget and Policy Priorities. It is not clear from this report, however, if the decrease (and reciprocal increase) is concentrated among children, below poverty, below 200 percent of poverty ,or above 200 percent of poverty. For the same period (1995–2001) the number of black children living in cohabiting households also rose significantly.

65. Dion, M. Robin (2005). Healthy Marriage Programs: Learning What Works. *Future of Children, 15*, pp. 139–156.

66. Ibid., p. 148.

67. Sowell, Thomas (1996). *Migrations and Cultures: A World View.* New York: Basic.

68. Becker, Gary S. (1996). *Accounting for Tastes.* Cambridge, MA: Harvard University Press; Coleman, James S. (1990). *Foundations of Social Theory.* Cambridge, MA: Harvard University Press, p. 595; and Willis, Robert J. (1999). A Theory of Out-of-Wedlock Childbearing. *Journal of Political Economy, 107*, pp. 533–564.

69. Brown, Sarah S., and Eisenberg, Leon (Eds.). (1995). *The Best Intentions: Unintended Pregnancy and the Well-Being of Children and Families.* Institute of Medicine: Washington, DC: National Academy; Donohue, John J., and Levitt, Steven D. (2001). The Impact of Legalized Abortion on Crime. *Quarterly Journal of Economics, 116*, pp. 379–420; and Gruber, Jonathan, Levine, Phillip, and Staiger, Douglas (1999). Abortion Legaliza-

tion and Child Living Circumstances: Who Is the Marginal Child. *Quarterly Journal of Economics*, 116, pp. 263–291.

70. Willis, Robert J. (1999). A Theory of Out-of-Wedlock Childbearing. *Journal of Political Economy*, *107*, pp. 533–564; and Becker, Gary S. (1976). *The Economic Approach to Human Behavior*. Chicago: University of Chicago Press.

71. Becker, Gary S. (1976). Ibid., p. 173.

72. Willis, Robert J. (1999). A Theory of Out-of-Wedlock Childbearing, pp. 547–548.

73. Brown, Sarah S., and Eisenberg, Leon (Eds.). (1995). *The Best Intentions.*

74. Jones, Rachel K., Darroch, Jacqueline E., and Henshaw, Stanley K. (2001). Patterns in the Socioeconomic Characteristics of Women Obtaining Abortions in 2000–2001. *Perspective on Sexual and Reproductive Health*, *34*, pp. 226–235.

75. Donohue, John J., and Levitt, Steven D. (2001). The Impact of Legalized Abortion on Crime.

76. Ibid., p. 386.

77. Ibid., p. 390.

78. Faler, Brian (2005, September 30). Black Baby Remark Causes an Outrage. *Washington Post*, p. 5.

79. Jones, Joy (2006, March 26). Marriage Is for White People. *Washington Post* , pp. B1, B5.

80. Ibid.

81. O'Crowley, Peggy (2002, March 17). For Women on Welfare, Marriage Might Not Improve Their Lot. [*Newark*] *Star-Ledger*, pp. 10–1, 10–6.

82. Jones, Steve (2006, May 17). Cosby Gives a Call Out. *USA Today*, pp. 1, 20.

83. Heckman, James (2005). Inequality in America: What Role for Human Capital Policies. *Focus*, *23*, pp. 1–10.

84. Jones, Rachel K., Darroch, Jacqueline E., and Henshaw, Stanley K. (2002). Patterns in the Socioeconomic Characteristics of Women Obtaining Abortions in 2000–2001. *Perspectives on Sexual and Reproductive Health*, *34*, pp. 226–235.

85. Boonstra, Heather D., Gold, Rachel B., Richards, Cory L., and Finer, Lawrence B. (2006). *Abortion in Women's Lives*. New York: Guttmacher Institute.

86. Newman, Katherine S. (1999). *No Shame in My Game*. New York: Knopf, pp. 25–26.

87. Haskins, Ron (2006). Welfare Reform Success or Failure?

88. Rector, Robert, and Fagan, Patrick F. (2003). The Continuing Good News about Welfare Reform. *Backgrounder #1620*. Washington, DC: The Heritage Foundation.

89. Zaslow, Martha J., Moore, Kristin A., Brooks, Jennifer L., Morris, Pamela A., Taut, Kathryn, Redd, Zakia A., and Emig, Carol A. (2002). *Future of Children*, *12*, pp. 79–95; and Chase-Lansdale, P. Lindsay, Moffitt, Robert A., Lohman, Brenda J., Cherlin, Andrew J., Coley, Rebekah L., Pittman,

Laura, Roff, Jennifer, Votruba-Drzal, Elizabeth (2003). Mothers' Transitions from Welfare to Work and the Well-Being of Preschoolers and Adolescents.

90. United States General Accounting Office (2001). *Welfare Reform: More Research Needed on TANF Family Caps and Other Policies for Reducing Out-of-Wedlock Births. (GAO–01–924).* Washington, DC: General Accounting Office.

91. Levin-Epstein, Jodie (2003). *Lifting the Lid Off the Family Cap.* Policy Brief No. 1. Washington, DC: Center for Law and Social Policy.

92. Henry, Gary T., and Mark, Melvin M. (2003). Beyond Use: Understanding Evaluation's Influence on Attitudes and Actions. *American Journal of Evaluation, 24,* pp. 293–314.

93. Weiss, Carol H., Murphy-Graham, Erin, Birkeland, Sarah (2005). An Alternate Route to Policy Influence: How Evaluations Affect D.A.R.E. *American Journal of Evaluation, 26,* pp. 12–30.

94. Edelman, Peter (2002, February). Reforming Welfare—Take Two. *The Nation,* pp. 16–24. See especially p. 22.

95. Heckman, James (2005). Inequality in America: What Role for Human Capital Policies. *Focus, 23,* pp. 1–10. See especially p. 9.

96. Patterson, Orlando (2007, January 7). Progress or Peril? *Washington Post* p. B4-5.

97. Edelman, Peter (2002, February). Reforming Welfare—Take Two, p. 22.

98. New Jersey Department of Human Services (2003, May 27). *Commissioner Harris Receives 2003 Public Policy Leadership Award.* Trenton, NJ: NJDHS.

99. Lazar, Kay (1996, March 17). Welfare Reformer Finds Himself a Changed Man. *The Home News Tribune,* p. A6.

100. McNicol, Dunstan (2006, October 3). Budget Cuts Cost Bryant Post at Rutgers. [*Newark*] *Star-Ledger,* p. 17; Ott, Dwight, and Moroz, Jennifer (2006, October 7). Schools Queried in Bryant Probe. *Philadelphia Inquirer,* p. 9.

Index